Kayaking the Inside Passage

Kayaking the Inside Passage

A Paddler's Guide
from Olympia, Washington,
to Muir Glacier, Alaska

Robert H. Miller

THE COUNTRYMAN PRESS
WOODSTOCK, VERMONT

Warning

This is a guidebook for an activity that is potentially dangerous. It is not a sea kayaking instruction book and does not replace proper instruction by a qualified instructor, nor does it replace the skill, proper equipment, experience, and judgment that every sea kayaker needs.

Library of Congress Cataloging-in-Publication Data

Miller, Robert H. (Howard), 1949-
    Kayaking the Inside Passage : a paddling guide from Olympia, Washington to Muir Glacier, Alaska / Robert H. Miller.
      p. cm.
    Includes bibliographical references and index.
    ISBN 0-88150-642-7
    1. Sea kayaking--Inside Passage--Guidebooks. 2. Inside Passage--Guidebooks. I. Title.
    GV776.115.M55 2005
    797.122'4--dc22

                        2005041259

Book design and composition by Faith Hague
Cover and interior photos by the author unless otherwise indicated
Maps by Catherine Moody, © 2005 The Countryman Press
Line illustrations by Zackery Zdinak

Published by The Countryman Press, P.O. Box 748, Woodstock, VT 05091
Distributed by W. W. Norton and Company, Inc., 500 Fifth Avenue, New York, NY 10110

Printed in the United States of America

10 9 8 7 6 5 4 3 2 1

For my mother, Mina;
my lover, Tina;
and my sister, Nani.

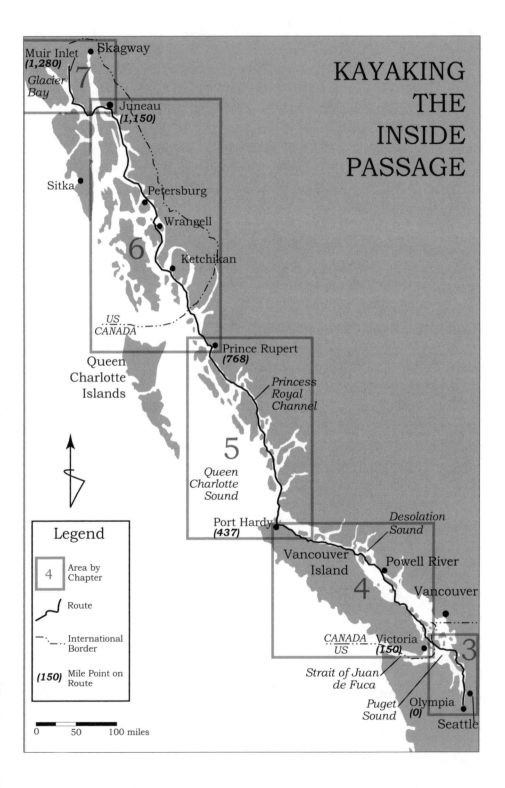

KAYAKING
THE
INSIDE
PASSAGE

Muir Inlet
(1,280)
Skagway

*Glacier
Bay*

7

Juneau
(1,150)

Sitka

Petersburg

6

Wrangell

Ketchikan

*US
CANADA*

Queen
Charlotte
Islands

Prince Rupert
(768)

*Princess
Royal
Channel*

5

*Queen
Charlotte
Sound*

Port Hardy
(437)

*Desolation
Sound*

Vancouver
Island

Powell River

4

Vancouver

*CANADA
US* Victoria
(150)

3

*Strait of Juan
de Fuca*

*Puget
Sound* Olympia
(0)

Seattle

Legend

| 4 | Area by Chapter |

Route

International Border

(150) Mile Point on Route

0   50   100 miles

Contents

Note: Numbers in parentheses indicate mileage from point to point.
Bold numbers indicate cumulative mileage.

Foreword

IN RECENT YEARS the body of literature about the Inside Passage, much like the number of people discovering sea kayaking, has increased exponentially. The objective and subjective aspects of this long-distance human effort achieve the best balance in *Kayaking the Inside Passage.* This select guide provides more detail dedicated to kayakers' interests than any other book to date and is the necessary companion to invite on your trip through the Inside Passage.

Like the Inside Passage itself, Robert Miller offers up moments of slap-your-head comprehension; glimpses of fin, flipper, and paddle receding into timeless mists; and a wealth of plain, rock-hard detail. This guidebook will aid kayakers in planning and carrying out trips on the rugged Pacific water artery that pulses along the western edge of North America. From the riches of the densely packed introduction to the surprise—under the heights of the Muir Glacier—found in the final sentence printed in words of but two syllables, there's the feel of a fine tool, sharpened by requisite data and personal experience, ready to cut a keen course of one's own.

In the first paddle strokes out of Boston Harbor at Olympia, Washington, at the southernmost end of Puget Sound, there's reference to the introduction of smallpox to the Western Hemisphere by a Cuban slave in 1520; George Vancouver's population estimates; the 1818 Treaty of Ghent; a discussion of bridge construction vis-à-vis underwater topography; and the geographic distribution of red-barked madrona trees—all this on the first 6 miles northward on the Cascadia Marine Trail's 150-mile portion of the 1,200-plus-mile-long Inside Passage. Two harbor seals tail along for the discourse.

Still life with slug

Robert Miller was first bitten by the Inside Passage in 1973 on his way to a Denali climb. More than 20 years later—probably highly infectious and with his wife catching the fever to go north as well—he was journeying by kayak. You may, as I did, get a case of Inside Passage fever reading this book. To fully enjoy this siren song of the Northwest, surround yourself with maps, charts, tide tables, and a dictionary, at least, to take the place of raven and eagle, bear and whale, cedar, cliff, and sand. Whether this book is a short reach from a living room armchair or drybagged on a kayak deck, the pull of powerful currents lies within its covers.

Kayaking the Inside Passage is an excellent compendium, achieving an expert pilot's trim. The Inner Passage cannot be traveled without an awareness of historic human use and misuse of coastal and inland resources; the shaping power of the aquatic and land mammals topping their food chains; the geological and meteorological forces constantly at work; or the challenges of one's own life. Reading and learning from this book are the first strokes of an Inside Passage adventure.

Reed Waite, Executive Director
Washington Water Trails Association
& Cascadia Marine Trail

Preface:
How This Book Came to Be

Number of strokes required to paddle the Inside Passage:
1,536,000

YOU SHOULD WRITE A GUIDEBOOK," Tina, my wife and paddling companion, suggested.

Paddling—like walking—stimulates the imagination, loosens the tongue, and invariably generates creative conversation. This morning we'd already exhausted practical topics—the day's objective, course and strategy, even what to have for dinner—and had tired of our well-worn stock of more imaginative themes: our dreams and aspirations, relationships and old gossip, public policy and architecture.

"No," I automatically retorted.

Tina answers every proposal with a *no,* and I'd acquired the odd habit. Not that we actually mean *no.* It probably started out as a protective adaptation to growing up in a large, contentious family. Now it's instinctive and seems to be just a displacement response to gain time to contemplate whatever has just been suggested. Every two or three days between Olympia, Washington, and Prince Rupert, British Columbia, the topic would resurface. As the full impact and magnificence of this most wonderful of adventures sank in, the idea of a guidebook grew from a modest, practical application of our research and experience to a celebration of the journey of a lifetime.

"I should write a guidebook," I declared one day.

"Great idea," Tina concurred.

Why write a guide? In a word, because I wish I'd had a comprehensive guide before undertaking my own Inside Passage trip. My own research, though extensive, time-consuming, and in-depth, was often unfocused or unproductive. Much of it I did not retain—it was too unmanageable and meant little without a sense of place. Moreover, a glance at a contiguous Inside Passage map will quickly overwhelm even a systems analyst. The complexity of landmasses and water passages rivals a Pollock painting. In order to chart a dependable route, navigational guides and maps require not only a thorough study and integration before embarkation but also comprehensive editing for on-board pilotage. A full set of topo maps; charts in varying scales; specialty maps (such as Forest Service and special interest maps); *Sailing Directions*, *Pilots*, and *Coast Pilots* books; small-craft and kayaking guides; tide tables; and other essentials are an unwieldy bunch to stow and grapple with in camp on a daily basis, much less on the water. Daily navigation prepping is very time-consuming. Finally, add bird, fish, plant, invertebrate, mammal, historical, and various other interpretive guides along with more general resource materials to the lot, and I was pressed to find room for extras such as tent, food, or sleeping bag.

Just north of Bella Bella, at the top of Reid Passage, on a cold and drizzly afternoon, we ran into a Canadian kayaker, traveling alone, making his way south. He exuded confidence but was hungry for some company. After exchanging pleasantries we immediately got down to business: picking each other's brains for route and campsite information. The coast of central British Columbia is the most isolated, wildest, and steepest section of the entire Inside Passage. He carried only 1:250,000 series topo maps, well annotated throughout. Campsites were traded like nuggets of hot gossip. But when he described his route south out of Prince Rupert we became alarmed.

A glance at the map makes Grenville Channel—the most direct route, along the east side of Pitt Island—jump out and rattle you. It is so perfectly straight and uniformly narrow for nearly 60 miles that you wonder just what is going on. Our friend had assumed the worst: precipitous walls, no landings, unmanageable currents without eddies, an endless wind tunnel subject to hellish chop. So he steered clear of it and went down Principe Channel along the west coast of Pitt Island. It nearly doubled his distance. We hadn't planned on an extra four days to Prince Rupert. With some apprehension we decided to double-check his assumptions and premises as best we could, given our limitations on the water. In situ exploration is a necessary complement to biblio, telephone, and Internet research, but it has its disadvantages. In a kayak, far from informants and sources and with little chance of making any informed connections, successful research can be elusive. But perseverance, often its own reward, this time yielded pay dirt. We concluded that the Canadian's detour proved unnecessary. A guidebook minimizes the need for on-the-fly research.

Sometimes there seems to be an inverse relationship between the amount of gear one lugs and the degree of expertise and knowledge one possesses. The irony is that most of the kayakers we met were trying to simplify their lives and valued going light, yet, due to a reliance on either inadequate gear or improperly thought-out strategies, ended up with needless complication. Perhaps this guide can help one find a balance.

In 1997, *Sea Kayaker* magazine ran an article about a Texan on his own Inside Passage quest. Though not too experienced, he had all the latest equipment, some of it donated. His commitment was wholehearted: he had both quit his job and gone into debt. But he had bitten off more than he could chew. Bad weather, bear encounters, too much solitude, and a melancholy disposition conspired to end his trip. The Inside Passage is inconceivably overwhelming. There are real, objective dangers out there. The trick, as with taxes, is to avoid them, not desperately attempt to dodge them while thick in their throes. Once in the jaws of danger, though, successful mitigation is the only solution. This guide ought to help—on both counts.

Guidebooks are sometimes criticized for eliminating a sense of adventure by providing too much information. Rubbish. Certainly some people like to challenge their ingenuity by venturing into the unknown clueless, but most want some idea of the scope and portent of their endeavor. Knowing the location of the next campsite, point of interest, resupply opportunity, potential danger, or alluring side trip allows the paddler to make the best use of precious time. A guidebook is a tool, plain and simple. Use it when you want it, stash it when you don't. A guidebook that withholds information is like a saw lacking teeth or a ladder missing steps.

Less prosaically, I hope this book puts within the reach of many an aspiring paddler a once-in-a-lifetime trip that might otherwise seem unreachable. Nothing compares to the total immersion of one's very being into the endless meditation of repetitive paddle strokes, come rain or shine, swell, chop, or glassy seas. The mantra is broken only by the explosive puff of a whale; the unexpected flourish of a leaping salmon; the scrutiny of an eagle, penetrating and vigilant, like a B-52 on the hunt for prey; the *kraw-kraw* of a raven; a solitary loon's ghostly lament; or the shy curiosity of a seal. Surrounded by impenetrable, snow-clad mountains, constant navigational challenges, and the minutiae of camping, the mind, by concentrating on the mundane, becomes flooded with the sublime.

Introduction

A good day is defined not by what happens to you,
but by what you do to it.
—R. H. M.

Straits of Georgia, April 1973, Alaska State Ferry USS *Malaspina*.
My new Ford F-100 pickup and I had been commandeered to, literally,
ferry all the gear and food to Alaska for a Mt. McKinley attempt. Of
course I agreed, volunteering to drive while the rest of the team flew to
Anchorage. Nonetheless, I wasn't looking forward to driving 4,000
miles, much of it along the still unpaved Al-Can Highway, mud-bogged
and potholed during the spring melt-off. That's when I found out
about the Alaska Marine Highway: an intricate system of long-haul ferries that penetrates where no road has dared.

Making the ferry arrangements and reservations had been cake: call
up, show up, and we were on our way. Back then, demand didn't seem
to exceed capacity and prices were downright cheap. The route was
shorter, too: only three days from Seattle to Haines. The ferry trip forced
a much-needed respite from the hectic planning and cross-country driving. And what a revelation those three days turned out to be! I had
never been on a ship before; never been to Canada or any northern latitudes. All my tensions and stresses drained away. The majesty of the Inside Passage, for thus had the improbable easement been knighted,
flooded my consciousness. I was overwhelmed.

Nothing quite focuses the mind like a serious climb. It is a time to
reflect on the undertaking; one's commitment, focus, and balance. At
the time, the proportion of failed attempts, and even fatalities, was quite

high. Was I really ready for a McKinley attempt? It was a time to take stock of life, what I was doing with it and question whether I'd change anything if I knew only a short time was left me. In such a frame of mind, it was inevitable: I was seduced. The Inside Passage (I didn't even know it had a name) infected me like a cunning succubus.

The previous winter, 14 of us, mostly friends and students from Prescott College in Arizona, had attempted to kayak the inside coast of Baja California. Sea kayaking, to us, did not exist then; we were inventing it—or so we thought. Our boats were Klepper doubles, skin-on-frame collapsibles, with sail rigs, shipped from New York. We'd been using them on the local rivers and the lower portion of the Grand Canyon and had been smitten by their simplicity and water-worthiness. Roy Smith, the college's Outdoor Action Program Director had come up with the idea (it was a whole new spin on phys-ed). He did not have a shortage of takers.

We didn't know what we were in for. The first day out of San Felipe, stunningly calm with a mother-of-pearl sea and sky, rendered all of 10 miles. We were exhausted; river currents had spoiled us. Huddled around the campfire, dispirited, with charts and pencils we worked out the math: 600 miles @ 10 miles/day = 60 days. We had planned on three weeks. Despair gripped the group. The trip was categorically impossible. Roy, a seasoned mountaineer and survival instructor for the British Army, gave us a pep talk. But there was no way to spin 10 miles today into 30 for every day thereafter. Yet, with dogged determination, our mileage slowly increased, in spite of downtime due to windstorms. Our spirits were further steeled by the futility of an expedition of three from Wyoming who were attempting the same trip in one double Folbot. While two paddled, one backpacked along the shore. Talk about one man's genius being another's folly! They didn't last long. At least most of us made it to Santa Rosalia, about two-thirds of the way down the coast. Another four persevered to Loreto. Two of us made it to La Paz, by which time we were ticking off 45 miles per day. But at what price!

We were paddling from 7 AM to 7 PM and arrived at La Paz Harbor burnt, rickety, and with a boat whose skin decomposed as we took it apart. At least we'd learned the difference between the possible and the improbable.

Leaning over the guardrail of the *Malaspina,* I wondered what it would take to kayak the Inside Passage. Had it been done? My God, it was more than 1,200 miles! I recalled the silent vow in La Paz never to paddle in the sea again. I had meant it; and my thoughts now were strictly speculative.

Sea kayaking (or canoeing, as the Brits call it) was the Inuit, Aleut, and Northwest Coast Native Americans' adaptation to a seashore environment. It was so effective (and they so adept) that whale and walrus were regularly hunted from these pilot fish–like crafts. After the Russian conquest of Alaska, sea otter hunting expeditions ranged as far as Baja California, more than 2,000 miles south of New Archangel—present-day Sitka—the capital of the colony. In fact, following Mexican independence in 1821 and the relaxation of trade barriers, entrepreneurs developed a salt rendering plant on Carmen Island, opposite Loreto, halfway up the Sea of Cortez, to supply the Russians with a pelt preservative.

During the Russian Imperial Administration, in the winter of 1852–53, three indentured servants, sick of the weather, Tlingit attacks, and the ham-handed policies of Governor Michael Tebenkov, went so far as to steal a native canoe with hopes of reaching the United States. Over the course of many tribulations and with only a hand-drawn map, they paddled to Astoria, Oregon, and freedom. But in a context other than subsistence or survival, sea kayaking, as a sport, would have to wait until the prosperity of Victorian Britain.

In 1865 John MacGregor designed and built a 15-foot-long, 28-inch-beam, 9-inch-deep sea kayak that drew 3 inches of water and weighed 80 pounds. He took his newly christened *Rob Roy* on a variety of "jaunts" (his term) throughout Europe and the Middle East, always later publishing his exploits in best-selling books. Sea kayaking became the rage in England. About 40 years later, Fred Fenger set out on what was probably the first great long-range sea kayaking adventure. In 1911 he left Grenada bound for the Virgin Islands in his homemade *Yakaboo*.

The Great Depression fathered a renaissance, out of circumstantial necessity, in human-powered conveyances. With little thought or credit to those who had gone before, some people sought escape or opportunity in setting out simply and, from today's perspective, with minimal planning in a paddle-powered boat, sometimes with a destination in mind, sometimes with only a direction. On October 9, 1933, Ginger and Dana Lamb embarked from San Diego in a homemade kayak, headed for Panama. As they recount in their fascinating 1938 book, *Enchanted Vagabonds:*

> *We had dreamt about this day. Ginger and I had talked about adventuring ever since we were kids together. The depression-ridden world was sunk in a morass of its own making. Like thousands of young men and women, we had come to maturity in such a world—and we were tired of it. This jaunt off to the wilds was not the result of a sudden impulse, nor was it conceived as a stunt. To both of us a life of routine was distasteful, and we had always planned to avoid it.*

Their boat, built in a garage, was "a mongrel boat, a sort of cross between an Eskimo kayak, a surfboat, and a sailboat with a canoe." They christened it *Vagabunda*. What little money they had they planned to supplement with gold panning, odd jobs, and hunting. It took them three years, to the day, to reach Panama, and they returned home richer than when they had left.

That same year, 1936, four Boy Scouts from California (Ken Wise, Gene Zabriskie, Wilfred Cash, and Phil Fallis) set out from Seattle in two canoes, without tents or stoves, headed for Alaska. In *Cruise of the Blue Flujin*, Wise minimizes their travails, always finding humor in adversity. It is difficult to discern whether his nonchalance reflected their wealth of experience, was a cover for their poverty, or was simply a literary conceit popular during the Depression. At Skagway, following in the footsteps of the 1898 Klondike prospectors, Wise and Zabriskie packed their kit over Chilkoot Pass and paddled down the Yukon River to Fairbanks, by which time encroaching winter overtook them. Having had their fill of the trip, they hitchhiked back to Los Angeles.

Not long after I'd been contemplating the magnitude of kayaking the Inside Passage from the deck of the *Malaspina,* Ed Gillet, a quiet but very intense San Diegan, with a custom-designed SEDA kayak (the company had just started laying up boats in his neighborhood), embarked from Skagway for Seattle—solo. He didn't intend to set a speed record. But, without company and with nearly 20 hours of daylight—not to mention his obsessive target fixation—Gillet ended up paddling every day for 16 hours at marathon pace. He reached Seattle in a month. It was to be the beginning of a lifelong sea kayaking odyssey that, so far, has resulted in a phenomenal solo paddle from California to Hawaii.

Only a cynic would assert that familiarity breeds contempt; in truth, familiarity is the foundation upon which greater feats are essayed. Arguably—but without diminishing previous exploits—the Inside Passage is becoming a much more familiar paddling objective. In 2002, New Zealand brothers Garth and Kevin Irwin set out not only to paddle the Inside Passage but also the Outside Passage. They departed Victoria, B.C., on March 11 bound for Glacier Bay, Alaska. On their return south they braved the swells of the open Pacific to follow the rugged and spectacular Outer Coast, returning to Victoria on October 21.

In the intervening years, though I had, in my mind, unfairly relegated sea kayaking to the realm of "old duffer" sports (along with golf and bowling—something I *might* pursue in my autumn years), the Inside Passage had bewitched me and wouldn't let go. Meanwhile, kayaking the Inside Passage gained in popularity. Seattle, Vancouver, and Alaska boaters explored, popularized, and commercially developed many sections of the inland waterway. Still, paddling the entire length of the archipelago was expedition-caliber kayaking.

Every journey is a compromise of conflicting objectives. Ought speed and endurance be the focus, à la Gillet, for the sheer joy of pushing oneself to unknown limits, or did I want to simmer in the bouillabaisse of the Northwest Coast, absorbing the flavors of the culture, history, and environment? Since paddling alone was out of the question, what would be the objectives of my prospective companions? I'd discovered, after many years of paddling, that 15 miles per day, average (with some big days of 30 or more miles, and some days off for weather, sight-seeing, and unforeseen circumstances), was the pace that most appealed to me. At that rate, an Inside Passage expedition would take more than 70 days. Could we accommodate this schedule with our work commitments? Should we go Spartan—light and fast is not only appealing, it can also be a safety edge—or would we be a tad more Dionysian, with some creature comforts, which carry home wherever one finds oneself?

My wife, Tina, is self-employed. The self-employed tend to have slave drivers for bosses; it's part of the territory. My work schedule at the local community college was extremely accommodating; I could leave for three months. After much discussion, research, and agonizing we realized that we could structure the trip almost any way we desired (sometimes more of a complication than a simplification). Additionally, there were some prospective co-expeditionists who were interested in joining us for different sections of the trip but couldn't take the time for the entire passage. It slowly emerged that our best bet would be to break up the trip into discrete sections, each paddled during portions of the summer for succeeding years during optimal weather and work windows. Upon reflection, it seemed somewhat arrogant to contain such a demanding and magnificent undertaking into a package of our own design, yet the piecemeal approach heartened us by scaling the venture within our reach. And there was precedent for this approach. None other than George Vancouver, pioneer explorer and mapper of the archipelago, resorted to a seasonal approach. He parsed the Passage into three discrete sections, charted during benign weather, and wintered in Hawaii between sections. The Inside Passage thus became a series of "Inside Jaunts."

In late June of 1996 Tina and I embarked from Boston Harbor in single kayaks, bound for Glacier Bay National Park, Alaska. Bursting out of our skins in anticipation and apprehension, our sentiments were tempered by the knowledge that our first leg—Olympia, Washington, to Victoria, British Columbia—would be a good shakedown cruise. We looked like characters from *The Grapes of Wrath.* Cart wheels, spare paddles, personal flotation devices (PFDs), pumps, deck bags, and chart cases covered our decks. Our plan was to tackle succeeding sections in yearly seasonal increments, each about three weeks in duration, to accommodate job and family responsibilities, to fine-tune equipment for changing conditions, and to regenerate depleted reserves.

So what is this book about? Basically, it is a select guide to kayaking the Inside Passage. It is "select" because a complete guide to all the possible routes and styles of kayaking would be beyond my ability. It is primarily a guide to the route we chose, emphasizing the strategies that worked best for us and the interests that motivated us. These ought to be helpful to a broad spectrum of potential Inside Passage paddlers.

Paddling the Inside Passage need not be a white-knuckle, quit-your-job, major expedition commitment. With proper planning, the right strategies, adequate skills, and suitable equipment, anyone can sample it. This guide emphasizes accessibility and breaks down the component parts of the challenge into attainable goals by partitioning the nearly 1,300 miles between Puget Sound and Glacier Bay into self-contained, logistically independent, bite-sized portions. These are stitched together by a primary route that is an ideal compromise of safety, comprehensiveness, brevity, and interest. A variety of alternate routes, some (for example) stressing interest over safety, or safety over brevity, offer optional choices.

But this book goes much further. By identifying the considerations involved in setting a route and configuring them into a useful algorithm, the reader can better customize his or her own route out of a bewildering number of possibilities. Along the way the book identifies and evaluates different tactics and approaches to objective conditions that facilitate good planning, for example, exactly where or when to cross a particular channel; how to approach and cross major river deltas; basic orientation for approaching big towns with overwhelming commercial traffic from low in the water; potential shortcuts; approaches to resupplying and camping when facilities are not conveniently spaced; border crossings; and much more.

Besides a kayak and an unquenchable lust for the journey, just what skills and experience do you need to paddle the Inside Passage? *Kayaking the Inside Passage* stresses three essential skills as the minimum for setting out: a dependable roll, competent navigation, and good seamanship. On the protected waters of the Inside Passage, in balmy weather and conditions of one's picking, the need for a roll is rarer than sasquatch. Nonetheless, a dependable Eskimo roll is the best safeguard against ever needing to use it and instills confidence and comfort in any situation. Competent navigation is not just the ability to read a map, the topography, and hydrography, but also being able to conform one with the other so you can determine where you're at and get to where you're going. Finally, good seamanship is that ineffable quality that is part experience tempered by an acute sense of place, and part self-knowledge combined with the sort of critical judgment that promotes risk assessment better than any actuary. Together, these will keep you out of trouble.

And experience? Just how much do you need? Experience is like capital: some people can wisely invest a small grubstake and turn it into a fortune, while others can squander a fortune and have nothing to show for it. It's not how much experience (or money) you have that will determine your success, but rather how you use it. In the late 1960s the National Park Service held public hearings to establish skills, proficiency, and equipment requirements for boating the Grand Canyon. During the discussion, some veteran river runners became concerned that the proposed regulations might be too restrictive. In a thinly veiled reference to explorer John Wesley Powell, Vern Taylor, a geologist who had spent years studying travertine deposits in the canyon, innocently asked: "So would a one-armed army veteran, without any previous experience or maps, and rowing a wooden boat, be disqualified?" The room fell silent. Subsequently, many of the proposed requirements were dropped. The only way for a novice to gain experience is to plunge into the task, preferably under controlled conditions but always reaching just a tad further than previously. This book cannot determine whether your experience and temperament are up to the challenge—only you can do that. Fortunately, this guide starts in Puget Sound, the most benevolent and forgiving portion, and wends its way north to more demanding locales. The incremental approach allows for experience to accumulate slowly, the better to invest wisely.

Suitable equipment can make or break a trip, or at least strike the difference between grim endurance and actual comfort. This guidebook makes some strongly opinionated recommendations that minimize the misery and maximize the fun.

Finally, the organization of the information makes for a very userfriendly experience. Reams of scattered and disparate data have been collated into a seamless compendium easily accessed on the go. Points of interest and challenging conditions, along with their background and strategies for making the most out of them, are woven into the mile-bymile description. Book maps note campsites, parks, points of access and resupply, and trip distances along the main route and alternate routes.

How to Use This Book

The first two chapters of this book provide general and specific information for paddling the Inside Passage: overall history, environment, equipment, weather, safety, and other considerations for the entire journey. The route has been divided into logical sections, each easily accessible and all approximately of equal length except for the first and last. Chapters 3 through 7 each correspond to one major section of the Inside Passage. Each trip chapter/section (3 through 7) is, by and large, self-contained and covers one discrete geographical area—including historical, political, and natural background. The trip chapters/sections are divided into two parts, each also—more or less—independent of the other. The first part of each trip chapter/section illustrates some major aspect of the region—regional history, economy, ethnology, and the like—and often applies to the entire Inside Passage. The second part of each of these chapters constitutes the mile-by-mile meat of the guide and includes necessary logistical arrangements for getting to and from starting and ending points. Where there is some cross-referencing among the chapters, it is noted in the text.

I do not belabor certain popular guidebook themes such as camping etiquette, menu planning, guided trips, and the admonition to get professional instruction; or provide exhaustive gear and clothing lists. Most are matters of common sense, inclination, or ubiquity, and I have nothing original to add. The book concludes with a list of resources and an annotated bibliography for those readers wishing to explore themes barely touched in this guide. Some of these are absolutely essential reading, either for enrichment or basic research, by anyone contemplating the Inside Passage.

The book opens with an Inside Passage map that indexes each trip section. Each trip section corresponds to one of chapters 3 through 7 and opens with its own overview map. Routes, points of interest, campsites, and other notable features pepper each map. The main route is calibrated in 15-statute-mile increments, a handy, though admittedly arbitrary, day's paddle. The mileage notation used in this guide is *not accurate*; rather it is merely a convention and a handy scale to measure progress. Navigation on a liquid medium precludes exact precision. The mileage is measured twice: once from each section's starting point, and—in **bold**—cumulative from Olympia, Washington. Alternate routes continue the main route's mileage notation from divergence to convergence, and then revert to the main route's mileage. Mileage discrepancies between alternate and main routes are noted and then ignored as the two rejoin and the main route continues. Points of reference and interest, towns, and settlements are also marked with their respective mileages. Port and rapids detail maps, wherever possible, accompany the text. Though all are scaled, they are for orientation, not navigation. I use statute miles because I will advocate primary reliance on 1:250,000 topographic maps for navigation. Unlike charts, these have the advantage of retaining the same scale from one map to another. In the text, "miles" will refer to statute miles. Here are the conversions:

> *1½ statute miles = 1 nautical mile*
> *1.13 statute miles = 1 nautical mile*
> *1 statute mile = 0.88 nautical mile*

Campsite notation on the maps is a tricky exercise. There is no way to list all possible campsites. Some areas might require a portaledge for camping, while others offer virtually unlimited tentable space. One person's sylvan retreat might be another's toxic dump. Some campsites are official and well developed with amenities, while others require pruning to become habitable. Map campsite symbols reflect some of this variety, but not all. The major distinctions are among campsite "areas," "possible" campsites, and specific campsites. These and other details are mentioned in the text.

Don't overlook the appendices and bibliography. Appendix A lists all the 1:250,000 topographical maps required for the routes in this guide. Appendix B lists all the resources (and then some) for equipment items recommended in chapter 2: map and chart dealers and agencies; government agencies such as Customs, Coast Guards, land managers, weather services, etc.; ferries, lodging, and vehicle storage facilities and some boating retail shops along the way. Appendix C is a very basic primer on marine radio use. Finally, appendix D helps you to identify the various salmon species and some of the more confusing small mustelid mammals. The bibliography includes not only my own research resources but also a thematic, annotated list of suggested reading.

1
The Big Picture

Observation is at best approximate;
ideas are tools,
and all judgement is provisional.
—*The Economist*

The "Inside Passage" became the Inside Passage during the Klondike gold rush of 1898. The name was coined, through common usage, to differentiate it from the "Outside Passage." Alaska-bound steamers, carrying hordes of would-be prospectors, instinctively avoided the sinuous channels, strong currents, and largely uncharted shoals of the Inside Passage, opting instead for the navigationally simpler open Pacific. (Although both James Cook, and especially George Vancouver, had definitively charted most of the Inside Passage, their focus had been on possible Northwest Passages, not so much a north-south thoroughfare.)

As the avalanche of demand for passage to the goldfields gathered momentum, smaller boats—oftentimes little better than motorized coracles—owned and run by skippers desperate for any source of income started plying the more protected inside waters. The onset of winter weather on the Outside Passage, with its low-pressure fronts goose-stepping across the Gulf of Alaska like waves of Soviet Army battalions on a May Day parade, pummeled the big boats, which were now, with the increased demand, freighting in the off-season. They too turned inside.

Thus was the Inside Passage invested. Seattle became the preferred port of departure; Skagway, the nearest harbor to the Yukon River, the terminus.

Natural History

But the Inside Passage is more than its historical definition. Much more. It is, first of all, a distinct geographic and climatic biozone bounded by the vast Pacific on the west and the continental Coast Range on the east, and by the limits of protected navigation at the distal ends. It includes not only a vast archipelago, created by rising sea levels after the last glacial epoch, but also the playas and pediments of the Coast Range piedmont, itself thrust up by the collision of the Pacific Plate with the North American Plate. With most frontally colliding tectonic plates, the crasher pushes against the stationary plate, causing compression and lift. A good example of this is India. Its advance into China is shoving the Himalayas upward. (Everest rises about 2 inches every year.) The Alaskan and Canadian Coast Ranges, North America's densest concentration of high mountains, are the products of a similar process.

Some geologists see Alaska as North America's India. It was a wandering mendicant from somewhere out in the South Pacific. As the Pacific Plate moved like a rotating conveyor belt, immature Alaska hitched a ride. On its journey north it picked up pieces of South America, Mexico, and who knows what else. It first came into contact with North America at California, where it left skid marks. Afterward, like an overly affectionate cat, it kept shoving itself into North America while sliding north. On its way it left more bits of itself: scraps of the Wrangell Mountains, Glacier Bay, Chichagof Island, and the entirety of the Queen Charlotte Islands. The largest of these abandoned vestiges is Vancouver Island. When it reached its present location, it nuzzled deep—so deep that it shoved Alaska's North Slope up into its present location and pushed Beringia and the Chukchi Peninsula, once part of North America, over to Asia.

Imitating the plate movements, Pacific weather patterns also smash into this landmass barrier. Like the Gulf Current (its Atlantic counterpart), the Pacific Current circumnavigates the continental rims, warming in the tropics and tempering the North American coast on its clockwise descent. Meanwhile, northern Pacific cyclonal fronts pick up oceanic moisture on their relentless eastward march and, crashing into the Coast Range, saturate the Inside Passage with the highest rainfall in North America, sometimes in excess of 200 inches per year. The resultant combination of temperate climate and heavy precipitation generates North America's only rain forest. At higher latitudes and altitudes the saturation begets glaciers instead of forests.

Repetitive, multiple glacial episodes over many millions of years have carved deep valleys between higher landmasses. Glacial recessions, with their concomitant sea level rise, on the other hand, have allowed the ocean to inundate some of these lower valleys. These advances and retreats are still going on and can be experienced, in vivo, at Glacier Bay National Park. No one knows their exact cause other than a slight correlation with sunspot activity. When Vancouver charted the Inside Passage in the 1790s, Glacier Bay did not exist.

For the kayaker, this cycle has practical implications. During a glacial recession, the glaciers retreat inward (inland) and northward (away from the temperate zones). The U-shaped valleys of relatively newly exposed and inundated shorelines tend to be steep and difficult to camp on, especially if they've had enough time to be recolonized by botanical invaders. This is the case along much of the middle reaches of the Inside Passage. More ancient glacial topography—such as Puget Sound—has had its rough edges softened by erosion. Alternatively, land areas underneath very recent glacial retreats, and bare due to melting, are subject to isostasy, the rebounding of the land once the glacial weight has been lifted, exposing the ice river's bed and flat campsites. The Beardsley Islands, just north of the Glacier Bay National Park headquarters, are rising at the rate of 2 inches per year. So, geomorphologically speaking, the temporary homes we call campsites are ineluctably in tune with deep time.

In the sea, tidal variations sometimes exceeding 30 feet, and tidal currents that can reach 14 knots, some with rapids, superimposed on deep, glacially carved canyons in the continental shelf—which alone can cause extreme sea temperature differentials—create a turbulent though ideal environment for plankton, the biotic foundation of this fecund paradise. These tiny but countless minions support large populations of minke and humpback whales, and provide the first link in a food chain that supports truly phenomenal numbers of salmon year-round. February brings the first spring run of king (or Chinook); mid-summer the sockeye (or red) and a second run of king; fall the silver (or coho) and—every other year—the pinks (or humpbacks). Finally, at the end of the year, the chum (or dog) salmon make their run. (Consult appendix D for salmon—and mustelid—identifying features.) It is the salmon that feed the predators at the top of the food chain: orcas, bears, pinnipeds, raptors, and man. And all of these have been able to achieve astounding population densities.

Not one hour after our initial departure from Olympia, two harbor seals were tailing us. One day we counted 67! We saw seals every day. Just north of Wallace Island Provincial Marine Park, we counted more than 70 bald eagles in a day. One, fussing over the carcass of a baby seal, even let us approach within 20 feet, more protectively than permissively. Two days out of Sydney, camped on the rocky promontory of an island, we saw five pods of orcas, each numbering five or six individuals, promenade past our bivouac, one after another, nearly overturning a small Bayliner that intersected their course. At Brown Island in Smith Sound, while we recuperated after sprinting through the exposed waters of upper Queen Charlotte Sound, another pod of orcas unabashedly used one of the intertidal rocks adjacent to our camp as a belly scratcher.

A one-bear day (usually black), about twice a week, north of Vancouver Island, was common. But in Griffin Pass we had a five-bear day—thankfully while paddling. Stopping to check out a potential campsite at Deer Island, I discovered the bear scat density was so astounding that I called out for my companions to come see: every 5 feet, in every direction, lay a fresh, huge black pile, as far as we cared to walk. Between Five Finger Islands and the Brothers, feeding humpbacks encircled us. For nearly 300 degrees the flukes, dorsals, and occasional breach of at least 30 whales repeatedly crashed into the atmosphere all afternoon. We'd heard apocryphal tales of salmon so thick you could walk across rivers. Well, they're true. In late July, just south of Juneau,

Salmon run up an unnamed creek just south of Juneau, Alaska.

one creek was so engorged with fat fish that the banks were strewn with hurdlers that had inadvertently jumped out of the channel. And the creek was so shallow that you literally could have walked across the stream on the backs of spawning salmon.

In Glacier Bay, endangered Steller's sea lions were not aware of park rules forbidding approaching wildlife close enough to alter their behavior. About eight of them decided to inspect and unabashedly play with us.

Ethnohistory

Homo sapiens opportunistically and, most probably, randomly, invaded the Americas from the Old World perhaps as early as 50,000 years ago. He undoubtedly walked across what is now known as Beringia, a broad swath of exposed continental shelf resulting from lowered sea levels—it is only 300 feet deep today—during a glacial advance (the missing water being concentrated in growing polar and montane ice). This first wave of immigrants became today's Amerindians, ancestors to nearly all aboriginal cultures in the Americas and, more specifically, the North West Coast cultures, which comprise six to nine cultural/linguistic groups, depending on whether you're a lumper or a splitter.

They are, from south to north: 1) the Coast Salish, who inhabit most of western Washington State and both sides of the Strait of Georgia as far north as Johnstone Strait; 2) the Makah (sometimes lumped with the Coast Salish) are on the Olympic Peninsula; 3) the Nootka (a.k.a. Nuu-chah-nulth) live along the west coast of Vancouver Island; 4) the Kwak-iutl (kwa-*cute*-ill), a.k.a. Kwagiulth or Kwakwaka'wakw', straddle northern Vancouver Island and the central British Columbia coast; 5) the Bella Bella (a.k.a. Heiltsuk) and Bella Coola (a.k.a. Nuxalk), along the valley of the same name, are sometimes included with the Kwakiutl, though they speak Salish; 6) the Tsimshian (*Chim*-shin), a.k.a. Gitksan, reside around Prince Rupert and, since 1887, at Metlakatla on Annette Island, Alaska; 7) the Haida (*Hy*-da) occupy the Queen Charlotte Islands and the southern half of Prince of Wales Island, which they invaded in the 1700s, displacing the Tlingits; 8) the Nishga (sometimes lumped with the Tsimshian), a.k.a. Niska or Nisga'a, are in the Nass River area of the Alaska–British Columbia border; 9) the Tlingit (*Clink*-it), a.k.a. Chilkat, inhabit all the rest of southeastern Alaska beyond Yakutat.

A second wave of Asian immigrants, hypothesized on linguistic and DNA evidence, came over later, perhaps around 15,000 to 10,000 years ago. These were the Athabascans, modern-day interior Alaskan and Canadian indigenous peoples. Two small groups kept going all the way to the southwestern United States and became the Navajo and Apache. The last wave of immigrants, the Inuit and Aleut, probably came over in kayaks and baidarkas after the seas had risen and inundated Beringia, perhaps as recently as 5,000 years ago.

At the time of initial contact with westward-expanding Europeans, Amerindians, in what is now the Lower 48 states, were distributed in an east-to-west pattern of decreasing social and political organization. This roughly correlated with an east-to-west pattern of decreasing precipitation and increasing climatic harshness. The confederations, chiefdoms, and tribes dependent on agriculture east of the Mississippi gave way to smaller hunter-gatherer groupings west of the 100th Meridian, from bands on the plains to roving nuclear families along the Great Basin and lower Colorado River deserts. The exception to this pattern—this time proving the correlation—was the stratified chiefdoms of the Northwest Coast. The mild climate and marine cornucopia facilitated a population density otherwise associated only with agricultural societies. Cultures of elaborate technology, architecture, art, and a sociopolitical organization approaching incipient statehood—complete with sometimes-recreational martial feuds and even slavery (the Haida regularly raided Puget Sound)—were built on an economic hunter-gatherer foundation: a rare phenomenon indeed, and a testament to the fecundity of the environment. Europeans, of course, were taken aback and temporarily held at bay by the unexpected sophistication of the Northwest Coast chiefdoms.

But not for long, though the respite proved beneficial. Each European colonizer recognized aboriginal rights to varying degrees, but all claimed sovereignty over and possession of territories, a practice imposed by the Spanish right from Columbus's very first voyage. This pattern, in turn, had been forged during the 800-year *Reconquista,* or reconquest, of the Iberian Peninsula from the Moors. Spain imposed unambiguous territorial annexation and total cultural hegemony, always initiated by military subjugation and forced religious conversion modeled on Inquisitional methods. Other European powers, sometimes at first loath to conquer, annex, or do battle, and coveting only trade and commercial advantage, were forced to adopt more realpolitik methods just to compete with the Spanish. If another country's explorer did not lay claim to newly discovered territories, Madrid would. And Madrid's claims knew no bounds. Balboa, "discovering" the Pacific from Panama, in one pretentious declaration extended Spanish sovereignty to all lands abutting that piece of water.

Spanish social policy ran the gamut from annihilation through slavery to integration through exploitation. After absolute slavery wrought nearly total genocide in the Caribbean, government imposed a more coherent policy. Under the direction of Fray Bartolome de Las

Casas, the Convention of the Indies decreed that, albeit within a context of conquest, yes, the American Indians were human beings and should be fully integrated as citizens of the empire. Fortunately, Spanish ethnocentrism was not racist, and the host and guest populations intermingled with abandon.

Spanish exploratory forays along the northern Pacific coast date from Juan de Fuca's discovery, in 1592, of the strait that bears his name but did not develop in earnest until 1774, when Juan Perez was instructed to sail to latitude 60 degrees N and take possession in the name of Carlos III, King of Spain. The effort was short-lived. By 1790 Spain had effectively abdicated what few claims it had above the 49th Parallel in the Nootka Convention (a settlement with the British concerning territorial suzerainty). Soon thereafter they further conceded the northern limits of their territory at the 42nd Parallel, the present Oregon-California border.

Following Vitus Bering's discovery of Alaska in 1741, Russia was driven not by the desire to expand its empire or to extend Christianity, but simply, and very much informally, in order to acquire sea otter pelts for sale to the Chinese aristocracy, who were willing to pay exorbitant prices for this delicate fur. Russian traders, *promyshlenniki,* were not known for their social graces except perhaps while intoxicated, when a vestigial empathy would metastasize into a maudlin fatalism. The product of a sociopolitical milieu that emphasized submission and resignation, cruelty and indifference; and with a temperament forged by repeated Mongol invasions and the regimes of Ivan the Terrible and Peter the Great (an even crueler autocrat), they forcibly impressed Aleuts in the hunt for pelts or massacred them if they did not take up paddle and harpoon. Catherine the Great, upon ascending the throne, rationalized government policy by formally annexing Alaska, codifying rule, and appointing a governor, Alexander Baranov. He set out to protect native rights and traditions while pursuing commercial gain.

Russia's modest occupation coupled with Tlingit sophistication and resistance also ensured a more measured coexistence. Like the Spanish, the Russians were not racist. (Siberian physiognomy, after all, was not so different from Alaskan.) Baranov himself took a native wife and reared a family. Liquor was banned. Religious conversion was very successful, mostly due, ironically, to the Orthodox missionaries' initial reluctance, their subsequent gentleness and ultimate adaptability to native ways.

British policy was perhaps the most enlightened—after all, the Enlightenment *had* dawned. Their claims to the area were based on Cook's and Vancouver's explorations in 1778 and 1792, respectively, but, critically, turned on Alexander McKenzie's phenomenal transcontinental trek in 1793, which established a Canadian presence on the British Columbia coast.

The American and French Revolutions had rattled societies to the core, and all premises were being reevaluated. British foreign policy had been suddenly infused with the idealism of the new liberal ideas, in an overt attempt to reform and preserve the empire. Central to these ideas was the dignity and sovereignty of all peoples. Still, Spanish precedent—claiming and annexing new lands—could not be abandoned unilaterally by London without dire consequences, so they too annexed according to international realpolitik practice. In the interests of tranquillity, alcohol trade with the natives was banned. And contrary to Russian commercial practices, in which the buyers' interests predominated, British traders created an atmosphere of incentive for the sellers. This spirit of equanimity was further enhanced by the Canadian traders' (they were mostly French voyageurs) inclination to take native wives. In stark contrast to US–Native American relations, which were punctuated by war, treaty, broken treaty, and subsequent banishment to reservations, Canadian–Native American relations were marked by mutual respect, treaties, and later, unfortunately, treaty attrition. In ensuing years this took the form of a concerted effort to integrate the Indians through the use of missionaries.

Why Great Britain allowed the United States a foothold in the Pacific Northwest, below Alaska, is anybody's guess. Vancouver had been commissioned to find and map a Northwest Passage. He approached from the south in 1792 looking for likely water channels piercing the western coast of North America. He missed nary a sea channel entrance but sailed right by every major river—the Columbia, Fraser, Skeena, Stikine, and Taku Rivers—without so much as a hint. Hot on his trail was Captain Robert Gray, skipper of the USS *Columbia*. Gray didn't miss the Columbia River. He sailed up the delta, traded with the natives, and named the river after his ship. When Meriwether Lewis and William Clark, in 1805, descended the Columbia to the Pacific, United States territorial claims became contiguous, connecting Gray's discovery with the newly purchased Louisiana Territory. John Jacob Astor sealed the deal when he established Fort Astoria at the mouth of the river in 1811 for the purpose of engaging in the fur trade.

Though pre–Alaska Purchase, American policy was also a product of the Enlightenment; individual traders, working the coast since the 1780s, sometimes tended to be a boorish, racist, greedy, and intolerant lot. Despite repeated requests by the Russians to desist from selling liquor and arms to the natives, Washington refrained from such overtly patronizing legislation. After the US purchase of Alaska in 1867, benign neglect, mostly due to preoccupation with post–Civil War Reconstruction and enforced through contemptuous military rule, was the order of the day. By the time good government was established at the turn of the century under Federal Judge James Wickersham, Alaska natives had successfully, and partly due to Russian stipulations in the purchase treaty, avoided relegation to reservations.

Today, native affairs in Canada, Alaska, and the Lower 48 vary radically from one jurisdiction to another. In the contiguous US, we are still saddled with an obsolete reservation system, lately worsened by the delivery into Indian hands of the Bureau of Indian Affairs, where varying degrees of competence and conflict of interest muddle administration. Canada, lacking the legacy of conquest but saddled with conflicting treaties that either promised too much or whose clauses have not been strictly observed, is in the throes of negotiations and lawsuits that, all parties hope, will lead to a "final" solution. The Alaska Native Claims Settlement Act, though no panacea, has provided a "final" solution (at least where basic citizenship and legal and property rights are concerned) to the native people's integration that allows cultural self-reliance somewhat along the lines of the Amish or Hooterite models. The act essentially removes government from the role of "Great White Father" and turns reservations into corporations with proprietary and financial interests converted into individual shares that can be manipulated at will by the owners. These can then pursue strategies anywhere along the individualistic-communitarian continuum.

An enchanting mini-archipelago flanks the once inhabited native village on Tongass Island, on which we discreetly and carefully camped one late-July day. Though it displays few signs of its ancient occupation, it exudes an atavism that draws one's gaze over the western isles on sharp lookout for Haida war canoes. Abandoned aboriginal settlements dot the Inside Passage, mostly identified on topographic maps, but nearly unidentifiable in situ due to lush overgrowth. Today, almost half the smaller roadless towns along the North Coast are native communities. Most, such as Bella Bella, Port Simpson, and Metlakatla, are more or less recent agglomerations due either to missionary or government influence and little affected by tourism. While most of these rely chiefly on fishing (and were a friendly source of water, provisions, and advice during our jaunts), others are cultural preserves and theme parks complete with museums, reconstructed long houses, old and new totems, and salmon bakes (Blake Island, Alert Bay, and Saxman Village). All well worth the time and cost of a visit.

The tentative nonnative toeholds (once-manned lighthouses, homesteads, and turn-of-the-20th-century canneries), some in ruins, some barely hanging on, and others bursting with promise, evoke images of overwhelming perseverance in the performance of duty and overarching dreams both disintegrated and inchoate. The Inside Passage is not a wilderness trip, though outside the traffic corridors, in isolated inlets and deep in the rain forests, it can be. Your companions are a constant promenade of purse seiners, gillnetters, and trollers (often with an errant salmon to offer); tugs and barges full of garbage, sawdust, timber, or ore; sleek sailboats with cryptic names; menacing container ships seemingly on autopilot; Coast Guard cutters with their reassuring presence of safety; tour boats—there is nothing more otherworldly than a fully illuminated, USS *Enterprise*–size cruise ship floating by at 1 AM, during a drizzly, foggy night (when you and all the world ought to be ensconced in a protective cocoon), waking you with the faint strains of an orchestra fading in the distance like a surreal dream—ferries; and, yes, kayaks, often manned by Japanese or Germans, seeking adventure and respite in a milieu they could once barely imagine and can hardly believe they're experiencing.

2
Details

*Survival is not so much a question of enduring adversity
as of avoiding it.*
—R. H. M.

Where to Go

Exactly where to begin or end an Inside Passage journey, what route to
chart, and even in which direction to travel can be points of contention.
The northern terminus presents few options: Lynn Canal or Glacier
Bay. Going to Skagway, at the head of Lynn Canal, has the attraction
both of being the historical objective and the longest route. Not only is
the town well connected both by road and by the Alaska Marine Highway but also the Yukon–White Pass Railroad has recently been re-
opened. For the really adventurous, Chilkoot Pass and the Yukon River
still beckon.

With Glacier Bay, however, one still has to choose between Muir
Inlet and the West Arm, the longer of the two. Both have tidewater glaciers and lots of wildlife. The phenomenally rapid retreat of Muir Glacier, the most often visited glacier in North America until the National
Park Service (NPS) stopped motorized travel at the head of the inlet,
has left a spectacularly vertiginous canvas of scoured and naked rock
with few places to camp. It now barely qualifies as a tidewater glacier
(one whose ice is actually advancing into the sea). Johns Hopkins Glacier in the West Arm, on the other hand, is the largest, most impressive
tidewater glacier in Glacier Bay National Park, constantly calving icebergs at an almost predictable rate. The heads of navigation in Glacier
Bay, should one choose to end his Inside Passage trip here, are wilderness destinations and require either paddling back to park headquarters

at Bartlett Cove afterward, or arranging for a commercial shuttle (offered on a daily basis).

We chose to finish our trip in Glacier Bay because we'd already been to Skagway, had never visited the park, and wanted to end on a note of solitude and reflection within the denouement of a 2½-day paddle back to Bartlett Cove. We chose Muir Inlet for its natural and historical significance.

Off the exposed headlands of Cape Caution, in Queen Charlotte Sound, we met a pair of Japanese riding the swell in a tubby double kayak. They had lots of cameras, engaging smiles, but not a whit of English. Forty days out of Skagway, they were white-knuckled for Vancouver. They chose Vancouver not just to lessen their overall mileage but also to avoid, for them, yet another international crossing with its enervating formalities. Additionally, they had a nonstop Vancouver–Tokyo flight back home. The options for a southern terminus are many. Vancouver and Seattle are the historical nexuses. Unfortunately, really big cities present their own logistical problems for the low-profile kayak traveler, and Vancouver eliminates Puget Sound, not only a stellar paddle but also a profitable shakedown cruise, if chosen as the start. Most Inside Passagers start or end in Seattle. We, on the other hand, didn't want to miss a single possible mile and so embarked from Olympia, the southernmost point on Puget Sound.

Choosing a route between Olympia and Muir Glacier, after a cursory glance at a map (for which map is best suited to this exercise, see The Bottom Line I: Navigation), can leave one bug-eyed and befuddled. A simplifying algorithm is necessary. First, pencil in the absolutely shortest distance between your start and finish, irrespective of whether it coincides with a ferry route or conventional navigation channel (after all, we are kayakers). Why the shortest? For one thing, one has to start somewhere and, in a paddling trip of more than a thousand miles, shorter has its logic. This route also has the advantage of being randomly picked, so a true sampling of the Inside Passage is guaranteed.

Next, pencil in any alternative routes that might be preferable from a safety aspect, for example, fewer crossings, less current, protected shore, and so forth. Then circle specific destinations along the way that you want to visit (such as McKenzie's Rock, The Brothers Islands, Baird Glacier, Pack Creek, Ketchikan, etc.) or avoid (e.g., Seymour Narrows, Vancouver, rapids, etc.). Next, conform what you have into a route.

Finally, wish really hard while looking at the map and note where ideal time-saving portages ought to be, and, voilà, they may appear. This is not as crazy as it sounds. At the head of Seymour Canal, connecting it to Oliver Inlet, is the most endearing little portage tramway on Admiralty Island, about a mile long, that's a real hoot to use. A portage also connects Port Frederick with Tenakee Inlet on Chichagof Island. Some portaging (or lining) will be inevitable due to tides or rapids. These may possibly include sections of Gastineau Channel, Griffin Channel, Dry Strait, the Skeena River delta, the Couverdeen Islands, and campsites with a dry foreshore at low tides. But take heart, we welcomed most portages as a delightful respite from the paddling. You'll now have a route with some out-and-back detours such as, for example, McKenzie's Rock or Baird Glacier. Decide whether these detours will really enrich your trip and either excise them or plan on visiting them via some alternative means, such as floatplane or hired boat minitour. Now you've got a route you can work with, and although it may not coincide entirely with the primary one in this book, it'll probably share many large portions.

For some people, deciding whether to go north-to-south or south-to-north is a serious concern. Not for me. I could no more start in Glacier Bay, headed for Puget Sound, than I could run a river against the current, climb a mountain from the summit down, or watch a movie in reverse. Sea voyages always start at home ports bound for the nether regions. A south-to-north trip recapitulates both the early explorers' efforts and the Klondikers' quest. Additionally, as one progresses north, the transition from temperate climes to a more antipodal environment is experienced firsthand. Lush and diverse forests of the Puget Sound–Vancouver Island region give way to the giant red cedars of British Columbia, so beloved by turn-of-the-20th-century loggers and now nearly gone; then to western hemlock and Sitka spruce (now heavily logged) in the Alaska Panhandle; and finally, to the receding glacier, alder-recolonized bare rock of Glacier Bay, the icy jewel of this paddling crown. The return trip home makes for a good "decompression" interval and a fitting resolution to a magnificent adventure, especially if it takes place on a ferry.

The justification for a north-to-south voyage might be if your home port is Skagway or Juneau or, more commonly, to follow prevailing winds. Fortunately, during the paddling season—May to mid-September—Inside Passage weather is generally benign, with prevailing winds evenly split from both directions, though there is much controversy on this matter. An informal (and, admittedly, very restricted) survey of north-to-south paddlers indicates that their primary motivation was to "paddle home," usually the Vancouver or Puget Sound area. And a satisfying finale that would make. Unfortunately, most returned with the *impression* that the prevailing winds blew against them. Admittedly, one might expect such a conclusion. However, south-to-north paddlers (again, in a very limited and informal survey) concluded that they mostly ran with the wind.

Weather and When to Go

The Gulf of Alaska is the point of conception and maternity ward for virtually all North American low-pressure systems. The Japanese Current brings warm water from the tropics and, as it passes Bering Strait, draws in cold water from the Arctic Ocean, which then mixes in promiscuous eddies. These in turn affect atmospheric air directly above them by altering its temperature and humidity. Extreme temperature, humidity, and pressure gradients close to each other generate winds and instability. These infant storms crash into the Coast Range (global weather, due to the earth's rotation, always moves eastward—the Coriolis effect) and often nestle for weeks in the crescent-shaped cradle of the Alaskan-Canadian coastal embrace, their movement further impeded by the Coast Range. When they're finally ready to move on, lows don't always go due east. Exactly where they go is a function of nearby high- and low-pressure systems that, like features in a pinball machine, can attract and repel. But they always follow the path of least resistance.

This constantly fluctuating, sidewinder-like path is the Jet Stream. Meteorologists have labeled its major crests and troughs "Pacific High" and "Aleutian Low." Every equinox they take turns setting the stage for climatic events in the region.

Certain practical implications follow from this model. One is that precipitation decreases from north to south and west to east, since lows are always moving eastward. The mountainous barrier eases a bit between Cape Scott, at the northern end of Vancouver Island and at the Seattle area, allowing storms to slip through. As a storm ascends a mountain barrier, its rapidly rising air cools and loses its ability to hold water. Phenomenal precipitation results. Areas in the lee of a mountainous land barrier—which has already sucked some of the water out of a storm—can be dramatically drier, such as the Gulf Islands.

Average annual precipitation from north to south:

Glacier Bay, Cape Fairweather, AK	170 inches
Glacier Bay, Bartlett Cove, AK	75 inches
Skagway, AK	26 inches
Juneau, AK	55 inches
Little Port Walter, Baranof Is., AK	221 inches
Kake, AK	57 inches
Ketchikan, AK	162 inches
Prince Rupert, B.C.	100 inches
Port Hardy, B.C.	70 inches
Powell River, B.C.	42 inches
Texada Island, B.C.	35 inches
Vancouver, B.C.	45 inches
Victoria, B.C.	27 inches
Olympic National Park, WA	150 inches
Port Townsend, WA	20 inches
Seattle, WA	35 inches
Olympia, WA	52 inches

Winter storms are more intense and more numerous because the temperature differential between the Japanese Current and winter arctic air and sea is much greater. Not that one would ever kayak the Inside

Passage in winter. But how early to start and how late to stay might be of greater concern.

Because winds blow from high-pressure systems to low-pressure systems, when there's a low in the Gulf of Alaska it'll blow from the southeast; when there's a high, winds will come out of the northwest. I hesitate to say this but, ceteris paribus, winds are not a major concern for the paddler along the Inside Passage. Having spent close to 24 weeks kayaking in the Sea of Cortez (and about 16 along the Northwest Coast), I've spent many more wind-borne down days in Mexico (sometimes as often as every three to four days for as many days) than I have along the Inside Passage (none). Not to say it can't happen! When a narrow channel constricts a breeze, it can intensify, and if it opposes a strong current—watch out! The chop can not only be unnerving, it can turn downright dangerous if coupled with cliffy shores and their resultant clapotis (the maelstrom produced by waves breaking and reverberating off walls). Katabatic winds, caused by warm air rapidly rising as it hits a mountain barrier and then, when cooled, shooting down its flank, are very local but very strong. (We never experienced worrisome katabatics in the Inside Passage but have, often, in Baja California.) Temperature differentials take time to build up, so calmer conditions prevail during the early morning. This is the optimum time to paddle. Exposed shores, subject to Pacific swells generated by winds a quarter of a world away, can also wreak havoc in the form of surf.

Superimposed on the natural trend for temperatures to vary according to latitude and altitude is variation according to distance from the tempering influence of the warm Japanese Current. Inside Passage temperatures, in spite of the constant pummeling of winter storms, remain mild. Juneau's average winter temperature, at 29 degrees Fahrenheit, is warmer than Chicago's (or for that matter, Moscow's—and both are considerably farther south). Summer averages are in the 60s, with many days reaching into the high 70s and low 80s. At Glacier Bay it is considerably cooler. Mid-40s to mid-60s are the daytime summer averages, with temperatures dropping further at night or near glaciers. South of Princess Royal Island it can get downright hot. Although July daytime averages in Seattle, Victoria, and Vancouver hover around 72 degrees, windless heat waves can raise the temperature into the high 90s. In fact, the mainland side of the Straits of Georgia is known as British Columbia's Sunshine Coast.

"I'm never sleeping with you again!" declared Tina, more frustrated than angry. We were camped on a cobble beach along Broughton Strait opposite picturesque Pulteney Point lighthouse. It had been a long day. Fog—formed when warm air moves over relatively colder water (more commonly in late summer and fall)—materialized like a spectral apparition, making time stand still. What a soothing delight. But just as our heads nestled down in our stuff-sack pillows, the loudest tuba in the firmaments cold-cocked us. Our earplugs were about as useful as adopting a positive attitude. It never crossed our minds that lighthouses become foghorns (duh!) when visibility is impaired. Don't let fog add discord to your marriage. Otherwise, it's only a nuisance when contemplating crossings. Better to wait until it lifts.

Just exactly what is fog? How can you get a sense of when it's likely to form or, more importantly, dissipate? There are two sorts of fog: radiation and sea fog. Both are easily understood, more or less predictable, and reasonably managed. Along the Inside Passage, during the summer paddling season, radiation fog is the primary occurrence. Precipitation can be categorized along a continuum from its mildest forms, fog and dew, through drizzle, all the way to a driving deluge. Lee Moyer, in his excellent *Sea Kayak Navigation Simplified,* has explained it quite succinctly:

> *All fog is formed in the same way: air cools to the point where it can no longer hold all its water vapor and the vapor condenses out as small droplets that are so small they are held in suspension and do not fall. If they get big enough to fall, they are called rain. Warm air can hold more moisture than cold air, which is why we use warm air to dry things. If it cools, the water comes back. The fraction of the total capability of the air that is actually used to absorb the vapor is called the relative humidity. Fifty per cent*

relative humidity means the air holds half of what it could hold. You get that sticky, clammy feeling when the air is holding about all the water vapor it can hold, and nothing will dry. As the temperature drops and the ability of the air to hold moisture decreases, eventually the temperature reaches a point where the air can hold no more moisture. That temperature is called the dew point. Dew will form on items that are cooler than the air. Typically, as surfaces radiate their heat away in the evening, they reach a point where they cool the air they touch and dew forms. When the air itself reaches that point, fog forms. Thus, fog will form in the cool of the night, be there in the morning and maybe burn off as the day warms up.

Radiation fog, as this type is called, forms as heat radiates away and air cools. It cannot coalesce when the wind blows, as the turbulence would mix the temperature variations and prevent fog from forming. Likewise, warming air in the morning or a building breeze will cause it to dissipate.

Sea fog, on the other hand, though materializing in the same way, is a different phenomenon. It forms offshore, is brought in often by strong winds, and comes in a big wall called a fog bank. Neither does the wind die quickly, nor does the fog burn off any time soon.

During the summer months, Inside Passage weather follows a pattern that is quite predictable: a series of clear days with a moderate headwind, followed by a few days of rain accompanied by a moderate tailwind. Diurnal micro-weather is also reassuringly dependable. Nights are calm and quiet, with fog or low clouds moving on shore. Mornings are God's gift to sailors. In the afternoon, moderate breezes pick up, dissipating the fog and clouds and creating a 1- to 3-foot chop, until evening when conditions calm again.

But weather is not the only concern when timing an Inside Passage venture. Nature's tides are also worth catching. Salmon runs occur in mid- to late summer. They are not to be missed. And neither are the bears taking advantage of them, particularly at Pack Creek and Anan Creek. Human salmon fishing season is a bit earlier. You can participate in the harvest either by catching your own or grubbing off the commercial and subsistence fishermen. The summer solstice is June 21. Berries ripen in August. Various cultural events, from the Tulip Festival in La Conner (spring) and Chief Seattle Days in Suquamish (August) to the West Coast Sea Kayaking Symposium in Port Townsend (September) and Canada Day (July 1) throughout the provinces, pepper the paddling season.

If attempting the entire Passage in one go, it's probably best to begin in early May. This avoids the really high temperatures possible in midsummer on the southern half and the "paddler's conundrum," that is, dressing for water temperature instead of for air temperature. Warm weather in this context, ironically, can be a hazard. Who wants to dress for 50-degree water when the air temperature is 90?

If you're doing the trip piecemeal, Puget Sound can be done anytime, though the above considerations still apply. All the other sections have no particular "best" time within the paddling season (although below Desolation Sound, the paddler's conundrum is still a concern) except for Glacier Bay. Late May and early June seem to offer the clearest weather at the northern terminus.

Getting To and From There

Part of the appeal of the Inside Passage is its relative inaccessibility by car. Ironically, the Passage is also the easiest medium for accessing this complex coast. The geomorphology of the area precludes bridges and makes road building extremely difficult and costly. Loggers have even resorted to helicopters to retrieve their harvest. This handicap has been the source of an ongoing controversy over the location of Alaska's capital, Juneau. Should it be moved to Anchorage or Fairbanks or, perhaps, some new spot in between? Engineering proposals already exist to extend the highway south from Skagway to connect with Juneau. Local resistance has put this option on hold for now. Juneau residents fear an influx of undesirable elements and a loss of their small-town atmosphere.

Coming up from the south, direct vehicular access to the coast extends as far north as Vancouver. On the central coast, Bella Coola, Kitimat, Prince Rupert, and Stewart have arterial connectors from the Alaska-Canada Highway. One can also drive to Skagway and Haines at the northern end.

The solution to the motorized access problem has been the development, in all jurisdictions, of some very sophisticated ferry systems for both cars and, in some instances, pedestrians only. Two short ferry rides connect the southern highway terminus with another 80 miles of road up to Lund, B.C. (on the mainland), while another single one opens the door to the entire length of Vancouver Island. Intricate ferry networks connect virtually all settlements along the Inside Passage and Puget Sound.

The three main ferry systems—Washington State Ferries, B.C. Ferries, and the Alaska Marine Highway—are government owned and operated. Washington State Ferries are first-come, first-served, short-run affairs, connecting nearby communities that would otherwise require a long drive or are located on unbridged islands. The ferries are the missing bridges and operate only in the State of Washington, with one important exception. Washington State Ferries also operates internationally between Anacortes, WA, and Sidney, B.C.

The Alaska Marine Highway, as its name implies, is southern Alaska's highway system and, consequently, sticks strictly to long haul (mostly). Along the Inside Passage, the Alaska Department of Transportation operates 8 ferries serving 14 communities. It also links with both the British Columbia (at Prince Rupert) and Washington State (at Bellingham) ferry systems. In 2002, the Bellingham-to-Skagway haul ran once a week at a cost of $900 for one adult with a vehicle, one way. These big, long-haul ferries can accommodate up to 625 passengers and 134 vehicles. All have restaurants, bars, lounges, gift shops, and even staterooms. At about 16 knots, the trip takes about 62 hours.

B.C. Ferries are both short haul and long haul and operate only in British Columbia. The province runs 40 ferries, some as far afield as the Queen Charlotte Islands, though most operate around small communities near southern Vancouver Island.

(continued on page 53)

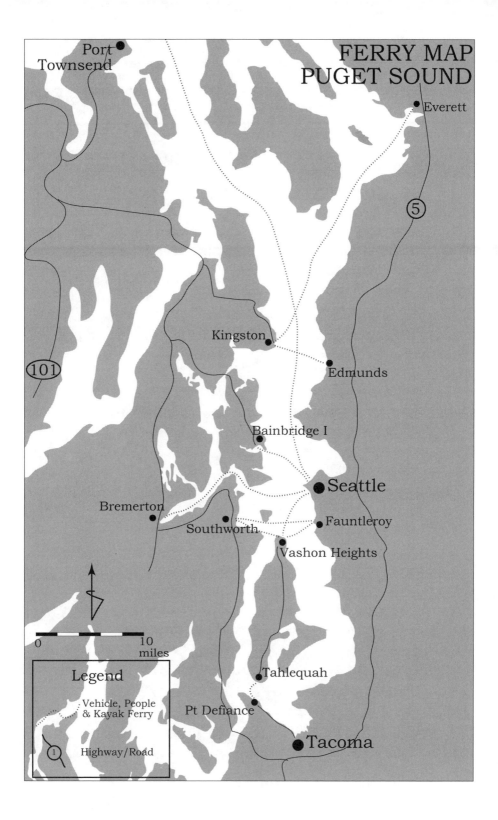

FERRY MAP
PUGET SOUND

Port Townsend

Everett

⑤

Kingston

Edmunds

Bainbridge I

Seattle

Bremerton

Southworth

Fauntleroy

Vashon Heights

⟨101⟩

N

0   10
        miles

Tahlequah

Pt Defiance

Tacoma

Legend

········· Vehicle, People
           & Kayak Ferry

① Highway/Road

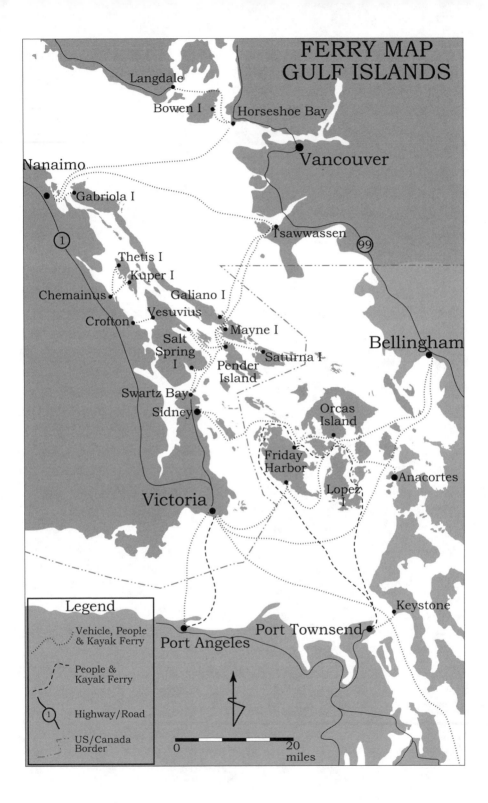

FERRY MAP
GULF ISLANDS

Langdale

Bowen I

Horseshoe Bay

Vancouver

Nanaimo

Gabriola I

Tsawwassen

99

① 1

Thetis I

Kuper I

Chemainus

Galiano I

Vesuvius

Crofton

Mayne I

Salt
Spring
I

Saturna I

Bellingham

Pender
Island

Swartz Bay

Orcas
Island

Sidney

Friday
Harbor

Anacortes

Victoria

Lopez
I

Keystone

Legend

Vehicle, People
& Kayak Ferry

People &
Kayak Ferry

Port Townsend

① 1   Highway/Road

Port Angeles

US/Canada
Border

0   20
                  miles

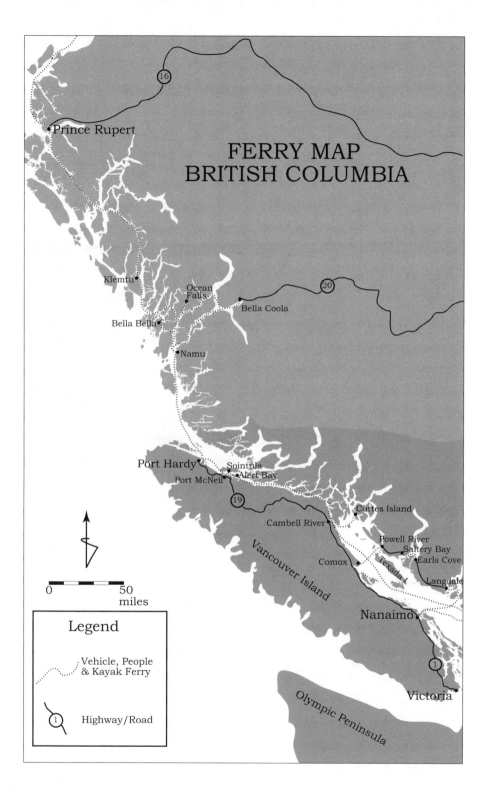

FERRY MAP
BRITISH COLUMBIA

Prince Rupert

⑯

Klemtu

Ocean
Falls

Bella Coola

⑳

Bella Bella

Namu

Port Hardy

Sointula

Alert Bay

Port McNeil

⑲

Cortes Island

Cambell River

Powell River

Saltery Bay

Comox

Texada I.

Earls Cove

Langdale

Vancouver Island

Nanaimo

①

Olympic Peninsula

Victoria

0   50
    miles

Legend

⋯⋯⋯ Vehicle, People
      & Kayak Ferry

①   Highway/Road

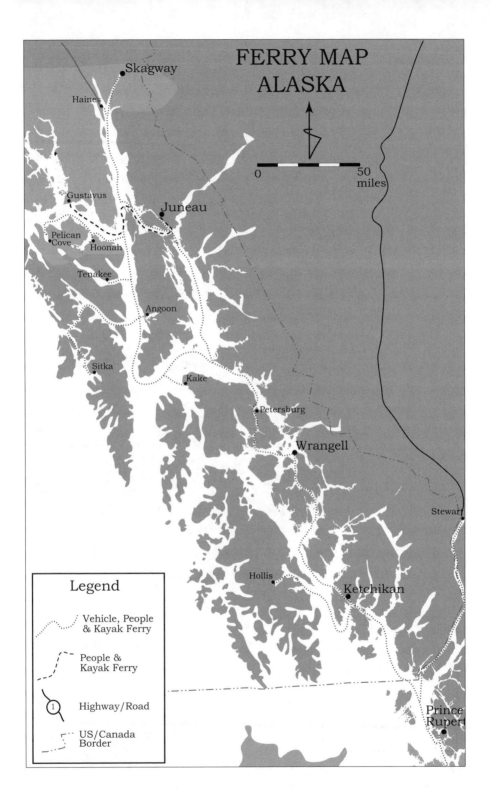

FERRY MAP
ALASKA

0   50
miles

Skagway

Haines

Gustavus

Juneau

Pelican
Cove
Hoonah

Tenakee

Angoon

Sitka

Kake

Petersburg

Wrangell

Stewart

Hollis

Ketchikan

Prince
Rupert

Legend

Vehicle, People
& Kayak Ferry

People &
Kayak Ferry

①   Highway/Road

US/Canada
Border

A small but important selection of private ferries fills specialty niches that the state and provincial ferries overlook. Most of these connect Victoria, B.C., with various cities in Washington; others service the San Juan Islands and one, the Auk Nu Ferry, is a people shuttle between Juneau and Glacier Bay National Park. Consult the route map for a full layout of all ferry routes.

All car ferries will carry kayaks and most people-shuttle ferries will also. All charge a nominal fee. When possible, ferry your boat and trip gear without a vehicle. It may not be as complex as you imagine, even when solo. With kayak wheels you can lade a fully loaded kayak onto or off the ferry without help. Long-haul ferries accommodate campers on the covered (and heated, when necessary) solarium deck and provide hot showers. Long-term parking is usually available—double-check this—at ferry terminals.

For short-haul ferries, taking the car along is not much of a problem. However, with long hauls (including the Washington State Ferry between Anacortes, WA, and Sidney, B.C., and all private ferries between Puget Sound and Vancouver Island), during peak season, car reservations are a very good idea, and the expense is much greater. In all situations, notify the ferry that you are carrying a kayak. By the way, only one kayak per passenger is customarily allowed for walk-ons. Arrive early so the crew can make necessary preparations.

People-shuttle ferries require a different approach. Empty the kayak and consolidate your dunnage. Wheels are unnecessary—the kayaks are usually loaded over the rails, with the gear remaining with the passenger as luggage. Here again, notify the ferry that you're carrying a kayak and be there early.

If you're traveling from the Lower 48, flying may be a good option but requires a folding boat. Virtually all communities are serviced by commercial airlines. Even getting somewhere without a commercial airline is doable with a bush pilot. In Canada, bush pilots are allowed to carry an external load (a hard-shell kayak) with inboard passengers. In the United States, Federal Aviation Administration (FAA) regulations do not allow this maneuver.

To contact most of the ferry services mentioned, here is a list of Internet addresses:

Sites that consolidate all information: www.ferrytravel.com and www.youra.com.

Individual ferry sites: www.wsdot.wa.gov, www.pugetsoundexpress.com, www.akferry.com, www.bcferries.bc.ca/ and www.glacierbaytravel.com (for the Auk Nu Ferry).

The Bottom Line I: Navigation

A friend of mine (let's call him Bob Ursurrun, to protect the author) once paddled 500 miles in Ethiopia using a Michelin road map and WWII vintage British Ordnance Survey maps (with all the accuracy of a gambler's hunch) to navigate. Bob was a good map reader. He had seen two tours of duty in Vietnam as a Marine Forward Observer. Just prior to and during an infantry assault, a Forward Observer, armed with map and radio, advances as close as possible to the enemy, often on his belly. With little chance to stand up and survey the territory (sometimes heavily forested and featureless) and always under threat of discovery, he pinpoints enemy troop locations and transmits the coordinates back to the artillery. The artillery then "softens" the position. Before GPS (Global Positioning System) and modern computers to aim the ordnance, this system was prone to error. Bob's life and those of his fellow advancing troops depended on the accuracy of his map reading (after all, the distance between opposing factions during an assault narrows to nil). Bob could pinpoint any location, anywhere, with the most rudimentary map and intuitive sensibilities forged under fire. Paddling the Inside Passage also requires impeccable map reading skills. Your confidence, sanity, and life depend on it.

Even if you're as skilled as Bob, you'll need more than a road map to paddle to Alaska. Traditionally, sea voyages rely on nautical charts and coast pilots, and so do we as two resources in our arsenal. These focus on marine and coastal features with a smattering of prominent interior landmarks—fine for oceangoing vessels. But kayaks are a coastal adaptation, and kayakers rely on land for sleeping, eating, safety, and even going to the bathroom (by and large). We also need to know the lay of the land, and only topographic maps can provide that. Additionally, a kayaker needs one map of the entire Inside Passage, not only to plot his overall route while planning the expedition but also to keep the big picture in focus while on the water. Add cruising guides, tide and current charts, and specialty maps and you'll be lucky to have room for food, tent, and sleeping bag. Some serious editing is required.

First, the overall map. R.O. Malin's two-portion *The Northwest Coast* map, published by the Sobay Company, is widely available, handsome, easy on the eyes, and great for figuring and plotting the entire route at home. It's too big and ungainly to carry in a kayak, but it looks sharp hung on the wall. *Alaska & Canada's Inside Passage Cruise Tour Guide,* published by Coastal Cruise Tour Guides, is an excellent alternative that you can carry with you (plus, it has lots of interpretive stuff in the margins). Both are available from Armchair Sailor, 2110 Westlake Ave. N., Seattle, WA 98109, 1-800-875-0852.

Now for the meat. Nautical charts come in a bewildering array of scales. Exactly which to pick is mind-numbing. Although the largest scale (that which shows the greatest detail) is the most useful, you can't practically carry them all (and neither might your wallet). Armchair Sailor has compiled a list of necessary charts, both US and Canadian, for the Inside Passage. With this list in one hand and the chart catalog (Armchair Sailor can provide these, too) in the other, you can start editing from and adding to the list. US nautical charts and catalogs are also available from the source, Distribution Branch (N/CG33), National Ocean Service, Riverdale, MD 20737, 301-436-6990, while Canadian charts are published by Canadian Hydrographic Service, Department of Fisheries and Oceans, Institute of Ocean Sciences, Patricia Bay, 9860 West Saanich Road, P.O. Box 6000, Sydney, B.C. V8L 4B2, Canada.

Compromise and decide on a selection that will at least cover your entire route with a mix of some small- and mostly medium-scale charts. Add a smattering of large-scale charts to cover problem areas such as small island archipelagos, congested commercial navigational routes, complex bays and ports, and areas subject to drying at low tides. A cheaper and simpler alternative might be Armchair Sailor's Chart

Portfolios. These are full-size, black-and-white copies of the latest editions of official government charts, printed on bond paper at less than half price. Each portfolio includes all the sailing, coastal, and harbor charts you're likely to need. Another reasonable compromise is the *Marine Atlas*, Volumes 1 & 2, published by Bayless Enterprises, Inc., a complete set of charts in book form at various convenient scales. While not as easy on the eyes and focusing on major cruise routes, and with a sometimes glaring lack of detail, these are considerably cheaper than a full set of nautical charts.

Topographic maps—both US and Canadian—are published in uniform increasing scale. A full set of the 1:250,000 scale gives good coverage at a reasonable price and volume. Though charts often note the character of the shore, they don't always at larger scales. Topo maps show stream locations (a must for fresh water) and allow one to infer the shore character from the lay of the land hindshore. Additionally, the 1:250,000 scale (if you shop smartly) will cover alternate routes you might decide on in the heat of the paddle (we changed routes three times and reconsidered a fourth). If expense is a concern—after all, you can spend close to $1,000 on charts and maps—stick, at least, to a full set of topos at this scale, and, if you can afford it, add some well-chosen charts.

United States topo maps are available from USGS Information Services, Box 25286, Denver, CO 80225, 1-800-USA-MAPS, as are indices. For Canadian equivalents, contact the Canada Map Office, Department of Energy, Mines and Resources, 615 Booth Street, Ottawa, Ontario K1A 0E9, Canada, 613-952-7000. For a full list of the 1:250,000 scale topo maps required for the proposed route, see appendix A.

Finally, there are a variety of specialty maps that can be more or less helpful. US Forest Service maps of the Tongass National Forest, Misty Fjords National Monument, and Admiralty Island National Monument have some features that are very useful, for example, Forest Service rental cabins (these are available for rent at a very nominal fee, though they require advance booking), public shelters (a bit of a disappointment—they provide shelter from rain, not bears; available on a first-come, first-served basis), and, for Misty Fjords, highlighted areas where it's nigh impossible to land. All are put out by the USDA

Forest Service, Information Center, 101 Egan Drive, Juneau, AK 99801, 907-586-8751.

International Sailing Supply (320 Cross Street, Punta Gorda, FL 33950, 1-800-423-9026) publishes a set of waterproof charts covering Puget Sound and the San Juan Islands that are compact and reasonably priced, with detail insets. (They may now publish more charts of relevant areas.) In Canada, Coastal Waters Recreation (Suite 547, 185–911 Yates St., Victoria, B.C. V8V 4Y9, Canada, www.coastalwatersrec.com) has a handful of specialty kayaking maps replete with backcountry campsites, provincial parks, sea caves, government wharves, native reserves, hiking trails, wildlife viewing sites, and so on, for Bella Bella, the Gulf Islands, Desolation Sound, Johnstone Strait, and many more areas.

No list of maps would be complete without Stephen Hilson's two-volume historical atlases of the Inside Passage, *Exploring Puget Sound & British Columbia* and *Exploring Alaska & British Columbia*, both published by Evergreen Pacific Publishing Ltd. These are actual charts (though technically not for navigation, as their information is not updated) reconfigured into book form, with a good color scheme, profile pen-and-ink drawings, and aerial color photographs. But the real purpose of these volumes is the etymology of place-names and history associated with the sea and landforms. Want to find out something about the Sukoi Islands just north of Petersburg? Open the folio to the appropriate chart and you'll find: "Fox farms on Big and Little Sukoi operated in 1923 under the name of Sukoi Is. Fox Co. *Sukoi* is the Russian word for dry." This information, aside from its intrinsic value, implies that not only is a landing possible here but that reasonable camping may be available. The texts are printed right on the charts using shores as margins.

On top of every successful map lies a compass. Sea kayakers need two. For technical orientation, especially in like-sized and like-shaped, island-studded mini-archipelagos, where disorientation can occur for absolutely no reason at all, a good handheld compass is a must. It helps if the compass comes equipped with a bearing-sighting notch in conjunction with a mirror so it can be held up for an accurate sight-reading. Also indispensable, both for target fixation and gauging drift, is a deck-mounted compass. There are many models, some more readable than others. Make sure yours is mounted to enhance its readability.

Indispensable for on-board navigation is a homemade tool I call Rosie. I do all my navigation off magnetic readings; I never correct for true north, as I would invariably befuddle myself and make mistakes. Rosie is a small compass rose copied from a chart onto a rectangular plastic transparency. Additionally, along one edge, I inscribe a mileage scale from a 1:250,000 topo map. Rosie should depict magnetic bearings prominently, while her up- and downsides ought to align with true north so she can be easily aligned with longitude lines on the map. Rosie has a sister named Audrey (after Audrey Sutherland, her inventor). Audrey is a transparent, gallon-size baggie with parallel lines drawn across it every 5 miles (again, scaled from a 1:250,000 topo map) with an indelible marker. Audrey serves as a set of foldable, disposable parallel lines for setting courses and doubles as a portable scale (remember that scale varies on charts, so either have more than one Audrey for different charts, or read distances only from the 1:250,000 topo map). Audrey can store Rosie. Commercially available Rosie-Audrey combos are known as "coursers." (For a detailed discussion on the construction and use of Rosie—with a photocopiable compass rose—see "The Kayaker's Course Plotter" by Dennis Fortier in the December 2003 issue of *Sea Kayaker*.)

There are many more aspects to kayak navigation in addition to map reading. David Burch, in *Fundamentals of Kayak Navigation*, covers them all. We carried his book on two legs of our trip. Few can master all the tricks and techniques he discusses—and not all are essential—while many are unnecessary when in view of highly featured terrain. Starting in Puget Sound is a good strategy if in the least bit of doubt about your navigational acumen: you can always resort to the ignominy of asking for directions. GPS is no substitute for ability. Though I own one, we never carried it. It really comes into its own in featureless terrain (always stay within sight of shore), during blind—fog or night—navigation (ditto), when requiring pinpoint precision (you're not digging for treasure or directing mortar bombardment), and, if in doubt, to verify your position. But if you need GPS to verify your position, your skills are inadequate for kayaking the Inside Passage.

The *Coast Pilot* (called *Sailing Directions* in Canada) may seem like a quaint eccentricity to those brought up on terrestrial navigation. Just exactly what is its function? Do we really need a running commentary on the marine cartographer's work? In his *Log of the Sea of Cortez,* John Steinbeck wrote:

> *In the first place, the compilers of this book are cynical men. They know that they are writing for morons, that if by any effort their descriptions can be misinterpreted or misunderstood by the reader, that effort will be made. These writers have a contempt for almost everything. They would like an ocean and coastline unchanging and unchangeable; lights and buoys that do not rust and wash away; winds and storms that come at specified times; and, finally, reasonably intelligent men to read their instructions. They are gratified in none of these desires. They try to write calmly and objectively, but now and then a little bitterness creeps in.*

Notwithstanding the sardonic commentary, Steinbeck admired the terseness of *Coast Pilot* prose, which—besides dealing with navigational details (such as shipping lanes, local customs, rights-of-way, Customs procedures, etc.) and variable conditions not reliably rendered on charts—gives a succinct, technical summary of weather patterns (and extremes), tidal and current advisories, verbal descriptions of coastlines, protected harbors, and port descriptions. *Coast Pilot* is updated annually, on a more regular basis than charts. Unfortunately they are promiscuous. Written for every type of craft, from a kayak to a supertanker, they take on all comers. Without a *Coast Pilot,* commercial shipping (and the mobility of anything larger than a skiff) would be seriously hampered. Fortunately, kayaks can slow down and reverse faster than a dreadnought, won't sink when colliding with a reef, don't suffer prop damage when impaled by a deadhead, and are usually dry-docked overnight. Before (figuratively) weighing anchor, at least read the relevant volume, highlight information you might find helpful, copy it, condense it, and take it with you.

More useful for the kayaker, because they're written for small, mostly recreational craft, are the privately published cruising guides such as *Charlie's Charts North to Alaska* by Charles E. Wood, *A Cruising Guide to Puget Sound* by Migael Scherer, and the multivolume Northwest Coast series by Don Douglass & Reanne Hemingway-Douglass. These mostly incorporate the pertinent *Coast Pilot* information; delete the mostly—from the paddler's perspective—irrelevant material, and greatly expand on stuff definitely useful to the kayaker. Overall, the Douglass guides are the most informative and may merit being taken along (we did, though selectively edited). *Charlie's Charts North to Alaska* is strong on ports and rapids sketches—definitely a useful feature. These and a variety of lesser gunkholing guides for selected sections of the Inside Passage are all available from Armchair Sailor.

A variety of general outdoor activity and strictly paddling guides have also been published for selected areas of the Inside Passage. These cover the gamut from what to do, to where to stay, to where to eat and what to see. The majority of paddling guides, in addition to covering discrete portions, are organized in "loop-trip format," mostly short loop outings with detailed information on access, camping, and return. For a list of these and other references of even more limited scope, check the bibliography.

The good news is that tide tables, in a 3 x 5-inch booklet, are complimentary at marine retailers in Alaska. In Canada, you'll have to buy them along with current tables. For Puget Sound, both are available at the many kayak shops in the area. Current tables are particularly important in the San Juan Islands and Desolation Sound. Tidal flows move away from and toward the Pacific, into and away from shore. Tidal height variation and current strength increase in proportion to the distance from open ocean and constriction of the passage up which the water must travel. A good example of this phenomenon is the head of navigation in the Sea of Cortez, where the Colorado River delta is located. Tidal heights at Ensenada, on the open Pacific, are minimal, while at San Felipe, directly across the peninsula in the Cortez, tides rise more than 20 feet. This is because during the six or so hours that the tide rises a foot at Ensenada, it must duplicate the same feat at the head of the Gulf, negotiating the length of the Baja Peninsula and the constriction of the Midriff Islands in the attempt. So, to compensate, the tide rushes in at a much greater speed. But it has no brakes, so it over-compensates and piles up (late, at that, since the obstacles succeed in delaying it) at its destination. Then it must duplicate the process in reverse when departing. The tide only slows and stops when it accomplishes its goal—being in or out. This respite is known as the "slack."

One might then logically conclude that slack water would therefore always coincide with high or low tide. And in a perfect world—and some real locations—that is, in fact, the case. Unfortunately, geography and hydrodynamics complicate matters in counterintuitive ways. A good analogy is a person taking a bath. If he or she moves forward to adjust the hot/cold water mix, their torso pushes a pillow of water forward, creating a "high tide." Instantly, the two narrow spots adjacent to their hips lower significantly, and water rushes in to fill the voids. At their lowest point, the voids experience no slack as water constantly rushes in to equalize levels. So, in the real world, what is the relationship between tidal extremes and slack? During neap tides, tidal extremes and slack tend to coincide; during spring tides, because of the greater volumes of water being exchanged, slack will typically trail high and low tide, sometimes by as much as an hour.

When tides collide with an oblong island lying perpendicular to the inflow (as at Vancouver, Princess Royal, and the Pitt Islands), they split and do a flanking maneuver around both ends. Exactly where they meet (see the current tables) will determine where the current reverses. Some spots are downright weird. In some channels the current always flows in one direction—for example, Colvos Passage in Puget Sound. We found this to be the case in Griffin Pass, a narrow channel on the central B.C. coast. Though technically "uncharted," due to its inappropriateness for craft larger than kayaks, it is still worth traversing for its shortcut and isolation. (The exact nature of its tides and currents await a modern-day Vancouver.)

It is better to go with the current than to buck it. But if you have to buck it, buck up; it's often not as bad as it's been made out to be. By and large, most locales are subject to flows of nil to 2 knots current; a few, 3–4 knots. Many are manageable by working the shore, nearly always scalloped (sea kayaking is best along shore, anyway), where the flow is slowed due to friction against the land and even reverses sometimes, due to the formation of eddies. Our experience, over a day's paddle, was that one hour more or less, or a bit more exertion (or coasting) was negligible—just part of the trip. A very few places dictate when you can paddle, and at these you must work with the current, or actually avoid them. Seymour Narrows has currents clocked at 16 knots. Yuculta, Whirlpool, and Greene Point Rapids in Desolation Channel must be timed for slack water. Many channel crossings also either require a strategy—such as bracketing the slack, or even ferry gliding (Portland Canal, for instance)—or at least an awareness of what the tides and currents are up to.

When winds mate with currents, sea states metamorphose. Downwind currents have their swells minimized by the flattening effect of the breeze. Conversely, when wind opposes current, wave frequency is shortened; waves steepen, froth, and break. Under both situations, sea states are at variance with one's intuitive expectations. These conditions achieve exquisite hellishness at headlands where currents converge or separate, creating tide rips.

Rips are first sensed as a low roar, like an imminent rapid. The waves become irregular and pyramidal, leaping up and disappearing chaotically. Take evasive actions so as to avoid them. If you cannot avoid the rip, head straight through it, paddling hard, à la Major Powell, to maintain balance.

The worst current conditions are encountered at major outflow channels. Extensive marine incursions, such as Portland and Butte Inlets, suck in and disgorge huge amounts of water during the tide cycles. Time your major inlet crossings with slack tide. But even more catastrophic are the outflow deltas of big rivers. The Skeena River, for example, dumps a continuous and unremitting volume of discharge into the Pacific. There is no slack. Eddy lines, with gargantuan whirlpools, can measure 50 feet or more across. Opposing currents clash and can cause aggregate differentials exceeding 8 knots, unpredictable wave flourishes, and a maelstrom best avoided by choosing a route far from the constriction of the channel proper, well at the verges of the delta's funnel mouth.

More than once we dreamed of floating the Inside Passage. Unfortunately, it was no dream. At least three times we woke up bobbing on our Thermarests wondering what the world had come to. Our campsites had been flooded by the wee hour's high tides. It was an undignified, disoriented, and naked scramble to move the tent and retrieve our paraphernalia—an ordeal better prepared souls ought to miss. Just refer to the article "Gauging High Tides: The Rule of 12s" by Bob Hume in the June 1999 issue of *Sea Kayaker.* Hume presents a rule-of-thumb approach to estimating how high the tide might encroach at any one particular spot when somewhere betwixt high and low tides. Though this is not easily committed to memory, and calls upon full concentration when all you want is a place to sleep after a miserable day of paddling in full conditions, better to have it and compute your situation than not.

Back home, a watch is unnecessary; out where the blade meets the swell, it is an essential navigational tool. Gauging tides for one, and determining slack—which at Yuculta Rapids opens a window of opportunity only minutes long—is impossible without a watch. Dead reckoning would be truly moribund without a timepiece. Sometimes paddling along a featureless shore, ensconced in a downy quilt of fog (say near False Head on the north shore of Vancouver Island), the only way to gauge progress is by counting the hours of steady paddling. Crossing straits wider than 2 miles is a test of faith without a watch. If you can, carry a watch with a few bells and whistles. Alarms are great for catching early tides. Waterproofness is de rigeur. I'd wear mine on my kayak's deck bungee so it wouldn't interfere with the drysuit gasket or chafe my wrist. There I could glance at it without breaking rhythm, and its thermometer could measure air temperature without the influence of a warm body. Whenever we approached glaciers, the chill was noticeable.

Passing McBride Glacier, my hands went numb; the temperature had dropped 16 degrees, to 48 degrees Fahrenheit.

The barometric tendency line on the Suunto altimeter/watch is a great wind and rain predictor. It shows barometric pressure trend for the previous six hours, with the trend for the last three subject to a separate indicator. If it was clear with a northwesterly breeze, and the second half of that little indicator line went limp, the wind, without fail, would calm or back around and the humidity would hit dew point within the hour. If both sides of the barometric tendency line pointed down, it was time for a real weather report.

The Bottom Line II: Safety

A VHF radio is a handy gadget to have along, especially now that new Federal Communications Commission (FCC) regulations have made them simpler to own and operate. During wretched evenings we'd gather round the console like Depression-era families hanging on to FDR's every word in hopes of better prospects for the morrow. Of course, you can just carry a weather radio, but these don't seem as powerful as a good VHF. When only receiving, a battery charge lasts about two weeks, so we brought along an AA battery adapter and spare batteries. During transmission, power consumption is much greater, and, particularly for Luddites like us, manipulation is much more complicated. But if you can master the button-pushing/releasing, talking/ listening sequence, the stylized jargon and the self-conscious trolling for strangers monitoring their radios, you too can transmit over the airwaves. You can even make telephone calls through a marine operator. That tenuous electronic link with the outside world can be a real lifesaver, but don't depend on it. Although the coast is peppered with relay stations, often only line-of-sight communication is dependable. Great for contacting passing traffic. Transmission and reception both improve with altitude and proximity to settlements. See appendix C for basic marine radio protocol for kayakers.

Cell phone coverage is very patchy, subject to overlapping jurisdictions, and won't provide a weather report. Satellite phones are a better bet. Not much larger than ordinary cell phones, Iridium and Global-star satellite phones provide full coverage anywhere, anytime for a reasonable price. For the full lowdown on these see Gary Lai's "Keeping in Touch from Anywhere: Two Affordable Handheld Satellite Phones for Sea Kayakers" in the December 2003 issue of *Sea Kayaker*. Nonetheless, electronic technology and seawater don't mix well; the prudent paddler will rely primarily on himself.

Since logging a float plan with the relevant authorities is impractical, your first line of defense must be a prudent and conservative approach to potentially dangerous situations (note the quote at the heading of this chapter): Stay out of trouble. Your second line of defense is to stay upright. Next is an absolutely bombproof Eskimo roll. In my opinion, like the admonition concerning navigation skills, don't go if you can't roll. That was the logic behind the roll's invention. Inuit hunters *never,* ever left their boats because the consequences were just too dire. So they developed rolls for virtually any predicament into which they might be cast. These ran the gamut from assisted rolls (other kayaks or device-aided rolls), through various paddle rolls, to hand and body English rolls. Modern kayakers can profit from this approach.

Conventional river kayaking emphasizes the screw (or C-to-C) roll because it's quick and doesn't require hand placement changes. With a small, light boat, close to shore, failure is no big deal: just try again. In a fully loaded sea kayak, with deck impedimenta resisting your efforts (God knows how far from land), and the panic of impending doom overwhelming your already strained disposition from battling gnarly conditions, the screw roll is not my first choice. If you go over, you must get up; if not on the first attempt, you've got to have the confidence in your system that allows success very soon. First, ensure you and your kayak are as tightly mated as an abalone to its shell; a kayak is virtually uncontrollable if you're lounging in it as if it were a bathtub. Then, go as light as you can, and carry nothing on your deck. I realize that this is easier said than done, but some compromises are possible. Say you normally carry spare paddles, charts, a pump, a tow/rescue line, and a deck bag on top. (If you have other gear on deck, get a bigger kayak.) At least make sure the deck bag is small, not floppy, hydrodynamic, and bound to the deck like a limpet; that way, if you have to roll, it won't thwart your efforts. If you purposely take a calculated risk and head out in questionable conditions, clear the decks and stow everything inside. After all, bigger boats do the same, and, as Louis Pasteur once said: "Chance favors the prepared."

The trouble with the screw roll is its poor leverage and indeterminacy of blade angle. So I prefer a different approach: get the most leverage by using the entire length of the paddle and position the blade exactly, for the most resistance, by holding the blade in your hand and adjusting its precise angle. These types of rolls—there are many—are generically known as extended paddle rolls. I favor two: the Pawlatta, for its ease of execution and similarity to the screw roll; and the put-across, because it's the only paddle roll I find intuitive. Two resources that have merit are *1st Roll: Eskimo Roll for Sea Kayakers,* a video produced by Outer Island Kayak and focusing on a simplified approach to learning the extended paddle roll; and "The Vertical Storm Roll: Trick or Skill?" by Doug Alderson in the December 2001 issue of *Sea Kayaker.* Even if you master these rolls, some additional aids are available, and I'll review them here because, like the Inuit, I believe that exiting the boat is out of the question.

The Petrussen maneuver. This is a fancy name for a very simple technique that allows a kayaker to get a breath while upside down. It requires dislodging oneself from the viselike grip of your fit by pushing slightly away from the seat, twisting the body sideways around the capsized kayak, and then raising the head above water to breathe, cry out for help, or wait for an assisted roll. For a detailed description see Greg Stamer's article, "The Petrussen Maneuver; A New Twist on an Old Technique" in the August 2000 issue of *Sea Kayaker.*

Assisted rolls. Assisted rolls have a long pedigree in rescue instruction but are little if ever used. I suspect they evolved as a response to capsizes due to Inuit hunting mishaps. In calm water, with other hunters nearby, the assisted roll was a viable option. In modern sea kayaking, capsizes are due to violent conditions. Violent conditions require full concentration and necessitate a greater spacing of paddling companions to allow for unimpeded maneuvering, thereby rendering an assisted roll more improbable. The Petrussen maneuver could prove useful in these conditions.

Air bladders. Another take-off on Inuit ingenuity is the Backup by Roll-Aid Safety, Inc., P.O. Box 72005, Vancouver, B.C. V6R 4P2, Canada. Inuit hunters carried an inflated seal bladder on deck, attached to the harpoon, to prevent speared game from escaping by diving. This rendered retrieval a snap. In the event of capsize, the bladder also provided rescue buoyancy. The Backup is a compact, CO_2 cartridge-activated nylon bladder that can be carried on deck unobtrusively and inflates in seconds. Just deploy, place your hands on the 80 pounds of buoyancy, pull up (or hip-flick), and you're up. It is reusable with a new CO_2 cartridge. For what to do in the maelstrom with the resultant beach ball, consult the instructions. Although we both have a variety of dependable rolls, we each carry a Backup.

Underwater supplementary air devices. Back in the 1970s someone came up with the idea of using the fetid air inside a kayak to extend the time a paddler could spend upside down. This was accomplished by extending a flexible rubber hose from an opening in the sprayskirt to the mouth. At the sprayskirt, the hose had about a 2-inch rigid end that extended through the neoprene so that, when upside down, any puddle of water in the kayak would not be aspirated. The seal consisted of off-the-shelf PVC screw fixtures with plastic washers. The mouth end was a snorkel bit. You could unscrew the hose and cap the rigid tube if you did not require it deployable, or you could just keep the whole thing on the sprayskirt and out of the way under a bungee. This device requires a tight-fitting (torso-wise) spraydeck. It was marketed for a short time and died an unsung death, probably because it was aimed at the whitewater market. It wouldn't be hard for the do-it-yourselfer to reinvent, perhaps not by attaching it, but simply by placing the hose through the sprayskirt tube against the paddler's chest. That way the mouthpiece is always close to the chin. An EPA analysis of cockpit air quality is still pending.

Yakerz! used to market a refillable air bladder that attached to the PFD. The KUBA (Kayaker's Underwater Breathing Apparatus) was a supplemental air system designed to decrease water acclimation anxiety by providing one to ten breaths with hands-free access through a standard hydration-system bite valve. It could be refilled on the spot and retailed for about $159. Unfortunately, Yakerz! seems to have disappeared. But the idea of the KUBA has merit and may soon be resuscitated under a different guise. See also Chris Cunningham's review in *Sea Kayaker,* October 2002. Rapid Air markets an emergency air supply that provides 15–20 breaths, is very compact, and refillable from a compressed-air source. It is available from Rapid Products, Inc., at 303-761-9600 or www.rapidair.net.

This is as good a place as any to mention nose plugs. Before you dismiss them as totally déclassé, consider that none other than Derek Hutchinson, one of the great expedition sea kayakers, is an advocate of their use. They weigh nothing and are totally unobtrusive worn around the neck. The only way, sans nose plugs, to keep water out of your nose while upside down is to exhale precious air. Not a good strategy when dumped unexpectedly. They can be attached during extreme conditions, prophylactically, in anticipation of disaster.

Reentry techniques after an exit are a last resort. There are many, assisted and unassisted, with and without aids. Learn the ones appropriate for your boat, but don't depend on them. I cannot emphasize enough: *Don't exit your kayak* unless you're close to shore and braving the surf is the easier option. Conditions that flipped you don't facilitate reentry.

Tina and I had drifted apart. Not metaphorically, but purposefully and determinedly. We were crossing the junction of Frederick Sound and Stephens Passage, between the Brothers and False Point Pybus on Admiralty Island. Morning had dawned calm and foggy. We set out. Currents are known to do strange things at points where they split or converge. Never mind that the map labeled this a "false" point. Then the wind picked up, against the tide. With the currents mixing, the wind in opposition, Pacific swell impinging, and clapotis adding to the anarchy, a large portion of sea looked like a punk hairdo moussed by a drunken stylist. The trough-to-crest height (not that this was clearly discernible, what with rogue wind and regular swell adding to the confusion) was only 6 to 8 feet. But the currents were stronger than we were, and the chaos required the reflexes of a boxer. We tried to bore away at sprint speed but were ineluctably sucked in. So as not to collide, we put more distance between us after a fleeting, knowing glance. Every stroke was a compromise between staying upright and making headway for shore. Time dissolved.

"I was sure I'd have to roll," Tina blurted when she hit the beach.

"Me too," I retorted.

Having a bombproof roll provides the confidence necessary to tackle such conditions and to execute braces with total commitment, not halfhearted lily-dips. During the entire trip, we never had to roll; but the self-assurance instilled by its integration into our tool kit enabled us to face many a planned—and unplanned—situation.

The Bottom Line III: Seamanship

When the ancient Germanic tribes who would become the Angles and the Saxons were confronted by a novelty, instead of making up a new word to describe it or borrowing a word from a neighboring tribe, they would join old words to form a new, compound word. Whale + road = whaleroad = sea. Likewise, Old English took sea + man + ship and created seamanship, a word whose meaning is neatly summed up by the three individual concepts in sea, man, and ship but implies much more. Seamanship is the characteristic that describes the successful adaptation of an individual to the marine environment through the use of a boat.

For the sea kayaker (as for any mariner), seamanship means proficiency in the operation of your craft and knowledge of the stage upon which it performs—the sea. Exercise of the two in tandem yields experience, which in turn is maximized by self-knowledge and common sense. A highly developed degree of seamanship often expresses itself intuitively. But don't be fooled; always check your intuition with reality—it can only make you wiser.

Your seamanship needs work if your weather predictions are no better than a crapshoot; if waves and clouds, like penguins, all look the same; if you can't talk and stay the course at the same time; if your dead reckoning is way off not only in distance but also in direction; if boat wakes panic or even capsize you; if it's always a revelation what the tide is doing; if you need to ask directions from passing boats; if you need to ask directions from passing boats but refrain out of fear of ridicule; if you are disproportionately plagued by rotten luck; or if you don't know the difference between a *guyot* and a *gyre*. So, what degree of seamanship is essential for kayaking the Inside Passage? There are no absolutes; seamanship is a journey, not a destination.

Bears

You will encounter two species of bears, grizzly *(Ursus arctos horribilis)* and black *(Ursus americanus),* and, if you're very lucky, a subspecies, the white (not albino) Kermode *(Ursus americanus kermodei),* a variant of the black bear most common on Princess Royal Island. Though they are technically the same species, brown bears are the coastal complement of grizzly bears. Adaptation to a different environment has created differences in behavior and size: incipient speciation. The coastal brown bears subsist on a rich diet of berries and fat-flush salmon, gathered from a crowded littoral; consequently, they are larger yet more tolerant of each other, requiring less territory per individual than their inland relatives. Some giant males on Kodiak Island can weigh as much as 1,400 pounds, though on Admiralty Island they seldom exceed 700 pounds. At Yellowstone National Park, a grizzly requires about 500 square miles of forage territory, nowhere near Admiralty Island's tolerant density of one bear per square mile.

Much has been written on bear behavior, bear attacks, and bear safety. Read it. (The best of the lot is *Bear Attacks: Their Causes and Avoidance* by Stephen Herrero.) I'll confine my comments to my experience, reliable anecdote, and the conclusions of my unplanned research. Though the two species' behaviors and habitats differ, for practical purposes, mitigation of encounters is about the same. We en-

Black bear

countered more black bears than grizzlies along the Inside Passage.

Bears are very much like humans in that their behavior varies according to their nature and nurture and can vary tremendously from individual to individual. So prepare for anything. This said, there are four broad categories of bears:

Wild bears. These are the bear equivalent of Rousseau's natural savage. Most bears fall into this category. Most of the material written concerning bear behavior applies to these bears. If you're a good camper and follow all the bear camping rules, you'll have little problem, for instance, give plenty of notice concerning your presence and do not make food a point of contention with Mr. Bear. Most wild bears will leave you alone and avoid potential trouble. The more curious will follow suit after a more cursory smell-over.

People-accustomed bears. These bears like to mingle, though many may lack social graces. They are the ones often found in national parks such as Yosemite and Yellowstone. To them, people are little different from trees. They'll mostly leave you alone and are totally blasé about your presence. The only likely locales for these bears are the Pack Creek and Anan Creek Bear Observatories, Glacier Bay National Park, especially on the Beardsley Islands, or perhaps, developed campgrounds. A very thin line separates people-accustomed bears from the next category.

Food-accustomed bears. Luckily, the NPS authorities (in the park alone, of course) have done an excellent and very successful job of managing human behavior so as not to create this type of bear. A food-accustomed bear has either been given a handout or has discovered, on his own (due to either bad camping behavior or improper garbage disposal), people food. This bear will walk through you to get food or what he expects to be food. You're in trouble only if you give him food, on purpose or inadvertently. Or if he thinks you're holding out. Public authorities exile these bears when they get too aggressive. You might run into them close to settlements or fish camps.

Bad bears. These are rare. One grizzly, in Montana, had acquired the reputation of attacking, and maiming or killing, any living thing he ran into. Yet his behavior was not hunting, per se, as he'd abandon the kill site. Not at all like a typical grizzly (they don't even hunt people). After one too many sprees, he was finally hunted down and killed by the authorities. The necropsy revealed an ingrown tooth. Poor bear, the pain must have turned him into a bully. But it's not the grizzly that makes a good bad bear candidate—it's the black bear that can develop a taste for human prey and actually stalk and kill people. Watch out for disingenuous black bears.

So should you take a gun? Pepper spray? A rubber President Nixon mask? I've never had to use the first two but had great results with the last. To kill a bear you need a big gun, and it must withstand the rigors of kayaking in the Northwest. Since handguns are illegal in Canada and a .44 Magnum would be strictly a mano a mano last resort, the gun of choice seems to be a stainless-steel, 12-gauge shotgun with as short a barrel as you can get away with and a capacity of five to seven solid slugs. The problem is that, inside a small dome tent, with a bear tearing through the wall—admittedly an improbable scenario—a shotgun just doesn't have the turning radius of a handgun. Any gun is an absolute last resort. Shooting a bear when it is charging at you is not recommended. The bear almost always lives long enough to maul the shooter severely. If you do take a gun, think of it as protection for your buddies, not yourself. Whatever you choose to take, you must always have it at the ready, and know how to use it, both safety-wise and for effectiveness.

Dances with Bears: I

Once, while portaging a waterfall on the Thelon River in the Northwest Territories of Canada, I tired of lugging the damn shotgun on every single carry (there were many). We had decided to break up the portage into relays and, for the first relay, were stockpiling gear atop the escarpment that defined the river channel's gorge. We would then do a second relay and negotiate the steep final descent down to the put-in eddy. After doing the penultimate trip down to the river, we trudged back up for one more load. Suddenly, I turned to Martha, my companion. "Look!" I screamed in a whisper.

There, only about 20 yards above us (it was a good 45-degree slope), stood a black bear, enthroned among the blueberry bushes, with a foot-long purple drool swinging from his mouth, legs splayed atop my shotgun like the Colossus of Rhodes. We backed away slowly just as every bear-warning pamphlet advises (*never* turn your back to a bear!), and decided to execute a very wide and slow end run around the spot. Luckily, he didn't give chase. We were hoping that, by the time we circled around, he'd have moved on. On our second (and much delayed) approach, this time arriving in a different spot—against all odds—he surprised us again. Martha panicked and ran. The bear charged. I was right in his path.

It wasn't a malicious charge, nor did it seem premeditated. It was instinctive, automatic. Instead of my life flashing before my eyes, all the potential lovers I had ever known but never consummated flooded my mind. At the same time, my mind reviewed all the possible effective strategies I could now call upon. Warrior mode took over. I put on a terrifying face, waved my arms, screamed, and counter charged. The bear ran off. The Nixon mask worked.

This is supposed to be a good strategy, in extremis, for dealing with a black bear. Not so with a grizzly. If these charge, at best it's a bluff: he'll stop short of you or run past you. Make not a sound, cower, give up, and assume the fetal position to protect your vitals. At worst, he'll thump and scratch you—no small thing. Just don't resist.

Pepper spray is the repellent of choice for Canadian park rangers. But it takes guts to deploy, because you trigger it earlier than you intuitively think you ought to. Spray before a charge (*nothing* can stop a charging grizzly at close range). Bears will usually echo- and olfactory-survey the scene (rumor has it they're myopic), often standing up to do so (mainly grizzlies), and swing their heads back and forth. (Actually, bears have damn good eyesight, and this combination of behaviors is now believed to be the bear's way of integrating visual, olfactory, and auditory clues into one seamless whole.) Spray now. The objective is to have the bear inhale a bit of the capsicum to irritate his mucous membranes. If he does, voilà, he'll turn and run. But consider two things: proximity and wind strength/direction. Getting pepper spray on you is harmless (just as for the bear) but a hell of a bad trip. At least *you* know it can't hurt you. Rinse with water.

Bear avoidance is a lot better than bear evasion. Do you announce your presence or keep a low profile? When hiking, the former; when camping, both strategies should be taken into account. Never hike in dense ground cover, and always make plenty of noise. Don't rely on in-effective little bells: sing loudly, argue politics, or recite, fortississimo, your best rendition of *The Cremation of Sam Mcgee.*

Camp in an unobtrusive and open place—from the bear's point of view. No scat and no bear trails or scratching trees (an obvious way they mark territory). An unobtrusive spot lacks a stream, often a corridor for his rounds. Points and peninsulas are better than bays. Because all coastlines are more or less scalloped, when bears work the shore, they'll have a tendency to straighten out the irregularities, especially around

Shelf camp, Admiralty Island, Lynn Canal, Alaska

rocky or distant promontories. This will give them a chance to become aware of you and avoid you. Or camp on a rocky shelf along a shore that is not conducive to beachcombing (see photo). Better yet, camp on small islands, far from larger landmasses. And even better yet is to camp on a small island close to a seal or sea lion colony. Pinnipeds and bears seem to have worked out a détente as to where each hangs out. Though bears swim well, distance, orcas, and the magnitude of the enterprise make it slightly less likely that they will. And never camp anywhere near any dead animal or close to a berry patch!

Dances with Bears: II

Kent, a Canadian Game & Fisheries warden, tells the story of one hapless grizzly attempting to swim a channel. The distance was, perhaps, less than a mile. Mr. Bear was beavering away at the swim. Up the channel, the dorsal fins of a small pod of orcas sliced the water—two bulls, some females, and get. The whales spotted the bear first. The moms and pups held back, while the bulls circled in. The bear weighed his options. First he looked to the far foreshore and then he looked to the back-shore. He rubbernecked back and forth. Realizing both were too far, he tried to paddle straight up like a missile coming out of a nuclear sub. The whales did not circle (after all, they're not sharks) and did not sprint. They simply swam straight for the grizzly. In seconds, Mr. Bear turned into a red oil slick.

Food, of course, is a major attraction, and great care must be taken with it. It seems as though most bear warnings are predicated on the camping habits of high-impact campers: great big slabs of meat and bacon sizzling on a barbecue and lots of freshly caught fish with offal everywhere. Sea kayakers don't really fit that mold. We took dry goods double wrapped in Ziploc freezer bags, gravy packets, tinned meat, and Mountain House freeze-dried meals. If you score a salmon, pack it in a Hefty-type plastic garbage bag, clean it well before camp, and, preferably, boil it. Burn the Hefty bag.

Dances with Bears: III

We'd just come out of Cordero Channel. It was late. There were no campsites, just vertical rock with forest at waterline. Tina pulled out her binoculars to check a small bay across the sound. It looked promising, so we headed there. The little bay had a small stream at its head and a shingle beach that would accommodate a tent above high tide. It looked to us like prime bear diggings, but pickings were slim, and there was no scat. We pitched the tent. To announce our presence, we built a roaring fire, pissed around the perimeter, and even defecated, near waterline, at the far ends, where we also pulled up the boats. All the gear and food were packed in the holds. We retired with the shotgun nestled between us.

About 2 AM, intuition awoke me. About 30 yards away, a black bear was fiddling with a branch in the shallows. He'd walked right over our boats to get to where he was. I put on my shoes and a scary face, exited the tent, and lifted my arms in the V-for-victory sign and gently urged him to beat it. After turning to me and seemingly mulling it over, he scampered away. Score two for the Nixon mask. I didn't sleep much after that. Fortunately, he didn't return.

Dances with Bears: IV

Early August. A white sandy beach. I was laid up with a bad back in our North Face dome tent. The shotgun lay between us, and we lay absolutely naked on top of our sleeping bags. It was a sweltering and, this being the northern latitudes, not very dark night. The no-see-um netting zipper had given up the ghost, so the ripstop door was closed, blocking any possible breeze. Tina leaned over and whispered, "There's someone outside the tent."

"See who it is," I smart-assed back. With the door closed, there was no way to see out. Then I heard what sounded like the grunt of a pig right next to the fabric of the tent wall. Tina was terrified (it was on her side). I had wrenched my back and was in the land of lumbago and Percocet. Suddenly our guest thumped the ground loudly and repeatedly, not 18 inches from poor Tina. And then he did it again. It had the same rhythm as a gorilla beating his chest. We cringed quietly. After what seemed like ages, the presence left. When we finally gathered the courage to go out, there, right next to Tina's side, were the paw prints of a huge mama grizzly, as clear as only damp sand can preserve. About 20 feet away were the cub prints.

A few details of these incidents bear noting. Our food, already described, besides being stored in the bulkheaded compartments of the kayaks and double Ziploc-bagged, was liberally peppered with mothballs within rubberized waterproof bags. Either they didn't smell the food, or they were a fifth sort of bear: the retarded bear. Either way, we'll always take moth- (bear) balls with us. The theory behind their use is that the strong, piercing smell masks food odors. Just don't put them adjacent to food, as the essence is contagious and makes the affected item inedible. Not only were the bears oblivious to the fire, our visual presence, and body waste (in the first incident); but even Tina's menstruation (during both events), an often-noted aggravating circumstance, did not seem to deter or unduly attract. Still, I wouldn't advocate food storage in kayaks while at camp. The risk is too great. Late in the trip we reverted to the more conventional bear canisters cached a distance from camp and slept much more peacefully.

Pinnipeds

Pinnipeds come in three varieties, roughly: seals, sea lions, and walruses. Not a day will pass without a visit from a Pacific harbor seal. These are so ubiquitous that a day without one would be an omen that something in the world is amiss. Less common are sea lions. Both Steller's and California sea lions are present. The Steller's sea lion ranges along the entire Inside Passage. Though threatened, its population is stable, while some colonies, particularly in Glacier Bay, are thriving. Male California sea lions can range as far north as the southern coast of Alaska, while females remain near California rookeries year-round. Sightings along the Inside Passage are infrequent but increasing. If you see a walrus you're off route.

Seals lack external ears; males and females are indistinguishable at a glance. Locomotion on land is an ungainly, undulating, caterpillar-like heave. Harbor seals are quiet, sometimes spookily so. More than once I had the feeling I was being watched. Sure enough, just outside my peripheral vision were the low dome, deep sockets, and penetrating stare, like a memento mori, of a solitary seal. Sea lions, on the other hand, have ears and a pronounced sexual dimorphism. Males are crowned with proud sagittal crests and ringed with thickened necks. On land they are agile and quadrupedal; and everywhere they are endearingly vocal. Steller's sea lions are brown and grumble, whine, growl, and roar but don't bark. California sea lions are black; their bark is reminiscent of a dog's.

Pinnipeds can be playful, and therein lies their potential danger. Sea lions are curious and will inspect you en masse with much alarm, surprise, neck craning, discussion, indignity, feints, even play, particularly from the younger visitors, and much general hubbub.

Harbor seal

Seals, on the other hand, are more solitary, yet shy *and* curious at the same time. When I saw an article in *Sea Kayaker* (April 2002) on seal attacks, I was incredulous and flipped right to it. Kayakers have usually associated a seal's reservation with their long history of human predation. Perhaps. But maybe that legacy is changing, and seals seem to be adapting. Documented "attacks," on kayakers, divers, and swimmers, are confined to bumping and light nipping—no skin breaks: classic signs of play behavior. After all, a seal is a predator and could inflict serious harm if that were its intent. The kayak "attacks" have occurred only around Texada Island in the Strait of Georgia and near Anacortes, Washington (in Puget Sound), where one seal seems to like to play pirate and boards kayaks.

The danger to the paddler, besides being in possible abeyance of myriad laws and regulations, consists of potential viral and bacterial infections. Seal pox, "seal finger," tuberculosis, and other infections can and have been transmitted by contact close enough to include exposure to a seal sneeze. So beware the killer seals and check out Michael Koerner's excellent article in *Sea Kayaker* for the full lowdown.

Killer Whales & Mosquitoes

Shamu and Namu have performed a real disservice. Humans, instead of fearing and respecting these 8-ton carnivores, seek them out for photo and petting opportunities—kayakers included. Orcas were not nicknamed killer whales for nothing (see Kent's anecdote above).

At 10 AM on June 15, 1972, the 43-foot schooner *Lucette,* skippered by Dougal Robertson (with his family), was attacked by a group of 20 orcas in the Pacific and sank in 60 seconds. His book, *Survive the Savage Sea,* doesn't even speculate about why the attack occurred. But he does wonderingly reflect on the Miami Seaquarium's trained whales. There are no recorded instances of orca attacks on kayaks. We can only speculate why not. Orcas are extremely intelligent. Are they clueless about kayaks? Probably not. Do they practice restraint? Who knows?

Cruising off Nelly Point in Whale Channel, we encountered three males working the rocky shore. They were headed right for us at breathtaking speed. We both wanted dorsal fin-cum-kayaks photographs, but Robertson's book's lesson took the wind out of our sails. We made for shore, yet still managed a couple of good shots. Use good judgment.

Mosquitoes, gnats, white sox, deerflies, and blackflies are not much of a problem along the Inside Passage. When present, they are not wholly intolerable. Campsites with some exposure to the breeze are preferable. Although insect repellent, bug shirts, and head nets are unnecessary, a bugproof tent is a must.

Campsites

Part of every day's ritual (and for us it would begin about 3 PM—and once lasted till nearly 8 PM) is looking for a campsite. Many times we'd settle for just about anything (taking into account, of course, bear and bug behavior). Campsites can be divided into three categories: shore, forest, and developed. Shore campgrounds include white sand, shell midden or shingle beaches, grassy foreshore areas, rocky shelves and points, and exposed tombolos. (A tombolo is an isthmus, either on a peninsula or before a point, that comes close to inundation during high water.) These all lack arboreal cover due to marine influence. Be careful with grassy foreshore areas, which are inviting from a distance. Though often adequate, they're buggy, and the salt-resistant grasses are no indication of the high tide line. Also be careful with sandy beaches. Low tides can leave you with a quarter-mile schlep. Our favorite is an elevated, flat rock shelf, out on an exposed point, on an island with a 360-degree view.

Sometimes there is just no way to camp on shore, and you must penetrate the rain forest. What a revelation! And what a contrast between areas that have been historically logged for the giant cedars (mostly in British Columbia) and those that haven't. Both seem rather unexploited from shore, but inside, the discarded rubbish and the spectral, monumental stumps, with their loggers' planks' niches, hewn to facilitate a stance for the wielders of giant crosscut saws, haunt the forest with a sad nostalgia. In the Tongass National Forest, by contrast, undergrowth is dense, mossy, and attractive with few, if any, stumps. Either way, it is an experience not to be missed.

One German couple we met in Griffin Pass always made a point of camping in the forest. They carried an ax and a saw so as to be able to homestead a tent site just about anywhere. A small, folding pruning saw is handy for cutting errant vines and little stumps.

Developed campsites play a most important part of this journey and come in a wide variety of forms. In Puget Sound, stick to the Cascadia Marine Trail sites. In lower British Columbia, developed campsites are also your best bet. Though the provincial parks are not as handily spaced, they often sport showers and firewood. Farther up, in the wilder regions, homestead ruins and abandoned logging landings offer flat, cleared spaces.

Private cabins pepper the Passage. Adhere to the code of the North when considering these. Most are trappers' or fishermen's redoubts, or vacation cabins. If the cabin is locked, you're not welcome but can probably camp outside. If it's unlocked, visitors are generally welcome to take shelter and, under duress, to use necessary supplies. Local word of mouth is the best source of information about usable cabins. Use your judgment, leave everything as it is, and reimburse and leave a note when appropriate.

The US Forest Service maintains more than a hundred cabins in southeast Alaska for public use. These can be reserved on a first-come, first-served basis for a very nominal fee. You can reserve cabins or, as Randel Washburne has suggested, "Take your chances that they will not be in use. Doing the latter is fine, so long as you understand that you will have to get out if someone with a reservation shows up." Cabin locations are marked on the Tongass National Forest map, and reservations can be made by mail or in person at agency offices.

In small settlements such as Namu, Meyers Chuck, or Big Bay, ask around for a place to camp. We were offered lawns, piers, and unused school buildings. Larger towns either provide a municipal campground or have a selection of public accommodations. These offer a good opportunity to shower, dry out gear, resupply, and play tourist.

Sometimes, along the lower Vancouver Island coast, a handy campsite can be as rare as pay dirt. Fear not! Canadian law stipulates that the intertidal zone is public property. Be discreet. Camp where you must, and be prepared for diplomacy and shuttling camp during the graveyard tide shift.

Equipment

One philosophy dominates our equipment complement selection: each boat ought to be as self-contained as possible. Not that we plan to separate. But circumstances have a way of dictating contingencies. So we each have a full complement of food, a stove, and even shelter. This approach has served us well more than once.

Kayaks. Our various crews took a variety of kayaks, from large expedition boats, through medium cruising craft to small, Greenland-style, British kayaks, on different sections of the Inside Passage. All worked well. Bombproof bulkheads and hatch covers are essential. Avoid foam bulkheads; they have a tendency to separate after much use. Don't rely 100 percent on the bulkheads and hatch covers; waterproof absolutely essential items such as food, clothing, and sleeping bags inside your kayak's compartments. For long cruising, we prefer rudders—they facilitate paddling meditation. Sprayskirts should fit snuggly and not come off when you're hit by a rogue wave or forced to capsize. We like the neoprene deck with nylon tube style. I modify them by sewing a piece of bungee across the deck, about midway, to hold the chart down. I also sew (with just a few stitches and straight across the middle in a line perpendicular to the keel of the boat) a small rectangular patch of light neoprene with Velcro along two opposite sides (also perpendicular to the keel), at the deck/tube junction. This is my paddle park. I can lay the paddle on it and, by rolling up the Velcro ends, enclose the paddle shaft.

Cart wheels. In general, wheels are handy only on the Puget Sound portion, with its many campsite boat ramps. And they can be carried on deck, if you must, when the danger of capsizing is minimal. Wheels are also popular to lade fully loaded boats onto and off ferries, particularly when accessing the upper sections of the Passage. Resist this temptation. The initial and final convenience is counterbalanced by having to carry the strap-ons either inside the boat, where they take up precious space, or on deck, where they can impede your roll. Even if traveling solo, you can offer a kindly looking stranger a few bucks to help you tote the kayak on or off board.

Deck bags. To facilitate rolling, the smallest, most hydrodynamic deck bag you can get is best. Dagger makes one that can be attached and removed quickly. It comes with welded seams, a waterproof zipper, and compression straps. Cascade Designs, Watershed, and Voyageur also make waterproof deck bags. Some kayaks, such as Azul's Triumph, feature a day-hatch on the foredeck—no need for a deck bag at all.

Paddles. Light is better, and take-apart is handy. Of course, take a second set for a spare. We like the versatility of a broad-bladed paddle complemented by an Eskimo-type narrow blade for glassy seas and shoulder R&R. A great addition is an adaptable canoe handle for half a kayak blade. Werner Paddles markets one that mates with their paddle's shaft.

Wetsuits. Wetsuits are designed for warmth while immersed in water colder than body temperature. They require the infusion of ambient water upon immersion. The cool fluid inundates the space between the skin and the neoprene, and is then warmed up by body heat. This process is inevitably chilling and is better avoided. The warmed water more or less stays put because it has few exits. The snugness of the wetsuit aids in this process. Unfortunately, a svelte, full-body rubber leotard also constricts muscle response, producing a continuous isometric exercise that can lead to premature fatigue while paddling. Additionally, wet suits without water can chafe areas of repetitive motion—in the armpits while paddling. And they don't breathe, thereby increasing body temperature and discomfort while exercising out of the water. Wet suits are great for diving but a marginal compromise for kayaking. Instead, invest in a good, breathable drysuit.

Drysuit & shoes. For most of the Inside Passage a drysuit is a necessity. I've always hesitated to put on a drysuit. They're hot, sweaty, a pain to get in and out of (forget going to the bathroom), the gaskets are delicate, and, in the wilds, the damn things can snag and tear. And what about your feet? They're more than just an afterthought! Kokatat has come up with a Gore-Tex drysuit that addresses all of my concerns. The breathability increases its comfort by minimizing the paddler's conundrum (cold seas and warm air), and its two-piece design makes it extremely versatile. The bottoms, actually a set of bibs, reach up to the armpits and are held by suspenders. They are so practical that we wore them even when we had no intention of donning the tops and creating a full drysuit. The outer layer of the Gore-Tex sandwich is tough Cordura; we could traipse through brambles and sharp rocks with impunity and wade at will. Kokatat offers a variety of integral foot treatments, a vinyl or Gore-Tex sock, a neoprene bootie, or the traditional vinyl gasket. We chose the bootie for its warmth, comfort, and durability. Worn with any number of paddling shoes commercially available, we could segue from paddling to wading in water up to our chests to serious hiking without any shoe changes, while our feet remained dry and comfortable under any conditions. For boots, the Chota Brookie has felt midsoles for traction on slick intertidal rocks, drains well, has good ankle support, and comes with a removable insole for greater flexibility in fitting when worn with or without the booties. For an extra $100, Kokatat will install a relief zipper. Don't leave home without it! Though I'm not well endowed enough to use it while in the kayak (and women will have to resort to a urinary device such as the Freshette, which allows—nay, requires—that they urinate like a man, standing up), not having to disrobe to go solves my biggest problem with a drysuit. One can also now get a crescent-shaped rear zipper, though I have not tried it. The tops are lightweight, mate to the bottoms via a roll-up tube, come with gasket guards, and can be used without the bibs, mated to a neoprene sprayskirt as simply a drytop. Kokatat's drysuit was so comfortable—and precipitation so frequent—that we ended up wearing them much of the time.

Hat. A hat must keep out rain and sun, be cool but warm, not blow off in a gale, and adjust enough to allow for the addition of a warm skullcap when it's really cold. It's hard to beat Outdoor Research's Seattle or Sitka Sombrero.

Gloves. A review in *Sea Kayaker* magazine (June 2001) highlights the problems with commercially available paddling gloves. After testing half a dozen neoprene gloves, the reviewer confessed that, although she'd add a pair to her repertoire, she was not going to retire her vinyl dishwashing gloves with thin polypro liners. Neoprene gloves are thick, insensitive, and, if not loose-fitting, not only a pain to get on and off but also downright cold because they constrict finger circulation. In sea kayaking, gloves need to go on and come off often, for taking pictures, snacking, putting on sunscreen, getting a drink, operating a zipper, picking one's nose, any number of things, with a minimum of exposure to getting wet. Though I like the reviewer's liner/rubber glove system, the liners inevitably end up wet when they come off and go on repeatedly. Some people like Poggies. Alaskans use long, loose, fisherman's rubber gloves, lined with fuzz inside, and available (cheap!), in many models, from any hardware store. These seemed like the ticket. Fortunately, gloves are seldom needed. I resorted to them only in Glacier Bay when the air temperature fell below 50 degrees, and it was raining and windy.

Paddling tops. In the southern reaches of the Passage, in sunny, warm weather and calm, protected conditions, you'll not need nor want to wear the drytop. When it's really hot I'll wear a long-sleeve, khaki-nylon blend work shirt that you can buy at Sears or JCPenney. I can turn up its collar to avoid becoming a redneck. In-between conditions call for some of the newfangled fuzzy rubber tops. This material refuses to get wet, is not clingy, and remains relatively cool in warmish temperatures yet provides comfy, fuzzy warmth when it turns cool. In all but the worst downpours it doubles as raingear. And you can wear it as insulation under the drytop.

Shelter. Take a good four-season tent: freestanding (on rock shelves it may be impossible to drive a stake), roomy, bug-screened, bathtub-floored, and capable of withstanding serious winds. A tarp, or some such supplementary shelter, for interminably rainy days, turns a depressing experience into a delight, and offers a sheltered place for hanging out and changing into and out of drysuits, stockpiling gear, and working on charts. But tarps require trees or poles and some expertise in setting them up properly. One couple we met, a 50-year-old man with his 70-year-old father, each carried a tent. One was a conventional two-man, freestanding affair, while the other, instead of the tarp, was a freestanding, cheap, family-style big dome where they could congregate in inclement weather. After experimenting with many systems and designs, Tina approached Kelty for a custom shelter that was freestanding, light, and large in area. They came up with what is now marketed as the Kelty Sunshade, and they gave it to us in return for photos and this plug. Thank you, Kelty (and Tina). The large Sunshade weighs only 12 pounds, has standing room, and goes up in seconds. Carry a few long, beefy stakes for use in loose sand and gravel for both tents.

Sleeping pads. The Inside Passage is a very wet place. Even the best bathtub-floored tents, after any use in constant rain, end up with puddles inside. Camping on bare rock and cleared forest also adds tiny nicks and punctures that can leak. If for most outings you use either a closed-cell foam pad or a regular, three-quarter-length Thermarest, then consider, for Northwest sea kayaking, a 1½-inch-thick, full-length Thermarest. This way the sleeping bag is fully protected from interior tent puddles due to rain, saturated ground, or unplanned rising tides.

Water. When my water purification pump isn't handy or I'm disinclined to use it for some reason, I rely on veterinary-strength liquid iodine in a plastic dropper instead of purifying pills. The small dropper easily fits in the deck bag or a survival kit. Two drops per quart do the trick unless it's really nasty water, in which case you double the dosage. Be aware that some purifying pumps add iodine to the processed water. One new purification method uses two pills: the first one to purify; the second one to neutralize the taste of the first. For drinking while paddling, Gaia, by PI Outdoors, PO Box 1067, Athens, TN 37371, 1-888-746-1313, has designed the POD, a dual-bladder hydration system that attaches to the top back of the PFD. I like it so much that I put it on there permanently. It's insulated and has two 40-ounce bladders.

Fire. Always carry a stove for cooking. Many areas, especially in Puget Sound and the Gulf Islands, are unsuitable for fires either due to restrictions or forest fire danger. Farther north, however, fires are a treat for warmth, ambience, or drying clothes. Getting a fire going in the drenched Northwest can try even the most skilled fire starter. Traditional sources of kindling such as pine cones, dry grass, or dead twigs off evergreens tend to be soaked beyond use. A couple of items can help. Chemical fire starters or stove gas (carefully sprinkled) usually work. I like to carry, besides the small pruning saw, a large knife with a blunt back edge. Not only can this fillet a salmon, but you can also shave driftwood down to the dry part for tinder shavings. The blunt reverse side is for careful nudging or hammering.

Auditory enhancement. There is no substitute for the sounds and silences of the sea, wind, wildlife, and paddling companions. Cut out nature's symphony and you may as well travel by motor craft. Your ability to respond to subtly changing conditions is compromised without auditory feedback. That said, there are certain times and situations where sound enhancement can enrich the paddling experience, particularly when used judiciously. *Sea Kayaker* markets a rugged 10-ounce hydrophone for listening underwater. At the approach of whales, plop it in and eavesdrop on their chatter. Perhaps Judy Collins used a pair when she recorded her version of *Farewell to Tarwathie.* The old Scottish air, already evocative of cold northern seas and the loneliness of the whale hunt, gained immeasurable impact with the counterpoint of whale song.

Consider taking a Walkman-type, waterproof tape or CD player for your occasional private concert. Certain types of music blend well with the paddling experience. Some, like Smetana's *Die Moldau* actually paint a symphonic picture of the environment. Baroque concertos, with their melodic, abstract tunes, turn paddling into a dance—particularly useful when energy lags. I recommend Bach's *Brandenburg Concertos,* anything by Vivaldi, and Pachelbel's *Canon* (one version is recorded with sea sounds). For the full dervish—the waltz on the swells that dizzy and swoon, the intense sense of place that raises the hair on your neck, and the transcendence of your own limits (like Neil Armstrong venturing where no one has been)—nothing beats Celtic music. Airs, hornpipes, jigs and reels, sea chanteys and marches—especially with plaintive bagpipes—grab the soul, wrench the heart, and double the energy.

If your prerecorded music player has an AM/FM radio, it's fun to tune in to local radio stations in the towns and hamlets along the Inside Passage. Far-flung rural areas in Canada and Alaska stay in touch and trade information and gossip via programs such as the *Tundra Telegraph.*

3

Puget Sound

Olympia to Stewart Island (Roche Harbor)

150 miles

> *The sea is in high spirits today*
> *promising adventure for those*
> *who would cut their moorings and follow.*
> —Unknown *(from Eric Stoller,* Keep Australia on Your Left*)*

George Vancouver entered Puget Sound escorted by a light breeze and a warm sun on a stunning spring day in early May. For a man who had pretty much been there and done that—after all, he'd been around the world with James Cook—Puget Sound so surprised and delighted him that you can sense his struggle to find the right words to describe it:

> *To describe the beauties of this region, will, on some future occasion, be a very grateful task to the pen of a skilful panegyrist. The serenity of the climate, the innumerable pleasing landscapes, and the abundant fertility that unassisted nature puts forth, require only to be enriched by the industry of man with villages, mansions, cottages, and other buildings, to render it the most lovely country that can be imagined. . . . I could not possibly believe that any uncultivated country had ever been discovered exhibiting so rich a picture. The land . . . rose . . . in a very gentle ascent, and was well covered with a variety of stately forest trees. These, however, did not conceal the whole face of the country in one uninterrupted wilderness, but pleasingly clothed its eminences, and checkered the vallies; presenting, in many*

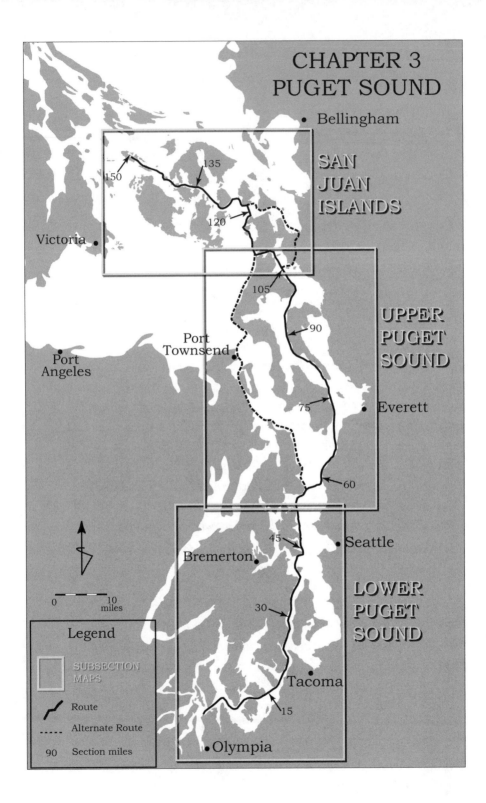

CHAPTER 3
PUGET SOUND

Bellingham

SAN
JUAN
ISLANDS

150   135

120

Victoria

105

UPPER
PUGET
SOUND

Port
Angeles

Port
Townsend

90

75

Everett

60

45   Seattle

Bremerton

LOWER
PUGET
SOUND

30

Tacoma

15

Olympia

0   10
          miles

Legend

SUBSECTION
MAPS

Route

Alternate Route

90   Section miles

directions, extensive spaces that wore the appearance of having been cleared by art, like the beautiful island we had visited the day before. ... A picture so pleasing could not fail to recall to our remembrance certain delightful and beloved situations in Old England.

Unfortunately, on the launch ramp at Boston Harbor, on the north end of Olympia, Tina and I were oblivious to the "pleasing eminences" and "delightful situations." We were victims of absorption-induced myopia. Our perspective had been blindered by adrenaline-fueled bloody-mindedness. Packing; unpacking and repacking; organizing and editing; arguing pros and cons; tracking the tides; charting; nervous snacking; photographing; arranging long-term parking; undressing and dressing; and, eventually, embarking consumed the morning. Thank Neptune Joemma Beach State Park, our first campsite, was only 6 miles away. Even though we knew that the scope of the first leg was modest, it was impossible not to be overwhelmed by the gravity of what we were ultimately setting out to do: paddle the Inside Passage.

More History

The gate to Puget Sound—and, indeed, all the protected adjacent waters—is the Strait of Juan de Fuca. Juan de Fuca, a scant 100 years after Columbus, may have discovered it. But because he was sailing at the limits of his possibilities, the find was much too early for any practical use, and was lost for nearly 200 years. Some say it was never really found or lost. De Fuca's real name was Apostolos Valerianos; he was a Greek alleged to have commanded an expedition on behalf of the Viceroy of Mexico in pursuit of the Northwest Passage. His claim comes down to us from an account by English trader Michael Lok, who met him in Venice in 1596 and recorded the details for posterity. Unfortunately, no records of his commission exist, and most historians dismiss the claim. James Cook missed it in 1778.

In July of 1787, five years before Vancouver's entry, Captain Charles Barkley of the *Imperial Eagle,* while on a fur-trading excursion, rediscovered the Strait. According to his 17-year-old wife, Frances (he himself was barely 28):

> *In the afternoon to our great astonishment, we arrived off a*
> *large opening, extending to the eastward, the entrance of which*
> *appeared to be about four leagues wide, and remained about that*
> *as far as the eye could see ... which my husband immediately*
> *recognized as the long lost strait of Juan de Fuca, and to which*
> *he gave the name of the original discoverer, my husband placing*
> *it on his chart.*

Over the course of the next five years, English, American, and Spanish traders and explorers tentatively inched their way up the strait. By the time of Vancouver's entry in late April 1792, the Spanish were already busy building the first settlement in what was to become the state of Washington, a fort at Cape Flattery (on the tip of the Olympic Peninsula), in present-day Neah Bay. Vancouver's ships, *Discovery* and *Chatham,* and the Spanish vessels *Sutil* and *Mexicana* (engaged in much the same task) danced an intricate but friendly minuet around the islands and inlets of the southern Strait of Georgia. At one point (after a night of conviviality) they even agreed to collaborate on further explorations.

Vancouver was a self-made man. He'd gone to sea at 14 and accompanied James Cook on two voyages, including the pioneering Northwest Coast trip of 1778, where he'd proved his mettle both as a navigator and chartmaker. It was these very extraordinary surveying skills that led the Admiralty, with Cook's forceful recommendation, to appoint him to lead the *Discovery* expedition: two ships, 144 men, and the commission to, once and for all, determine whether or not a Northwest Passage existed. The trip got off to a bad start. Vancouver did not inspire, much less engender affection among, his crew. Jonathan Raban, in *Passage to Juneau,* recounts:

> *At 34, Vancouver wasn't naturally a commanding figure. He*
> *was a short man, glandularly fat, whose weight was increasing*
> *noticeably during the voyage. He had lost most of his hair. He*

*had protuberant, thyroidal eyes. He sweated a lot. In gentle
weather, Vancouver's rattling graveyard cough made itself heard
from bow to stern. His explosions of temper were frequent, and
famous: puce-faced and bawling, he seemed possessed and
transformed by some inner demon. In a period when symptoms
of extreme psychological disturbance usually could pass as
acceptable eccentricity, several gentlemen aboard Discovery
diagnosed Vancouver as suffering from fits of temporary insanity.*

It didn't help that these "several gentlemen," 15 well-connected scions of patrician families, aged 16 to 22 and out to make reputations and fortunes for themselves, were openly and snobbishly disdainful of their nerdy leader. Never mind. His mathematical acumen (particularly in determining longitude, which required heinously complex calculations of lunar vis-à-vis solar distances so as to keep the newly developed chronometers honest) and by-the-book adherence to duty carried the expedition (with not a little—and a sometimes excessive—application of the lash).

Expeditions can be like marriages, and Vancouver's wasn't even graced by a honeymoon. After the initial affinity of shared ideals and anticipation of exploring uncharted territories wears off, the accomplishing of the task begins. And no small task that. Vancouver had to follow every convoluted twist and turn the coast flourished so as not to miss any possible Atlantic-bound channel. It was a topological puzzle requiring both vessels and their tenders: 20-foot cutters rigged for sail or oars, under Lieutenants Peter Puget and Joseph Whidbey. The stresses of on-board life, personality differences magnified by constant close-quarters friction, and the inevitable setbacks associated with any great undertaking are apt to irritate the most unflappable dispositions. Whidbey, Puget, and the other regular navy officers, accustomed to such difficulties, found themselves "in the delicate and uncomfortable position of mediators between the young bluebloods and the apoplectic captain," as Raban further observes.

That Vancouver was the first European visitor into Puget Sound is a widely held but erroneous assumption. One week after having entered the Strait of Juan de Fuca, while anchored in Discovery Bay, next to Port Townsend, he thoughtfully remarked:

> *The character and general deportment of the few inhabitants we occasionally saw... were uniformly civil and friendly, without manifesting the least sign of fear or suspicion at our approach; nor did their appearance indicate their having been inured to hostilities. Several of their stoutest men had been perfectly naked, and contrary to what might have been expected of rude nations habituated to warfare, their skins were mostly unblemished by scars, **excepting such as the small pox seemed to have occasioned; a disease which there is great reason to believe is very fatal amongst them. It is not... easy to draw any... conclusions on the... cause from which this havoc... proceeded.** [Bold added for emphasis.]*

Smallpox invaded the American continent proper in 1520, using an infected slave from Cuba as its landing craft. By 1618, the native population of Mexico, estimated at about 20 million before the conquest, plummeted to 1.6 million. Exactly when it first reached the Pacific Northwest is unknown; it spread erratically and episodically and annihilated approximately 95 percent of the American aboriginal population. One particularly bad outbreak, during the American Revolutionary War, started in Mexico City and spread north both east and west. It killed five times more people on the entire continent than the war did in the east. The worst outbreak along the Northwest Coast occurred in 1863, when an infected Californian landed in Victoria, which, at the time, was full of native trading parties. City officials, in a well-meaning but absolutely disastrous move, hurriedly sent them home. The newly infected spread the disease north and inland. Over the course of two years, more than 20,000 died.

Just what Vancouver meant by "few inhabitants" depends on what his expectations were. He had passed about 15 villages along the south shore of the strait. In Hood Canal he reported about six villages. The 1855 treaty, which ceded the Seattle-Everett area to the United States, is cosigned by 82 Native American leaders representing the Dwamish, Suquamish, Sk-tahlmish, Sam-ahmish, Snoqualmoo, Skai-wha-mish, N'Quentl-ma-mish, Sk-tah-le-jum, Stoluck-wha-mish, Sno-ho-mish, Skagit, Kik-I-allus, Swin-a-mish, Squin-wha-mish, Sah-ku-mehu-Noo-wha-ha, Nook-wha-chah-mish, Mee-see-qua-quilch, Cho-bah-ah-bish, and "other subordinate tribes." To what degree the scourge had decimated the sound's population at the close of the 18th century, or even 50 years later, is the subject of much extrapolation. Whatever the density, before the invasion of smallpox the protected waters east of the strait must have nurtured a human population commensurate with the paradise that it is.

Today that population has rebounded and surpassed whatever it may have been. As of this writing, about 4.4 million people reside in the Puget Sound area. (There are about 88,000 Amerindians in the entire state of Washington.) Add the Vancouver and Victoria metropolitan areas, and the total goes up to 7 million. Fortunately, most of the population is concentrated in the cities of Olympia, Tacoma, Bremerton, Seattle, Everett, Bellingham, Vancouver, and Victoria. Though no wilderness, the thoughtful, and even affectionate, settlement and development pattern on the nook-and-cranny, hill-and-dale topography would still remind Vancouver of England.

It might have remained English. American claims were few but strong. Following Barkley's trumping of Vancouver in discovering the mouth of the Columbia, Lewis and Clark strengthened that tenuous claim with their Corps of Discovery expedition. One single, solitary settlement followed. In 1811, John Jacob Astor, fur capitalist extraordinaire, established a trading fort, Astoria, at the mouth of the Columbia, to extend and facilitate his enterprises. It fell to the British the following year during the War of 1812.

If, as Von Clausewitz so insightfully observed, "war is diplomacy by other means," then the obverse must to some extent be true. The United States annexation of the Oregon Territory (which included what are now the states of Oregon, Washington, and Idaho, as well as small portions of Montana, Wyoming, and Canada) bears this out. Through very astute statesmanship, minimal territorial claims or colonization, and lots of luck, the largest chunk of territory ever ceded to the young republic was acquired without war or purchase.

The War of 1812 was officially resolved by the 1818 Treaty of Ghent. Though most authorities consider it a draw, the United States turned out the winner. The treaty set up a joint British-US occupation over the territory, with neither power allowed to establish a separate official government. The race was on. The Hudson's Bay Company, royally chartered (with monopoly powers) to both organize commerce and rule western Canada, undertook a program of expansion into the disputed area. Fort Vancouver was established (in 1824) at the junction of the Willamette and Columbia Rivers to be the headquarters for the entire Columbia region, as the Oregon Territory was then known. Under the enlightened administration of John McLaughlin, the settlement became a retirement community for the fur industry, attracting French-Canadian trappers with their Indian wives and American mountain men intent on a more settled way of life. In 1833, McLaughlin expanded into Puget Sound with the building of a trading post on the Nisqually Delta next to present-day Olympia.

McLaughlin's evenhandedness backfired. By 1843, Willamette Valley residents voted out the Hudson's Bay Company and opted for a closer relationship with the increasingly avaricious United States. North of the Columbia the HBC still ruled.

"Manifest Destiny," a term first coined in a newspaper editorial, was originally the idea that republican government was inevitable throughout the continent. For some it soon metamorphosed into an insatiable United States appetite for American (the continent) real estate. The 1844 presidential campaign was a contentious squeaker with a Reform Party spoiler. Democrat James K. Polk, an ardent expansionist, urged the annexation of the entire Northwest, including British Columbia, up to Russian Alaska ("54/40 or fight!" [a reference to the degrees and minutes of latitude to which the nation's northern border ought to be extended]); a merger with Texas; and the purchase of Mexico's northern provinces. He faced Whig Henry Clay, a Jeffersonian and reluctant interventionist. Joseph Smith, founder of the Church of Jesus Christ of Latter Day Saints, led the Reform Party on an abolition platform. Polk won. He immediately began negotiations to acquire both Mexican and British territory—lame-duck President Tyler having completed the Texas bit.

On the domestic front, the "twin evils of barbarism," polygamy and slavery, polarized the electorate as today's drug war threatens to do someday. A state of civil war in all but name, which would culminate in the assassination of Mormon leader Joseph Smith, raged in Missouri and Illinois. Slave or free? Maintaining parity in the Senate was a question that gridlocked Congress as new states and territories were considered for admission. Both issues would have a bearing on Northwest developments. The 1843 Willamette Valley vote not only designated the land south of the Columbia free, it excluded people of color in a feeble attempt to avoid the controversy in its entirety.

Oblivious to the ban, George Bush, a free black from the previously Spanish colony of Louisiana, led a mixed group of 32 Missouri pioneers out the Oregon Trail in 1845. Running from the religious conflicts and racial prejudices back home, they chose to settle north of the Columbia, at the head of Budd Inlet, where British hospitality welcomed blacks. Thus was Olympia founded.

Smith's murder had galvanized the Mormons to evacuate Missouri. To strengthen their hand, Brigham Young made friendly overtures to the British, who were looking to shore up their territorial claims in the Pacific Northwest (most of the 30,000 saints were British Isles converts), exploring possible settlement on Vancouver Island. When war with Mexico finally erupted in 1846, Young threw his support behind the US in return for safe passage west for his refugees. To avoid war on two fronts, the US and Britain agreed (mostly—the San Juan Islands retained the ambiguous status quo ante) to the present border along the 49th Parallel. Once victory over Mexico was secure, US troops occupied the now vacant HBC trading post next to Olympia and renamed it Fort Nisqually.

People poured in. Seattle, Tacoma, and Port Townsend were all founded in 1851. By 1853, Congress organized Columbia into the Territory of Washington (cocking a snook at the Brits). Two years later, the Indians of Puget Sound ceded their lands to the US in the Treaty of 1855.

The exact border separating Canada and the United States was not established until 1872, when Kaiser Wilhelm I of Germany, the neutral arbitrator chosen by the antagonists to settle one final point of contention, ruled in favor of the US. The dispute arose in 1855, when tensions over fiscal jurisdiction in the San Juan Islands led to a diplomatic confrontation. In this atmosphere, a Hudson's Bay Company sow chose the wrong moment to wander over to a US settler's potato patch and root with impunity. The settler shot the pig. The English demanded compensation. The US sent troops to occupy San Juan Island, founding Fort Pickett in the process. Cooler heads prevailed, and a joint military occupation was agreed upon until a suitable arbitrator could be found. Congressional obsession with post–Civil War reconstruction delayed the Kaiser's proxy for 13 years.

Natural History

Whenever I arrive in the Northwest my mood changes. I feel boundlessly energized and overwhelmingly relaxed. Today the Northwest retains a certain ambience, a certain subtle iconoclasm undergirded by an appreciation for tradition. Victorian homes and a passion for formal landscaping coexist with a strong entrepreneurial bent. Eccentricity, not for its own sake but as a flowering of individuality, abounds. Celtic music and tearooms are popular along with the ever-present obsession with coffee. Aristocratic sports, such as sailing, mountaineering, skiing, and kayaking trump stock car racing, cock fighting, or monster truck mud derbies. Vestiges of the fur trade remain. Fishing is serious business. Logging is still an honorable profession, though tempered, more and more, by a concern for preservation of dwindling forests and resources. Industrialization, in the form of defense, both maritime and aeronautic, and information technology now generates a truly dynamic economic diversity. Yet, you can still find miles of uninterrupted beaches and lots of undeveloped coves and bays, particularly on the more than 300 islands dotting the sound. Why? Roadways have not spanned many of the waterways.

The unique underwater topography of the sound, carved out by Pleistocene glaciation, and not yet shallowly sedimented, has depths of more than 800 feet and some of the strongest currents in the world. Bridge building is a challenge. The first Tacoma Narrows Bridge, designed light for a greater span, dramatically collapsed on November 7, 1940. During winter storms, the roadway would pitch and heave in waves so high that one would lose sight of the vehicle ahead. Engineers tried parking heavily loaded trucks along the bridge to dampen the oscillations. It didn't work. So they tried floating bridges. On February 13, 1979, the Interstate 90 floating bridge across Hood Canal sank. Now the sound relies on a well-designed (but sometimes overburdened—mostly at rush hour) network of cross-channel ferries, along with a few strategically placed bridges (where depth and currents allow). Many islands and isolated coastal bits are left not easily accessible—a paddler's paradise.

Puget Sound area weather and, at least in the sound itself, the state of the sea are just about the most accommodating along the entire Passage. Virtually anytime during the spring, summer, or fall is suitable for paddling south of Port Townsend and east of Whidbey and the San Juan Islands and along the mainland coast where the waters are most protected. Just be alert around the equinoxes, when the Aleutian Low asserts itself. Daytime high temperatures between April and October are about 60–72 degrees Fahrenheit. Summer is also the driest season. But the region is relatively dry anyway (compared to the rest of the Inside Passage), being in the weather lee of the Olympic Mountains and Vancouver Island. The more in the rain shadow, the drier: Port Townsend gets two-thirds of Seattle's precipitation, while Seattle gets only two-thirds of Olympia's, which is just south enough to miss the Olympics' full protection.

This warmth and dryness are expressed in the greater biotic diversity of the Passage's southern terminus. Prickly pear cacti and golden grasslands are not uncommon. But perhaps the most eccentric inhabitant is the beautiful madrona (in Washington; madrone or madrono farther south; arbutus in Canada). A close relative of the manzanita, which it resembles, though straighter and much taller, it is the only broad-leafed evergreen native to Canada and favors open banks along saltwater shores where, battered by storms, it twists into picturesque shapes. The madrona keeps its leaves, which resemble a rhododendron's, but sheds its bark, which is dry and thin and peels back like onionskin. The wood is very hard and burns extremely hot. With white flowers in the spring, red berries in the winter, and the pistachio green of young growth, the tree is a decoration all year long.

Sea states in Juan de Fuca Strait, the San Juan Islands, and Deception Pass are another matter. These waters must be negotiated in optimum weather, with suitable defensive strategies and seamless navigation, at just the proper interval in the tide cycle. Water temperatures hover around 48–54 degrees Fahrenheit year-round. Strong currents and dangerous crossings, however, can be virtually eliminated by hugging the mainland. With a very conservative route and time-of-year strategy you could even (contrary to my earlier advice) eliminate the drysuit south and east of Deception Pass. Plan well. Average tidal variation ranges from 15 feet at Olympia to 8 feet at Port Townsend, with 11 feet at mid-sound Seattle.

You won't need a gun or pepper spray, except perhaps for the raccoons, curious to a fault, who will go so far as to invade your tent, even while occupied, to burgle. Be firm.

The biggest obstacle to paddling the sound is the human density. (On the other hand, with so many people the chance of an outside rescue is much more likely.) One manifestation of this is the intense and sometimes overwhelming commercial and naval traffic along what is essentially a marine interstate. Since kayaks tend to hug the shore, container ships and tugged barges are little more than colorful photo ops—except, however, when that highway must be crossed. The slow-motion nature of the undertaking, no matter how hard you paddle, is surreal and unnerving. Kayaks are invisible to large ships, which are, moreover, the metaphor invoked to paint a picture of an extremely slow reaction

Tug and barge under Tacoma Narrows Bridge, Puget Sound

time. Even if they did see you, evasive action on their part, no matter how well intentioned or executed, would be about as effective as casting a spell. You must give these Godzillas wide berth.

The first concern in crossing shipping lanes is that, unlike interstates, they don't really physically exist. They're convenient fictions agreed upon and, mostly, adhered to by all parties involved. The first task is to find their "exact" location. Nautical charts delineate traffic lanes and directions, in red or purple. In Puget Sound, inbound and outbound lanes tend to span half a nautical mile, separated by a 0.25-nautical-mile median. For practical purposes, don't depend on the imaginary safety of the imaginary median. Figure that, for the crossing, you can maintain a 3- to 4-knot speed. A half hour, tops, should get you across.

Pick a transect for your crossing. I like to cross where the lanes are adjacent to or hug a headland, so I can land and study the situation closely without distractions. I also don't have to factor in the additional time required to reach the lanes. Timing is everything. Big ships can be surprisingly speedy. If there's no traffic, go for it. If there is, you need to gauge a safe crossing opportunity. I undertake an exercise analogous to counting wave sets for a surf exit. And this is best done ashore. From a standing position, look up or down the highway to the horizon for the first discernible sign of a big ship. Measure the time it takes from when you first see one to when it intersects your planned route across. Now you know how much time you have to cross, and you won't have to sweat bullets once under way.

Washington State Ferries (and B.C. Ferries, as well) are another story. Although these can see you and are endowed with quick reaction times, they cover fetch like a skipped rock. Make no attempt to cross their 20-knot path, no matter how far away they appear. Go around or wait for their passing. One long horn blast signals their impending departure from the dock. Perhaps the safest strategy is to cross their path below their docks between the pylons. There is usually enough space and water.

Density also creates access problems. Aside from the environmental considerations, applicable to any intensively exploited area, camping and use are subject to private property and selected public lands restrictions, for instance, Indian reservations, wildlife habitats, and national security areas. On the other hand, parks and campgrounds are plentiful. There is even a national park commemorating the 1859 Pig War, San Juan Island National Historic Park (though it does not provide camping facilities). With these considerations in mind, the Washington Water Trails Association was founded in 1989 by a group of enthusiastic paddlers committed to a vision of a marine trail system designed for human- and wind-powered beachable craft.

Cascadia Marine Trail

In 1993 that vision came to life with the establishment of the Cascadia Marine Trail (CMT). This is a network of campsites administered by a variety of public and private entities that together make up the only Marine National Recreation Trail in the country, an award and designation on a par with the Appalachian Trail. Since its creation by the Washington state legislature, the trail has won many awards, including the White House's National Millennium Trail Award, one of only 16 trails so honored. How does it work?

Heretofore, membership was pretty much a requisite for use. For a $25 annual fee you got guaranteed access, pretty much, to a campsite, often primitive (but who cares?) at the end of a day's paddle. Some campsites, such as those administered by city or county parks, provided the guaranteed access but for an additional fee. The guarantee is subject to a first-come, first-served proviso, though crowding—all parties willing—is dependent on consent. Today, you no longer have to become a member. Simply pay the overnight camping fee that the land manager charges. At Washington State Parks Cascadia sites, the fee is $10 for a party of six. Campers not arriving in human- or wind-powered beachable watercraft are not eligible to use the designated sites. Due to a scarcity of funds, the system will continue to evolve. Nonetheless, priority access (and conservation) will still be the centerpieces of the trail. Either way, I urge you to join so as to support and maintain the good work the Washington Water Trails Association is achieving.

Contact the Washington Water Trails Association, 4649 Sunnyside Avenue North #305, Seattle, WA 98103-6900; 206-545-9161, fax 206-547-0350; www.wwta.org. E-mail: wwta@wwta.org.

Once you join, the WWTA provides a guide to all the campsites with beaching details for each spot. As of this writing, 52 campsites are on line. Cart wheels and earplugs are dandy extras to have along. The WWTA was organized in tandem with the British Columbia Marine Trails Association, with the same objectives in mind. Together they hope to establish a trail and network of campsites for human-powered craft that reaches all the way up the Inside Passage. It will be known as the Cascadia Marine Trail.

The Route: Overview

The Cascadia Marine Trail, established, as of now, only in Washington, is the apéritif for a multicourse repast that, for some, will be difficult to digest at one sitting. The first leg of this hegira, for it *is* a mystical experience, tallies 150 miles and is divided into three portions: Lower Puget Sound, Upper Puget Sound, and the San Juan Islands. The route is a balanced compromise among many competing objectives. Beginning in the calm reaches of the sound's southern extremity, it wends its way, avoiding extreme urbanization, past the verges of the Strait of Juan de Fuca's unnerving reach, and, upping the ante, through the idyllic maelstrom of the San Juan Islands' invigorating channels right up to the Canadian border. Who could ask for a better introduction to the Inside Passage?

Two alternate routes offer, on the one hand, a more challenging alternative—up the exposed west coast of Whidbey Island—or, an even more protected passage than the main route—up Swinomish Channel. The alternate routes are described in detail at the end of this chapter, following the description of the main route.

Boston Harbor, a satellite of Olympia 8 miles north of the head of Budd Inlet, is the perfect launch. This out-of-the-way cove has some distinct advantages over putting in at Olympia itself, not the least of which is a lack of congestion and a relaxed, unhurried atmosphere at the boat ramp—essential for good organization. And right across the street, suitably close for lugging loads, is a long-term parking lot. Purists can paddle up the inlet to Olympia for a grand view of the state capital.

The aesthetic and logical end point for this portion would be Victoria or Vancouver, B.C., depending on whether one is ultimately aiming to go up the Vancouver Island or mainland coast. Hugging the continental shore, theoretically, has many advantages. There are no crossings, and, by a tad, it's the shorter distance. On the other hand, intense urbanization, from Olympia to the northern suburbs of the city of Vancouver, severely limits or actually precludes camping. Between Point Roberts and Plumper Cove Marine Park are 45 miles of full-on Vancouver with, sometimes, no spot to spread a tent. And fatally, the Fraser River creates extensive mud flats 5 miles out to sea and, during the freshet (May to August) can combine with tidal fluctuations and prevailing winds to make the broad delta a challenging, tiresome, and dangerous enterprise.

The main route, going to Victoria, gets you out of this mess and into the San Juan Islands archipelago, where the WWTA has arranged for many convenient campsites. The currents and crossings are challenging but, after all, this is the shakedown portion of the Inside Passage, and negotiating these must become second nature. It's also a compellingly comely and engrossing kayaking paradise, much more interesting than paralleling the mainland coast, with the added advantage of ending up on the lee shore of the Strait of Georgia.

But logistical considerations impinge and dictate a few alterations. Getting back to your car from Victoria, crossing the border twice, disembarking, and making all the necessary arrangements from a big city is quite complicated and convoluted. Additionally, there is a technical glitch. Once across the border, you must not exit your boat until you reach a customs station, as Canadian officials may confiscate your boat and subject you to charges. (If you do decide to paddle on, the closest customs entry is at Bedwell Harbour on South Pender Island about 5 miles north of Stuart Island's Turn Point.) A much simpler alternative beckons.

The Puget Sound Express, specializing in whale-watching tours and willing to ferry kayaks, makes daily stops at Roche Harbor in the San Juan Islands. By paddling to Stuart Island, the northernmost San Juan Isle closest to both Roche Harbor and the US-Canada border (you can count coup by nipping up and back), one need only paddle 5 miles south to the Express terminal at Roche Harbor. The ferry can then shuttle you to Port Townsend, where a 30-minute walk south along the main drag brings you to Budget Rent-a-Car.

Meanwhile, where do you store your kayak? Take advantage of the newest addition to the WWTA repertoire, Land Lunch Launch (L^3). These are places where, if you must leave your kayak unattended, you may do so with some peace of mind. In Port Townsend the participating member of L^3 is Kayak Port Townsend, an outfitter located just about next door to the Puget Sound Express in a beige metal warehouse with a red kayak sticking out of a planter and a blue kayak hanging from the gutters. Leave your kayak(s) along the east-northeast side of the building (after all, it *is* a working business) and go rent a car (or hitchhike) down to Olympia to pick up your vehicle back at Boston Harbor.

Lower Puget Sound: Boston Harbor (mile 0) to Fay Bainbridge State Park (mile 53)

To reach Boston Harbor, take Exit 105B (Plum Street) off Interstate 5 in Olympia and drive straight north. After about 1 mile you'll see the waters of Budd Inlet on your left. Plum Street becomes East Bay Drive, which eventually becomes Boston Harbor Road. At 73rd Avenue Northeast, turn left (about 8 miles from the interstate, total). The marina, ramp, and parking lot are 0.25 mile beyond. Water, ice, and some groceries are available.

When you're all packed up and ready to go, launch your boat into Dana Passage. South of Tacoma Narrows, Puget Sound waters are at their warmest and calmest. An underwater ridge, the foundation for the Tacoma Narrows Bridge, impedes the tidal exchange of water between the north and south sound, keeping conditions south of Tacoma very mild. Nonetheless, when spring tides flood, currents can run at nearly 3 knots by Briscoe Point on the southern tip of Hartstene Island.

Just north of Boston Harbor you'll pass Squaxin Island, an Indian reservation since 1854. Until 1993, its south end was a public park, but a dispute between the Squaxin tribe and the Parks and Recreation Commission terminated access. Somewhere near Johnson Point, on the south shore, you'll need to decide whether to detour north 2 miles to Joemma Beach State Park (mile 5), the first CMT campground, or head on up the sound (south) for 4 additional miles to the Anderson Island CMT campsite (mile 9).

Joemma Beach has water, sanitary facilities, a fishing pier, and overflow camping. It is located at the north end of Whiteman Cove on the Case Inlet side of the Key Peninsula. The CMT campsite is above and north of the day-use picnic shelter. Another 2.5 miles farther up Case Inlet is McMicken Island State Park. Although there is no camping here, McMicken is wild and solitary with a network of braided trails and a sandy foreshore, a reminder of just how sensual walking and beachcombing can be.

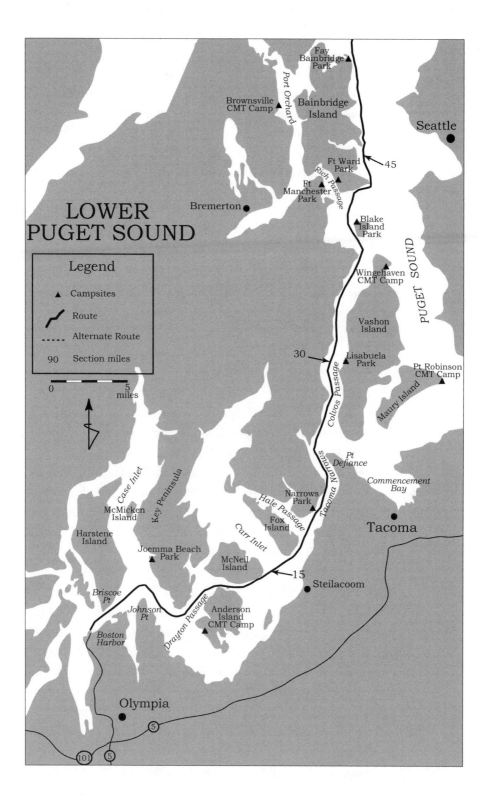

LOWER PUGET SOUND

Legend

▲ Campsites

⌇ Route

- - - - Alternate Route

90   Section miles

0   5
        miles

Fay
Bainbridge
Park ▲

Brownsville
CMT Camp ▲

Port Orchard

Bainbridge
Island

Seattle ●

Ft Ward
Park ▲ ← 45

Rich Passage

Ft
Manchester ▲
Park

Bremerton ●

Blake
Island ▲
Park

Wingehaven ▲
CMT Camp

PUGET SOUND

Vashon
Island

30 ← Lisabuela ▲
Park

Colvos Passage

Pt Robinson ▲
CMT Camp

Maury Island

*Pt
Defiance*

*Commencement
Bay*

Tacoma Narrows

Case Inlet

Key Peninsula

McMicken
Island

Narrows ▲
Park

Hale Passage

Harstene
Island

Fox
Island

Carr Inlet

Tacoma

Joemma Beach ▲
Park

McNeil
Island

*Briscoe
Pt*

15 ← ● Steilacoom

*Johnson
Pt*

Anderson ▲
Island
CMT Camp

Drayton Passage

*Boston
Harbor*

Olympia
●

(5)

(101) (5)

Past Devil's Head, on the southern tip of the Key Peninsula, enter Drayton Passage. To the east lies Anderson Island, wholly private and mostly rural. The Anderson Island CMT campsite (mile 9) is on the southwestern shore, just beyond Treble Point at the end of a gravel spit in Carlson Bay. There are outhouses (a challenge to get to at high tide) but no water. Reservations are recommended. Since camping is for WWTA members only, Anderson Island can be quite popular with overnight kayakers. There is an eight-person limit, and a one night maximum stay.

Going up the west coast of Anderson Island, pass Amsterdam Bay on the right. Here, even the tidelands are private. Curve around Otso Point and enter Balch Passage. Eagle Island State Park, 0.5 mile straight ahead, beckons with rustic day-use trails for a leg stretch and snack.

McNeil Island: The north verge of Balch Passage is defined by the south coast of McNeil Island, a rehabilitation center for both our dwindling wildlife and 1,700 of Washington's minimum- and medium-security convicts. With only 100 acres dedicated as a prison, the remaining 4,400 are a true wildlife refuge. McNeil is home to 13 mammalian (including close to 500 blacktail deer), 16 shellfish, 19 finfish, and 80 avian species. Citizens of the largest seal rookery in the south sound, numbering about 350, ply the waters around Still Harbor. Though a ferry calls on the island for necessary support, both its functions require absolute isolation. Signs warn boaters to maintain a 300-yard distance. Don't pick up hitchhikers. The cold waters and high fence have discouraged escapes. The last one was in 1983.

Approach Tacoma Narrows up its west side, first crossing Carr Inlet, coasting by Fox Island, and then crossing Hale Passage. On the east side of the sound, Steilacoom is the threshold for an intensively developed coastline that, with few breaks, stretches all the way north to Vancouver. Tacoma Narrows are narrow both horizontally and vertically. The sill, which provides the foundation for the bridge, constricts tidal flows, and currents may exceed 5 knots. Hug the shore. But even if going with the flow, you'll want to keep a good distance from the heavy shipping.

About 0.5 mile before the Tacoma Narrows Bridge, on the western shore, lies Narrows Park (mile 20), under the jurisdiction of Pierce County Parks, a CMT campground at the end of Lucille Parkway NW, also known as the Doc Weathers site. Identify it by the presence of a little stream (partially constrained by a culvert) and a CMT sign. Water and a chemical toilet are available. Doc Weathers offers a good base for exploring Point Defiance Park (mile 24), which unfortunately has no camping. The next CMT campsite is at Lisabuela Park (mile 30), 4.5 miles up Colvos Passage on Vashon Island.

Tacoma: Across the channel, on the east side, lie Point Defiance, Commencement Bay, and the city of Tacoma, named after Mt. Rainier (née Tahoma, wife of Kulshan [Mt. Baker]), which, in all its Vulcan-rooted and skyline-defining glory, dominates the view. Point Defiance Park (mile 24), 700 acres of award-winning preservation and interpretation, occupies the entire point. The park is well worth investing an entire day. Point Defiance Park is unusual in that it specializes in Pacific Rim exhibits. Reconstructed Fort Nisqually brings the Hudson's Bay Company and the fur trade during the mid-1850s back to life with exquisite detail. Period piece replicas of toothbrushes, tea blocks, musket balls, trade mirrors, and countless quotidian items line the gift shelves, while demonstrations of cooking, construction, and gardening techniques (among others) transport the participant back in time. The aquarium alone is worth the stop. Get a close look at puffins, seals, sea lions, walruses, and a beluga whale. There's even a zoo highlighting Pacific Rim species, a logging museum, and an extensive trail network through formal and natural gardens, also with a circum-Pacific theme. There is no campground.

For a day visit, using the Doc Weathers site as your base, land along the pebble beach just around Point Defiance on its northwest shore, about halfway to the marina. Alternatively, moor your kayak at the park marina, 2 miles into Commencement Bay, and splurge on a B&B. Bay Vista B&B (253-759-8084) is only a 1-mile walk from the marina. The proprietor, Fran Borhek, comes from a seafaring family and will do her best to accommodate kayakers. She might even let you roll out your bag in her backyard if her rooms are full.

Across from Point Defiance, at the end of the Narrows, lies Gig Harbor, technically on the mainland and flanked by a sand spit with a privately maintained lighthouse. All services (except camping) are available, including boat-accessible restaurants. Head due north into relatively undeveloped Colvos Passage and don't worry about whether the tide is ebbing or flooding. Colvos Passage is one of those rare locales where currents always run in one direction—in this case, north. Lisabuela Park (mile 30) is just past Point Sandford, on Vashon Island. The CMT campsite is the grassy area at the north side of the park. There are five sites that receive heavy day use and occasional loud night parties. Water is not available, and fires are not allowed. If for some reason you decide to go up the east side of Vashon Island, there is a new CMT campsite at Point Robinson (about mile 30 also—actually on Maury Island)—right next to the lighthouse. The same limitations apply.

Just on the east side of the northernmost tip of Vashon Island, outside Colvos Passage, is another CMT campsite, Wingehaven (mile 38, plus 1 mile off route). The campsite is located in the first bay south of Dolphin Point and 0.75 mile from the ferry terminal. There are three spots but no water. Although Blake Island (mile 40), the next CMT campsite, is nicer, Wingehaven might better fit your needs depending on conditions and your exact itinerary. When crossing from Vashon Island to Blake Island, watch out for the Southworth–Fauntleroy–Vashon Heights ferry.

Blake Island: If you didn't lay over in Tacoma, you'll have an opportunity to do so at Blake Island State Park (mile 40), at the head of Colvos Passage. Blake is rumored to have been the birthplace of Seattle, chief of the Suquamish. Chief Seattle sided with the settlers during the skirmishes that followed the 1855 treaty that ceded much of Puget Sound to the United States. So the nascent settlement, New York, was rechristened Seattle. The chief was a complex character. About 11 years old when Vancouver visited, he developed a strong antipathy to the newcomers. Hudson's Bay Company records often refer to him as a "scamp...and a villain." In 1838, Father Modeste Demers baptized him Noah Sealth into the Catholic faith. Perhaps he had a Pauline epiphany or perhaps he saw the writing on the wall. Either way he underwent a profound change to the benefit of the invaders and, perhaps (some might argue), to the benefit of his own people.

The park does him justice. The island is a gem with manicured lawns and docile deer. All 475 acres are public land with the centerpiece, Tillicum Village, built around a Coast Salish longhouse, anchoring the minimal but graceful development. Sign up for an alder-smoked salmon bake followed by traditional dances. Flush toilets and pay showers are available. The three CMT sites are located just east of the northwest tip of the island a short distance past site #13 in the public camping area, which has 48 sites. See the ranger for overflow camping. Beyond Tillicum Village the island is all forest, with interpretive trails that explain how the Indians exploited the lush environment.

North of Blake Island the main route continues with no major technical challenges other than traffic. And traffic does increase. Seattle and Tacoma generate ferries and commercial shipping the way a Roman candle shoots sparks. And that's not all. Defense—from the Spanish American War forts located on strategic points to the modern naval construction, testing, and deployment installations—permeates the mid-sound area with a resolute vigilance, ghosts of duty long past and history yet to be made.

Make a beeline from Blake Island due north to Bainbridge Island, but look both ways before crossing. Rich Passage, separating Bainbridge from the Olympic Peninsula, is the gateway to the Navy's Bremerton Shipyards, home base for the aircraft carrier *Nimitz*. Submarines, tugs with tows, and attack and support tonnage of all sizes parade through at all times. Add to that the more than 10 daily runs of the Seattle–Bremerton ferry and you've got a real obstacle course. The *Coast Pilot* warns that the collision hazard here is "considerable." In 1841 Charles Wilkes, leading an expedition commissioned by the US Congress to survey Puget Sound, noted that Sinclair Inlet, where Bremerton is located, was "perfectly protected." Built prior to WW I, Forts Manchester and Ward (mile 42), now both state parks with CMT campsites, guard the entrance to Rich Passage. The two CMT sites at Manchester are in the wooded area above the lawn between the day-use rest rooms and the wooden picnic shelters. Showers are available. The five Fort Ward

CMT sites are just inland of the trail along the water, south of the ranger houses and north of the picnic area.

For the full naval defense monty you might consider a side trip up and back to Bremerton or go all the way up the west coast of Bainbridge. Bremerton is impressive and, as of recently (all things considered), more visitor-friendly. Still, remember to keep at least 600 feet from all naval vessels and facilities. The naval shipyard has operated for more than 100 years and hosts a fairly extensive mothballed fleet, including the aircraft carrier *Midway,* the USS *Missouri,* and the Vietnam War–vintage destroyer *Turner Joy,* which is open to self-guided tours. The Naval Museum is one of the few of its kind. For a visit, park at the marina just north of the ferry dock, between it and the destroyer. Farther up Port Orchard Channel is the Naval Undersea Museum and, *heads up,* a torpedo testing range between Brownsville and Keyport (hug the Bainbridge shore). This detour adds 5–8 miles (depending on just how much you decide to take in) to the route up Bainbridge. Agate Passage, at the top of Port Orchard Channel, is steep, narrow, and subject to 6-knot flows. There is a CMT campsite halfway up the Port Orchard Channel at the Port of Brownsville.

But back to our route. Coasting up Bainbridge Island's eastern shore, you'll pass Blakely Harbor and Eagle Harbor on your left, with spectacular views of Seattle. Watch out for the Winslow-Seattle ferry running in or out of Blakely, a port fully stocked with all services except camping. Fay Bainbridge State Park (mile 53), straddling Point Monroe on the north end of Bainbridge Island and only a short 12 miles from Blake Island, is the next likely layover. This CMT campsite has five spots, water, flush toilets, and showers. It is south of the picnic shelter on the east side near the volleyball court, about 100 feet from shore at high tide.

Upper Puget Sound: Fay Bainbridge State Park (mile 53) to Deception Pass (mile 112)

Fay Bainbridge lies at the mouth of Port Madison, a large bay rich with native history. The inner bay is an old village site, while the flat point at

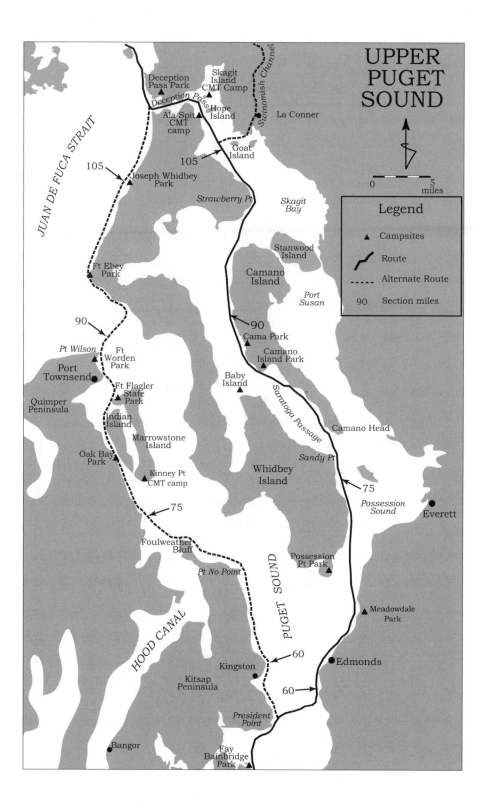

UPPER PUGET SOUND

Legend

▲ Campsites

Route

Alternate Route

90 Section miles

0   5
   miles

Deception Pass Park

Skagit Island CMT Camp

Swinomish Channel

Hope Island

Ala Spit CMT camp

La Conner

Goat Island

Deception Pass

105

Joseph Whidbey Park

105

JUAN DE FUCA STRAIT

Strawberry Pt

Skagit Bay

Stanwood Island

Ft Ebey Park

Camano Island

Port Susan

90

90

Cama Park

Camano Island Park

Pt Wilson

Ft Worden Park

Port Townsend

Baby Island

Ft Flagler State Park

Quimper Peninsula

Indian Island

Saratoga Passage

Marrowstone Island

Camano Head

Oak Bay Park

Sandy Pt

Kinney Pt CMT camp

Whidbey Island

75

75

Possession Sound

Everett

Foulweather Bluff

Pt No Point

Possession Pt Park

PUGET SOUND

Meadowdale Park

HOOD CANAL

60

Kingston

Edmonds

Kitsap Peninsula

60

President Point

Bangor

Fay Bainbridge Park

the entrance was called "Where Corpses Are Put." The deceased were laid out in boxes and hoisted into the trees to await the afterlife. Guarding the entrance to Agate Passage stands the modern village of Suquamish, final resting place of Chief Seattle and Tribal Center of the Suquamish. Chief Seattle Days are celebrated in August with traditional games and dances, canoe races, and a salmon bake. The public is welcome.

Throughout Puget Sound, before the introduction of guns, Indians employed an ingeniously novel and evidently effective method for hunting ducks and geese. One of these sites was in Agate Passage: "After dark or on foggy days, Indians would startle ducks off Agate Pt. and send them flying down Agate Pass. At the appropriate time, large nets would be raised on high upright poles, catching the fleeing, squawking birds. Nets were dropped and birds were killed." (T. Waterman, as quoted by Stephen Hilson in *Exploring Puget Sound & British Columbia.*)

Now is the time to consider whether you'll continue on the main route (or its even more protected alternative) or opt for the sportier route. The sportier alternate separates from the main route above Port Madison, just below President Point (mile 56), and goes up the west side of Puget Sound's main body via Port Townsend. It then rejoins the main route at Deception Pass.

While neither is shorter, the main route is well protected except for very strong currents in Deception Pass, which must be negotiated at or near slack water. The Port Townsend alternate is more interesting but much more challenging. (See the concluding section of this chapter for alternate route details.) From Fay Bainbridge, the next campsite on the main route is 13 miles away at Meadowdale (mile 66), while along the Port Townsend alternate it is 24 miles to the next camp at Kinney Point CMT campsite (mile 77).

From Fay Bainbridge, cross or coast Port Madison to President Point (mile 56), the point of divergence between the main and primary alternate routes. While the alternate route continues north along the Kitsap Peninsula, the main route crosses the sound to slip in behind Whidbey Island. The distance from President Point to Richmond Beach, across the sound, is about 3 miles. Look both ways, plan your crossing well, and go for it.

Once across, head up the well-developed Seattle coast. About 5 miles north of the Edmonds Ferry Terminal lies Meadowdale (mile 66), a CMT campsite that was once a country club. From the water the site is somewhat indistinct—although there is a sign—because the railway line blocks the view of the park proper. A small stream flows to the sound under a trestle at the spot and provides access to the main grounds. Water and toilets are available. Although the CMT membership entitles you to camp, reservations are required 72 hours in advance. (Call Meadowdale Beach County Park at 425-745-5111.) Camping is limited to one night, but there is overflow camping and the ranger is resident so, if you missed the call, you might be able to negotiate with him for a spot.

About 2 miles north of Meadowdale, Picnic Point, on the south tip of Whidbey Island, guards the entrance to Possession Sound. Although not a major traffic lane, the entrance to Possession Sound can congest with small craft—this route is the most popular and protected for going up into the San Juans. Cross over to Whidbey Island, the second largest island in the Lower 48 states. Just east of the point lies Possession Point State Park (mile 69). There is a chemical toilet but no water. Be aware that the next CMT site is 20 miles away at Camano State Park (mile 87).

Head up Whidbey to Sandy Point, and cross Saratoga Passage to Camano Head at the southern tip of Camano Island. Avoid going up the east coast of Camano Island. Although a kayak can get through at the north end between Camano and Stanwood, the Snohomish, Stillaguamish, and Skagit Rivers all drain into Port Susan and Skagit Bay, creating deltaic mud flats. During the freshet, strong freshwater outflows impede approach. Add wind and tides to the shifting shoals, and the currents and chop become a hazard, if not downright unnavigable.

Coast up the west side of Camano Island to Elger Bay and Camano Island State Park (mile 87) on Lowell Point, for the next CMT campsite. Water, toilets, and five tent sites are available at the far south end of the Point Lowell day-use area. For a more undeveloped—and free—camping experience, Baby Island (mile 86), about 2 miles off route across Saratoga Passage, is mentioned in some older sources as a possible camping spot. Two miles farther along lies Cama State Park (mile 89). Cama was recently purchased and is not yet quite developed or open, though there are plans to integrate it into the CMT network. Get an early start the next day, as the next CMT campground, Ala Spit (mile 107), is 20 miles away (it will be 18 when Cama State Park comes online). Continue up the Camano Island coast to Rocky Point, cross over to Whidbey Island, and head for Strawberry Point at the entrance to Skagit Bay.

The Skagit River, second largest in the western US, debauches into Skagit Bay, making much of the north and east portions unnavigable mud flats. Stick to the Whidbey Island side. Between Dugualla Bay and Goat Island, near mile 105, the main route forks again into the second, even more protected option, through Swinomish Channel. (This second alternate route is also described at the conclusion of this chapter.)

Continue up Whidbey to the channel between Ala Spit and Hope Island. Ala Spit CMT campsite (mile 107) is at the south end of the spit above the bulkhead. Do not approach from inside the small bay, as low tide exposes a big, muddy carry. There are four tent sites and a Sanican, but no water. Finding the exact location of the CMT allotment can be problematic. The spit itself is either too narrow or exposed—we camped just before the spit (closest to the Sanican) on either of two grassy areas or the pebbly foreshore in front of the low concrete breakwater.

Hope Island State Park covers most of Hope Island. There are picnic tables, pit toilets, even a restaurant, and hiking trails among the giant cedars of some honest-to-goodness old-growth forest. Skagit Island (mile 108), just to the north, is also a state park with a CMT campsite that was inaugurated in 2004. Swift currents surround both islands at most times. At the head of Skagit Bay, tidal flows accelerate as they constrict upon entering Deception Pass.

The changes in topography, hydrography, and ambience at Deception Pass are striking. The flanking abutments are steep, rugged, and dramatic. Deception Pass channels a phenomenal amount of tidal exchange. Currents can exceed 8 knots during spring tides; averages run about 6. Speeds decrease rapidly within half a mile each side of the pass. Paddlers of all abilities can often be found here, ferry gliding and whirlpool riding. Consult the Deception Pass current tables for direction and slack. Slack does not coincide with high and low tides and only lasts about 15 minutes. Expect some current at all times, and watch out for traffic during slack. Deception Pass is the preferred north-south route for small craft.

Hug the shore up to Hoypus Point to evade flood tides. Here, too, survives one of the last stands of precontact old growth in what has been designated a natural forest area. Better yet, round Hoypus on a waning ebb, and island-hop from Ben Ure Island to Strawberry Island to the Fidalgo Island shore. Traverse Canoe Pass, between Fidalgo and Pass Islands, at the end of the ebb or during the short slack. Turn Lighthouse Point and Reservation Head to Bowman Bay (a.k.a. Reservation Bay). Once north of Deception Island, the current lets up.

Deception Pass State Park (mile 112), straddling both the Whidbey and Fidalgo Island coastlines, is the most heavily used park in Puget Sound. The CMT campsite is on the Fidalgo Island side at the back of Bowman Bay, between the picnic shelter and the head of the pier, about 100 yards south of the pier. Water, flush toilets, and showers are available. There are ten tent sites, and overflow camping is at the ranger's discretion. Don't miss the hike across Sharpe Cove to Rosario Head, where the Maiden of Deception Pass stands guard. The wooden story pole commemorates the Samish princess who, by marrying the Prince of the Sea, saved the land and her people.

San Juan Islands: Deception Pass (mile 112) to Stuart Island (mile 150)

The San Juan Islands are the most popular sea kayaking destination in the Lower 48. They consist of 786 islands at low tide but only 457 at high tide, according to the 1927 USGS survey.

Together they comprise San Juan County, the only island archipelago county in the United States. It is also one of the richest, per capita. The main cities, Friday Harbor and Roche Harbor, along with the beautiful scattered homes, are an architectural delight. The normal population of about 10,000 swells to more than 35,000 during the warmer months, which are quite dry—average yearly rainfall is only 25 inches.

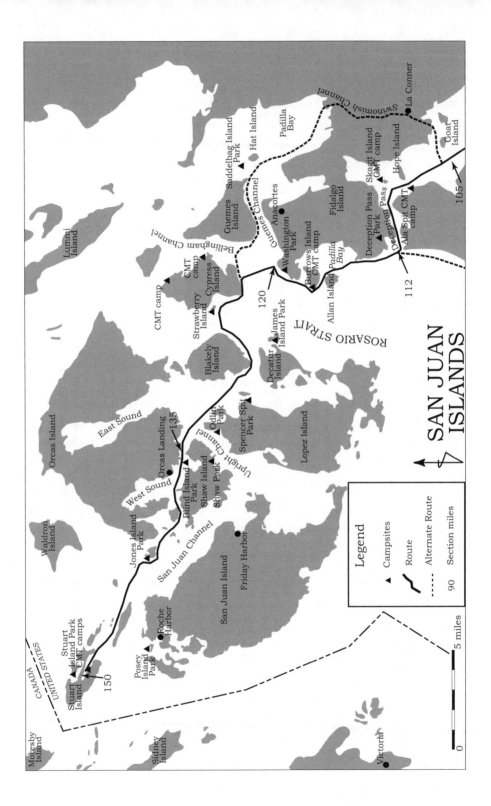

SAN JUAN
ISLANDS

Legend

▲ Campsites

Route

Alternate Route

90 Section miles

0   5 miles

Where the international border along the 49th Parallel hits the San Juan–Gulf Islands archipelago all hell breaks loose, at least from the perspective of diplomats, mapmakers, and bureaucrats. Drawing the line was a riddle tackled by procrastinators driven by expedience. At this point, the elegant frontier becomes a sieve, which smugglers have arbitraged. At first, the commodity was illegal Chinese immigrants. During the reign of the Volstead Act it was alcohol. With Canada moving toward decriminalization, its marijuana industry becoming more sophisticated, and prices south of the border skyrocketing due to intensified prohibition, pot is now the smugglers' choice. Between October 1999 and October 2001, law enforcement agencies confiscated more than 640 pounds of cannabis from boaters—most of them Canadians. About 100 pounds of that was seized from kayakers. Don't become a casualty of the drug war.

North of Rosario Head the shore is steep and rocky, a pleasure to coast. Guarding the entrance to huge Burrows Bay are Allan and Burrows Islands (mile 117). Both are private, including the tidelands, except for a once seldom-visited, 40-acre state park established around the abandoned light station on the western end of Burrows Island. In 2004 a new CMT campsite was opened. The stunning views should make it quite popular. Best access is from the gravel beach just north of the facility. Only very small craft can land.

Continuing on, whether along the north or south passage of Burrows Island, pick a flood tide or slack in which to paddle. Ebbs can run 2 knots and flow east through these channels. Going through the north channel, you'll pass Flounder Bay just before Fidalgo Head. All facilities except camping are available. Round Fidalgo Head and Green Point. Washington Park (mile 119), an Anacortes city park encompassing all of Fidalgo Head, is best accessed from the shallow bay between Green and Shannon Points. Though not part of the CMT network, it has extensive campgrounds, water, toilets, showers, and picnic tables close to the launch ramps. Sites are $12, and the Flounder Bay facilities are a close 10-minute walk.

Paddling through kelp in the San Juan Islands

East of Shannon Point you'll enter Ship Harbor, the west end of Anacortes proper. Since Cypress Island is your next objective, study conditions carefully. Generally, floods run north while ebbs flow south. At 2 miles, making a beeline from Shannon Point to the south shore of Cypress is the shortest distance, and a reasonable strategy with a flood tide. Alternatively, heading east toward Anacortes proper, crossing Guemes Channel to Guemes Island, coasting north, and then crossing Bellingham Channel to Cypress is longer but only requires two 1-mile crossings. During ebb tides, follow this route. Either crossing requires vigilance, not only for the San Juan and Sidney ferries, which dock at Ship Harbor, but also for tankers that ply the Guemes Channel waters delivering oil to the Anacortes refinery, end of the line for Alaskan crude.

Cypress Island is mostly public recreation land and harbors three CMT campsites, one on a tiny satellite off the west coast—Strawberry Island (mile 124). This is the next campsite en route. The island is steep and only a quarter mile long. Access is from a minuscule gravel (at high tide) or rock (at low tide) beach at the south end, while the three tent sites are halfway up the island. No water is available, though pit toilets and picnic tables are provided. Draw up the boats well high, as traffic wakes and tides reach higher than you might imagine. The Strawberry Island campsite is a perfect location for studying Rosario Strait, the next piece of the paddling puzzle to be worked out, and probably the route's biggest challenge in the San Juans.

Rosario Strait is a serious body of water. You'll be certain of it as you watch the constriction rapid at the southwest end of Strawberry Island surge, die, and reverse direction with the tide, if you camp here. Three-knot currents are the rule. As if that were not enough, Black Rocks (your approximate destination when crossing), off the east end of Blakely Island, create heavy swirls and strong tide rips. But the icing on the cake is the well-used shipping lane with tankers, tugs with barges, and all manner of shipping. Prepare for the full fry. Fortunately the crossing is only 1 mile, 15 minutes if you're psyched up properly. Bracket the slack and, once across, hug the Blakely shore to avoid Black Rocks and you're home free. Head south to Thatcher Pass and calmer waters.

Blakely Island is entirely private and has no public ferry service or even county roads. It is precipitous and rugged. Coast up its west side to Willow Island, a national wildlife refuge (keep 200 yards away), and choose a good route and time to cross over to Lopez Island. Though conditions here are placid, this remains the route of the San Juan ferry, so make sure to give it a wide berth. The James Island State Park (mile 127) CMT campsite lies about 1 mile off route to the south. Three sites, an outhouse, picnic tables (no water), and robber raccoons lie at the southwest corner of the dog bone–shaped island. Stairs mark the landing. Just behind Frost Island, on Lopez, lies Spencer Spit State Park (mile 131), the next CMT campsite on route, located on the south side of the hill directly west of the spit, among wild roses and up the lane from the log picnic shelter. Beware of the wild rabbits! There are three sites (with some overflow camping), water, flush toilets, picnic tables, and a telephone.

Coast up through Swifts Bay to Humphrey Head. As you pass tiny Flower Island, stay 200 yards away—another national wildlife refuge. (All other tidelands along this stretch are private.) Cross Shoal Bay and continue on to Upright Head at the very north tip of Lopez Island. Watch out for the ferry terminal on Upright. On the southwest shore of Upright Head's neck lies Odlin County Park (mile 132), one of the CMT's newest additions (and about 1 mile south, off route). There is water and a vault toilet. The crossing to Hankin Point on Shaw Island should be uneventful.

Shaw County Park (mile 134), a CMT campsite, is situated about 3 miles off route, due south of Hankin Point on South Beach at Indian Cove. There is water and a vault toilet at the 60-acre park. Enter Harney Channel. Currents generally flow west on flood and east on ebb. Shaw Island is lightly populated (fewer than 200 souls, Franciscan nuns, mostly) and mostly off limits. Blind Island State Park (mile 136) lies at the head of Blind Bay. This CMT campsite is just west of the ferry dock and has four tent sites, picnic tables, and a composting toilet. There is no water. Adjacent to the ferry dock is a small, picturesque store run by the nuns and stocked with dairy items produced on their farm.

Orcas Island: To the north lies Orcas Island, largest of the San Juans, second in population and home to the tallest peak in the archipelago—2,400-foot Mount Constitution. Orcas Landing, almost due north of Blind Island, is the ferry landing and commercial center of the island. Next to it is West Sound, a large indentation up the south coast of Orcas. Inside is Skull Island State Park. Many place-names in West Sound—Victim Island, Massacre Bay, Haida Point—memorialize Haida slave-raiding expeditions to the San Juans. In 1858, Stikine Tlingits from Alaska raided a Lummi village here. The Stikines referred to Puget Sound as "place of slaves." This time they encountered fierce resistance at a dear price. Reports indicate that more than 100 bodies littered the beach after the battle.

By now your navigational skills will have been tested. Distinguishing islands as distinct landmasses while zigzagging through passes and channels with a constantly changing perspective, not to mention the distraction of spirited conversation (just as conducive as during a good amble) and the occasional spacing-out on the wild beauty of the archipelago, can try one's navigational concentration. Out of Blind Island, head for Broken Point west up Harney Channel and, farther on, to the

Wasp Islands. Pick any route through these, but don't miss Yellow Island.

Wasp Islands: Yellow is owned by The Nature Conservancy and has been managed as, primarily, a plant preserve: there has been no grazing or resident deer population. Consequently, the grasses and wildflowers have reached a natural climax that is not only rare here, it is also exceptionally contemplative. Shore access is best from the gravel spit on the east. Visiting groups are limited to five individuals. Camping, picnicking, smoking, and fires are not allowed. The caretaker lives on the southwest shore. McConnell Rock, off the northwest tip of McConnell Island and adjacent to Yellow Island, is an undeveloped state park. No camping is allowed here either. All the other Wasp Islands, as inviting and scenic as they beckon, are off limits.

Jones Island State Park (mile 141) is my idea of the perfect campsite. I'm not alone; it is one of the most popular CMT campsites in the entire system and well situated as an ideal last camp before the end of this section at Roche Harbor. The site is midway up the west coast and includes fire pits, picnic tables, a composting toilet, and a two-log custom kayak ramp up to the two elevated tent sites. If the site is full, paddle over to the north or south coves for overflow camping and where water is available between May 15 and September 30.

Strong currents and tide rips obstruct any route up and back to Stuart Island, the final objective for the Puget Sound portion of the Inside Passage. San Juan Channel can run currents of 5 knots. The junction of Spieden and San Juan Channels is the worst, with rips 100 yards off Limestone Point and next to Green Point on Spieden Island. Make the 2.5-mile crossing from Jones to Spieden bracketing the slack. Amply circle Green Point on the north and coast up Spieden along New Channel. Spieden Island is private.

Stuart Island: Stuart Island, though mostly private, includes Turn Point and Stuart Island State Parks (mile 150). The latter has two components, one in Reid, the other in Prevost Harbor. The entrance into Reid, flanked by Cemetery and Gossip Islands, is elegantly proportioned and symmetrically nuanced—it takes your breath away, slowly. Gossip was originally slated to become the Stuart Island CMT campsite, but discovery of rare lance-leafed sedum, prickly pear cactus, chocolate lilies, camas, and native bunch grasses caused it, instead, to be turned into a Natural Protected Area within the Washington State Parks system. Feel free to land and walk.

Though both Reid and Prevost have water, camping, and toilets, the CMT site is in Reid Harbor (mile 150), with overflow into Prevost Harbor. The campsite lies at the head of the bay, a muddy walk through the marsh at low tide. Protected all around from breezes by the steep horseshoe landform, it's also an insect preserve. If you're lucky, Reid will be full and you'll be forced to camp at Prevost, where the tent sites are especially appealing, each with its own beach access and lovely views.

Don't finish your trip without circumnavigating Stuart and hiking up the bluff at Turn Point State Park for tantalizing views of Sydney, Vancouver Island, and the Gulf Islands, the next section, which, for some, won't come soon enough. Turn Point State Park encompasses 53 acres around the 10-acre Coast Guard installation on the northwest corner of Stuart Island. A now-automated lighthouse and US boundary triangulation monument man the point. The best landing is 0.25 mile south of the point. Access is also available along trails from Stuart Island State Park. There are no facilities at Turn Point.

Good show. If you've chosen to paddle the Inside Passage in sections, you must now work your way back to your car in Olympia. The entire return paddle to Roche Harbor is only 5 miles. Head for Spieden Bluff and cross Spieden Channel at its widest point, heading toward Davidson Head at the top of San Juan Island, about a 2-mile crossing. Posey Island State Park, at the entrance to Roche Harbor and 1 mile from it (just off the northwest corner of Pearl Island), is the last CMT campsite on this stretch and a well-situated staging point from which to explore Roche Harbor. It gets lots of day visitors. There are two sites with a maximum of 16 people allowed. There is no water, though two picnic tables and a composter are provided.

The startlingly white, 120-year-old Hotel de Haro dominates Roche Harbor. It is flanked by white clapboard cabins, a chapel, and a restaurant, all remnants of another, long-forgotten colonial era, like something out of a W. Somerset Maugham tale. The effect is starker for the rich green forests that frame the resort and, with the crowded harbor and busy waterfront, evokes latitudes farther south. Transient showers are available right on the pier.

Call the Puget Sound Express and make arrangements (if you haven't already done so), in advance, for a pickup. Inquire from the harbormaster about where the ferry customarily docks. Empty the kayaks and pack your dunnage separately, for the boats will have to be lifted by hand onto the cabin roof. The run back to Port Townsend is along Haro Strait, dining room and parlor for the resident and visiting pods of orcas. Don't miss them.

Alternate Route #1: President Point (mile 56) to Deception Pass (mile 112) via Port Townsend

The alternate route via Port Townsend is no longer than the main route; however, it is much more scenic, interesting, and challenging. Between Port Townsend and Deception Pass, the route is exposed to the full brunt of Juan de Fuca's ire. The 4-mile crossing from Port Townsend to Whidbey includes one serious rip and all the traffic entering and exiting Puget Sound. Whidbey Island's west shore boasts the only surf in the sound. In good conditions, this is my preferred route.

The next camping opportunity after Fay Bainbridge State Park (mile 53) along the alternate route is 24 miles away at Kinney Point CMT campsite (mile 77), so get an early start. After President Point (mile 56), where the routes diverge, continue up the coast past Kingston inside Appletree Cove on your left. Keep an eye out for the Kingston-Edmonds and Kingston-Everett ferries. Head for Point No Point and Foulweather Bluff, which not only caps the Kitsap Peninsula but defines the southwest corner of Admiralty Inlet and the eastern rampart of Hood Canal, which now must be crossed. Colvos Rocks makes a good objective. Larger boats avoid them, and seals often haul out on them.

Bangor, in Hood Canal, is the US Navy's Trident submarine base. Keep an eye out for nuclear subs. Trident-class subs are 560 feet long and gestate a clutch of nuclear missiles in their bellies. Out on patrol for 70- to 90-day tours, they are completely overhauled at the base and their crews rotated between missions. Give them a very wide berth.

Kinney Point CMT campsite (mile 77), on the southern tip of Marrowstone Island—with 68 acres and no road access—is a great spot from which to catch the right tide to take you through the Port Townsend Canal separating Indian Island from the Quimper Peninsula. Unfortunately, there is no water. Alternatively—though more crowded—Oak Bay County Park (mile 79) has pit toilets and water and is located on the west side of the north end of Oak Bay, immediately south of the Port Townsend Canal. Ebb and flood do not occur here at the same time as in Admiralty Inlet, and they near 3 knots. Because the canal is straight (it's man-made), shore-hugging eddies are minimal and it's best to catch a favorable current. Once through, you can follow the western shore of the bay to Port Townsend for an uneventful transit. Or you can coast up the Indian Island shore for a much more interesting but challenging approach to Port Townsend.

Indian Island: The southern reaches of Indian Island are wild and have a sculpted sandstone foundation peppered with hoodoos and handles. Seals and river otters hang out on the many offshore rocks. As you approach Walan Point, stay 600 feet away from the navy's ammunition depot on the northwest end. All landings within station boundaries are strictly prohibited.

The island is aptly named. Archaeological excavations indicate a continuous occupation for more than 3,000 years. When Vancouver approached the beach where the CMT campsite is now located, at Fort Flagler State Park (mile 85), he saw 17 long poles erected on the beach:

> They were uniformly placed in the center of the low sandy spit, at the distance of about eighty yards from each other... They were, in general, about six inches in diameter at the bottom, and perfectly strait; and, when too short, a piece was added... very neatly scarfed on; the top of each terminating in two points like a crescent... these posts I should suppose to be about one hundred feet... Between several of them large holes were dug in the ground, in which were many stones that had been burnt.

These were probably fireplaces used to create smoke to conceal nets used to catch the fowl when fog did not collaborate. The nets were probably strung between the two points of the crescents.

Fort Flagler State Park (mile 85), lies at the north end of Marrowstone Island, Indian Island's twin. There is plenty of camping, showers, and a commanding view of Port Townsend and Admiralty Inlet. The six CMT campsites are in the woods, east of the lower campground, just inland from the north beach.

Pick a target well west of Point Hudson for the crossing of Port Townsend Bay, about 1.5 miles across. An underwater ridge just outside the bay can cause extra turbulence during big ebbs. You'll also be positioned to avoid the Port Townsend–Keystone ferry.

Port Townsend: Fort Worden State Park (mile 89), the Port Townsend CMT campsite, is on the northern edge of the town, just south of the pier on the beach below the main fort area. All facilities are available, including a marine science center right on the pier with a "touch tank" so you can fully familiarize yourself with many of the spiny and squiggly creatures encountered along the Inside Passage. Bus service connects the fort with the town.

If only to ensure yourself of a good opportunity for crossing Admiralty Inlet, plan on a layover day at Port Townsend. Paddling up to it has got to be one of the most thrilling approaches in Puget Sound. The town, like a tiered wedding cake baroquely ornamented with Victorian storefronts and mansions, thick with coquettish plumage, reveals its delicate details only if explored on foot. The hundreds of sailboats, often under full billow, give the impression of upright, folded linen napkins guarding the confectioner's edifice. Port Townsend, Seattle, and Tacoma were all settled concurrently in 1851. All aspired to be the continental railroad and oceanic shipping hub of the Northwest. When the railroad bypassed Port Townsend, the town died and remained frozen in time until discerning cranks and eccentrics revived it with wooden boat festivals, kayak symposia, Libertarian conferences, Green politics, eclectic bookstores, B&Bs, and the occasional on-location film shoot. Not quite close enough to Seattle to serve as a bedroom community, Port Townsend remains fiercely independent and low-key.

Fort Worden, along with Fort Flagler on Marrowstone Island and Fort Casey on Whidbey Island, command and dominate the entrance to Puget Sound. All three were built in 1900, during the Spanish-American War, to defend the sound from enemy invasion. Don't miss exploring at least Fort Worden. Intricate tunnels and battlements with oversize guns and concrete pillboxes dedicated to Civil War heroes evoke an era and type of defense otherwise nonexistent in the United States today. The installation became obsolete with the development of aerial warfare, but the army held on to it until 1972, when it was transferred to the State Parks Commission. Vast parade grounds, refurbished officers quarters available to the public for rent, and the 248th Coast Artillery Museum round out the attractions.

You are now about to exit the protected dead-end waters of Puget Sound. From Point Wilson all the way to Point Gustavus at the entrance to Glacier Bay, swirling, converging, and diverging currents from diverse Pacific origins will be your foundation. Studying the sea state and psyching up for our crossing at the base of the Point Wilson lighthouse (built in 1879), I was struck by Migael Scherer's observation in her excellent book, *A Cruising Guide to Puget Sound,* about how these beacons continue to reassure: " 'You have arrived at this point,' each seems to say. 'May you continue safely to the next.' "

The featureless sweep of the Whidbey Island scarp does not invite; it is simply a target. Aim for the indistinct point halfway between Admiralty Head and Point Partridge, about 4 miles distant (an approximate due-north magnetic bearing). Choose your time to cross carefully, as you'll be exposed to the full brunt of Juan de Fuca Strait and all of Puget Sound's inbound and outbound traffic. Luckily, the traffic lanes just about graze Point Wilson, allowing for near-perfect timing, in terms of shipping, for the crossing.

Beware of the nasty rip that forms due true north of Point Wilson during current runs. Native Americans aptly named it "Rough Water." When traversing the area they sat very still, maintained silence, and paddled carefully. Menstruating women had to walk around the point.

It has claimed the life of at least one kayaker. Make note of it during your layover and skirt it on the right. Begin the crossing at the end of flood, so that slack finds you in the middle and ebb pushes you up toward Point Partridge.

Ebey's Landing, about where you'll be aiming for, was the objective of another Inside Passage paddling expedition, one which ended in carnage and death. On the night of August 11, 1857, a war party of Tlingit Indians from Kake, Alaska, landed here. They were seeking retribution for the murder of one of their chiefs by a US warship. Colonel Isaac Ebey, unfortunately available, became the scapegoat: he was decapitated. In a startling display of temperance and understanding, no punitive counterattack was deployed. Instead, Captain Charles Dodd, commander of the *Labouchere,* sailed for Russian America and undertook to resolve the dispute. After laborious negotiations he untangled the misunderstanding, set the record straight, and returned to Washington with the remains of the grisly trophy for proper interment.

Whidbey Island is the second largest island in the Lower 48 states. Its western shore is the only place in Puget Sound where you can actually surf. Fort Ebey State Park (mile 97), a CMT campsite, is just around Point Partridge at the southern edge of the day-use area and north of the lighthouse. Water is available. Seven miles up the coast is Joseph Whidbey State Park (mile 105), another CMT campsite, this one without water. The site is located north of the grassy picnic area. There is a sign marking the location. By now you'll have become increasingly aware of the crescendoing roar of US Navy jets either practicing touch-and-gos or just making noise like cruising teenagers. Unfortunately, Joseph Whidbey State Park, just south of Rocky Point, is adjacent to the US Naval Reservation, so if you camp here, remember your ear plugs. The eagle never sleeps.

The last 5 miles of shoreline before Deception Pass consist of white sandy beach with, at best, gently breaking Pacific swell. On warm summer days bathers pack the surf and slopes. It's a great place to practice surf landings, especially if you want to recon Deception Pass and/or wait for slack. Just don't suffer the ignominy of a dump or, worse yet, pummel a swimmer.

Avoid crossing Deception Pass anytime during flood lest you be swept in, as well as when ebbs combine with westerlies. Once past Deception Island, the current wanes and you have rejoined the main route.

Alternate Route #2: Ala Spit (Mile 107) to Cypress Island (mile 122)

This alternate routes you through the even more protected confines of Swinomish Channel. It is 8 miles longer than the main route. I would recommend it for the charms of La Conner and during adverse conditions on the other routes, but only when used with favorable currents.

From the Ala Spit CMT campsite (mile 107), retrace your steps 2 miles. The dredged passage into Swinomish Channel parts company with the main route at about mile 105 and runs adjacent to the north shore of Goat Island on a range east-northeast from Dugualla Bay. It is well marked. At higher tides make a beeline directly for Goat Island (don't worry, there are high-water openings in the levee); at lower water the sand flats north of Goat preclude passage, and you must head directly to the channel opening. Swinomish Channel, an old Skagit River distributary connecting Skagit with Padilla Bay, is the safest, most protected route up to the San Juans, especially when conditions "outside" beg for respect. Rafts of logs, both berthed and under tow, congest the southern extremities. The channel proper is 7 miles long, with La Conner and the state highway bridge about 1 mile north of the entrance.

Goat Island: Steep and imposing, Goat Island includes Fort Whitman, an inconspicuous component of the coast artillery defenses built at the turn of the 19th century. Concrete rooms, three gun emplacements, and connecting tunnels fortify the northwest shoulder. To get a perspective of the channel, delta, and sand flats or perhaps wait for a tide change, hike the 250 yards up to the battery. The trail begins at the old dock along the island's north shore. A rough path, angling right, heads up from the rocky but muddy beach behind the pier.

The strong current in Swinomish Channel is deceptive and irritating. According to Scherer in *A Cruising Guide to Puget Sound:* "No one seems able to explain or predict it. Some say it floods north and ebbs

Harbor seal

south, about an hour before (or after) Anacortes. Generally. Others say it floods and ebbs from both ends. Usually. Where it meets is anybody's guess." My own experience is illuminating: Ebb tide at the south end, current flows south at south end. Flood tide at the north end, current flows south at north end.

Though on the chart, Swinomish Channel—being straight and narrow—does not seem a good candidate for paddling against the current, it in fact actually is. The dredged center channels most of the current's force while the shallow, leveed verges slow the current substantially between the not-infrequent eddies. The secret is to hug the shore. Still, it is better to go with the current than against it. Enter the south mouth during a rising tide. Don't fret about the direction of the channel's current. Wait for the tide change in La Conner so as to exit the north end on an ebbing tide. Then the current will not only be with you in the channel, it'll push you all the way across Padilla Bay—a tiresome exercise if attempted against the current, especially since it must be accomplished at mid-bay, where progress is difficult to gauge and tidal currents are at their strongest.

La Conner: La Conner is a small, attractive tourist, farming, and fishing community, vibrant in spite of its preservation in the National Register of Historic Places. Like Dutch towns along the Rhine's delta, it has built dikes to reclaim rich river sediment deposits for agriculture and boasts a tulip festival in the spring. There are two or three "public beaches" for docking. These are actually floating public docks connected by stairs to decked waterfront parks along the main street. Right next to one park, you can get Indian smoked salmon cured with three different spices. The La Conner Pub has unfiltered Mack & Jack's African Porter on tap and excellent fish and chips. Across the channel lies the Swinomish Indian Reservation.

Follow the channel markings for 2 more miles past land's end into Padilla Bay. Head due north through Padilla Bay's center, avoiding the sand flats to the east, and don't angle northwest across Fidalgo Bay to Anacortes. Instead, avoid the traffic, congestion, and 3- to 4-knot currents in Guemes Channel by heading up to Hat Island (private), tiny Dot Island, and then Saddlebag Island, another 0.25 mile north.

Saddlebag Island State Park (mile 118), a CMT campsite, fronts the National Estuarine Sanctuary of Padilla Bay, itself part of the Skagit River estuary. Adjacent Dot Island is a national wildlife refuge (keep 200 yards away). More than 240 species of birds including black brant geese use both facilities on their migrations between Alaska and Mexico. The CMT camp has two tent sites in the forest behind the west end of the beach on the south side of the island; overflow camping is on the north side. There are outhouses but no water.

Out of Saddlebag Island, aim for Southeast Point on Guemes Island and follow the south shore around to Yellow Bluff. As you pass the town of Guemes, beware of the Guemes–Fidalgo ferry. Cross Bellingham Channel to Cypress Island and rejoin the main route at mile 126.

4
Vancouver Island

Sidney to Port Hardy

287 miles

> *Oh Canada!*
> *Our home and native land!*
> *True patriot love in all thy sons command.*
> —*Robert Stanley Weir*

"Are you bringing in any liquor, beer, wine, or tobacco?" In spite of the businesslike punctiliousness of the question, the Canadian Customs agent's carside manners were leagues ahead of those of his US counterparts, who give the impression of having trained under sadistic proctologists.

Indeed we were: wine and pipe tobacco, one slightly in excess of the allowed limits. No matter. An honest declaration rendered a generous individual exemption.

"Are you carrying any self-defense devices such as guns, pepper spray, or mace?" This time the eyes narrowed suspiciously, homing through the response to detect revealing body language.

Our shotgun passed muster without a glance, but the US-made pepper spray was apologetically confiscated. Curiously, although pepper spray is legal in Canada for bear protection, it must be labeled "for bears." Perhaps the label inhibits its use against other predators. We later forked out $80 for two Canadian-made capsicum bear repellents.

Not one question about drugs or suspicion concerning illegal stowaways. Canada's border priorities are obvious: first, an unfailingly polite

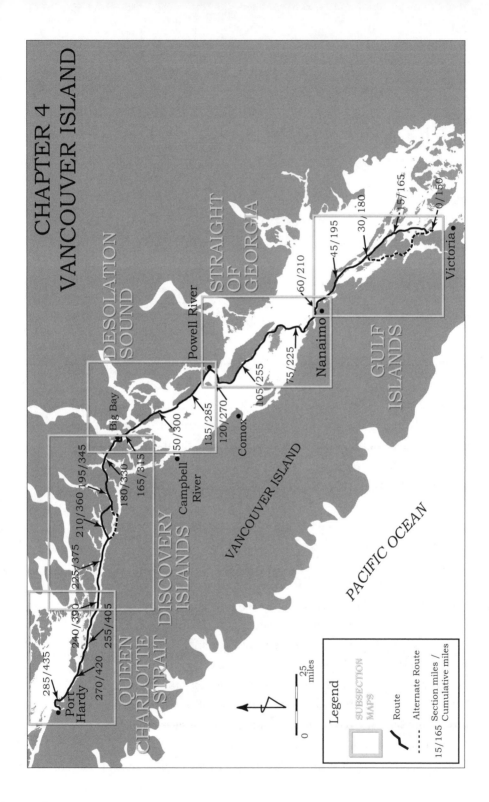

CHAPTER 4
VANCOUVER ISLAND

DESOLATION
SOUND

STRAIGHT
OF
GEORGIA

Powell River

Big Bay

Campbell
River

Comox

DISCOVERY
ISLANDS

VANCOUVER ISLAND

QUEEN
CHARLOTTE
STRAIT

Port
Hardy

GULF
ISLANDS

Nanaimo

Victoria

PACIFIC OCEAN

0/150
30/180
157/165
45/195
60/210
75/225
105/255
120/270
135/285
150/300
165/315
180/330
195/345
210/360
225/375
240/390
255/405
270/420
285/435

Legend

SUBSECTION
MAPS

Route

Alternate Route

15/165   Section miles /
          Cumulative miles

N

0   25
     miles

welcome, then liquor and tobacco smuggling—vice taxes are not only an important source of revenue, they embody a long tradition of reformist social policy that discourages unhealthy habits—and, finally, handgun prohibition. Canadians are proud of their civil society and deathly afraid of contracting what they perceive as a US epidemic of handgun violence.

By law, you are now required to carry a passport. However, you may be asked to produce only a driver's license or nothing at all. Remember that admission and duration of stay are at the discretion of the immigration officer at the border.

It is a pleasure to be in Canada. The towns and countryside are spotless and never crowded. Canadians are patient, tolerant, and egalitarian to the core. A leisurely civility and understated formality barely conceal an endearing earnestness—about the most trivial of life's minor curiosities—that disarms even the most irascible visitor. Finalizing preparations for the second leg of our Inside Passage trip could not have been more pleasant. In sharp contrast to our apprehension at embarking from Boston Harbor, we were impatient to resume our trip and discover what surprises Vancouver Island held along its eastern verge.

The only way to get to Sidney from the mainland with a vehicle and kayaks is via ferry. Ferries depart from Port Angeles; Seattle; Anacortes; Bellingham, WA; and Tsawwassen, B.C. All but two converge on Victoria. The Anacortes and Tsawwassen ferries dock in Sidney.

Tina expressed minor concern over the slight gap in the continuity of our route. Actually, the beginning of the second leg is south of where the first leg ends, and the route north comes within 4 miles of it. Stuart Island's northern tip lies at latitude 48 degrees, 40 minutes, while Island View Beach Regional Park, the start, is at 48 degrees, 35 minutes. Island View, about halfway between Victoria and Sidney, is an ideal staging point from which to get organized and take off. The park itself is undeveloped except for a parking lot and launch ramp, but adjacent to it is a private campground. The setting is rural, reasonable, and relaxed. Drive north from Victoria on Highway 17 and turn off onto Island View Road. Follow it to the park at the road's end. One can either engage long-term parking right there or rent a car at the nearby Sidney–Victoria airport for a shuttle to Port Hardy, this leg's northern terminus. We spent a day getting ready and spent another day shuttling our vehicles with a rented car to Port Hardy. After returning the rental car, we took an airport taxi to complete the 5 miles back to Island View.

An alternate start is located just north of Sidney at McDonald Provincial Park. Although the setting is not quite so rural and the park is not actually on the water (the shore is just across the road), McDonald Park has 39 sites and all the amenities. Just continue north on Highway 17 until you reach the park.

There are at least four options in Port Hardy for long-term vehicle parking. At the bottom of Hardy Bay is the Sunny Sanctuary Campground (250-949-6753) near the south end of town, at 8080 Goodspeed Road, just off the trans-island highway. Although it's located on the water, you'll probably not be able to paddle right in at the end of the trip, as the tidal mud flats are extensive and only covered for a short period during high tides. No problem, as the road parallels the bay. Sunny Sanctuary charges about $50 Canadian for vehicle storage. Next up is the town's public pay parking at the Fisherman's Wharf, 6600 Hardy Bay Road. This is the lot adjacent to the public docks that most boaters use. It has several advantages including public rest rooms, showers, a launch ramp, and a central location and is easily spotted from several miles away, low in the water. Near the north end of town, just north of the Government Wharf, the public beaches of Carrot and Tsulquate Parks provide an excellent launch and take-out spot. Debbie Erickson, in *Kayak Routes of the Pacific Northwest,* suggests checking with the Northshore Inn (corner of Market Street and Highway 19), less than a two-minute walk away, for parking. Just out of town and at the north end of Hardy Bay is the Scotia Bay RV Campground. Access is north off Market Street/Park Drive and straight through the Tsulquate Reserve.

Canadian History, Eh?

Canadians believe that their history is short,
boring and irrelevant.
—historian Desmond Morton

Residents south of the border would probably agree. (But then they also believe that Canadians all want to be Americans.) Such a verdict, if not already based on ignorance, inevitably leads to it. One museum curator in Powell River couldn't even specify just what Canada Day, July 1, exactly commemorates. Canadian politics are even more enervating, somewhat like watching concrete set, and in slow motion at that. And this is no exaggerated metaphor. The United States can proudly point to July 4, 1776, as Independence Day, an event unambiguous in its explicitness. When did Canada become independent? A nation? Is it independent? Who knows? You decide:

1791: The ink was hardly dry on the Treaty of Paris (the one that confirmed US independence) when Britain, so as to preclude similar events farther north (and not a moment too soon) decided belatedly to remedy the ills that had wrought revolution among the 13 southernmost colonies. In 1791 the British Parliament passed the Constitutional Act extending the rights of the British Constitution, and thus representative government, to the remaining North American colonies. Thenceforward, taxation would be *with* (limited) representation. At the same time they created a separate English Canada (distinct from French Canada), namely Upper Canada, the future Ontario.

1840: Two of the North American colonies, Lower Canada (the future Province of Quebec) and Upper Canada become one Canada under the Act of Union. The remaining colonies, clustered around the mouth of the St. Lawrence River, were known as the Maritime Colonies (see below).

1848: All remaining British North American colonies—Canada, Newfoundland, Nova Scotia, New Brunswick, and Prince Edward Island—achieve self-government (internally).

When the US-Mexican War broke out, Britain realized that its interior North American colonies were hopelessly indefensible. The US Civil War further underscored that impotence. It didn't help that Britain actively aided the Confederacy, not only by recognizing it but also by trading with it to the extent of running the North's naval blockade. Moreover, Canada, as ever, promiscuously welcomed refugees of all stripes, from escaped slaves, Union draft dodgers, and deserters to Confederate combatants, both active and on the run. Britain's support for the South is usually attributed to its cupidity—the sale of manufactured goods in exchange for cotton (with not a little revenge for the Revolutionary War thrown in) the desire to weaken US power so as to declaw the eagle next door. Actually, idealism also played no small part. Let me explain.

A political and philosophical upheaval, rooted in the Scottish Enlightenment ideals of John Locke, David Hume, and Adam Smith, and the republican principles of the American and French Revolutions, had swept the Kingdom in the mid-1800s. It demanded uncompromising liberty for all. The first casualty was slavery. Britain not only abolished it in 1837, it then set out, with its control of the seas, to eradicate the slave trade. It was so successful that it forced the US to follow suit, at least in outlawing the slave trade. But slavery was only a small part of a larger perspective.

Britain had also come to believe in the political self-determination of all peoples and absolute free trade, not only for its own sake but also as the only way to foster economic development and lift the poor out of poverty. It was these ideals that led not only to support of the South but also to an active effort to divest itself of its colonies. By 1863 Britain was pushing for an independent Canada responsible for its own defense. Looked at another way, the US had to revolt to free itself of Britain, but it was Britain that had a revolution to rid itself of Canada. (At this point, a cynic might point out that much of the British Empire survived for a very long time. It's a long story. Suffice it to say that, like Nixon withdrawing from Vietnam "with honor," Britain sought to free its colonies "responsibly.")

1867: The British North America Act creates the Dominion of Canada, a union of Nova Scotia, New Brunswick, and Canada (Quebec and Ontario). Prince Edward Island refused to join until 1873; Newfoundland didn't join until 1949. It was supposed to be the Kingdom of Canada. But ever the politically correct and inoffensive good neighbor, the new entity did not want to offend republican sensibilities south of the border, especially since, at the close of the Civil War, the US had the largest standing army in the world. Leonard Tilley, Premier of New Brunswick and a very devout Christian, turned to his Bible for inspiration. His thumb fell on Psalms 72:8: "He shall have dominion also from sea to sea . . ."

Canada quickly expanded westward. In 1869 Britain facilitated the transfer of Rupert's Land (named after Prince Rupert, first governor of the Hudson's Bay Company) to the new Dominion for £300,000. This huge expanse, which included much of future Nunavut, Manitoba, and Saskatchewan plus parts of Ontario, Alberta, and the Northwest Territories, had been separately jurisdictioned to the Hudson's Bay Company. Manitoba was then quickly organized into a province and admitted in 1870. The far west, consisting of the future British Columbia, the remaining portion of the future Northwest Territories, and the Yukon, was claimed by Britain and held under a status separate from that of Canada proper. But not for long. British Columbia, after a short identity crisis during which it considered joining the US, became a province in 1871. The 1897 Klondike gold rush drew a huge influx of population into the Yukon watershed. But not enough to warrant provincial status—the Yukon Territory was admitted in 1898. The Northwest Territories joined piecemeal in 1870, 1876, and 1895. Alberta and Saskatchewan joined as provinces in 1905. Nunavut became a separate territory in 1999. The Dominion was now whole.

1919: Following World War I, the victors chartered the League of Nations, forerunner of the United Nations. It was to include all nations and serve as a forum for conflict resolution, particularly since the Great War had not turned out to be the "war to end all wars." But what was a "nation"? Canada, with Britain's support, insisted on being seated. After all, Canada, under Canadian Prime Minister Robert Borden's demand, had put its own signature on the Treaty of Versailles rather than have Britain sign on its behalf, as was previously done. The US was furious, and saw this as a ploy to use mere colonies to give Britain extra votes.

Though President Woodrow Wilson reluctantly withdrew his objections, the US Congress demurred and petulantly refused to join.

1923: Canada was still a British colony. Foreign affairs were conducted through the British Foreign Office. In anticipation of handling its own foreign affairs, Canada had created the Department of External Affairs in 1909. In 1923 Canada concluded (without the British Foreign Office's imprimatur) its first independent treaty—the Halibut Treaty—with a foreign power, the United States. This was soon followed, in 1927, by the opening of a legation—not a full-fledged embassy, mind you—in Washington, DC.

1931: The British Commonwealth of Nations is founded by "autonomous nations (Canada included) of an Imperial commonwealth" with control over their own internal affairs and "an adequate vote in foreign policy and foreign relations." The British Privy Council, however, remains the final court of appeal.

1947: The Citizenship Act redefines citizens as, primarily, Canadians. Heretofore they had been, first and foremost, British citizens.

1949: The Supreme Court of Canada becomes the final court of appeal, replacing the British Privy Council.

1965: Under pressure from an ever restless Quebec, the Canadian flag—with its imperial banner of the crosses of St. Andrew and St. George—became the red and white maple leaf.

1982: Queen Elizabeth II signs the Constitution Act, severing Canada's anomalous dependence on the British Parliament *and* formally entrenching the monarchy's position.

2005: The Canadian Head of Government is the Prime Minister in a parliamentary system; the head of state remains Queen Elizabeth II (the one who lives in Buckingham Palace in London). On the beat, she is represented by her viceroy, Canada's Governor General.

The US-Canada border has been described as the longest undefended frontier in the world. It wasn't always so. For nearly a century, Canadians feared a US invasion. At the start of the US War for Independence, which colonies would join the revolt and which would remain loyal was an open question. French Canada, ironically, had no doubts—they had no quarrel with the king. For one, they perceived the dispute as a ruction between the English speakers. More importantly, the Quebec Act of 1774 had just guaranteed the French many rights they had been clamoring for. This did not sit well south of the St. Lawrence, especially since the act also gave the Ohio Valley and the Great Lakes to Quebec.

For 10 years a growing estrangement between Americans and the king, caused by British attempts to assert greater control over colonial affairs, had been poisoning relations. For the crown to suddenly address French grievances while ignoring those of the English speakers was as much a casus belli as the Tea Tax (imposed, by the way, to help recoup revenue deficits due to Britain's recent conquest of New France). The very first act of the American Continental Congress, when it first convened in 1775, was not to declare independence but to invade Canada. Generals Richard Montgomery and Benedict Arnold marched on Montreal and Quebec, respectively. The invasion polarized the indecisive. Loyalists poured across the border. English Canada and the Maritime Colonies joined loyal Quebec. Though Montreal was captured, the Americans were routed at Quebec. On July 2, 1776, two days before the Declaration of Independence, the soon-to-be United States withdrew from Canada.

The Treaty of Paris in 1783 did not really settle anything; it was more a cease-fire than a resolution. Neither side adhered to its commitments. No one expected it to be the last word on the American revolt; after all, there was absolutely no precedent, anywhere, for such a precipitous divorce. John Graves Simcoe, governor of Upper Canada (a.k.a. English Canada, later Ontario) certainly was skeptical. Convinced that Americans would soon repent, he greased the skids by offering free land to anyone renouncing the Revolution and swearing allegiance to the Crown. "Late Loyalists," many torn between free land and independence, poured into Canada.

The Treaty of Paris transferred the Ohio Valley from Quebec to the US. However, its ill-defined borders and US settlers' infringement on aboriginal rights that the English had implicitly guaranteed at the treaty were still a source of friction. Border skirmishes and territorial disputes, erupting into outright battles—with Indian surrogates bearing much of the brunt—flared up in 1790 and disrupted the peace in the Old Northwest Territories of Ohio, Michigan, and Indiana through 1795. Meanwhile, presaging the country's future role as cultural trendsetter, the US's revolution was spreading like a virus. France caught it in 1789; Haiti in 1804. Soon it spread to all of Latin America. Britain felt cornered and besieged. The result was war with France.

The War of 1812 was inevitable. Britain's unceremonious boarding and confiscation of US commercial vessels bound for France (added to the still smoldering embers of the northwest frontier dispute) sparked the conflagration. The US reignited hostilities and upped the ante. Henry Clay, Speaker of the US House of Representatives, boasted "that the militia of Kentucky are alone competent to place Montreal and Upper Canada at (our) feet." President James Madison concurred: "There would be a second War of Independence." The US Congress authorized the raising of 100,000 troops and invaded Canada to drive out the British.

The war was a draw. Though Britain quickly and decisively reestablished rule of the seas, rebuffed northward incursions, and even managed to burn and sack the new capital at Washington, it made no territorial gains. Much to the chagrin of Canadians, she was more anxious to concentrate on European concerns. The Treaty of Ghent reaffirmed the status quo antebellum: no changed boundaries, no reparations, and no wrongs avenged. Ironically, according to Canadian historian Desmond Morton: "By insisting on war, the American warhawks helped cancel a process that would probably have led to peaceful absorption of the colony (Canada) into the United States." American isolationist doves, on the other hand, nearly succeeded in rejoining a chunk of New England back to Britain.

US designs on Canada remained very much alive. With Manifest Destiny morphing into actual territorial seizure, Canada remained vulnerable and vigilant. The Aroostook Wars of 1840 contested territory along the Maine frontier. That dispute was finally resolved with the Webster–Ashburton Treaty of 1842. By 1844, presidential candidate James K. Polk was advocating the annexation of British Columbia and adjacent territory all the way up to Alaska. The Mexican War saved Canada. The US, unwilling to fight a two-front war, agreed to the 49th

Parallel border in 1846. In 1855 the San Juan Islands Pig War kept confrontation alive.

The last bellicose incident between the two neighbors occurred just after the Civil War. The Irish potato famine of 1846–51 had driven many emigrants to the New World. Those who landed in the United States were soon enlisted in the Mexican War and then conscripted during the Civil War into the Union Army. Victory after victory instilled confidence. Conspiring with Irish immigrants in Canada, they hatched a bold but harebrained plot. By enlisting hardened veterans with ready access to arms and American sympathy, the Fenian Brotherhood (precursor to today's Irish Republican Army) planned to form an army to conquer Canada and hold her hostage for Ireland's freedom. In April of 1866, Fenians invaded New Brunswick. The next month, 1,600 Fenians defeated two forces of Canadian militia near Fort Erie. US authorities intervened. They apprehended 1,800 Fenians in Vermont before they could act. By June 3 the invasion was over and done. The era of armed confrontation was over.

The next 74 years were not particularly warm. As late as 1911 you could still hear the following in the halls of Congress, by none other than Champ Clark, Speaker of the US House of Representatives: "We are preparing to annex Canada, and the day is not far off when the American flag will float over every square foot of the British North American possessions—clear to the North Pole." Both countries tried to out-tariff the other and, contemptuous of its northern neighbor's ambiguous sovereignty status, the United States either ignored or thumbed its nose at Canada. Adolf Hitler changed all that. When he invaded Poland in September 1939, Canada dutifully declared war. By June of 1940, with continental Europe overrun by the combined might of Germany and the Soviet Union, Canada was the second most powerful (after England) of Germany's adversaries. The US took notice. President Franklin D. Roosevelt and Canadian Prime Minister Mackenzie King signed an agreement at Ogdensburg, New York, for the joint defense of North America.

When Japan attacked Pearl Harbor, the US finally invaded Canada. A force of 33,000 men marched north for the construction of the Alaska–Canada Highway. The road, built straight through in the phenomenally short time of nine months and six days for the defense of Alaska, is now the closest road access to the Inside Passage.

After the war, Soviet expansionism strengthened and broadened US–Canadian North American defense commitments. Canada joined NATO in 1949 and the North American Aerospace Defense Command (NORAD) in 1958. In return, the US finally recognized Canada's historic claim to its arctic islands.

Instead of scuttling the mutual defense arrangements at the close of the Cold War, both decided to enter into an even more intimate relationship, including Mexico this time, with the launching of the North American Free Trade Agreement (NAFTA) in 1993. Mexico's president, Vicente Fox, has even floated the idea of sharing a common currency.

The Salmon Wars—Fish Wars, in some quarters—however, still disrupt the honeymoon. Mark MacGuigan, one-time Minister of External Affairs, has declared that "the most serious dispute we have with any country is with the United States over fish." Canada accuses US fishermen of harvesting a disproportionate share of salmon returning to their spawning grounds, thereby both reducing Canada's take and depleting overall stocks. Confrontations have escalated to the point that, for a short time, Alaska ferries were refused docking privileges at Prince Rupert, B.C. The Salmon Wars are not over yet, but interim treaties have defused the antagonism, and ferry service has resumed.

If truth be told, Canadian history, boring or not, is enviable in at least one respect: Canada managed to avoid most of the wars the United States fought. To some degree this is due to the different temperaments of the two populations. At the time of the American Revolutionary War, complacent conservatives (Tories) gravitated north, while dissatisfied radicals (Whigs) sorted themselves south. While the American Declaration of Independence celebrates "life, liberty and the pursuit of happiness," Canada's founding document promises "peace, order and good government."

Reluctance to join the War for Independence was well founded. At that time, revolutions had no track record. The US Articles of Confederation turned out to be a failure marred by instability and conflict, such as the Whiskey Rebellion. The subsequent French, Haitian, and Latin American revolutions were all disastrous. The Mexican and Spanish–American Wars, or anything analogous, never tempted Canada. Canada had no Indian Wars. Indian relations, barring a few minor conflicts, were pursued much differently. The Vietnam War was roundly condemned, both popularly and officially, much to the displeasure of President Lyndon Johnson, who summoned Prime Minister Lester Pearson and dressed him down: "Lester," he told the Canadian, "you peed on my carpet."

The Canadian art of war avoidance reached new pinnacles of creativity in its dodging of anything resembling our Civil War. Quebec separatism has always threatened to dissolve the union, but Canadians would never, like their more bellicose neighbors to the south, go to war over it. The Canadian Supreme Court has even spelled out the proper procedure for secession. Unthinkable in the USA.

Perhaps what makes Canadian politics so frustrating, unintelligible, and yes, even boring to Americans, is the more than usual lack of congruence between political parties and any sort of principled political philosophy. Consistency has been sacrificed to national unity, growth, and development that, in such a geographically sprawling and climatically extreme country, all parties promote through vigorous federal intervention and subsidies. Each election seems to be contested by politicians with a big wish list of concrete promises that expediency and the demands of a fractious confederation often reverse 180 degrees within days of victory.

The inviolability of the dominion, or Canadian unity, has always been a vexing problem. That word, dominion, doesn't help—and lately confederation has been favored. Most countries are republics, kingdoms, or some such neatly identifiable entities. Canada is the only dominion in the world. In an effort to more clearly define Canadian cohesiveness, Prime Minister Pierre Trudeau initiated a process to develop a new constitution for the confederation. The latest proposal, the Charlottetown Accord, and its predecessor, the Meech Lake Accord, both failed at the last second.

The main problem was Quebec. It had never experienced parity with the other provinces and rejects it, on principle. In spite of many efforts to relegate it to the status of just simply another province, Quebec demands special status; co-equal with all the other provinces en masse, as a culturally different founding nexus, with its own language and traditions, and greater power in the federation. When the Meech Lake delegates swallowed their sense of fair play and conceded Quebec's demands, the First Nations piped up and decided they too wanted a special status within the newly proposed constituency.

The First Nations, precontact inhabitants who had never been subjugated by war but had instead been co-opted by treaties, decided to reassert their prerogatives. They came in four competing groups: "status" and "non-status" Indians (those who lived on and off reserves), Metis (French–Indian half-breeds), and Inuit. The First Nations reasoned that if Quebec's claims preceded those of the other provinces, their claims certainly preceded all others. The ensuing fudges, half-measures, and compromises ended up being unacceptable to all parties. The new, improved constitution did not pass.

If you think this is a lot more Canadian history than you bargained for, consider that not only is half the entire length of the Inside Passage in Canada but, conversely, the Inside Passage encompasses Canada's entire Pacific coast. And, after all—in spite of all the muddles—Canada, according to the UN, is the best country in the world in which to live (for the seventh year in a row).

Vancouver Island

Spain based her exaggerated claim to all circum-Pacific lands on Balboa's "discovery" of the Pacific Ocean. When she got wind that Russia was not only exploring but also settling territory in the Pacific Northwest, she sent an expedition under Juan Perez to strengthen her claims and counter Russian expansion. By 1774 Perez had reached the Queen Charlottes and traded with the Haida.

Into this finely balanced though straggly détente, Britain thrust its curious nose with an innocent expedition commissioned to search for a northwest passage connecting the Pacific with the Atlantic above or through North America. History credits James Cook with the discovery of Vancouver Island, though it is likely that others—perhaps Sir Francis Drake; more likely Japanese fishermen—preceded him. In 1778 he anchored at Nootka, cut wood, brewed spruce beer, repaired his vessels, and set up an astronomical observatory. Even while his ships were searching for anchorage, canoes began approaching, seemingly without fear or distrust of the strange vessels. Subsequent visits by Americans, Russians, French, more English, one or two nominally Portuguese and Austrian ships, and even small Spanish and English settlements invested a global importance on the small village. Spain was not happy.

By 1788 Spain had decided to expel all foreign interlopers and trespassers from the Northwest Coast. Ensign Esteban Jose Martinez singlehandedly set out to enforce the empire's integrity. A spark looking for a fire to ignite, he was possessed of a hair-trigger temper (particularly while drinking) and a foppishly pompous self-importance and was given to big talk and braggadocio. He was the chip on the shoulder of Spain's empire. At Unalaska, in the Aleutians, under the very noses of his Russian hosts, he had the audacity to take formal possession of Alaska.

At Nootka, he seized three British ships intent on establishing a trading settlement and arrested their captains and crew. It didn't help when one of the skippers, Captain Colnett, roundly insulted him. Britain prepared for war. Prussia and Holland, under the terms of the Triple Alliance, backed her. Spain appealed to France, but King Louis XVI, about to take a short walk to the guillotine, was indisposed. Spain had no choice but to capitulate. The Nootka Conventions of 1790, 1793, and 1794 were the beginning of the collapse of the Spanish colonial system. Spain retreated south to California while Britain promised not to settle Vancouver Island in the immediate future, leaving Nootka a nominally free port.

Before the founding of Victoria in 1843, Nootka Sound—slightly more than halfway up Vancouver Island's west coast—was unquestionably Canada's western capital. Explorers, traders, and diplomats gravitated to its well-positioned harbor and hospitable inhabitants. Maquinna, chief of the Nootka, rose to the occasion.

An imposing, sophisticated, and intelligent man, whose long administration lent stability and continuity to the tentative but inevitable new contacts, he rolled with the punches wisely and admirably. By 1792, he more than likely spoke a good deal of Spanish. According to Juan Francisco Bodega y Quadra, his table manners were near perfect and he was well aware of the political and acculturational situation in which he and his people were involved. But he was no doormat. When treated treacherously, he would counterattack, with success. He even held white slaves whom he treated equitably, not only according to his customs but also with some consideration for their European sensibilities.

One of the last important Spanish expeditions, co-led by Dionisio Galiano and Cayetano Valdes in the *Sutil* and *Mexicana,* circumnavigated Vancouver in 1792, proving once and for all that it was in fact an island. Their charts of Desolation Sound actually show more detail than Vancouver's charts. Both expeditions probably unofficially collaborated as they worked their way up the east side of the island. In the diplomatic spirit of the ongoing Nootka deliberations, the island was christened "Quadra's and Vancouver's Island."

In the intervening years the Hudson's Bay Company had concentrated development of its westernmost district in the Oregon Territory, with the capital at Fort Vancouver, just north of the Columbia River. US expansionist pressures in the 1840s and the anticipation that Puget Sound might soon be ceded to the Americans caused HBC Governor George Simpson to look for new headquarters farther north. The recently surveyed harbors of Sooke, Victoria, and Esquimalt on the southeast coast of Vancouver Island were perfectly positioned as a strategic bulwark against further US encroachment. Fort Victoria was erected at the head of Victoria Harbour in March of 1843; the Songhee, a band of the Coast Salish inhabiting the area, were very pleased.

Victoria prospered. It was at the hub of a trading network that sent manufactured goods from England and the United States to Hawaii, Russian America, and Canada in return for raw materials. Victoria took a cut. In 1849 Britain made Vancouver Island a crown colony and put the Hudson's Bay Company in charge. Governor Simpson transferred HBC headquarters from Fort Vancouver to Victoria. In 1856, the HBC turned over administration to a locally elected legislative assembly and governor, James Douglas. Douglas, who also governed British Columbia as HBC factor, retired from both positions in 1864. The resulting separate dual governorships, heretofore held by one man, proved ungainly. The two crown colonies (BC had become one in 1858 and been officially christened "British Columbia") merged in 1866 with the united capital at Victoria.

Natural History

Vancouver Island is 279 miles long and 75 miles at its widest. The south and east coasts, where the majority of the population is concentrated, are mostly level while the interior consists of a rugged mountain chain exceeding 7,000 feet in altitude. Deep coves and bays indent the west coast, with Quatsino Sound nearly bifurcating the island near the north end. Vancouver indulged his sense of symmetry—and vanity—by nestling his namesake island between two bodies of water commemorating his sovereigns: the Strait of Georgia (I suppose the Strait of George might have sounded a bit prosaic) and Queen Charlotte Strait (Charlotte was wife to George III). Discovery Passage and Johnstone Strait separate Vancouver Island from the mainland by a scant 1.5 miles at the narrowest point.

Vancouver Island mountain ranges block and squeeze Pacific weather fronts, creating a relatively dry and sunny rain shadow along the Strait of Georgia. You can expect relatively clear skies about 60 percent of the time, with about five days per month of measurable precipitation during the paddling season. North of the city of Vancouver the mainland shore is known as the Sunshine Coast, while the Gulf Islands have been nicknamed Canada's Hawaii. Annual rainfall in the Gulf Islands rarely exceeds 32 inches, with only 25 percent of that falling between April and October. Galiano Island, the driest, gets less than 23 inches.

July and August are the warmest months with the average daily temperature range between the low 50s and low 70s Fahrenheit. During warm spells, 85-degree F temperatures are not uncommon, and highs of 95 degrees F have been recorded, though due to the cooling effect of sea breezes, maximum air temperatures on the water seldom exceed 73 degrees F. These same sea breezes are common during hot weather and are caused by differential heating between land and sea. They peak in the afternoon, sometimes causing uncomfortable chop for the kayaker. The predominantly clear weather generates gentle northwest breezes, when conditions permit, which is about half the time. Huge amounts of fresh water invade the straits and channels between Vancouver Island and the mainland during summer runoff, actually lowering the mean summer sea temperature of 58 degrees F by about 5 degrees F.

Tides behind Vancouver Island flood and ebb from both ends. The exact spot where they meet is near Stuart Island. North of Stuart, sea temperatures are a good 10 degrees cooler. Air temperature drops commensurately—you'll not see madrona trees anymore. And tides exhibit a marked diurnal inequality, for instance, one day's two low tides (or high tides) will be substantially different. In the Gulf Islands during the summer, the lower low tide generally occurs in the morning, while the higher high tide sweeps in at night.

The tremendous distance tides must travel behind Vancouver Island and the extreme constriction wrought by the archipelago separating the two landmasses create tidal currents in excess of 15 knots through Seymour Narrows. Currents follow the mostly southeast-northwest trend through the multitude of alternate passages and, though not as strong as in Seymour Narrows, still warrant due diligence. Saltwater rapids form and impede a kayak's progress in all of the channels that course north of the Strait of Georgia. All have to be negotiated at slack, with impeccable timing. Boats of all types and sizes will converge at narrow passes at this time. Most currents in the Gulf Islands seldom exceed 2 knots, except through some of the narrow passes between islands, such as Dodd Narrows and Gabriola Pass, where they can reach 9 knots. Very generally, if you want to coordinate your paddling with the tides, they ebb south in the morning and flood north in the afternoon. Queen Charlotte Sound and Johnstone Strait pose no extraordinary hazards other than a paucity of campsites—

mostly due to steep, highly vegetated ground cover—beyond Desolation Sound until the vicinity of Telegraph Cove.

South of Lund, population density and private property limit camping opportunities. In the Gulf Islands, most of the shoreline above the historical high-tide line is private property. However, in Canada there is no such thing as a private beach. In theory, all foreshore between high and low water is Crown land and legally accessible to the public. Still, no one wants to camp in front of a residence and possibly shift his tent during the wee hours of the night to avoid a high-tide soaking.

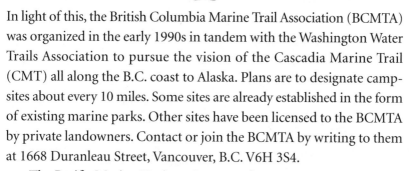

In light of this, the British Columbia Marine Trail Association (BCMTA) was organized in the early 1990s in tandem with the Washington Water Trails Association to pursue the vision of the Cascadia Marine Trail (CMT) all along the B.C. coast to Alaska. Plans are to designate campsites about every 10 miles. Some sites are already established in the form of existing marine parks. Other sites have been licensed to the BCMTA by private landowners. Contact or join the BCMTA by writing to them at 1668 Duranleau Street, Vancouver, B.C. V6H 3S4.

The Pacific Marine Heritage Legacy, a five-year program designed to expand an integrated network of Pacific Coast Marine Parks, was launched in 1995, dovetailing with the BCMTA objectives. The goal, involving both federal and provincial governments, is the acquisition of new lands that collectively will comprise a new national park system within the Gulf Islands. Paddlers are welcome on newly acquired lands regardless of their state of development. Besides coastal marine parks, there are several islets designated as public recreation reserves and one piece of Crown land (other than beaches) accessible to paddlers for camping: Blackberry Point on Valdes Island.

Ecological reserves in B.C. have different restrictions than their counterparts south of the border. Whereas casual, nonconsumptive, nonmotorized use is permitted on most reserves in the province, these areas are particularly delicate—some are pelagic bird rookeries—and are not intended for public recreational use. Landing, though not strictly prohibited, is discouraged.

A variety of policies govern public use of native reserve lands. The Lyackson band in Ladysmith administers the Valdes Island reserves. Call the band office at 250-246-5019 for permission to camp. The Penelakut Band on Kuper Island administers Tent Island, once a provincial marine park. Call 250-246-2321 or write the Penelakut Band, Box 3601, Chemainus, B.C., V0SS 1M0 for permission to camp on Tent Island. Native reserves, coastal marine parks, and ecological reserves are well marked on federal and provincial topo maps. Nautical charts frequently fail to designate them.

North of road's end, most of the lands along the B.C. coast are Crown lands, deeded to the province by the federal government at the time of Canada's confederation. Management is the responsibility of the B.C. Forest Service within the province's Ministry of Forests. Pacific Rim National Park, on Vancouver Island's west coast, is the federal government's only land management responsibility.

The Route: Overview

The Vancouver Island section of the Inside Passage is divided up into five portions: the Gulf Islands, the Strait of Georgia, Desolation Sound, the Discovery Islands, and Queen Charlotte Strait. Three of the subsections have alternate routes.

Starting out from Island View Beach Park, you are immediately confronted with two very attractive route choices: launch headfirst into the beckoning Gulf Islands with their promise of solitude, or head straight up the more protected Vancouver Island coast. The main route plunges out into the archipelago. Who can resist this cluster of spilled pearls? After the hassles of access and shuttle driving, border crossings, and the hubbub of cities, our first inclination was to get away. The alternate route winds through Sansum Narrows with camping opportunities on Saltspring Island, not an inelegant variation. Both reunite about 33 miles out—neither is longer than the other—off the northern tip of Saltspring Island and follow the Northumberland Channel funnel to Nanaimo. The alternate route is described immediately following their point of reunion.

The route then coasts north of Nanaimo for a short stretch until a suitable crossing is reached for the Ballenas Islands. A glance at the chart would logically suggest the route continue along the coast up into Discovery Passage or Sutil Channel. Instead, our objective is Lewis Channel. Seymour Narrows constricts Discovery Passage where tidal and shipping bulk converge, creating 16-knot currents and congestion. A local sailor, as a safer and more aesthetic alternative, suggested Lewis Channel. And so it is. From Ballenas, the route hits Lasqueti Island and courses up the west coast of Texada Island, to a final crossing for Powell River.

A scant 15 miles north of Powell River lies Lund, the end of the road and the beginning of Desolation Sound. Snow-clad mountains interspersed with deep fjords constrict any attempt to extend the coastal highway. Sweet desolation indeed! Isolated fishing and logging camps, with associated clear-cuts, are the only obvious signs of man's touch. The coastal verges are niggardly with campsites, and chilly mists descend from the heavens in an attempt to preclude further encroachment.

Many channels crisscross the Desolation Sound archipelago. All constrict tidal flows to such an extent that saltwater rapids guard all routes north, though none as dauntingly as Seymour Narrows. Our route up Lewis Channel and, in due course, through Calm, Cordero, Chancellor, Wellbore, and Sunderland Channels is only one of many possibilities. All lead inexorably into Johnstone Strait, where the route again follows the Vancouver Island coast. Only one minor alternate route is described: around the south side of Hardwicke Island, also described after its point of convergence with the main route.

At Telegraph Cove, the Vancouver Island highway reconnects with the shore, though not obtrusively. Here again, the seemingly logical route and our route diverge. A glance at the map would dictate heading north into the Broughton Archipelago to follow the mainland coast north. This would be the route of choice for the through-paddler, as the archipelago is stunning and no crossing of Queen Charlotte Sound is required.

This leg, however, ends at Port Hardy, another 30 miles along the Vancouver Island coast. At the edge of a vast wilderness and before the longest piece of unprotected coast along the Inside Passage, Port Hardy is the perfect spot for a pause. Logistically, it is also the ideal terminus for this section, as all services are available and it sits at road's end with ferry service extending north.

Gulf Islands: Island View Beach Park (mile 0/150) to Newcastle Island Provincial Park (mile 54/204)

The Gulf Islands are a historical misnomer. Vancouver, at first believing the Strait of Georgia to be an inland sea, named it the Gulf of Georgia after King George III. Hence, the Gulf Islands. When the "gulf" was discovered to be a strait, the islands' name remained unchanged. The "Strait Islands" just wouldn't have the same ring. Many of the islands' and passages' names commemorate the naval vessels stationed there during the tensions of the 1850s—HMS *Thetis, Portland, Trincomalee, Ganges,* and *Prevost.*

Carved out of sandstone, often eroded into overhangs resembling petrified breaking waves (which mostly preclude impulse landings) and dotted with *huecos* and calcified nodules along their brims, the islands have a distinct personality. Rustic old farms and funky artistic communities lend continuity with the San Juan Islands. Numerous shell middens and petroglyphs attest to the thousands of years the islands have been inhabited. There is still an abundance of natural life, with an estimated 3,000 species of plants and animals, including hundreds of seaweed and fish varieties; invertebrates such as octopus, starfish, oysters, clams, green anemones, and spiny red urchins; and large marine mammals including orcas, porpoises, pinnipeds, and sea otters. Bald eagles rule, though there are more than a hundred species of birds among which are a wide array of ducks, great blue herons, ospreys, gulls, and cormorants.

The majority of the islands are private property, though with good planning an extensive marine provincial park system affords plenty of camping. All marine parks in the Gulf Islands have camping fees (usually about $5 per person per night, though some charge $14–$17 per group per night). It helps to carry small bills, $1 (loonie) and $2 (toonie)

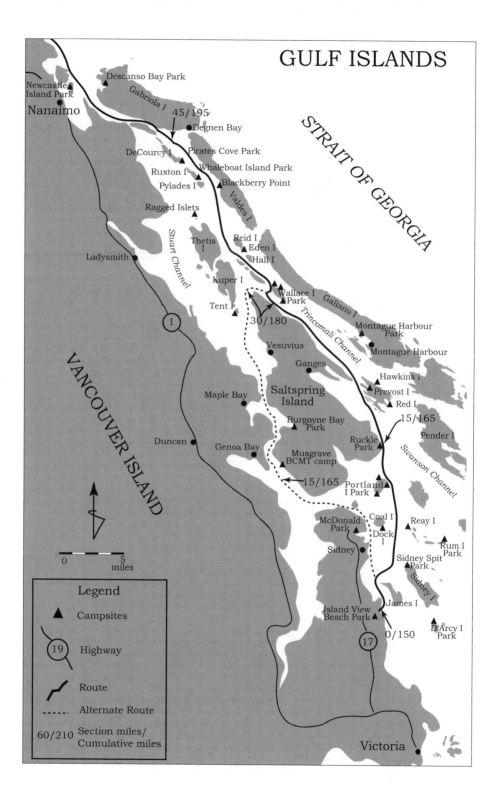

GULF ISLANDS

STRAIT OF GEORGIA

Newcastle Island Park

Nanaimo

Descanso Bay Park

Gabriola I

45/195

Degnen Bay

DeCourcy I

Pirates Cove Park

Ruxton I

Whaleboat Island Park

Pylades I

Blackberry Point

Ragged Islets

Valdes I

Stuart Channel

Ladysmith

Thetis I

Reid I

Eden I

Hall I

Kuper I

Tent I

Wallace I Park

Galiano I

30/180

Trincomali Channel

Montague Harbour Park

Vesuvius

Montague Harbour

Ganges

Hawkins I

Saltspring Island

Prevost I

Red I

Maple Bay

15/165

Pender I

Burgoyne Bay Park

Duncan

Ruckle Park

Genoa Bay

Musgrave BCMT camp

Swanson Channel

15/165

Portland I Park

Coal I

Reay I

McDonald Park

Dock I

Rum I Park

Sidney

Sidney Spit Park

Sidney I

VANCOUVER ISLAND

0   5
miles

Island View Beach Park

James I

0/150

D'Arcy I Park

Victoria

Legend

▲ Campsites

⑲ Highway

⌐ Route

----- Alternate Route

60/210 Section miles/ Cumulative miles

coins (change is not available), and a pen (usually missing) for self-registration.

Summer weather brings calm morning conditions, usually followed in late afternoon by brisk westerlies that whip up an uncomfortable chop. Plan for early crossings and carry plenty of water, as days can be hot and water sources are scarce. Fires are not allowed.

Standing on the beach at Island View Beach Park prior to launch, contemplating conditions and exactly where to set a course for, you'll be struck by the strength of the eddy currents rounding Cordova Spit. Don't worry. According to the *Sailing Directions,* tidal streams are weak. The spit's intrusion into the channel creates a Venturi effect that actually makes the eddies stronger than the current. Decide whether to follow the main route around the east side of Saltspring Island or take the alternate up along the Vancouver coast. If following the primary route, head for the light at the northwest tip of James Island or go around the south end of the island, depending on current direction. Directions for the alternate route will follow immediately upon reaching both routes' point of convergence.

> *A curved line is the loveliest distance between two points.*
> —Mae West

Bear with me with what might seem a somewhat confusing series of island descriptions and minor route variations. There is just a lot to do and visit here within very short distances, with none of it along a straight line.

James Island: James Island is the only island in the Gulf Islands that is completely surrounded by sand, in spite of its south end looking as if it has been hacked off by a giant meat cleaver. Feel free to land and linger. From 1913 until the mid-1970s, James was home to an explosives and ammunition manufacturing plant and storage depot. In the 1980s the island was decommissioned and cleaned up. Currently owned by a Seattle billionaire, it is now a resort with plans for a portion to be set aside as a public marine park.

Paddling in the Gulf Islands, British Columbia

From James Island it is difficult to discern a clear target on Sidney Island for which to aim. From a kayaker's perspective the low-lying spit, lagoon, and shoals at the north end, which encompass Sidney Spit Marine Park (mile 5/**155**), are a thin, monolithic, wavy mirage. One strategy is to head straight across Sidney Channel. Ebb tides in Sidney Channel can reach 3 knots; floods are not as strong. Once across, head north toward the light at the end of the spit. From this much closer perspective you'll be able to make out the park's public dinghy dock and approach channel as you coast north. This should be a snap if the tide is flooding. If it's ebbing, what the hell, go south around Sidney where you'll be within nipping distance of D'Arcy Island just across Hughes Passage. From the south end of Sidney, it's best to follow the east coast up Miners Channel to the park (see below—Sidney Island).

D'Arcy Island: D'Arcy Island, if you choose to visit, was a small Chinese leper colony until 1924 and a storehouse for bootleg whiskey. Leprosy was widespread in the Orient at the turn of the past century, and so occasionally Chinese immigrants coming to work on the railroads were found to be infected. Strict quarantine policies required isolation. Archaeological excavations in 1989 revealed six units of row housing. Since essential resupplies arrived only every three months, inmates kept chickens and gardens. Not much was done to relieve the patients' intense pain. Now it is an undeveloped marine park seldom visited by pleasure boaters, as there is no convenient anchorage. Head for the small bay just north of the light on the west shore. There are numerous fine beaches for camping. Deer and otters abound and a colony of seals inhabit the rocks in the passage between D'Arcy and Little D'Arcy (private) Islands. Camping fees are on the honor system. There is no water, though there is a pit toilet.

Sidney Island: Sidney Spit Marine Park (mile 5/**155**) is at the north end of the island; the rest is private. The park, this section's first possible campsite (not counting D'Arcy, which is just a tad off route), is very popular and, in parts, often crowded, though there is plenty of room especially if you camp away from the picnic tables. A small passenger ferry out of Sidney calls hourly. Toilets and water are available. Camp fees are collected by the camp host. A system of trails leads to a meadow and the remains of a brick mill that closed during WWI. One alternative, recommended by John Ince and Heidi Kottner in their 1982 guide (especially if you came up Miners Channel) is to head for the east side of the spit, just south of the piles, where no boats anchor and somewhat isolated camping can be found.

Mandarte Island: Going up Sidney's east coast is a treat. Miners Channel was part of the main canoe route for prospectors heading to the Cariboo Gold fields during the rush of the 1860s. Mandarte Island, about 1 mile to the east, is a gem. More than 15,000 nesting birds cover this massive bare rock, filling the air with their cacophonous calls and pungent stink. Glaucus-winged gulls, pigeon guillemots, and pelagic and double-breasted cormorants abound. But the real treasure is the tufted puffins. Mandarte is the only place along the Inside Passage south of Glacier Bay where they nest. Their subterranean burrows are sometimes difficult to spot.

North of Sidney Spit, head for the unnamed archipelago that includes Little Group, Dock, Reay, Forrest, Domville, Brethour, Gooch, and Rum Islands. Although the ultimate objective is Moresby Passage between Moresby and Portland Islands, I will linger—as perhaps you might choose to also—on this archipelago, for it demands attention.

Going north, Forrest Island will probably be your first target. Limit stops to below the high-tide line, as it is privately owned. Watch out for the twice-daily Sidney-Anacortes ferry.

Dock Island: Dock Island (mile 7/**157**), the easternmost member of the Little Group and slightly northwest of Forrest has been reserved as a public recreation site with unimproved camping. Land on the pebble beach at the northwest end. The grassy tent sites have magnificent views but no shade. Hike through scrubby Gary oak to the steeply banked inlet on the south shore. Graffiti, visible on a nearby rock face, commemorates when, in 1972, the *Nonsuch*, a replica of the Hudson's Bay Company's 16th-century vessel, used this location to re-create "careening," a method used to haul a sailing ship out before docks were constructed.

Domville and Brethour Islands, just north and slightly east of Forrest, are private. Farther east are the nearly contiguous Gooch and Rum Islands. Although Gooch is also private, Rum is a provincial marine park. A tad out of the way, it is truly a Gulf Islands gem.

Rum Island: Less than a mile from the US border, Rum Island was a contraband stepping-stone during Prohibition. Now it has been re-designated Isle-de-Lis Provincial Marine Park. Its main attractions are the spectacular views of Haro Strait, Boundary Pass, and the San Juan Islands and remarkable wildflower displays, including the chocolate lily. The only place to land is the steep gravel isthmus connecting it to Gooch. Tenting is restricted (to preserve the wildflowers) to a half dozen wooden platforms close by. Picnic tables, sanitary facilities, and a self-registration vault comprise the amenities. There is no water.

Reay Island: Reay Island (mile 7/**157**—the same on-route distance as Dock Island) is dead on route. The island, a public recreation site, is tiny with two small sheltered landing coves. Just a few tents fit: no water, picnic tables, privies, or fees, though there is shade. No fires are allowed. The commanding views of Boundary Pass and Mount Baker and the hubbub of the animal kingdom espied from this lordly spot exalt.

From Reay Island, head north into Moresby Passage. Currents here can reach 3 knots during both ebb and flood, so plan accordingly.

Moresby Island, on the east side, is private. On the other side however, Portland Island is a marine park.

Portland Island: Princess Margaret Marine Park (mile 11/**161**) encompasses the whole of Portland Island. Three designated camping areas with picnic tables and toilets are located at Princess Bay (Tortoise Bay), Royal Cove, and Shell Beach, though camping is not limited to these sites. Camping fees are on the honor system, and a water pump is located near the center of the island (best accessed from Tortoise Bay). Trails connect all the improvements, and orientation maps are posted at Royal Cove and Tortoise Bay.

Princess Bay, on the southeast corner of the island, additionally protected by Hood Island and the Tortoise Islets (private), has an old apple orchard, meadow, and blackberry bushes. This is the most popular small craft anchorage on the island, and the Sidney–Sidney Spit passenger ferry occasionally calls here. Royal Cove, on the north end, has a couple of camping areas. One is located in the subsidiary cove just south of Royal, while the other, best accessed from its own gravel beach, is on Arbutus Point, which is the northeasternmost point on Portland. Nearby Chad Island is private. On the southwest corner of Portland lies the third camp area, Shell Beach. Just offshore lies Brackman Island, an ecological reserve created by the Nature Conservancy of Canada. Old-growth Douglas fir, sea blush, camas, white fawn and chocolate lilies, otters, mink, and harbor seals reside; *Homo sapiens* are not welcome.

One improvement not included in the trail system is the sunken wreck M/V *G.B. Church* just off the Pellow Islets on the east coast. In 1991 the freighter was intentionally scuttled to create an artificial reef. Holes were cut in the hull to allow diver access. Anemones, sponges, and various other marine organisms have moved in and redecorated.

Coast Salish natives originally inhabited Portland Island. In the mid-1800s the island was deeded to Hawaiian natives, known as kanakas, by the Hudson's Bay Company. They chose to settle there after their work contracts with the HBC expired. In the 1930s, Major General Frank "One-Arm" Sutton acquired Portland; he settled and raised apples and thoroughbred horses. British Columbia got Portland in 1958 but then turned around and gave it to Princess Margaret Windsor in commemoration of her visit during the province's centennial. Three years later she returned it so it could become a park, which it was so designated in 1967.

Going north from Portland, cross the intersection of Satellite and Swanson Channels headed for Eleanor Point on Saltspring Island. Watch out for the Sidney-Tsawwassen ferry that runs twice hourly. Currents reach 1–2 knots.

Saltspring Island: Saltspring Island is the largest and most populous of the Gulf Islands. Its resident population of 11,000—mostly concentrated in the three villages of Ganges, Vesuvius, and Fulford—about triples during the summer months. Originally known as Klaathem by the Cowichans, it was renamed by the HBC for its brine pools, all of which lie inland. Saltspring was settled in 1859 by free American blacks seeking to escape prejudice in the US. Fat chance. An 1860 account reports: "The Indians always steadfastly refused to regard black men as entitled to any of the respect claimed by and shown to the whites. They also entertain the same feeling with regard to the Chinese."

From Eleanor Point follow the coast up to Beaver Point, where Ruckle Provincial Park (mile 15/**165**) provides yet another camping opportunity. Ruckle is unique in that it combines a fully operational farm (with most of the original buildings, including the ornately Victorian Ruckle family house, circa 1872) with recreation. The campsites are south of Beaver Point (accessible from shore) while the official docking area is just beyond the point in the small bay. Don't worry about noisy car campers, as all the campsites are walk-in only. Water and toilets are available, as well as picnic tables at every site. Don't miss the walk in the woods; some trees are more than 6 feet in diameter.

Out of Ruckle Park, coast up the peninsula to Yeo Point and a good crossing of the Ganges Harbour mouth over to the Channel Islands. Ganges is the population center of Saltspring, and all services (except camping) are available. Then cross Captain Passage over to Prevost Island. Watch out for the interisland ferry that plies this passage.

Prevost Island: Prevost Island has been in the Digby Hussey de Burgh family since the 1920s. They still farm here. But James Bay and much of Selby Cove (mile 20/**170**) are now a B.C. Parks protected area.

Undeveloped camping is allowed in a large meadow by the orchard next to the beach. Nearby Red Islets (south of Prevost) and Hawkins Islet (off the northeast coast) also have campsites.

From Selby Point, recross Captain Passage to Nose Point on Saltspring Island and head up Trincomali Channel along the Saltspring coast. Tidal streams in Trincomali Channel south of Wallace Island can attain 1.5 knots. Across Trincomali, on Galiano Island (hidden behind Parker Island) Montague Harbour Marine Park (mile 23/**173**—and 3 miles off route) has camping and fresh water. Pass Walker Hook and Fernwood Point, where the small store carries produce, dairy, a deli, and some staples. From Fernwood veer north to Wallace Island. Currents in Trincomali Channel north of Wallace Island, due to the constriction, can double to 3 knots.

Wallace Island: Wallace Island is a provincial marine park (mile 30/**180**) with three designated camping areas. Conover Cove is the first one you'll encounter and the focal point of the park. Water is available from a pump; there are picnic tables, toilets, and a shelter—part of the

Overarching sandstone cliffs, Wallace Island Provincial Park

old Chivers homestead—and also some gnarled fruit trees. For more isolated camping with powerful views, keep going up the southwest coast to Chivers Point at the north end of Wallace, where there are nine campsites. Probably the least visited campsite is Cabin Point (two sites), about half a mile from Chivers down the east coast of Wallace. Conover and Chivers have toilets, and all three are fee areas. A trail runs the length of the island. The alternate route rejoins the main route north of Wallace Island near mile 31/**181**.

Alternate Route: Island View Beach Park (mile 0/150) to Secretary Islands (mile 31/181) via the west coast of Saltspring Island

Instead of heading out into the islands from Island View beach Park, follow Cordova Channel up the Saanich Peninsula to Sidney, the second largest city on Vancouver Island if you don't count it as part of Victoria. Watch out for the Anacortes ferry, which docks at the north end of Bazan Bay. Another 0.75 mile north is the Sidney Spit and Portland Island ferry terminal. Cross Sidney Harbour, Roberts Bay, and Tsehum Harbour to Curteis Point. Lots of traffic. Inside Tsehum Harbour lies McDonald Provincial Park (mile 7/**157**), the alternate put-in. All facilities are available.

North of Curteis Point, head for Swartz Head through the congested little archipelago that guards Canoe Cove, a large marina complex. During spring tides, swift currents can course through here. Swartz Bay, besides harboring the B.C. Ferries terminal to Tsawwassen, is a very busy place. Course westward along Colburne Passage to get out of the congestion and cross Satellite Channel to Saltspring Island. Head for Cape Keppel below the impressive flanks of Mount Tuam. Tidal streams attain 1 to 2 knots through Satellite Channel.

As you cross Satellite Channel, spare a thought for unique Saanich Inlet astern. While the depth across its mouth does not exceed 13 fathoms (78 feet), its central basin plunges sharply to 40 fathoms (240 feet). The deeper the water, the heavier the salt content and the lower the oxygen content. Tidal exchanges, unable to displace the cold, heavy water at the bottom, have little impact on the lower 20 fathoms (120 feet)—a marine black hole. Consequently, the inlet is highly susceptible to damage from runoff and every other type of pollution.

Three miles north of Cape Keppel you'll hit Musgrave Rock or Island (depending on your map or chart), behind which is the only official campsite along the west side of Saltspring Island. The Musgrave BCMT campsite (mile 15/**165**) is in the forest above the rocky gravel beach facing Musgrave Rock. The remains of an abandoned road (not visible from the water), which doesn't quite reach the sea, allows for the flat space and clearing that make the campsite. There's an outhouse, and water (filter, boil, or treat it) is available from the creek a short paddle away at Musgrave Landing behind Musgrave Point.

Sansum Narrows begin north of Musgrave and Separation Points. South of Burgoyne Bay tidal streams can run to 3 knots; north of it, 1.5 knots. The fjordlike, precipitous walls of Sansum Narrows are a sneak preview of upcoming attractions. Paddle north past Burial Islet, an old Indian burial site, then Bold Bluff Point, and cross or coast past Burgoyne Bay (mile 20/**170**) to Maxwell Point. Much of Burgoyne Bay has just been added to Mount Maxwell Provincial Park, with camping soon to be allowed. Notice the rare Gary oak groves along the north coast of Burgoyne. Notice too that visitation is prohibited in an effort to preserve this unique environment. At Erskine Point, Sansum Narrows are left behind and Stuart Channel begins. Cross Booth Bay to tiny Vesuvius, where you can quaff a pint at the waterside pub overlooking the bay. Water is available at a public tap on the second flower box on Main Street. A small but quick-and-frequent ferry connects Vesuvius with Crofton on Vancouver Island.

North of Vesuvius, head for Parminter Point, turn the corner, and set course for Idol Island. Idol, once an Indian burial ground, has only recently been designated a park preserve. Notice the shell midden on its west point. Though it looks to have a good campsite, landing is discouraged, as it remains a culturally significant First Nations site. Tent Island (mile 28/**178**), across Houstoun Passage and just south of Kuper Island, is an Indian reserve and requires prior permission from the Penelakut band for camping. Southey Point marks the northern extremity of Saltspring Island. Cross Houstoun Passage over to Jacks-crew Island and the Secretaries to rejoin the normal route at mile 31/**179**.

Main Route: Continued . . .

Slip through the opening separating Wallace Island from South Secretary Island. These secretaries are charmingly inviting. Both, however, are private. A sandy tombolo connects the two at all but the highest tides—a camping opportunity for the confident tide table interpreter. Continue northwest to Mowgli Island and decide whether to favor eastward to Hall, Reid, and Valdes Islands, or hop along the reefs and islets north of Thetis. At this point Trincomali Channel widens progressively north and currents are commensurately weaker until one reaches the constrictions at the north end of the Gulf Islands chain. All possible routes have diverse attractions. I'll lay these out south to north; you can stitch your course.

Both Norway and Hall Islands are private. The drying passage (only at zero tides) between Kuper and Thetis Islands has a small marina with an ice-cream parlor. Farther west is a shoreside pub.

Reid Island: Tiny Eden Islet off the southern tip of Reid Island is a recreation preserve (mile 34/**184**). Land on the rocky south end, where exposed flat ledges provide somewhat awkward kayak access. Flat grassy mini-meadows on the south and northwest extremities make ideal campsites. There are no improvements. Up the east or west coast of Reid, that is the question. Though Reid is privately owned, about half a mile up its east side lies a small bay where camping is allowed. Alternatively, at the south end of the larger bay on the west coast, behind thick blackberry brambles, are the remains of a Japanese herring saltery built in 1908. During World War II all Japanese and Japanese Canadians were relocated and their properties confiscated. After the war, compensation was not provided. Going up the west coast of Reid also puts you in a perfect position to navigate through the Rose Islets, an ecological reserve with a seal haul-out spot, just making a comeback after too much human disturbance. The Rose and Miami Islets are pelagic cormorant rookeries, a species that has experienced an unexplained decline in recent years. Paddle lightly and at a distance. The Ragged Islets (mile 37/**187**) have a campsite.

North of these disparate islets and reefs, all of the Gulf Island waters are channeled into two major arteries, Pylades and Stuart Channels. These in turn squeeze tides through three very narrow openings at the north end of the island chain. I route you through False Narrows at the head of Pylades Channel, as it has the least traffic, the least current, and the shortest distance north. Both sides of Pylades Channel are dotted with interesting attractions, not all of which can be sampled by paddling in a straight line. First the west side of the channel, along the De Courcy Island group.

Pylades Island, all private, marks the south end of the group. The Coastal Waters Recreation map indicates a campsite on the east shore of Pylades; this has not been verified. Ruxton Island, also private, is next. Adjacent to its south east shore lies 7-acre Whaleboat Island Marine Park (mile 41/**191**). Though one can camp here, the park is undeveloped, difficult of access and short on space (best bet is on the northernmost point).

De Courcy Island: De Courcy Island, just north of Ruxton Passage, is mostly private except for its southeast appendage, Pirates Cove Marine Park (mile 43/**193**). There are two main access bays for the park, Pirates Cove on the north, and Ruxton Passage Cove on the south. Pirates Cove is the more popular anchorage as it offers greater protection; consequently, it can become crowded. At low tides it becomes a bug-infested and olfactory-assaulting bog trap. Kayakers should head for Ruxton Passage Cove, the closest access to the campground. A water pump, toilets, and fee collection site are all present.

Pirates Cove was once known as Gospel Cove, headquarters of the Aquarian Foundation, a millennial sect that made the island its home in the late 1920s. Edward Arthur Wilson, known to his followers as Brother XII, ran a tight ship. Converts were expected to pool their resources and contribute to the task of creating a self-sufficient colony. Some of the old buildings and an orchard along the western shore of De Courcy are all that remain from that era. From female converts the good brother expected sexual compliance, after which the whip-wielding Madame Zee,

Wilson's right-hand woman, would ensure the acolyte did her fair share of work. Cult conflicts soon involved the police and, inevitably, the courts. Tales of sordid sex, insanity, and misappropriation of funds became public. Wilson was tried but never convicted. He and Zee fled to Switzerland. No trace of the cult's half ton of gold (said to be buried in 43 boxes) has ever been found. Now for the east side of Pylades Channel.

Valdes Island: Valdes Island is almost completely uninhabited. About one-third of it is native reserve; the rest is private, with the exception of Blackberry Point (mile 39/**189**), an isolated piece of Crown land and a spacious, mostly undeveloped campground. The site has privy toilets and is maintained by the BCWTA, which charges a $5 per person fee. An extensive sandy beach surrounds the point; campsites— lots of possibilities—are either in the meadow or the madrona enclaves. To climb Mexicana Hill, the highest point on Valdes, paddle to an obvious little cove 0.5 mile north of Blackberry Point. Head up the old logging road and veer off on one of the many trails that lead in the general direction of the top. These are some serious views and it's well worth the effort.

According to Mary Ann Snowden in her excellent guide, *Island Paddling:*

> *Up until the beginning of this century, a large native population inhabited the southern shores of Valdes, living in one of three permanent villages. The largest village, Laysken, spread north and south of Shingle Point and had as many as ten houses and a population of two hundred. A smaller village at Cardale Point had five more houses and a total population of one hundred. The smallest site included three or four houses stretching from Cayetano Point to Vernaci Point (Rozen). The villages were abandoned when populations became so depleted that the remaining few inhabitants had to join up with related bands.*

The Valdes Island side of Pylades is a pleasant paddle that becomes spectacular at the north end of the island. Wave erosion has carved magnificent, intricately shaped sandstone galleries that stimulate the imagination. Sometimes though, you can't get very close. The area adjacent to and just south of Dibuxante Point is often used as a log booming berth by tugs awaiting suitable conditions to navigate Gabriola Passage. Still, it is quite an experience to paddle right next to millions of dollars worth of lumber on the float.

From Dibuxante Point, cross over to Gabriola Island at a respectful distance from the entrance to Gabriola Passage. Although the worst part of Gabriola Passage is between Cordero and Josef Points, expect turbulence, eddy lines, and funny water at the west entrance. Currents can run 8 knots, and their direction is seemingly counterintuitive. Ebbs flow west; floods flow east. Scope out your crossing well and, if in doubt, cross close to slack. Head for the protection of Degnen Bay, usually crowded and lacking any real facilities other than a government wharf. Degnen is the access point for a variety of prehistoric native petroglyph sites that are extensive, well preserved, easy to find, and now protected.

Degnen Bay, Gabriola Island: The first petroglyph, known as the "killer whale," is 16 feet below the high-tide line between the last two piers on the northeast shore at the head of the bay on a sloping sand-

Petroglyphs near Nanaimo, British Columbia

stone ledge. At low tide, land on the gravel beach between the afore-mentioned piers. Two other petroglyph sites, one with more than 50 glyphs known as the Weldwood Site, requires about a two-hour hike round trip. It is well worth the effort. Park the boats well high on the beach near the government wharf. Follow the gravel road west from the wharf to its intersection with South Road. Turn left. Follow South Road for about a mile until you get to the Gabriola United Church, at the intersection with Price Road. From the church parking lot a signed path leads to the Weldwood Site. In about 0.25 mile you'll come to a distinctive clearing with two stone boulders marking the entrance. The carvings are incised on a horizontal sandstone slab, and were discovered only in 1976, under a thin layer of grass and moss. Weldwood of Canada, the property owner, donated the site to the Crown. The depiction of a T-shaped labret on one of the carvings indicates a date (at least for that carving) of between 500 BC and AD 500.

A third petroglyph group lies about 0.5 mile to the west. To reach these, retrace your steps back to the church. Go west on South Road for 0.5 mile to the Wheelbarrow Nursery. Take the old logging trail north for about 800 yards to a trail intersection near a large tree. Then take the path to the east and in 400 yards arrive at the third site.

The passage between De Courcy and Link Islands is the last opportunity to slip over to Stuart Passage and Dodd Narrows; it dries only at low tide. Link and Mudge Island are connected by a tombolo that is covered only at the highest tides.

Time to slip through False Narrows. Dodd Narrows, boiling with whirlpools and rips, floods at 9 knots and ebbs at 8; much of the Nanaimo–Gulf Islands intermediate-size traffic favors it. Boats, from runabouts to tugs with log booms, congest the approaches prior to slack and the channel during the run. False Narrows, about a mile long, only runs at 4.5 knots and only during spring tides at that. Mostly small, local craft use it, as the channel is narrow, shallow, and choked with kelp. Although you need not wait for slack, you must, at least, go with the flow, though passage is not impossible at nearly any time.

Northumberland Channel, separating Gabriola from Vancouver Island just south of Nanaimo, is a de facto extension of Nanaimo Harbor and can be quite congested. The south shore is home to one of MacMillan Bloedel's pulp mills; the Gabriola Island shore is the storage yard for the log booms. Two ferries crisscross. The Nanaimo-Tsaawwassen ferry departs from a new terminal at Jack Point; the Nanaimo–Gabriola Island ferry crosses from the inner harbor to Descanso Bay on Gabriola. A good strategy is to hug the shore between Duke and Jack Points and slip through after the departing Jack Point ferry (or under the pilings). The fish petroglyphs that once graced the fingertip of Jack's Point have been removed and placed on display at the entrance to the museum in Nanaimo. Then work the foul south shore flats of Nanaimo Harbour until you can nip over to Protection Island behind, or well in front of, the Nanaimo–Gabriola Island ferry.

Don't overlook (in spite of the phalanx of log booms) the spectacularly eroded sandstone cliffs along the western edge of Gabriola Island. These reach their apogee at Galiano (Malaspina) Galleries just south of Malaspina Point at the north end of Descanso Bay (mile 52/**202**). When Spanish explorer Alejandro Malaspina discovered them in 1792, he compared them to monasteries and spent the rest of the day making sketches. Descanso Bay Regional Park, 0.5 mile north of the ferry terminal, is a popular developed campground.

From Gallows Point at the south end of Protection Island, it's best to head up the east coast of Protection to Newcastle Island Marine Park (mile 54/**204**), as this approach, regardless of tides, puts you in the best position to access the Newcastle Island campground.

Newcastle Island: Shoot for Newcastle's east shore just above Protection Island and south of Kanaka Bay (below MacKay Point). The campsites are in the woods behind the lawn. In contrast, the landing docks and boat ramp, at the very southeast tip of the island, are nowhere near the individual campgrounds. However, if you choose to land at the piers, there are wheeled carts available for dunnage transport, and an orientation map. Nearly the entire east coast of Newcastle, including the passage to Protection Island, dries at low tide, making for an inconvenient carry to camp.

Newcastle Island Marine Park (mile 54/**204**) is undoubtedly one of the prime jewels in the crown of the provincial park system. Newcastle has every convenience and then some. The absence of vehicle access and proximity to Nanaimo make Newcastle unique. Because it's next to the city, not many people camp here. And since day use is only via private boat or ferry, natural restrictions keep overuse at bay, though it can get busy on weekends. The island has been a park and resort since the 1930s, when it was owned by the Canadian Pacific Steamship Company and used for company picnics and Sunday outings. Many of the old buildings still serve as the park's headquarters. Gary oaks dot the manicured lawns. Rabbits and raccoons, including rare albino variants, abound. Twelve miles of trails to every conceivable point of interest, including the island perimeter, the old coal mines, Mallard Lake, and the sandstone quarry lace the island. Showers are available. A small footpassenger ferry runs hourly between the island and downtown Nanaimo.

Newcastle Island is an ideal layover stop. As a further enticement, the Dinghy Dock Marine Pub, adjacent to Protection Island and just across the narrow, unnamed passage separating the two islands, is open 11 to 11, serves excellent food, and is accessed by boat only. Literally, a 1½-minute paddle. Be sure to return before it gets too dark or you get too lit. A small shoreside store is adjacent.

Nanaimo: Nanaimo is Vancouver Island's second largest city with a rapidly increasing population of 100,000. It was founded in 1853 after the discovery of a high-grade coal seam and originally called Colville Town. The settlers eventually adopted the native name, meaning "big strong tribe" (a reference to the area's five villages). Today, fishing and forest products predominate. Once drab and depressing, the Nanaimo waterfront has undergone a transformation that makes an attractive excursion. A 2.5-mile, pedestrian-only waterfront promenade is lined with restaurants, parks, shops, museums, and historic sites. These include the Bastion, a defensive white octagonal tower built by the Hudson's Bay Company in 1853; the Swy-A-Lana Lagoon, a constructed tidal pool; and the Nanaimo Centennial Museum. Nanaimo must be the only place in the world to have erected a bronze statue to a real estate developer, Frank Ney, also an ex-mayor, who had the vision to redesign and carry out the waterfront's facelift. A short walk up Bastion Street lies the Old City Quarter, where restored brick-and-stone buildings line Fitzwilliam, Selby, and Wesley Streets.

A few miles south of downtown, at the mouth of the Nanaimo River, Petroglyph Provincial Park protects and displays prehistoric native rock carvings. Nearby is Saunders Bridge where, in 1990, Nanaimo became the first place in North America to feature bungee jumping. A 140-foot jump runs $100 Canadian; call 250-753-5867. Lastly, each fourth Sunday of July, Nanaimo sponsors the annual Bathtub Race to Vancouver across the 30-mile-wide Strait of Georgia. If your kayak is tubby enough, consider competing.

Strait of Georgia: Newcastle Island Provincial Park (mile 54/204) to Powell River (mile 123/273)

North of Nanaimo the journey's character changes. Though the Vancouver Island coast retains its hustle and bustle, adventure and some degree of isolation punctuate the interisland crossings of the Strait of Georgia. Meanwhile, Powell River will be the last city until Port Hardy. Coordinating camping (somewhat limited) along the remaining portion of the Vancouver Island Coast with the 5-mile crossing to Lasqueti Island requires some planning. Winds and seas can build up in the Strait of Georgia during the afternoon, so plan on early starts.

Head up the east coast of Newcastle Island and position yourself for a propitious crossing of the mouth of Departure Bay. Watch out for the Nanaimo-Vancouver ferry—eight daily trips—coming out of Departure Bay. Pass Horswell Bluff and continue north to Hammond Bay. Page Lagoon, on the southeast side of Hammond Bay, is a regional park. Coast the 6 miles past Neck, Icarus, and Blunden Points to the mouth of Nanoose Harbour.

Maude Island (mile 65/**215**), at the far end of Nanoose's mouth, is, according to Peter McGee in *Kayak Routes of the Pacific Northwest Coast*, the first potential campsite. Head for the beach at the southeast corner. Southey Island, 0.5 mile farther and just off Wallis Point, is another.

Other islands in the Winchelsea Archipelago are a Canadian Armed Forces base and off limits. Adjacent to the Winchelseas and clearly

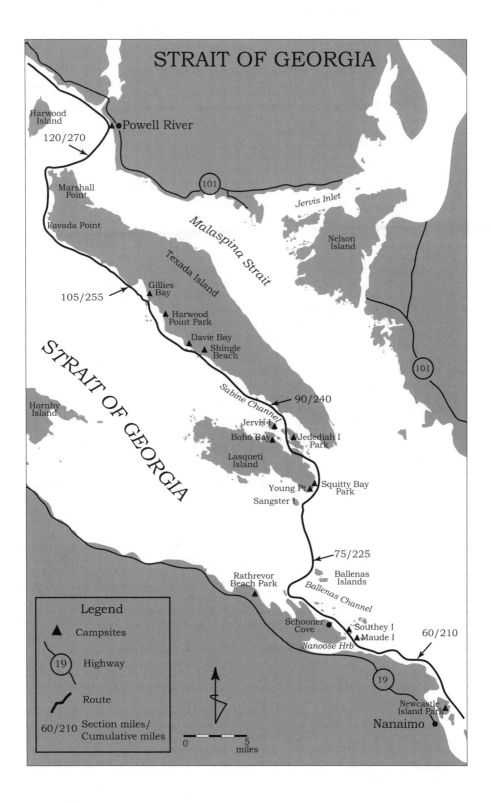

STRAIT OF GEORGIA

Harwood
Island

Powell River

120/270

Marshall
Point

Favada Point

Jervis Inlet

Malaspina Strait

101

Texada Island

Nelson
Island

105/255

Gillies
Bay

Harwood
Point Park

Davie Bay

Shingle
Beach

STRAIT OF GEORGIA

Sabine Channel

90/240

Hornby
Island

Jervis I

Boho Bay

Jedediah I
Park

Lasqueti
Island

Young Pt

Squitty Bay
Park

Sangster I

75/225

Rathrevor
Beach Park

Ballenas
Islands

Ballenas Channel

Schooner
Cove

Southey I

Maude I

60/210

Nanoose Hrb

19

Newcastle
Island Park

Nanaimo

Legend

▲ Campsites

19 Highway

Route

60/210 Section miles/
Cumulative miles

0   5
miles

marked on charts is the Whiskey Golf Canadian Forces Maritime Experimental and Test Ranges. The area technically extends across Ballenas Channel, includes the Ballenas Islands, and barely touches the Vancouver Island coast just south of Dorcas Point. Although the portion impinging on Vancouver Island and including the Ballenas is not transit-restricted, exercise caution. Heading northwest along the Wallis, Nankivell, and Dorcas Points coast make sure to hug the shore. Schooner Cove, just south of Nankivell Point, has a restaurant, marina, hotel, and grocery store.

The objective now is to use the Ballenas Islands as a stepping-stone for the crossing of the Strait of Georgia to Lasqueti Island. Plan the crossing far enough west of the Whiskey Golf Range to avoid any trouble. Dorcas Point, Cottam Point, and Mistaken Island are good launching points. If you camped on Maude or Southey Islands, get an early enough start to tackle the bulk of the crossing before noon. (Note: Remember that Canada is on Daylight Savings Time, and meteorological phenomena respond to actual solar conditions, i.e., real time.) Alternatively, you could camp at Rathrevor Beach Provincial Park (2 miles off route from mile 71/**221**), over by Parksville, and be slightly closer to the crossing. Rathrevor is a fully equipped campground. Unfortunately, it requires crossing the mouth of Northwest Bay twice and negotiating an extensive sand beach that gets even longer at low tide. Plus, between the last week of June and Labor Day, reservations are required. Do not be misled by the teepee symbol just inside Northwest Bay on the Cottam Point side on the 1:250,000 Canadian topo map. This park is a picnic-only site.

Launch early toward the Ballenas Islands. The north island has a lighthouse station that makes for an interesting visit and walkabout. From here, reassess the 5-mile crossing to Sangster Island. After the crossing, head for Young Point (mile 82/**232**) on Lasqueti Island, where there is an undeveloped kayak campsite. Squitty Bay Marine Park (mile 83/**233**), another mile up the southwest side of Lasqueti, has no facilities and is usually crowded with small craft.

Jedediah Island: Continue north into Bull Passage. A delightful archipelago, anchored by Jedediah Island, separates Lasqueti from

Texada Island. Jedediah Island Provincial Park (mile 87/**237**) was only recently acquired by the provincial parks system. Remains of an old homestead still add flavor, and, at least when we were there, feral goats somehow survive without water. Approach the camping area from Long Bay on the west side. Steep steps lead to a copse high on a grassy bluff overlooking the drying mud flats of Long Bay, where raccoons clam at low tide. Both arms of Long Bay have camping areas. A trail traverses the island to Home Bay on the eastern side of Jedediah. If Jedediah is not to your liking, Boho Bay, on Lasqueti just across Bull Passage and behind Boho Island, also has a camping area, as does Jervis Island a bit farther on.

Cross Sabine Channel to Partington Point on Texada Island. Sabine is often calm when conditions are somewhat choppy in the Strait of Georgia. Texada is mountainous and rugged with little traffic along its western shore. A military exercise area parallels the western shore about 1 mile out for 20 miles. Stay within the 1-mile distance, coursing north. Remember to keep a sharp lookout for Texada's "killer" seals.

About 8 miles up Texada from Partington Point lies a small island behind which is located the Shingle Beach (mile 97/**247**) campsite. Another mile on, behind a couple more islands, is the Davie Bay Campground (mile 98/**248**).

Five miles farther, at Harwood Point, is Harwood Point Park (mile 103/**253**). Water, campgrounds, picnic tables, and toilets are available. The launching ramp is on the northeast corner of Mouat Bay. And yet another mile up lies Gillies Bay, a small community with a private campground, post office, medical clinic, Royal Canadian Mounted Police (RCMP) office, grocery, and liquor store.

Continuing up the west coast of Texada, you'll pass what must be the largest kitty litter operation in the world, Texada Mines Ltd. Turn Favada (a curious name, as *fabada* is a traditional Spanish bean stew) Point, pass Crescent Bay to Marshall Point, and then Limekiln Bay to Kiddie Point. Blubber Bay indents the northern extremity of Texada. It is not inviting. The limestone plant runs an incessant and noisy 24 hours a day. The Texada–Westview ferry maintains a regular schedule. To complicate matters, the Comox–Westview ferry runs east/west close to Texada's north end. Avoiding the eastbound ferry is easy: once past Grilse Point, you and the ferry are on diverging courses, since you'll be heading farther north toward Powell River.

Avoiding the Comox ferry is more problematic, as you'll both be on approximately parallel courses that cross acutely about halfway across Malaspina Strait. Look both ways before starting to cross, and stick together to present a more visible target. Malaspina Strait is about 5 miles wide at this point. The Powell River–Westview urban area appears uniform from the kayaker's perspective. Where to head? Powell River's campground is at its northern end. From Grilse Point it lies at about a 40 degrees true north bearing. Since the magnetic declination is about 20 degrees east, set a compass course of 20 degrees and realign as visual clues come into sight. Another strategy is to aim halfway between Grief Point on the south and the giant chimneys—often spewing—of the pulp mill complex at the extreme northern end of Powell River.

The Powell River campground (mile 123/**273**) is well situated. Right on the water, big trees and broad lawns attract many of the area's residents on sunny weekends. The facilities include toilets and showers. About a mile down the road are laundromats, groceries, post office, liquor store, and every other urban convenience. Consider resupplying here, because neither Lund nor Squirrel Cove, farther north—nor, in fact, any settlement for the remainder of this stretch—is as well stocked. Nor are their camping facilities quite as accessible to their other resources.

Desolation Sound: Powell River (mile 123/273) to Big Bay, Stuart Island (mile 172/322)

Gird your hatches and resolve for a journey beyond the end of the road. Ten miles north, at Lund, the mainland highway hits the coast range and terminates abruptly. Though the Vancouver Trans-Island Highway continues north on the other side of the Strait of Georgia, its presence will not affect you until Telegraph Cove, many miles hence. George Vancouver, when navigating in these nether regions, was overcome with a sense of desolation and gloom, hence the name. Here the Vancouver Island tides converge and are thrown further into disarray by constricting

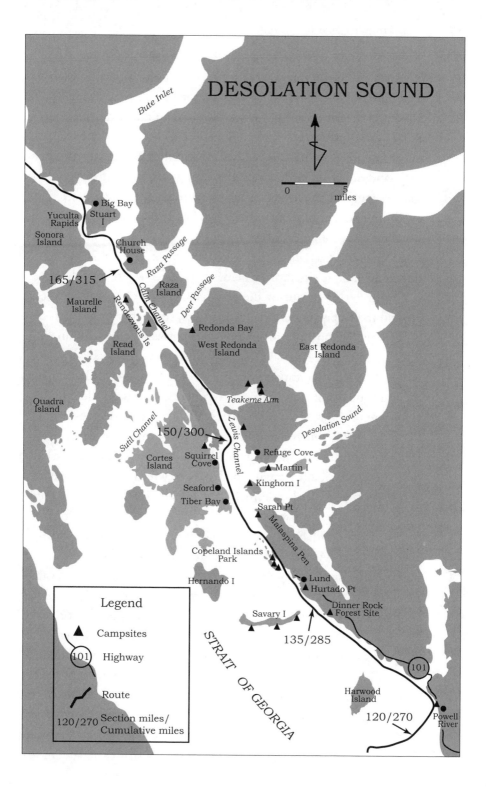

DESOLATION SOUND

Bute Inlet

Big Bay
Stuart I
Yuculta Rapids
Sonora Island
Church House
Raza Passage
165/315
Raza Island
Deer Passage
Maurelle Island
Calm Channel
Rendezvous Is
Read Island
Redonda Bay
West Redonda Island
East Redonda Island
Quadra Island
Teakerne Arm
Desolation Sound
Sutil Channel
150/300
Lewis Channel
Cortes Island
Squirrel Cove
Refuge Cove
Martin I
Seaford
Kinghorn I
Tiber Bay
Sarah Pt
Malaspina Pen
Copeland Islands Park
Hernando I
Lund
Hurtado Pt
Savary I
Dinner Rock Forest Site
135/285
STRAIT OF GEORGIA
Harwood Island
101
120/270
Powell River

Legend

▲ Campsites

(101) Highway

Route

120/270 Section miles/ Cumulative miles

0   5
miles

landmasses. The impinging mountains mirror the surface and subsurface topography, destabilizing the weather along with the tides and adding to the sense of disquietude and impending vague foreboding. Revel in the grandeur.

While the weather can be a sociopath in its constantly threatening—and, more often than not, delivering—attitude, it is the waters that are truly schizophrenic. After overcoming so many obstacles and exhibiting so much pugnacity to get here, the waters can't decide whether to stay or go. Some return as do most tides, creating constriction rapids and overfalls in their constant ingress and egress, but some, due to the unique situation of being at the place where the tides meet, end up loitering in out-of-the-way back bays and channels. These, around the Copeland Islands for instance, simmer in basins that undergo only the most pro forma tidal exchange, and so can attain tepid highs of nearly 80 degrees F. Oysters abound; they seem to favor warmer waters. If you do harvest oysters, beware of red tides—which can make them unsafe to eat—and respect commercial leases. At the other extreme are the newborn glacial waters, frigid at 32–34 degrees F, which flood the remote inlets and dilute and lower local water temperatures to nearly 50 degrees F. And then there's Yuculta Rapids, the biggest, baddest, most intimidating rapids you'll have to wrestle with on the entire Inside Passage. At slack, admittedly an awfully short time, you wouldn't even know they existed.

North of Lund, bears become a concern. As does the sasquatch—reported North American sightings are highest in Desolation Sound and the Broughton archipelago. Keep the pepper spray handy and camp defensively. The nature of camping and campsites also changes once the road is left behind. Not that private property ceases to exist or parks disappear, but without a road, man's impact is infrequent. Human density decreases due to naturally limited access, and encountering another human being becomes a welcome rather than a tedious experience. Ironically, though de facto unrestricted camping vastly increases north of Lund, beaches become very rare, shores are rocky scarps, and flat, accessible ground is difficult to find. If not using a designated campsite or one identified by this guide, start your search early each day. Due to the sometimes dry climate, fires are not allowed on most of the islands without a burning permit.

Just 1.5 miles north of the town of Powell River lies the Powell River proper, an extremely short river with an impressive gradient. MacMillan Bloedel has harnessed its latent power to run the world's largest pulp paper mill. Surplus WWII hulks chained together nestle millions of board feet of British Columbia forests for transformation into newsprint. And it smells funny. Harwood Island, just to the west, is a First Nations reserve.

Eight miles north of the Powell River campground, opposite Dinner Rock, lies the Dinner Rock Forest Site (mile 134/**284**), a camping area with pit toilets and road access. Just offshore lies Savary Island, surrounded by sandy beaches (all open to camping) and warm water. Likely campsites bracket Mace Point and lie east of Garnet Point. About 1 mile south of Lund, at Hurtado Point (mile 136/**286**) is another possible campsite, the closest camping opportunity to Lund.

Lund, a small settlement at the end of Highway 101, has groceries, liquor, water, lodging, a post office, a bakery, a laundromat, and a restaurant. Don't miss a visit to the local native carver working in one of the garage stalls right by the wharf. Though usually lacking much in the way of stock, he's always working on at least one or two impressive totem poles.

Copeland Islands: Two miles up the Malaspina Peninsula and only 500 feet offshore lies Copeland Islands Marine Park (mile 140/**290**). The Copelands, formerly and locally known as the Ragged Islands, were the last redoubt of Joe Copeland, a Confederate Army officer turned stagecoach robber. He lived out his days safe from extradition on these islands at the turn of the 20th century, making a living as a hand logger. There are good campsites on at least three islands, two with privies, and the odd picnic table, but no water. A narrow neck almost cuts through the southernmost island a little over halfway up. The first campsite is located here. Probably the best—and largest—campsite is on the middle island in the small, west-facing bay. The third large island also has a campsite on its western side. Not only are the waters particularly warm here, but flat rocky ledges abound just at, above, and below water level, making for inviting swimming platforms.

Sarah Point (mile 143/**293**), on the tip of the Malaspina Penninsula, is the absolute end of even the most minor dirt track and the actual gate to Desolation Sound. Though the point itself is rather rocky, camping is possible just to the south and past the point a bit farther east. Desolation Sound Marine Park encompasses parts of Desolation Sound, though the park is unusual in that it is not all public property. Tidal streams are inconsistent and weak, seldom exceeding 2 knots, until the constrictions of Cordero Channel are reached.

North of Sarah Point, enter Lewis Channel. Decide now whether to follow the Cortes Island shore or island-hop straight north to Kinghorn, Martin, and West Redonda Islands. Going up the Cortes side, pass the wannabe settlements of Tiber Bay and Seaford. Farther up, the community of Squirrel Cove (mile 149/**299**) preserves some vestigial counterculture traits. The store is just behind the giant pier spanning the extensive sand flat that dries at low tide. Water, a post office, and phone are also available. At the head of Squirrel Cove, about 1.5 miles from the wharf, is a short tidal creek connecting to a lagoon that reverses flows with the tide—a miniature whitewater course. The lagoon is a park, and camping is allowed.

Heading due north from Sarah Point, cross over to Kinghorn Island (mile 145/**295**), where possible campsites dot the north shore. Pass by tiny Station Island and make a beeline to Martin Island (mile 149/**299**), almost two islands. The connecting neck makes an excellent campsite. At the southwest tip of West Redonda Island, about a mile farther up the route, Refuge Cove indents the salient. This small community has a post office, grocery, marina, telephone, and showers, as well as a gift shop and liquor store.

About halfway up to Joyce Point, inside a small bay with an accessible shore, camping (mile 150/**300**) is possible. North of Joyce Point, Teakerne Arm nearly cuts West Redonda in half. Cassel Falls cataract down from Cassel Lake at the head of Teakerne's north arm. Although 5 miles off route (round trip), this side excursion is worthwhile. There

Cassel Falls, Teakerne Arm, Desolation Sound, British Columbia

is a small docking float with adjacent steps, and a trail leads to the lake. Both the falls and the lake are swimming-temperature warm. For the ambitious, a great campsite lies at the lake's outflow. Other camping possibilities are in a small cove at the southern end (east shore) of Teakerne's north arm; somewhat to the right of the dock; and about halfway along the west shore of Teakerne's north arm.

Enter the narrow portion of Lewis Channel and paddle north. Currents are not a concern here. At the junction with Deer Passage and just around West Redonda's northwest buttress lies Redonda Bay (mile 160/**310**—and about 0.5 mile off route). It has a small wharf, camping, and the remnants of an aboriginal fish weir in the creek.

Cross Deer Passage and enter Calm Channel. No current concerns here either. Raza Island, on the east side, is precipitously steep and high.

Rendezvous Islands: The west side of Calm Channel is bordered by the Rendezvous Islands; both have campsites. South Rendezvous Island (mile 161/**301**) has one or two old homesteads that are suitable for pitching a tent. North Rendezvous (mile 164/**304**), though mostly private, has a 10-acre park at the northern tip that includes the small, adjacent islet farther north. Both provide suitable campsites. A grassy track runs up the interior of the island past several homesteads and cabins. A small, hard-to-find but dependable spring is located about 500 feet east of the road in dense salal. There are also some hand-dug freshwater pools about 60 feet upstream from the beach.

Beyond Raza and the Rendezvous Islands, head for the Toba Mountain peninsula on the mainland along the east side of Calm Channel and forming the north shore of Raza Passage. This puts you in a good position to approach Yuculta Rapids and, if you have to, wait for slack water within a manageable distance. On the east side of Toba Mountain lies Frances Bay, a bit out of the way but offering a couple of possible campsites and a stream. On the west side of Toba, between Bartlett Island and Johnstone Bluff, Church House spectrally stands guard, like Vulcan's Anvil before Lava Falls, in mute warning of the dangers, different in kind, up Bute Inlet and Cordero Channel.

Church House, Calm Channel, British Columbia

Church House has seen better days. The docking float is officially considered unusable, though the white spire of the church and surrounding ruins attract all passersby. The settlement is an Indian reserve and quite overgrown with salal. This is a good spot to kill some time (for those who like their time dead) if slack at Yuculta is more than an hour's wait. One hour before slack, or longer if you're a cautious sort, cross the mouth of Butte Inlet to Stuart Island.

Just around Harbott Point lies the Stuart Island Resort. This part of the island is very steep and rocky; the only place to haul out and wait for the exact time to negotiate Yuculta is at the floating wharf. The resort affects airs of exclusivity, but in the spirit of things, puts up with kayakers gathering their thoughts.

Yuculta Rapids: To those with a whitewater background, the term "rapids" in this application is a bit of a misnomer, except for the actual speed of the water, which often reaches 8 knots. There are no standing waves and no real gradient to the channel. Instead, extreme turbulence in the form of giant eddy lines and whirlpools—with edge gradients of 3 feet or more—form when incredible volumes of water are squeezed into a very narrow channel which, not satisfied with the simple Venturi effect it produces, then twists, turns, and sprouts shoals and islands to further rattle the water's cage. "Rapids" such as these are no place for kayaks, no matter how hotshot the whitewater boater. As Ralph Keller warns in *Kayak Routes of the Pacific Northwest Coast*: "No amount of skill—rolling, bracing, or paddling—will guarantee you a safe passage through any of the region's rapids."

It is difficult for an expert Class V whitewater boater to imagine such conditions. The closest examples, in a river (that I have experienced), are the narrows in the Grand Canyon at high water. The exact same phenomena, albeit in miniature, occur there. Giant whirlpools, eddies, boils, and overfalls—none named rapids—appear and disappear randomly. Boaters who cruise through the rapids are often stymied, sucked, discombobulated, and capsized by these watery poltergeists. Imagine the same conditions magnified to a scale and volume so immense that a kayak would be like a twig in the Middle Granite Gorge of the Grand Canyon at 35,000 cubic feet per second. Curiously,

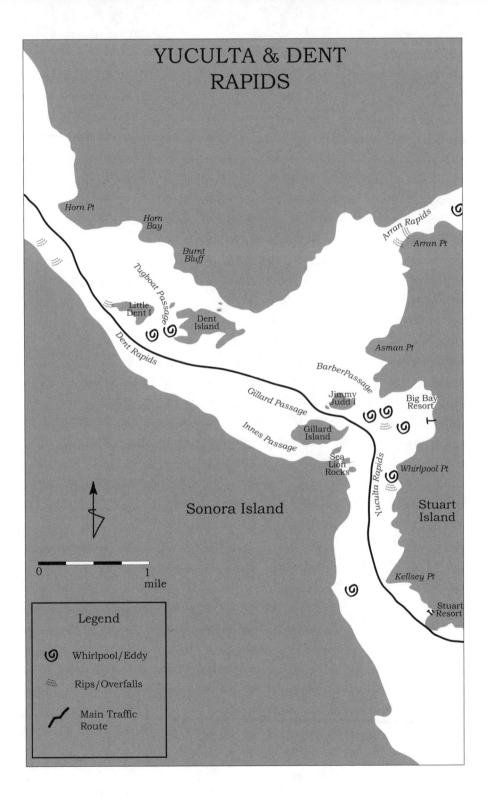

YUCULTA & DENT RAPIDS

Horn Pt

Horn Bay

Burnt Bluff

Arran Rapids

Arran Pt

Tugboat Passage

Little Dent I

Dent Island

Asman Pt

Dent Rapids

Barber Passage

Jimmy Judd I

Big Bay Resort

Gillard Passage

Innes Passage

Gillard Island

Yuculta Rapids

Sea Lion Rocks

Whirlpool Pt

Sonora Island

Stuart Island

Kellsey Pt

Stuart Resort

0   1 mile

Legend

Whirlpool/Eddy

Rips/Overfalls

Main Traffic Route

many of the whirlpools in saltwater rapids are stationary, rather like standing waves or holes in river rapids. Some of the nastier ones even have names, such as Devil's Hole in Dent Rapids.

If you've arrived at the Stuart Island pier well in advance of slack, anticipation and impatience will gnaw at your gut. Unable to see around Kellsey Point and get the merest glance (there is no roar) at these "rapids," you might be tempted to go out and have a look at Yuculta, especially when you see Boston Whalers with 50-horsepower outboards and 10-horsepower kickers coming and going, in all directions, seemingly with impunity. Don't. The shores are unlandable, and going around Kellsey is quite committing. Professional guides, who know the rapids well and are out every day during the season, skipper the powerboats, which plane across the surface at high speeds, with little draw for the eddies to act upon. Everyone aboard wears an exposure suit. Still, accidents happen, and these skipping stones sometimes go *kerplunk!*

It is possible to traverse the entire length of both Yuculta and Dent Rapids (Dent Rapids immediately follow Big Bay and will be covered in the following section) during one slack at one go. The total distance is about 4.5 miles. If this is your plan and you choose not to stop at Big Bay, leave the Stuart Island pier 30 minutes before slack. The current tables are essential for correct timing, because the change in current direction does not always coincide with the tidal change. This strategy will bracket the slack with one full hour in which to cover the 4.5 miles. The tide floods south at 5 to 7 knots in Yuculta, 7 to 9 knots in Dent; and ebbs north at 4 to 6 knots in Yuculta, 6 to 8 knots in Dent.

A better strategy is to paddle each rapid at different slacks, enjoying the amenities of Big Bay during the interval. With this plan, leave the Stuart Island pier 30 to 15 minutes before slack. The 1-mile paddle between Kellsey Point and Whirlpool Point is Yuculta Rapid. You wouldn't know it at slack. Once around Whirlpool Point, you're in Big Bay and safe waters.

Big Bay, Stuart Island: Big Bay (mile 172/322) is an idyllic maelstrom of contrasts. Although quite isolated, it boasts an international reputation for salmon sport fishing. A handful of serious angling resorts cluster both on Stuart Island and across the rapids at Sonora Island. No make-do floating barges converted into accommodations here. The architecture and landscaping are stunning and fit in well with the surrounding terrain. There is even a golf course, beautifully designed, at that. Big Bay itself is a community (year-round population 19, as of 1986) with a government wharf and a school. Some very fancy homes, mostly seasonal, surround the area. A small store with some produce, a restaurant, pub, showers, and laundry facilities are present. However, there is no campground. We camped, with permission, on the school grounds. With a little luck and the right attitude, you probably can, too. These facilities are located just behind the public wharf. Land either at the wharf or at the steep beach from which it originates. Walk northward along the forest trail just behind the beach until you reach the resort/store to inquire.

There are many superb walks from Big Bay. Mount Muehle, the highest point on the island at 1,710 feet, yields spectacular views of the rapids, waterways, and surrounding terrain. Approach Mount Muehle from the south, right behind Big Bay. Another trail south parallels the coast to the Stuart Island Resort. North of Big Bay, a trail inland forks either right, to a bay on the east shore, or left, to a view of Arran Rapids on the small north fork of Butte Inlet.

Discovery Islands: Big Bay, Stuart Island (mile 172/322) to Robson Bight (mile 240/390)

North of Stuart, say good-bye to the sensual madrona. Sea and air temperatures drop noticeably; fog and rain increase. Here, you will probably spot your first bear. This section, though quite isolated, is neither devoid of traffic nor exploitation. Barges with log booms, fishermen, and sailboats along with logging camps and small salmon pisciculture enterprises punctuate the isolation. The mountains drop straight into the sea. Camping is at will, yet campsites are few, tentative, and widely dispersed. Saltwater rapids require proper timing and negotiation. Once into Johnstone Strait you'll rejoin the Inside Passage's main traffic lane. Though always occupied, it is never crowded. The terminus, Robson's Bight, a world famous orca reserve and research area, is no

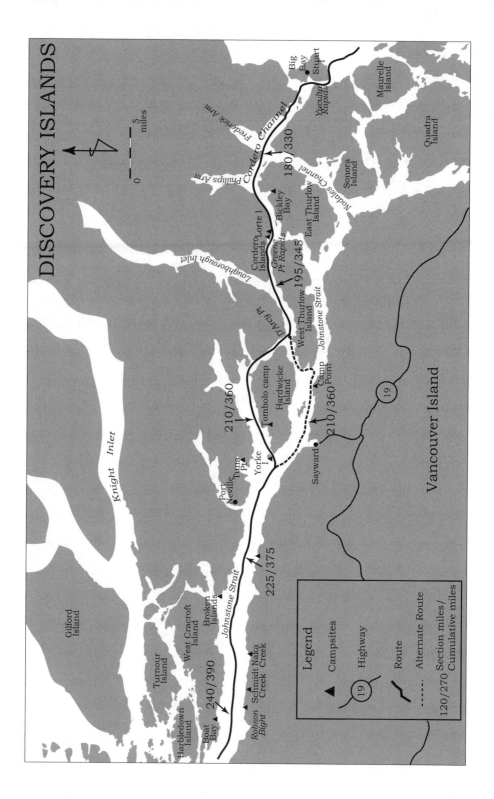

DISCOVERY ISLANDS

Legend

▲ Campsites

⑲ Highway

Route

⸱⸱⸱⸱⸱ Alternate Route

120/270 Section miles/Cumulative miles

N

0 ——— 5 miles

place to lay over, in fact, it must be skirted. Still, your chances of seeing orcas in the vicinity are quite good.

The route follows Cordero and Chancellor Channels and then, putting off merging with Johnstone Strait until absolutely necessary, veers up Welbore Channel, along the north shore of Hardwicke Island. Welbore turns into Sunderland Channel, which then enters Johnstone Strait. You can shave a mile by joining Johnstone Strait at its junction with Chancellor Channel via the south coast of Hardwicke. This option is the only alternate route in this section and will be described immediately following its main route alter ego.

Dent Rapids: Two miles out of Big Bay, Dent Rapids await. From the air, at full rush, Dent actually resembles a river rapid complete with standing waves and a cheater route. Depart Big Bay about half an hour to 15 minutes before slack at the end of a flood tide. Don't worry that *Sailing Directions* indicates a slack lasting only five minutes; the fudge time is greater. In spite of the presence of a cheater route, do not attempt Dent at times other than slack. The reason for this is that the waters between Yuculta and Dent are always fast and turbulent—except around slack. Head for the cheater route, the tiny, narrow passage between Dent Island and the mainland.

Because this dries at low tides, go at the end of a flood. Using this passage keeps you close to shore and out of the way of the bigger boats timing their runs. Local skiffs use this shortcut, but often have to negotiate a resident standing wave at times other than slack. Timed properly, the passage through Dent makes this paragraph seem like the ranting of Chicken Little. Once through, the ebb tide will escort you for the next six hours.

Good thing, too. The Douglasses, in their cruising guide to the south coast of B.C., describe Cordero Channel as a "two-way reversible 'river.'" It pays to go with the flow here. Pass Horn Point and work your way toward the Sonora Island shore, skirting Denham Islet before Hall Point. Look both ways before crossing. To the north, Frederick Arm, with its logging camps and booming grounds, penetrates the mountains. To the south, Nodales Channel is the quickest route to Johnstone Strait. Graze Channe Point and head for Channe Island.

Shoal Bay indents the northern tip of East Thurlow Island. Gold was once mined here, but the former settlement of Thurlow is abandoned. The public float accesses a resort in the meadow. Water and a few supplies are available at the lodge. Round Godwin Point and take in the magnificent views up Phillips Arm on the north bank of Cordero. Lined with salmon farms along its eastern shore, the rest of Phillips Arm is extensively logged.

Just past Bickley Bay (with possible camping at its head on small, grassy beaches) Cordero Channel narrows in anticipation of Greene Point Rapids. During tidal floods, with the current going east, swirls and zones of funny water from the tail end of the rapid extend nearly to Lorte and Erasmus Islands. Hug the north shore. Lorte Island (mile 189/**339**) provides protection for what must be one of the most unexpected encounters along this stretch, the Camp Cordero Lodge with its restaurant sign facing the channel. What is unusual is that the small lodge, besides soliciting as if they were on a busy roadside, is very attractively ensconced on a log floathouse, is family owned and run, *and* serves excellent German food. You can call ahead to inquire on Channel 73.

Barely a mile ahead, thanks to Earth's tectonic forces in conjunction with the Holocene climate, lie the Cordero Islands (mile 190/**340**), upon which you can not only camp, but camp in style. The islands are steep, white granite with one having just enough flat surfaces for a couple of freestanding tents. Just behind is a seal haul-out rock. Access the site—a bit steep and rough—from the back. Approach quietly and you'll get a great view of the seals. Halfway between Lorte and the Corderos, Tallac Bay indents the shore. The bay dries as far as the eastern peninsula and has a grassy meadow at its head, another possible campsite.

Mayne Passage, the upper part of which is known as Blind Channel, comes in from the south. It has a small settlement on West Thurlow Island's east coast, in a small bay about 1.5 miles south of the Cordero Islands. Water, laundry, showers, groceries (with homemade bread for sale), liquor, a post office, and an excellent restaurant nestle in the resort. Three trails lead into an old-growth cedar rain forest whose crowning attraction is the 800-year-old "grandfather cedar" a full 20 feet in diameter! If you're venturing into Blind Channel, tidal and current effects should be kept in mind. Rips and eddies can develop, especially in the narrower part during full-on ebb or flood. Think of this area as Upper (or Lower, depending on the tide) Greene Point Rapids.

Greene Point Rapids: Camping at the head of Greene Point Rapids puts you in a very favorable position to negotiate the difficulties at your convenience (slack, of course). Tidal streams can reach 7 knots. Plan on traversing during the slack following a flood. By the time you're through, you'll be going with the flow for a good six hours. Stick to the north shore. If the tide was high enough, you'll even be able to sneak through the tiny channel separating the westernmost Cordero Island from the mainland. If not, slip around the south side of that island. Greene Point Rapids intensifies with the size of the tide. Overfalls, whirlpools, and eddies wane and surge. On spring tides, a fairly stationary whirlpool 200 yards south of Griffiths Islet Light is the center of the action, dropping 3 feet for a width of 60 to 75 feet. West of Greene Point, Cordero remains narrow, and so the current stays strong for the remainder of its length.

Five miles west of the Cordero Islands, Loughborough Inlet joins Cordero Channel to form Chancellor Channel, bounded on the north by the mainland's Franklyn Range and on the south by West Thurlow Island. Loughborough has been extensively logged; because of its configuration, it can channel winds down Chancellor. Currents in Chancellor seldom exceed 2 knots. Campsites are about as common as coral reefs. One possibility, flat but not very aesthetic, is logging operation landings and clearings (both abandoned and still operative—if there are any).

D'Arcy Point (mile 200/**350**) marks the junction of Wellbore Channel with Chancellor Channel. You can continue down Chancellor and join Johnstone Strait in about 4 miles or go up Wellbore and avoid Johnstone for another 14 miles. The main route goes north; the alternate south route, described immediately after the point of convergence, is 1 mile shorter. Factors to bear in mind when choosing which route to take should include proposed camp location and weather, sea state, and the time of day for the crossing of Johnstone Strait. All other things

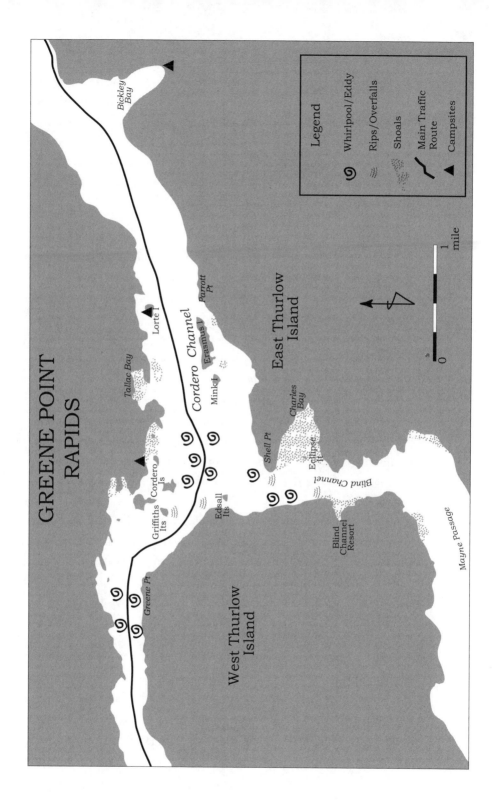

GREENE POINT RAPIDS

Bickley Bay

Tallac Bay

Greene Pt

Griffiths Itts

Cordero Itts

Lorte I

Cordero Channel

Edsall Itts

Mink I

Erasmus I

Parrott Pt

Shell Pt

Charles Bay

Eclipse I

Blind Channel

Blind Channel Resort

West Thurlow Island

East Thurlow Island

Mayne Passage

Legend

Whirlpool/Eddy	
Rips/Overfalls	
Shoals	
Main Traffic Route	
Campsites	

0   1
mile

being equal, the best time to venture across is early in the morning just before or at the start of an ebbing neap tide. Review the description of Johnstone just ahead to better decide on a strategy for your crossing.

Hang a right at D'Arcy Point into Wellbore Channel. Wellbore bypasses Current and Race Passages (on the alternate route), where wind against current—especially in the afternoon—can cause heavy tide rips. Two-thirds of the way up Wellbore, Carterer Point constricts the channel and creates Whirlpool Rapids.

Whirlpool Rapids: Whirlpool is the mildest rapid encountered. Still, whirlpools, upwellings, and strong back eddies occur. The best time to traverse is during a waning ebb. Wait for a propitious time, if you need to, at the small cove just south of Carterer Point. The window of opportunity here is broader than at Yuculta and Greene Point Rapids, particularly when the tides and currents are not large. Stick to the west shore so as to avoid the converging tidal influence out of Forward Harbour.

Once around Althorp Point, enter Sunderland Channel. Tidal Streams at Sunderland's east end seldom exceed 1.5 knots. Unfortunately, we found no possible campsites along Hardwicke's north shore until nearly its very end. Salmon farms abound. Some possible campsites might exist at either head of Bessborough Bay, around Thynne Point on the mainland.

Near the western end of Hardwicke Island, three small bights indent the shore. A small island connected to Hardwicke via a picturesque tombolo divides the easternmost cove. This isthmus is an artfully rendered and proportioned campsite. Tombolo camp (mile 212/**362**), as we called it, appeared just in the nick of time at the end of a long, 21-mile day. Does the tide cover it? Neap tides do not. I don't know about spring tides or intermediate tides. It didn't for us but it might for you. Apply the "rule of 12s."

The Rule of 12s: A basic tide cycle runs about twelve hours. For six hours the tide rises; for the other six hours it falls. For each six-hour half cycle, tides will advance or retreat half their distance during the middle two hours. During each of the first and last two-hour intervals the tide moves only one-quarter of its height. (For a more in-depth

Tombolo camp, Johnstone Strait, British Columbia

explanation of the "rule of 12s" and its application to campsite selection, see "Gauging High Tides: The Rule of 12s" by Bob Hume in *Sea Kayaker*, June 1999.)

Two miles farther, off the western tip of Hardwicke Island, lies Yorke Island (mile 214/**364**), the last possible campsite before Johnstone Strait. Yorke was a WWII military installation with gun emplacements. Two buildings remain, halfway up the slope on the southwest side.

Johnstone Strait: Johnstone Strait is the main tidal and shipping thoroughfare of the Inside Passage along this section. Crossing it is a big deal. Currents run 1–3 knots at the west end and increase to 2–4 knots near Hardwicke Island. During the spring freshet—May and June, mostly—when mainland rivers disgorge immense volumes of snowmelt, the fresh water runoff can be so strong that it sometimes overpowers the surface currents of flood tides, giving the impression of a continuous ebb. However, in high summer, the northwest winds prevalent during periods of high pressure tend to increase the flood and reduce the duration of the ebb tide.

To say that chop can be a problem here is a gross understatement. After the intimate channels and passages you've just navigated, Johnstone Strait is sobering. This is the ocean and it's big. Sometimes there is even locally generated swell from day upon day of pummeling wind. Add a contrary tide, some freshening erratic gusts, rain, and a sprinkling of slow tugs and fast cruise ships whose exact course and speed are indeterminate and pretty soon you're in full conditions.

Johnstone Strait must at some point be crossed. The question is, when? Three options present themselves. From east to west: (1) Tyee Point on West Thurlow Island to Vancouver Island, 1 mile—on the alternate route, and described immediately following; (2) Hardwicke Point on Hardwicke Island to Vancouver Island, 1.5 miles; and (3) at the west end of the strait, island-hopping across the Malcolm Island group where no crossing is greater than 1 mile. The last crossing is in the final portion of the Vancouver Island section and will be fully described there. Generally, crossing conditions intensify west to east, so the safest, easiest traverse is over by Alert Bay. However, coming from the east, you might encounter ideal conditions sooner and take advantage of them.

If, like us, you decide to cross Johnstone Strait from the Yorke Island/Hardwicke Point area, set forth early, preferably at slack or during the ebb. The cross-channel distance here, being 1.5 miles, is but a mere half hour.

Alternate Route: D'Arcy Point (mile 200/350) to Yorke Island (mile 214/364) via the south coast of Hardwicke Island

At D'Arcy Point decide whether to favor the Hardwicke Island coast or head south along the West Thurlow Island shore and across Johnstone Strait to Vancouver Island. Both have advantages and disadvantages. First, the northern option along the south coast of Hardwicke Island.

Cross the mouth of Wellbore Channel and hug Hardwicke Island's south shore to rejoin the main route at Hardwicke Point/Yorke Island, where camping is possible as described above on the main route. Helmcken Island, dividing Johnstone into Current and Race Passages, has a possible campsite in its north cove—a cabin and old logging operation along the bight's south shore. Tidal streams in Current Passage run 3–5 knots, so be sure to go with the flow and be wary if crossing over to Helmcken.

Now for the southern option, which heads directly for Vancouver Island. Head for Shorter Point on the north shore of West Thurlow Island, if you're not already coasting that shore. Turn Eden Point, making for Vere Cove and Tyee Point, which are good locations to observe conditions in Johnstone Strait. Ripple Shoal, a mile west of Tyee Point, can be an exaggerated microcosm of general conditions in the Strait.

The crossing of Johnstone Strait from Tyee Point is only 1 mile (see *Johnstone Strait* above). Soon after hitting Vancouver Island, you'll arrive at Camp Point (mile 206/**356**) which, as the name implies, has a grassy meadow suitable for camping. Beyond Camp Point, Hkusam Mountain steepens the coast along Race Passage. Just as in Current Passage, it is best to go with the flow in Race where currents run 3–6 knots.

Five miles farther west, around Graveyard Point, Salmon Bay, the estuary of the Salmon River, deeply indents the shore. Old ship hulks in the MacMillan Bloedel logging area form a breakwater. Kelsey Bay and Sayward are small logging settlements with a few stores and an RCMP detachment along the western verge of Salmon Bay. Rejoin the main route a few miles west of Kelsey Bay.

Main Route: Continued . . .

Johnstone Strait is not a body of water you'd zigzag back and forth across impulsively. Best to pick a side, north shore or south shore, and stick to it. At Johnstone's west end, where the main waterway segues into Queen Charlotte Strait, the Malcolm Island group provides a nifty series of steppingstones over to the Vancouver Island shore which, in due course, must be joined in order to reach Port Hardy. First, the north or mainland side of Johnstone Strait.

North Shore of Johnstone Strait

From Yorke Island hop over to Clarence, then Fanny Island and cross the mouth of Sunderland Channel. Sunderland's strongest currents, up to 4 knots—sometimes with heavy rips at the verges—occur here.

Check tide intervals and conditions before venturing across this 1-mile stretch.

Aim for the white cliffs by Tuna Point. Around the point, inside Blenkinsop Bay (mile 215/**365**), camping is possible. Cross the mouth of Blenkinsop to Point George and continue west between the mainland and Jesse Island. Round the Hardy Peak peninsula to Ransom Point and the entrance to Port Neville. Tidal streams at the entrance can attain 3 knots. Half a mile up the entrance from Ransom Point is the old Port Neville settlement. Before the completion of the Trans-Vancouver Island Highway, Port Neville was an important local marine outpost. The handsome two-story log store closed in 1960 but remains in excellent condition. The family, homesteaders since 1891, still run the small post office. Artist Peggy Sowden maintains an arts and crafts gallery on the hill across from the public dock. You can even commission a watercolor of your expedition.

Weave your way west between Neville Point and Milly Island. Round Nelson Ridge. This coast is steep; the native peoples referred to it as "(stone walls) put up on side of beach." Pass Stimpson Point and make for the Broken Islands (mile 230/**380**), a refreshing little gunkholing archipelago with, reportedly, some great campsites. The stretch between Neville Point and the Broken Islands is considered one of the windiest portions of Johnstone Strait.

Cross the entrance to Havannah Channel and Port Harvey, heading toward Forward Bay. Tlingit and Haida raids on the Gulf Islands and Puget Sound inhabitants were common before the incursion of Europeans. In the late 1860s, a British naval detachment caught up with a Haida raiding party that had attacked Saltspring Island. They were on the lam in Forward Bay. Swift but measured retribution followed. Such consistent and predictable response soon brought the raids to an end.

Continue along the south coast of West Cracroft Island to Boat Bay (mile 240/**390**), home base for the Robson Bight Patrol. Observers use the wooden platform and telescope on the point to monitor boat and orca activity across the strait in the reserve. There is a good campsite at the head of the bay.

South Shore of Johnstone Strait

If you crossed Johnstone Strait over to Vancouver Island from either Yorke Island or Tyee Point on West Thurlow Island, I last left you somewhere west of Kelsey Bay making toward Hickey Point along steep Newcastle Ridge. Like the route along the north shore, camping along this shore is also tenuous. Camp Point (mile 206/**356**), the last camp along this south shore, is 26 miles from the next certain campsite, Naka Creek (mile 235/**385**). Few distinctive landmarks other than St. Vincent Bight and the Adam River estuary break the sameness of the coastal physiognomy. Much of the immediate shore resembles the high cutbank of the current side of a swift river, which in some sense it is. Occasional abandoned logging operation clearings and road termini provide at least one intermediate campsite, near mile 225/**375**, depending on how extensively the alders have recolonized the clearings.

About halfway between Naka Creek and Robson Bight, Schmidt Creek (or perhaps a smaller creek farther west) reportedly has a small, campable pebble shelf above the high-tide line. These are the last camps before Robson Bight along the south shore of Johnstone Strait, though there are more immediately afterward. According to John Ince and Hedi Kottner, a couple of less well-known whale-rubbing beaches are situated just east of Robson Bight. One is the small indentation 1 mile east of the easternmost point of Robson Bight, while the second is a mile farther east from the first, at another small bay.

Queen Charlotte Strait: Robson Bight *(mile 240/390)* to Port Hardy *(mile 287/437)*

Beyond Robson Bight, local traffic noticeably increases. The Vancouver Island Highway reaches the coast at Telegraph Cove, providing access for small craft—including many kayak tour groups—to the Broughton Archipelago and the Robson Bight whale-watching areas. The communities of Alert Bay, Sointula, and Port NcNeill punctuate the passage. Camping, while pretty much still at will, requires a bit more discretion. As the coastal ranges diverge, the immediate lay of the land flattens and

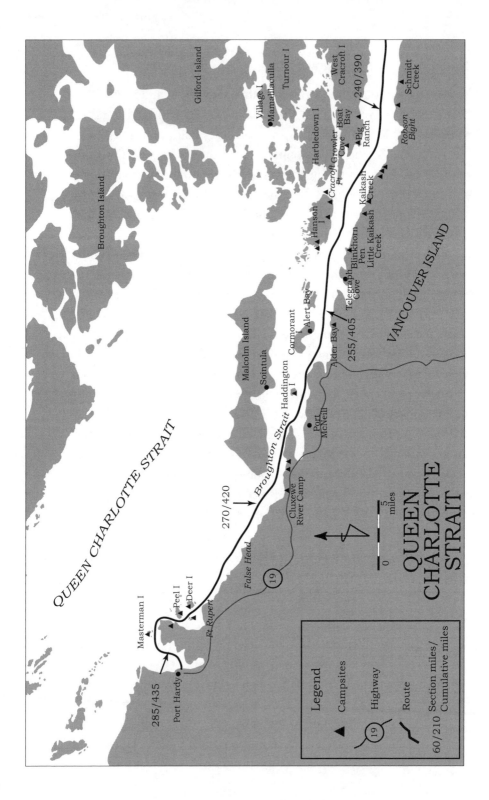

QUEEN CHARLOTTE STRAIT

Gilford Island

Turnour I

Village I
Mamalilacilla

West
Cracroft I

Schmidt
Creek

240/390

Broughton Island

Harbledown I

Growler Boat
Cove Bay

Cracroft Pt

Pig
Ranch

Robson
Bight

Kaikash
Creek

Hanson
I

Little Kaikash
Creek

Blinkhorn
Pen

Telegraph
Cove

Malcolm Island

Cormorant

Sointula

Haddington

Alert Bay

Alder Bay

255/405

VANCOUVER ISLAND

QUEEN CHARLOTTE STRAIT

270/420

Broughton Strait

Port
McNeill

Chuxewe
River Camp

False Head

19

Masterman I

Peel I

Deer I

Ft. Rupert

285/435

Port Hardy

0   5
          miles

QUEEN
CHARLOTTE
STRAIT

Legend

▲ Campsites

19 Highway

Route

60/210 Section miles/
        Cumulative miles

camping opportunities increase. The broadening Charlotte basin also weakens currents, easing tidal timing concerns.

Johnstone Strait terminates and becomes Broughton Strait, at which point the north and south shore routes rejoin. About halfway through this section at the tip of Malcolm Island, Broughton Strait joins Charlotte Strait. If you're lucky you'll see some orcas.

Orcas

Orcinus orca, also known as the killer whale, is a member of the dolphin family. Their seductive neoteny and atavistic appeal belie a predatory carnivorous palate, unique for a cetacean and catholic in its scope that includes fish, birds, squid, turtles, and marine mammals. The strikingly dramatic black-and-white, bipolar coloration is probably an adaptation providing camouflage, depending on the perspective of the viewer. Seen looking up from the depths, the white belly blends well with the light-colored rendition of the sky on the water's surface. Seen from above, the black back mimics the dark hues of the surface's light-refractive opacity.

Orcas may live more than 50 years and are very convivial, often traveling in matrilineal pods of 3 to 40 individuals and communicating with a wide variety of sounds. They often cooperate in hunting and feeding efforts. Adults average 25 feet in length. A marked sexual dimorphism, with males nearly twice the size of females, and further emphasized by the disparity in both the shape and size of the dorsal fins, indicates a polygamous family structure. Mating and birth occur year-round, with a gestation of 13–16 months.

Nearly 30 different extended family groups—pods—consisting of more than 300 individuals, total, range along the Inside Passage. (Some estimates are as high as 1,000.) About half frequent Johnstone Strait during the summer. "Residents" consume mainly fish, while "transients" seem to favor marine mammals. The two do not mix and even have their own vocal dialects. Orcas have a curious habit of self-grooming involving rubbing their sides and bellies close to shore on established "rubbing beaches" to rid themselves of parasites. Perhaps it just feels good. The most famous rubbing beach is at the mouth of the Tsitika River in Robson Bight.

Robson Bight: Plans to log the Tsitika watershed and boom logs in Robson Bight galvanized the B.C. government to protect this important whale habitat. In 1982 the Robson Bight (Michael Biggs) Ecological Reserve was established. Approximately 1.5 miles on each side of the Tsitika River and 0.5 mile offshore from the flanking headlands are closed to recreational traffic. Landing is not allowed.

Just what effect kayakers and other boaters have on orcas has not been systematically studied. In spite of the caveats in chapter 2, paddlers are inexorably drawn to these magnificent beasts. Many don't consider a simple sighting satisfying and strive for a poster-quality photograph of a closer encounter. Even if you're not concerned for your own safety, at least for the whales' sake, observe the following guidelines:

- Paddle no closer than 100 yards.
- Approach whales slowly and from the side.
- Remember that under section 71(A)(2) of the Canadian federal fisheries regulations it is illegal "to disturb or molest orcas."
- Limit your visit with any group to no more than 30 minutes.

Dances with Rangers I

It was as tranquil, windless, and clear a day as Johnstone Strait seldom but gloriously sometimes serves up. Solitary gulls, their squawks eerily amplified by the silence, languidly glided by, occasionally plopping down in our vicinity. Little groups of grebes, minding their own business, tried to ignore us, but the tension precipitated by our four kayaks inevitably gave way to repeated subsurface evasive scuttling. About a half mile from shore, adjusting to a lazy, post-lunch paddle in glassy conditions, we each sought our own space and rhythm. Contentment overrode conversation. Yet, beneath the surface, anticipation brewed muted excitement so we remained relatively close to each other. Robson Bight was just ahead. If ever there was a perfect place and moment to encounter orcas at close range, this was it.

We were aware of the Bight's ecological reserve status and visitation restrictions but were unsure as to its exact boundaries, as buoys do not mark them. Three fishing boats between shore and our heretofore projected course implied that we were well outside the boundaries of the reserve. Lance wasn't so sure. A quick conference among us failed to yield unanimity as to a course. He sensed that something was amiss and chose to head farther out, toward midchannel. Cat, Tina, and I continued bearing for the fishing boat nearest shore. Not a whale was in sight.

Before long our reverie was disturbed by the low hum of an outboard. A Zodiac, under full throttle, was approaching from West Cracroft Island and pretty soon skidded to a sideways halt next to me. A giant, in full orange exposure suit with red hair to match, manned the helm. In spite of the absence of any insignia of authority, I could tell something was up. Unfailingly and involuntarily, like Pavlov's dogs before food, my own conditioned responses to governmental scrutiny rose to the fore: guilt, fear, and vulnerability.

"Good afternoon," he greeted. I was struck by his stereotypical Canadianness: lantern jaw, inordinate proportions, lumbering grace, alabaster white skin, unthreatening mien, and unfailing courtesy: a veritable marine Sergeant Preston.

"Hello," I responded.

"Beautiful day to kayak, eh?" he retorted disarmingly. Canadians seem to go out of their way to avoid confrontation. We exchanged pleasantries. He asked about our trip, about us, putting off the purported reason for the visit until he was certain we were both comfortable with the situation. Then he asked me whether I was aware of my location and the regulations. I explained both my understanding of the regulations and the intent of the preserve and that we were uncertain as to its exact boundaries but thought that we were outside.

"You're actually a couple of hundred meters inside. Would you mind just angling out some?" he requested.

"Of course not," I responded.

In spite of the uneventful climax, something nagged at me. Something still didn't quite add up. All the pieces of the puzzle didn't quite fit. I asked him about the presence of the commercial fishing boats within the boundaries of the preserve.

Sergeant Preston paused while he searched for just the right words. With a straight face, the ranger explained that while kayaks can be very disconcerting to orcas, they are quite accustomed, even impervious, to fishing boats, motors, nets, and all. I was skeptical but passed up the opportunity to pursue the subject. Sometimes I know when to leave well enough alone.

Many miles later I uncovered the real dirt. Apparently the Articles of Canadian Confederation reserve the right to establish and maintain parks and preserves to the provinces. Navigation, shipping, and coastal fisheries, on the other hand, are the remand of the federal government. And there's the rub. Commercial fishermen do not recognize British Columbia's jurisdiction over potential fishing restrictions in the Robson Bight Preserve. Unwilling to push the issue until either the courts or the federal and provincial governments lay down some clearer guidelines, Sergeant Preston sticks to policing recreational boaters. Perhaps this jurisdictional impasse can soon be resolved to the benefit of all parties involved, particularly the orcas.

Past Robson Bight, both the south and north shore routes continue their separate trajectories until just past Port McNeill where they reunite. First the continuation of the north shore route.

North Shore of Johnstone Strait: Continued . . .

Out of Boat Bay, continue west around the light for 2 miles, at which point West Cracroft Island's coast turns north around a small point into a bight locally known as Pig Ranch (mile 243/**393**). Camping is best on the point, though the bay has a couple of tent pads and a small creek at the north end with dependable water. One mile farther north lies Growler Cove, another protected, though logged, campsite on the north shore on a small islet.

Continue on to Cracroft Point, the western extremity of West Cracroft Island and the entrance to Blackney Passage. Although beyond the scope of this guide, it is worth noting that Blackney Passage is the gateway to the Broughton Archipelago Provincial Marine Park, just due north.

Broughton Archipelago Provincial Marine Park: The center of the Broughton is a stunningly beautiful scatter of islands, coves, and protected passages with human occupation dating back a good 8,000 years. Much of it has been preserved as a provincial park while smaller portions remain Indian preserves. At the heart lies Mamalilaculla, an abandoned native village on Village Island. Fallen totems and ruined dwellings atop a 12-foot midden only hint at Mamalilaculla's importance. The village was the site of the last great potlatch in December of 1921. Hosted by Chief Dan Cranmer and lasting six days, it included more than 300 guests and many thousands of dollars worth of goods. The RCMP terminated the potlatch with prejudice under the infamous potlatch laws and prosecuted and jailed participants. All the goods, gifts, and artifacts were confiscated. New Vancouver on Harbledown Island and Mound Island also hold historic and prehistoric native sites. Check with the Mamaleleqala Que'Qwa'Sot'Enox band (250-287-2955) in Campbell River for regulations concerning visitation and camping on Indian reserve land.

From Cracroft Point, cross Blackney Passage over to Hanson Island. Currents in Blackney Passage can reach 5 knots during spring tides, so favor the wider entrance portion at the south end, where currents are not quite so strong (2–4 knots). During periods of strong opposing winds, overfalls and rips can occur off Cracroft Point.

Hanson Island: Hanson Island is home to two whale research stations and, on its north side, at least one floating fishing resort. Its first permanent settler was a Hawaiian native by the name of Kamano, who took up residence in 1885. He must have been an energetic and peripatetic entrepreneur (or a prolific father), as his name seems to be ubiquitous up and down the Inside Passage. On route along the south coast, Hanson boasts at least five different campsites. At mile 247/**397** there are two adjacent campsites. One is on the southern tip of the larger of the two islands off Hanson's east coast, while the second is just inside the small bay on the southeast corner of Hanson.

Two miles on, an unnamed bay (mile 249/**399**) indents the south shore of Hanson and also provides camping. At the southwest corner of the island a deep little bay defines the south shore of a prominent point (mile 251/**401**) just behind Weynton Island. Both the bay and the point are campable, though commercial kayak tour groups often use the latter. One more campsite on Hanson lies 1 mile due north from the latter one.

From Weynton Island, head due west across Weynton Passage to the Stephenson Islets, protected as a provincial park. Currents in Weynton Passage can attain 6 knots, so be wary. Aim for the Pearse Islands, another provincial park save for the west end of the largest island in the group, which is private. The waters around the Pearse Islands are particularly clear with underwater visibility sharp to a good 25 feet. Cross Pearse Passage to Gordon Bluff on Cormorant Island. Currents run 2 to 4 knots with extremes sometimes reaching 5 knots.

Cormorant Island: Boomerang-shaped Cormorant Island is a Nimpkish Indian Reserve and its capital, Alert Bay (mile 256/**406**) is well worth a visit. Many of the ceremonial potlatch goods confiscated during the 1914–1921 crackdown have been returned and are on exhibit at the U'Mista Cultural Center. One of the world's tallest totems, 175 feet high, anchors the town's center. All services, including camping, are available. Don't forget to visit Gator Gardens, a park displaying rain forest and cedar marsh flora.

Only 1 mile separates Yellow Bluff light on the southwest tip of Cormorant from Vancouver Island. Head for the unnamed, rounded point defining the northern verge of the Nimpkish River Delta across Broughton Strait and join the Vancouver Island, south shore of Johnstone Strait route near mile 259/**409**. Watch out for the Port McNeill–Sointula–Alert Bay ferry. Currents are not too consequential, just don't drift south into deltaic deposits.

South Shore of Johnstone Strait: Continued . . .

Continuing along the Vancouver Island shore, the paddling is relatively uneventful, with the homogeneity of the landscape broken only by watercourses. Campsites become more frequent.

Immediately west of the Robson Bight boundary lie three small campsites (mile 244/**394**), one right after the other. Though unmarked, the western boundary of the preserve can be accurately estimated. It lies about halfway between a prominent headland ("Old Man" to the natives) about 2 miles west of the Tsitika River and the waterfalls just past Old Man. The campsites are immediately west of the waterfall.

Continuing west, Kaikash Creek (mile 247/**397**) is very large, with room for nearly 30 tents, and very popular. Creek water, though dependable, must be treated. The B.C. Marine Trails Association and Ministry of Forests have installed a composting toilet. Another mile or so on is Little Kaikash (mile 248/**398**), another campsite intensively used by commercial kayak groups.

An hour's paddle west, the Blinkhorn Peninsula (mile 251/**401**) extrudes and indents the shore with two good pebble beaches, one on each side, which catch lots of winter driftwood. The name is apt: A light marks the tip, while the 185-foot hill hopefully shields the campsites from the not infrequent blasts from the foghorn. A creek provides water and there are some old buildings to explore. Cross Bauza Cove, round Ella point, and enter Telegraph Cove, 2 miles west of Blinkhorn.

Telegraph Cove: A short branch of the Vancouver Island Highway hits the sea here, and its influence is staggering after so many days in roadless areas. Coming in from the east, a new condo development far larger than the original stilted, cantilevered, and boardwalk-connected clapboard buildings jolts the senses. Originally established in 1911 as the island's northern connection with the outside world, Telegraph Cove soon developed a salmon saltery and small sawmill. Today tourism, both high and low impact, is causing a boom. With the popularity of kayaking, the whales of Robson Bight, and vehicular access, Telegraph Cove will not soon stop growing. Never mind. As you paddle up the cove, the sea level view of the old town is still charming, and the boardwalks worth a walkabout. All services (except seaside camping) are available.

Cross adjacent but much larger Beaver Cove—a major log booming and processing center and salmon hatchery—to Lewis Point. Halfway between the Kokish and Nimpkish Rivers, across from Alert Bay in a small bight, lies the Alder Bay Campground (mile 256/**406**), a private enterprise connected by road to the highway. Alder Bay has water, picnic tables, bathrooms, and even a kayak rental and tour company. Natives called the bight "Having Brant Geese."

You can hug the Vancouver Island shore for another mile west before turning sharply northwest to avoid the sand flats of the Nimpkish River delta. The flats foul and dry for up to a mile off the coast. Look for the two beacons that mark their edge and head for the rounded headland north of the river where this south shore route reconnects with the north shore variant near mile 259/**409**.

From the junction of the routes, continue west toward Broad Point. Here you can choose your best course toward Ledge Point. Haddington Island (mile 262/**412**), at the epicenter of the Port McNeill–Sointula–Alert Bay ferry and general traffic pattern, has good camping. Port McNeill, with a population of 2,641, is a large town with all services except (you guessed it) handy kayak camping.

Just past Lady Ellen Point, two road-accessible campsites (mile 267/**417**), in quick succession, front the shore. A third site (mile 268/**418**) at the Cluxewe River mouth also has water and toilets. Enter Queen Charlotte Strait. Beyond the Cluxewe River, not only does the intermittent hustle and bustle of this section abate (you'll find yourself blessedly isolated), but the shore also becomes devoid of landmarks, demanding navigation by chronometer and dead reckoning. Due to a shoal and a shallowing and level foreshore, even False Head is rather indistinct. Yet, as you approach Thomas Point, with the Port Hardy airport clearly visible, civilization and the terminus of this portion of the Inside Passage loom nigh.

Whether in order to delay your departure, simply crown your achievement, or just make up for the unprepossessiveness of Port Hardy—after all, the Indians variously referred to it as "Bad Smell Coming Out of It," "Bent Crotch Beach," and "Face Hanging"—Mother Nature has laid a sumptuous banquet along these last dozen miles.

Past Thomas Point the land rises, a score of islands appear, the coastline sinuously beckons, wildlife comes out of hiding, and even white, sandy beaches at the head of shallow coves lure like seductive naiads. The contrast with the previous dozen miles could hardly be greater.

Thomas Point guards the south entrance to Beaver Harbour, a large bay protected from the outside by a half dozen island groups and the setting of Fort Rupert, a Hudson's Bay Company trading post established in 1849. Unless you're planning to visit the native village (population 33), aim for Peel Island. Deer Island (mile 280/**430**), just to starboard, has a great campsite around the corner on its north shore. But the white sandy cove on the south end of Peel Island (mile 281/**431**), conspicuously on target since rounding Thomas Point, is difficult to detour away from. Truly an exceptional campsite. The Cattle Islands, between Deer and Peel, also have good campsites.

Round Peel Island, cross Daedalus Passage, and graze the lovely shore of The Seven Hills peninsula. Watch for puffins. The cove—variously known as Herald Rock or Basket Eater (mile 282/**432**), its head invisible from its mouth—flirts with one's curiosity. Inside there's a campsite with picnic table and an old trail out to Dillon Point.

Rounding Dillon Point, the Masterman Islands (mile 283/**433**), the last campsite before Port Hardy, appear. As you arc around the blunt peninsula, bejeweled by reefs, rocks, and islets, spare a glance at the subsurface environment. The water is particularly clear here. Orange and purple starfish splay about. Anemones, plump to their tentacle tips, quiver like fingers hungry for a piano.

Port Hardy: Past Daphne Point, you enter Hardy Bay. Port Hardy, the end of the line (for now), comes into full view. Whether you're target-fixated on the end or reluctant to terminate the reverie, practical considerations impinge. Head for the densest concentration of buildings and boats, the central part of the town with the wharf complexes. As shore detail emerges, angle toward the location of your vehicle. If you've left your vehicle at the Sunny Sanctuary, there are two options. (1) If the tide is flooding and near peak, head directly for Sunny Sanctuary at the southwest corner of Hardy Bay. Be aware that the inner recess of the bay dries to mud flats at all but high tides. (2) Get as close to your vehicle as you can and walk the remaining short distance. Although a road fronts the bay's western edge, mud and steep (albeit short) gradients can be an obstacle to a clean exit. Walk the short distance to Sunny Sanctuary.

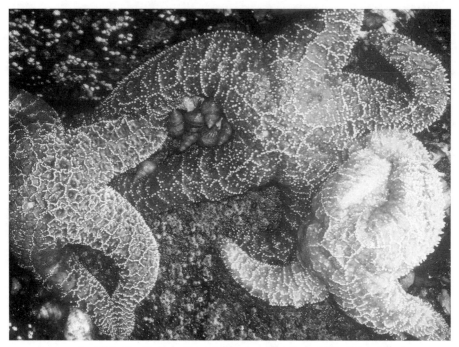

Starfish, Hardy Bay, Queen Charlotte Strait, British Columbia

Port Hardy is a medium-sized city with a population near 5,000 that relies, as its motto proudly states, on fishing, logging, and mining. Tourism ought to be added. It is the informal capital of northern Vancouver Island, founded in 1912 as a store and post office. The Hardy Bay Land Company immediately offered cheap land to attract settlers. Many were disappointed by the gloom of the Augean forest, the chill, and the wet. By 1920 there was a school, a church, and a sawmill, but the town grew very slowly for the next 50 years. When a copper mine opened in the 1970s, the population boomed to its present size. All services are available, including two large grocery stores, Overwaitea and Giant Foods. The Port Hardy Museum, at 7110 Market Street, displays artifacts from the early Danish settlement and, of special note (see chapter 5), results of the archaeological investigations at the ferry dock dating from 8,000 BC.

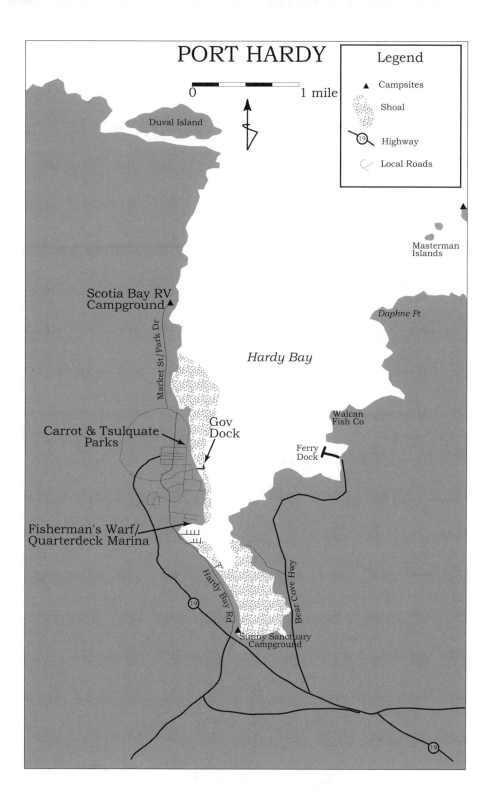

5

Central British Columbia

Port Hardy to Prince Rupert

331 miles

> *Wilderness is like first love:*
> *beguiling, seductive, addictive;*
> *humiliating, terrifying, sublime.*
> —R. H. M.

Dances with Rangers II

We'd found Louis Pasteur's observation, that "chance favors the prepared mind," to be spot on and its inverse, chance overwhelms the unprepared, doubly damning. Well, chance wasn't going to chop us up. We'd done our homework. Or so we thought, until we ran into Todd, a Canadian paddler out of Prince Rupert. So intimidated was Todd by the map's rendition of Grenville Channel that he detoured 40 miles around it into Principe Channel. Fear is contagious.

The 45-mile-long Grenville Channel, on the map, looked about as inviting as submitting to an MRI. Its laser straightness is correspondingly narrow, sometimes a scant quarter mile compressed by closely spaced, multiple contour lines with sirenic names such as Countess of Dufferin Range. Only one irregularity, Lowe Inlet, sticking out like a goiter on a giraffe, disrupted Grenville's symmetry. Were the shores landable? Would this southeast–northwest-trending canyon funnel and exacerbate prevailing blows? Would the tidal surges be navigable? None of this had crossed our minds.

We agonized and reassessed. Dignity went out the door; we offered passersby twice the going rate for large-scale charts of Grenville and

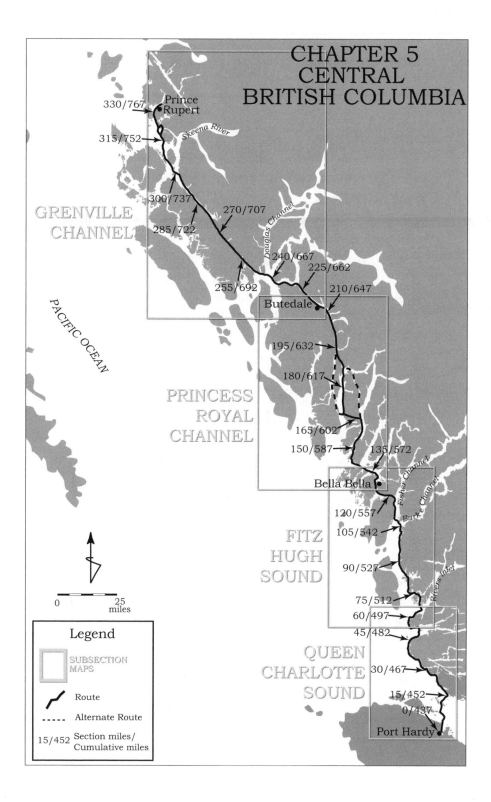

CHAPTER 5
CENTRAL
BRITISH COLUMBIA

330/767 Prince
Rupert

315/752

Skeena River

300/737

270/707

285/722

Douglas Channel

GRENVILLE
CHANNEL

240/667

225/662

255/692

210/647

Butedale

PACIFIC OCEAN

195/632

180/617

PRINCESS
ROYAL
CHANNEL

165/602

150/587

135/572

Bella Bella

Fisher Channel

120/557

Burke Channel

105/542

FITZ
HUGH
SOUND

90/527

75/512

Rivers Inlet

60/497

45/482

QUEEN
CHARLOTTE
SOUND

30/467

15/452

0/437

Port Hardy

0   25
      miles

Legend

SUBSECTION
MAPS

Route

- - - - Alternate Route

15/452 Section miles/
        Cumulative miles

begged for any scrap of information that might refute Todd's assessment. Exactly halfway up the channel, Lowe Inlet appeared to offer a safe harbor. With a freshly re-researched, seemingly sound strategy, we decided to rely on Lowe. Prescience, however, is a flaky friend that fails randomly and often.

The run to the inlet, going with the tide and very early, proved uneventful. Lowe was all that we expected: beautiful, calm, with three open and serviceable campsites at the head where the Kuwowdah River cascades in two majestic tiers into Nettle Basin. Two classic sailboats were anchored within its protected walls. We paddled over to the first flat spot, guarded by the scant remains of a long-defunct enterprise—a scatter of old pilings. Camouflaged in the shadows was a brown bear working the shore. Not a good omen.

The second campsite, near the base of the falls, was too close to the first for safety, so we aimed for the third. However, along the way we noticed a black bear rummaging in the undergrowth at the second site. Conditions weren't improving.

On the way to the third campsite we passed next to one of the anchored sailboats. "Looking for a place to camp?" one of the crew hailed.

"Yeah. Seen any bears over in that grassy area [the third prospect]?" we asked. He told us a grizzly had been showing up every evening to graze the young grass shoots.

All of a sudden, short of begging for deck space, our plans had been shot through with a big gaping hole. The crewmember sensed our dismay and told us to inquire at the other sailboat, a dark, ivy green schooner. A Canadian fisheries warden, busy on shore at a small, steep, thickly wooded peninsula, skippered the aptly named *Grizzly Bear*. We made our way over to him. Lashing on to his tender, a tiny inflatable with an outboard, we scrabbled our way toward the din of his task.

"You're in luck today!" the warden declared expansively. Kent was tall, honest, and handsome, a very fit over-sixty. He was busy froeing fir shingles for a new outhouse. "I've just finished this warden's cabin and you're welcome to use it. You're kayakers, eh? There are bears everywhere. Want to see one up close? Unload your kit and come over after dinner for tea, and Joannie [his wife] and I'll take you over for a closer look."

A sudden sense of relief deflated our qui vive. Kent finished shingling the outhouse roof, noted that we'd be the first to christen it, and nailed up a plaque over the cabin's small porch: Lowe Budget Motel. Then he took his leave. "See you in a few hours."

Kent and Joannie were instinctively self-reliant. They had homesteaded northern British Columbia's interior forests in the early 1960s but, discovering a greater affinity for building than farming, sold the homestead. Then they did it again, from scratch. The completion of the second homestead coincided with their children's maturity. After selling the second farm, they decided to homestead in a totally different place: the sea. Plans for the *Grizzly Bear* were commissioned to a naval architect. Kent and Joannie built it together. From scratch.

As planned, we went over for tea, brewed on the schooner's four-burner woodstove, and visited. As a federal fisheries warden, Kent undertakes a variety of tasks, including fish counting. I asked him just exactly how does one go about counting fish for a ministry? He explained that he either actually walks an entire stream course or random-samples sections. As he walks—mostly in the streambed—he has a digital counter in each hand and a third, ongoing mental count, for different varieties of salmon. This informs the government about the vibrancy of the salmon stocks. I was about to ask about the uncounted varieties when instead I asked about fish-counting bear encounters.

"That's a point of contention in this job," he said. Totally engrossed in the count, eyes scanning the streambed for fish and footing, he'd run into more bears than he cared to recall. Luckily he was usually the more startled at the standoff, but the whole experience was a bit too unnerving. He needed someone to ride shotgun, literally. The government wasn't about to expand the budget to include security for fish counters. So Kent hired Joannie out of his own pocket.

After tea the four of us piled into the tiny tender to get a closer look at the grizzly feeding on the young grass shoots. The little Avon was no bigger than a sheet of plywood sprouting a podium-style helm amidships. By 10 PM it was barely dusk. Kent turned the temperamental engine over four or five times before it cranked to life, and off we went to see the bear, a very large male. He was sitting on his haunches, facing the water, pulling grass out by the roots with alternate sweeps of his front paws and munching slowly and contentedly each pawful. He was oblivious—to us, our scent, the tender, the engine noise, to everything but each burst of tender young shoot flavor. He looked like the Emperor Nero at a banquet.

Kent cut the engine. The bear didn't seem to notice. With the wind at our backs, we drifted closer. I noticed that the foreshore below us had shallowed to just a few inches. Mr. Bear was now less than 50 feet away. Frankly, I was beginning to get nervous. We had no gun or pepper spray and were about to run aground at the feet of Jabba the Hutt, trusting our escape to a neurotic outboard that required foreplay. Surely one of the women would speak up.

We drifted within 40 feet of the bear. I repeated to myself that Kent knew what he was doing—after all, he was a game and fisheries warden. At 30 feet, the women still hadn't spoken up while I was rocking from one butt cheek to the other. "Kent, we don't want to disturb the bear, do we?" I finally stammered.

"He's too busy eating to care. We'll go over for a closer look at the falls." Kent pulled the cord on the motor. It caught the third time. He turned the Avon around, actually getting even closer to the bear during the maneuver—still no reaction at 20 feet, and off we went.

At 10–20 feet in height (depending on the tide's cycle) and leaning about 60 degrees, Verney Falls was a showcase for the salmon run. Already, at this early stage of the run, you could aim your camera, shoot randomly and be certain to catch at least one fat fish jumping. Perhaps that explained the bear density. At the height of the run, the fish are so dense that those in the water would damage your prop while those jumping in the air would certainly cold-cock you. And the bears—even more by the height of the run—are so busy fishing, they ignore both each other and human observers. But by then it was getting late so we headed back to the *Grizzly Bear,* our kayaks, and the snug warden's cabin.

Native Peoples

Kent's duties included law enforcement. He was at Lowe Inlet as a show of force. While there he was to build the "Lowe Budget Motel," a cabin, as a permanent, seasonally manned outpost. Native poaching at Verney Falls during the spawn had become a serious problem. The warden's presence was meant to be a deterrent.

It wasn't the first time natives had exploited the salmon run at Verney. Right next to the Kumowdah River's mouth, on the north side, lies a small, sandy bight. At the bight's mouth, just where the overflow of salmon waiting to jump the falls would congregate, lies an old underwater fish weir constructed out of standing rocks. It is plainly visible at lower tides. A wide arc, several dozen feet in diameter and too regular and strategically located to be natural, it was undoubtedly further enhanced with wooden frame members. During the run, one-way mazes and falling tides would trap fish within the enclosure. The stranded salmon could then be picked manually or with double-headed harpoons. Salted and smoked, the fish would easily last a year and constituted the natives' primary dietary staple.

Oolichan, a small, silvery fish also known as candlefish, because it is so engorged with oil that it will combust when held near a fire, was also a mainstay of the Northwest Coast economy. These were (and are) netted and rendered for their rich oil—definitely an acquired taste yet considered a great delicacy. Today, along the Nass River near the Alaskan border, the Nishga still harvest the oolichan during the great runs in March and April.

Numerous shell middens (incongruous white sand beaches) up and down the Inside Passage indicate an important reliance on shellfish, primarily clams and mussels. Halibut, those giant, one-sided bottom dwellers, were taken with large, elaborately carved, baited and weighted, wood and bone hooks. Seals, sea lions, dolphins, and sea otters were speared from canoes. The Haida, Nootka, and Makah even undertook whaling expeditions from their canoes. "Grease trails"— trading routes with interior tribes—provided a venue for the conversion of food surpluses into locally scarce, imported goods.

Archaeological evidence for Northwest Coast habitation goes back about 10,000 years. Sites at both extreme ends, at Dalles, Oregon, and at Ground Hog Bay village, Glacier Bay, Alaska, have been carbon-dated to 8,000 BC.

Namu, smack in the middle of the Inside Passage, has also rendered three dates clustered around 8,000 BC. Bear Cove, next to Port Hardy (where the ferry terminal is located), and Lawn Point, on the east coast of Graham Island in the Queen Charlottes, yield dates of similar antiquity.

Prior to the arrival of the Europeans, there was no wilderness. All the land along the Inside Passage was accounted for, claimed, and geographically subdivided into well-defined political entities with attendant property rights. White traders were annoyed to discover that even the taking of firewood or fresh water required payment to *someone.* These entities were independent of each other and had a "capital" village, with a contiguous, resource-rich, rural hinterland. Within each village-state, called a *qwan* by the Tlingit, settlement patterns followed an annual cycle determined by salmon runs, seasonal harvests, and the hunt. During winter, the population of each *qwan* would congregate in the principal village, while in summer, smaller groups would disperse to seasonal camps to exploit cyclical resources. Permanent winter villages were located in sheltered bays, inlets, and river mouths, in close proximity to good fishing and where canoes could safely land.

These village-states lacked any tribal or national meta-organization other than constantly shifting military alliances and commercial arrangements buttressed by infrequent ceremonial get-togethers, linguistic affinities, and shared customs. Villages consisted of warehouse-scale longhouses—rectangular gabled buildings of massive post-and-beam construction sheathed with cedar planks. Longhouses were built next to each other facing the beach. Some particularly large towns, however, would have a second row of longhouses behind the first. One exceptionally large *qwan*, Chilkat, at the upper end of Lynn Canal, had four large villages. The largest of these, Klukwan, had 65 houses and about 600 residents. In 1854, British naval officer W. C. Grant described a typical Vancouver Island Indian village:

> *No pigstye could present a more filthy aspect than that afforded by the exterior of an Indian Village... They are generally placed on a high bank so as to be difficult of access to an attacking party, and their position is not unfrequently [sic] chosen*

(whether by chance or from taste) in the most picturesque sites . . . A few . . . oblong holes or apertures in the palisades (generally not above three feet high) constitute their means of egress and ingress. They seldom move about much on terra firma, but after creeping out of their holes at once launch their canoes and embark therein . . . A pile of cockle shells, oyster shells, fish bones, pieces of putrid meat, old mats, pieces of rag, and dirt and filth of every description (the accumulation of generations) is seen in the front of every village. Half-starved curs, cowardly and snappish, prowl about, occasionally howling. And the savage himself, notwithstanding his constant exposure to the weather, is but a moving mass covered with vermin of every description.

Generally speaking, when not engaged in fishing, they pass the greater portion of their time in a sort of torpid state, lying beside their fires. The only people to be seen outside are a few old women cleaning their wool or making baskets. Sometimes a group of determined gamblers are visible rattling their sticks, and occasionally some industrious old fellow mending his canoe . . . any unusual sound will bring the whole crew out to gaze . . . They may wrap their blankets around them, and then sit down on their haunches in a position peculiar to themselves. They are doubled up into the smallest possible compass, with their chin resting on their knees, and they look like so many frogs crouched on the dunghill aforesaid.

Political power was vested in the chief of each village-state. The chief's ascendancy was determined by a combination of hereditary rank (emphasized in the north) and wealth (more important farther south). A variety of inherited and merited ranks, from chief down to slave, stratified society, which itself was organized, in descending order, along moieties, clans, extended families, and nuclear families.

Moieties are the two equal halves into which all Northwest Coast societies are divided. These are formally named—the Haida, for example, were either "Raven" or "Eagle"—and were represented by totemic or heraldic crests. Moieties are exogamous, for example, a Raven must never marry another Raven. To this day membership in a moiety generates the same sort of loyalty, enthusiasm, and friendly rivalry that identification with a baseball team often does in New York. Family lineage was reckoned matrilineally, patrilineally, or bilaterally, depending on local custom. Clans are lineages (hyperextended families) whose members all trace their origin to a common ancestor, much like the Campbells and McDonalds of Scots Highland fame. These too are formally named and exogamous—a form of marriage restriction that inhibits incest. Abortion and parricide kept nuclear families small, as Mr. Grant again elaborates:

> *The natural duration of life among the savages is not long, seldom exceeding 50 years. Indeed, a gray-haired man is very rarely seen. This may be partly accounted for by the horrible custom (universally prevalent) of the sons and relatives killing their parents when he is no longer able to support himself... Sometimes the wretches commit this parricide of their own accord unquestioned, but generally a council is held on the subject at which the... medicine-man presides. Should they decide that the further existence of the old man is not for the benefit of the tribe, the judges at once carry their own sentence into execution. Death is produced by strangulation by means of a cord of hemp or sea weed.*
>
> *Not less horrible is the custom, very prevalent among the women, of endeavoring to extinguish life in the womb. From this and other causes premature births occur with great frequency. The native Indian woman seldom becomes the mother of more than two, and very rarely indeed of more than three little savages or savagesses. Whilst on the other hand, the half-bred woman is almost invariably extremely prolific.*

These "savages" could make for an intimidating encounter. They were tall (5 feet, 8 inches average in the north) and lean with stocky chests and muscular shoulders topped with broad heads and broad faces elaborately mutilated and made up either to attract or repel. When young, a male's nasal septum was pierced, and a ring or length of bone inserted. Small holes around the outer circumference of the ear displayed bits of wool or feathers, while ornaments of shell, stone, or teeth hung from the lobes. Facial hair, already light, was plucked, while the coiffure, parted in the middle and impregnated with grease, hung loose over the neck. In addition, women pierced their lower lips to display labrets sometimes spanning four inches. Tattoos and elaborate facial paintings rendered with a pigmented seal oil base completed the arrangement.

Like the British, the Northwest Coast Indians named their houses. The names were not humble or subtle: *House Which Thunder Rolls Across, House Other Chiefs Peer at from a Distance,* or the unforgettable *House People Are Ashamed to Look at as it is so Overpoweringly Great.* Inside the longhouses, families would stake out and partition portions with their paraphernalia. A central cooking area and smoke hole served all the residents. Plank flooring lined the whole structure, including a recessed lower level somewhere near the center. Northern longhouses averaged 3,000 square feet; in the south, bighouses might run to 30,000 square feet. Fifty to 200 individuals, usually members of a single clan, inhabited each dwelling. While spring, summer, and fall were taken up with economic activity, winter, with its constant precipitation, provided a time for creative indulgence and consumption. Elaborate theatrical productions, based on religious themes and employing smoke, trap doors, and crawl spaces for heightened dramatic effect, warded off cabin fever. While you can still visit a longhouse and witness some of these reenactments—for example, at Blake Island in Puget Sound—you'll never participate in a potlatch.

Extravagant parties—actually orgies of conspicuous consumption—with many subtle undercurrents, potlatches were held to celebrate a birth or marriage; commemorate the dead; settle a property dispute; soothe hurt feelings or humiliate a rival; formalize a succession line; dedicate a new longhouse; or punctuate any important event. The

Northwest Coast Indians seem to have fully understood that it is better to give than to receive, and though some income redistribution ensued (important in its own right), the social ascendancy of the host was the primary objective of any potlatch.

At the previously mentioned potlatch hosted by Dan Cranmer of Alert Bay in 1921, the chief entertained 300 guests and divided his vast wealth among them: more than 450 ceremonial items including masks, dance capes, and coppers (shieldlike symbols of wealth), 24 canoes, billiard tables, musical instruments, sewing machines, motorboats, 400 Hudson's Bay blankets, 1,000 sacks of flour, and food and drink commensurate with the occasion. Some feast throwers achieved a truly Zen state of disdain for material possessions by actually burning—instead of giving away—assets, including killing (prior to European contact) hapless slaves. Potlatches could last for days and leave the host materially destitute (albeit some reimbursement was inevitable in the course of reciprocal potlatches) but inestimably prosperous in repute and radiant in cynosure. Such was the gravity of the enterprise that individuals would seldom host more than two potlatches in a lifetime.

Scandalized by the wanton destruction of property, some of it contributed as relief or compensation for past injustices, and under the understandable impression that penury would ensue, thereby exacerbating a vicious feedback cycle, the British Columbian government outlawed the feasts in 1884. By the time potlatches were again legalized in 1951, the custom had waned.

Perhaps the most evocative artifact of Northwest Coast native traditions is the totem pole. Although present prior to the arrival of Europeans, totem poles were smaller, less elaborate, and not as ubiquitous. In spite of the various depredations suffered as a consequence of contact, a minor renaissance ensued with the tremendous increase in trade and exchange of ideas. Metal knives and soft western red cedar, coupled with artistic vision and acumen and leisure time, gave rise to the totem pole efflorescence that continues to this day.

Traditional totem poles rarely exceeded 60 feet and were usually incorporated into the design of a house as entry posts. They were totemic in intent, that is, they depicted a mystical relationship between a family or individual and a totem, an animal or plant with a particular significance to a family's lineage. Much like a family emblem or heraldic crest, it served as a symbol of family pride and a historical pictograph depicting its entire ancestral history. Few of these poles remain today, as most cedar logs decay within 60 to 80 years, though some in the Queen Charlottes are more than 100 years old.

After contact, totem pole iconography burst its bounds. The Nisga'a of the Tsimishian led the way. Freestanding welcome poles at the waterfront invited visitors; mortuary poles, implanted with a box of the honored individual's decomposed remains, honored a significant person; memorial poles, erected either to commemorate a deceased chief's accomplishments or, like the apocryphal Lincoln totem pole, to commemorate Alaska's purchase by the United States, marked a peoples' rites of passage. Shame poles, carved with upside-down figures, were temporary fixtures and are found only in museums today. Closely related are ridicule poles, T-shaped with self-satisfied, buffoonish carvings along the top, intended to deprecate an individual's actions or aspirations.

New totem poles are rarely constructed for traditional or neotraditional purposes, but are instead commissioned as art for college campuses, museums, public buildings, the private market, and as public art to honor the First Nations and their outstanding artistry.

Consider for a moment the above ornament, which separates minor thematic transitions in this book. Deceptively simple, understatedly elegant, and soothing in its perfection, what function does it serve? Just exactly what is it? In this context, it's an elaborate, overgrown punctuation mark, a period, reminiscent of the opening capitals of medieval manuscripts. Stylistically, there is nothing quite like it in the world. It is unambiguously and quintessentially a Northwest Indian art motif. José Cardero, expedition artist for Galiano and Valdes on the *Sutil* and *Mexicana* in 1789, noticed it. The motif crops up in several of his sketches.

It is difficult to pinpoint the essence of a motif, as each of its component parts can vary so widely. In its many renditions, it is the fundamental design unit of all Northwest Coast Indian art. Focusing on their perimeter shape, Franz Boas, encyclopedic chronicler of North America's vanishing aborigines at the turn of the 20th century, called them "eye designs." Bill Holm, a leading authority on Northwest Indian art, calls them "ovoids." The ovoid typically frames some dismembered, stylized body part such as an eye, a claw, the front teeth of a beaver, or the dorsal fin of a killer whale.

Even their shape can vary to rounder, more trapezoidal, rhomboid, or even parenthetical. Topologically, however, all variations remain equivalent. Perhaps these ovoids are akin to the modern plastic grocery bag, varying in shape and size according to its contents (always of a certain provenance) but ever identifiable and never confused with, say, a suitcase. On a decorated item such as a blanket, oolichan dish, chest, or bentwood box, ovoids tend to fill the entire surface area being decorated, leaving little or no blank background.

What muse inspired such symmetrical and pervasive artistic abstractions uniformly throughout the Northwest Coast? Jonathan Raban, in *Passage to Juneau*, speculates incisively that

> *the maritime art of these mostly anonymous Kwakiutl, Haida, and Tsishimian craftsmen appeared to me to grow directly from their observation of the play of light on the sea . . . I saw a water-hauntedness in almost every piece . . . The simplest way of retrieving order from chaos is to hold a mirror to it . . . [like a] kaleidoscope . . . In the sheltered inlets of the Northwest, the Indians faced constant daily evidence of the mirror of the sea as it doubled and patterned their untidy world . . . Sometimes, especially in the morning, the water of the inlets is as still as a pool of maple syrup, its surface tension unblemished by wind or tide: then it holds a reflection with eerie fidelity, with no visible edge or fold along the waterline.*

Raban is onto something. The ovoids are the spitting image of the variations in sea-surface tension observed from the bow of a canoe or the cockpit of a kayak. Note the water surface patterns on the accompanying photograph. Rendered upon a blank canvas, they evoke Antonio

Can you spot the ovoids in the water's surface tension? CREDIT: T. COBOS

Gaudi's artistic philosophy of abstractly replicating patterns found in nature. Inside the ovoids, the designs, sometimes stylized vestiges of body parts or abstract renditions, are a collage of reflected images.

Natural History

To the Kwakiutl, Nuxalk, Heiltsuk, Nisga'a, and Haida, central British Columbia was *patria,* a home exuberant with people, settlements, resources, and the quotidian activities associated with making a living. To visitors it is a wilderness. And what a glorious wilderness it is: sparsely populated (now), teeming with wildlife, and seemingly—if not actually—remote from the centers of western civilization: a region that induces awe, introspection, contemplation, and spiritual renewal. Chances are it may remain this way. In 2001 the British Columbia government approved, in principle, the new 1,200-square-mile Spirit Bear Park, including Campania, Swindle, and Princess Royal islands, along with much of the adjacent mainland coast. In conjunction with the Fjordland and Kitlope protected areas, about 2,500 square miles are now permanently protected. A further 3,000 square miles have had logging deferred.

Central British Columbia is the most uninhabited section of the entire Inside Passage. Between Port Hardy and the Prince Rupert metropolitan area, along the waterway, there are very few towns: Bella Bella (Waglisla), Shearwater, Klemtu, Hartley Bay, Kitkatla, Ocean Falls, and Oona River. Some have fewer than 50 people. Not far away, the deep inlets of the interior verges cloister Bella Coola, Kitimat, Hagensborg, and Kimsquit. A handful of smaller outposts round out the settlements that together comprise a population of fewer than 4,000 residents, mostly native. Numerous smaller redoubts—fly-in fish camps, abandoned canneries with colorful caretakers, manned lighthouses, ad hoc logging camps, overgrown outposts, villages forgotten by all but a few, and even transient agglomerations of anchorage seekers—round out the settlement pattern. Even radio contact is sparse. Be fully self-sufficient. Any sort of rescue operation can take days instead of hours. Proper preparation can be the difference between confident self-reliance and grim survival.

Campsites are often limited to toeholds, many carved by previous itinerants. The coastal ranges dominate the littoral topography even more so than in southern British Columbia. Bare rock abounds, and not just because treeline is lowering. This is a steep and young landscape, not the best conditions for soil formation. In sharp contrast, extensive white sand beaches trim the Cape Caution surrounds like lace edging. Exposed to the churn of the breaking surf, much of this section of coast, over time, has been ground into sand by the Pacific swell.

Precipitation, in all its myriad forms, abounds. Fog lingers longer. Mists become drizzles, drizzles turn into showers, and rain can last for days. Snow arrives earlier and overstays its welcome. During summer, temperatures rarely hit 90 degrees. Though no one would nickname central British Columbia the "Sunshine Coast," it can be balmy, although seldom for more than one or two days at a time.

Ursus arctos horribilis, the brown bear, thrives here, especially where major river channels and inlets connect his home range in the mountains with the sea. You *will* encounter him. After landing at a likely campsite in Smith Inlet, we noticed what looked like a beaver swimming straight for us from an outlying island. The scale was deceptive; it was a grizzly. We tripped, fell, bumbled into each other, and even managed to rip open and spill our wine-in-a-box during the mad scramble to stuff our gear back into the boats and disappear. Black bears *(Ursus americanus)* are downright common. Along the more protected passages you'll run into more than one bear per day, any time of day, sometimes even at camp, where he'll run into you. However, you're not likely to see a Spirit Bear *(Ursus americanus kermodei)*, namesake of the proposed new park. A rare subspecies, only about a hundred survive on the islands and mainland north of Bella Bella, in an area centered around Princess Royal Island. Although technically a black bear, the Kermode's color ranges from snowy white to café au lait. It is not an albino but rather an occasional manifestation of a recessive—albeit persistent—gene that perhaps offered an evolutionary advantage during the last ice age.

Where there are bears, there are salmon. The seasonal runs in Smith and Rivers Inlets attract not only grizzlies from the high interior but also human subsistence, commercial, and sport fishermen. These are world-renowned salmon fishing waters. Both inlets are dotted with seasonal, fly-in, strictly angling resorts, some floating on reconditioned barges.

And salmon also attract orcas. Driven to Brown Island in Smith Inlet by the swimming grizzly not an hour earlier, we were called on by a pod of killer whales. Each whale, in turn, came over and scratched at a shoreside rock outcrop not 50 feet from our tent. A few days later in Whale Channel, three orcas led by a magnificent bull with a disproportionately large and eccentrically angled dorsal fin headed directly for us, nipping in and out from the shore, at an alarming rate. Windmilling for land, I suggested that Tina hold her position for some good photos. She reached shore before I did.

Wolves, too, are common. On one isolated beach, an adolescent wolf played tag with a rambunctious raven. And play it definitely was. This wolf wasn't looking to eat crow. Down would swoop the bird while, in response, the pup would run, splay his forelegs, and spin around for another pass. Back and forth along that quarter-mile stretch, the free-form waltz added a playful touch to our lunch.

Besides the nearly impenetrable Coastal Ranges, two other important obstacles bracket this bit of coast to maintain it in such splendid isolation.

To the north lies the international boundary with Alaska. At both ends, wide corridors—Dixon Entrance at the north, and Queen Charlotte Sound at the south—connect Inside to Outside. The exposed coastal areas, in the American vernacular, "separate the men from the boys." Casual cruisers cross these unprotected gaps only with due diligence and prudent haste. At both locales, Pacific sea states, unhindered by fringing islands, converge on the exposed shore and, in periods of inclement weather, let loose all hell. At the very minimum, in the best of conditions, Pacific swell will waltz your boat and tattoo the shore. Cape Caution, so christened by Vancouver after his own close call and observations, is no place for kayaks to linger. Monitor well the forecast, inventory all possible sanctuaries, avoid surf landings, crank out the miles, and hie for more protected waters.

The Route: Overview

This section of the Inside Passage is divided up into four more or less equal portions: Queen Charlotte Sound, Fitz Hugh Sound, Princess Royal Channel, and Grenville Channel. Up here the Cascadia Marine Trail is purely a dream held together by a vision, while the British Columbia Marine Trail Association's hand has touched only lightly, if at all. Fortunately both the route and the logistics are relatively straightforward, though there are two alternates to the main route about halfway up, near Klemtu. All three choices diverge and rejoin near the same spots; each is about 30 miles in length and is described at the appropriate point along the main route.

Queen Charlotte Sound has been derisively nicknamed the Queen's Pond in an ironic reference to its lack of tranquillity. The first 50 miles of this 335-mile portion, the crossing of Queen Charlotte Sound and the exposed coastline around Cape Caution, is the crux. That knowledge and the preparation for imminent total performance can create a hollow anguish in the gut, the result of commitment and resolution laced with fear. My high school football coach used to call it "the big eye." Use it to your advantage. It won't help that the boats are probably full to the brim, making them sluggish and unwieldy.

From the protected backside of Vancouver Island, the route immediately plunges across Queen Charlotte Sound over to the mainland via a series of opportunely spaced island groups. These steppingstones reduce the crossing to a series of short hops, none greater than 2 miles. The next 35 miles to Smith Inlet are the crux de la crux. Luckily there are plenty of protected harbors along the way. Once in Smith you have some protection but you're not fully Inside yet. Around Kelp Head, at Rivers Inlet, the route enters Fitz Hugh Sound and for the remaining 285 miles uses protected channels to wend its way to Alaska.

Heading north up Fitz Hugh to Bella Bella, the route marches in step with the ferries, cruise ships, and cargo bearers that ply the Inside Passage. Beyond Seaforth Channel, we part company with the masses. While the shipping route goes up Finlayson Channel, the kayak route cuts up Mathieson Channel. At Jackson Passage, the two alternate routes diverge. Following the route-setting algorithm outlined in chapter 2 (shortness and sweetness), the main route, after Jackson Passage, goes up Finlayson Channel to Hiekish Narrows, where it rejoins the main traffic route and the two alternates at Princess Royal Channel's Graham Reach.

Princess Royal Channel is deceptive. It is this portion's secondary crux. Finlayson and Tolmie Channels innocently funnel all traffic into this seemingly welcoming and protected watercourse. But Princess Royal's embrace also funnels and then constricts wind and tide within its plunging rock walls. Conditions can deteriorate quickly, and landing spots—especially north of Butedale—are nearly nonexistent. Problem bears trapped near Terrace and Kitimat are relocated along the mainland between Griffin Pass and Khutse Inlet in Graham Reach.

After Princess Royal, Grenville Channel looks like a Royal redux, only longer and narrower. Not a welcome prospect. It has deterred more than a few Inside Passage paddlers. Unlike Princess Royal, however, which becomes steeper as you progress, Grenville eases, never becomes impossibly steep, and the critical distances, if properly coordinated with the current and winds, are quite manageable.

Beyond Grenville, the route dodges the Skeena River's mouth and all the obstacles that a major river's delta holds—the Skeena is the largest river in British Columbia north of the Fraser— and heads up to Prince Rupert alongside the big boats. There you can catch the B.C. ferry back to Port Hardy.

Queen Charlotte Sound: Port Hardy (mile 0/437) to Rivers Inlet (mile 60/497)

If you've driven up, Port Hardy has at least three likely launch sites with nearby long-term vehicle parking, and a possible fourth. The closest to the Gordon Group Islands is the Scotia Bay RV Campground just out of town and at the north end of Hardy Bay. Access is north off Market Street/Park Drive and straight through the Tsulquate Reserve.

Centrally located are two possibilities, the public dock and Carrot/Tsulquate Park. In spite of all the hustle and bustle, Quarterdeck, the public dock and marina close to the center of town, is an excellent launch site, though you must be efficient so as not to congest the boat ramp. Here, and at the Prince Rupert and then the Port Hardy ferry terminals, a set of kayak wheels might be handy but not essential. The public dock includes public pay parking. The address is 6600 Hardy Bay Road. It offers several advantages, including public rest rooms, showers, a launch ramp, and a central location. For a more relaxed kit-up and launch, head for the public beaches of Carrot and Tsulquate Parks, with their "Port Hardy: Mining, Fishing, & Logging" carved wooden sign. The park complex is near the north end of town, just north of Government Wharf. We parked and got ready in the open area just north of and adjacent to the house on the north side of the park. Debbie Erickson, in *Kayak Routes of the Pacific Northwest,* suggests checking

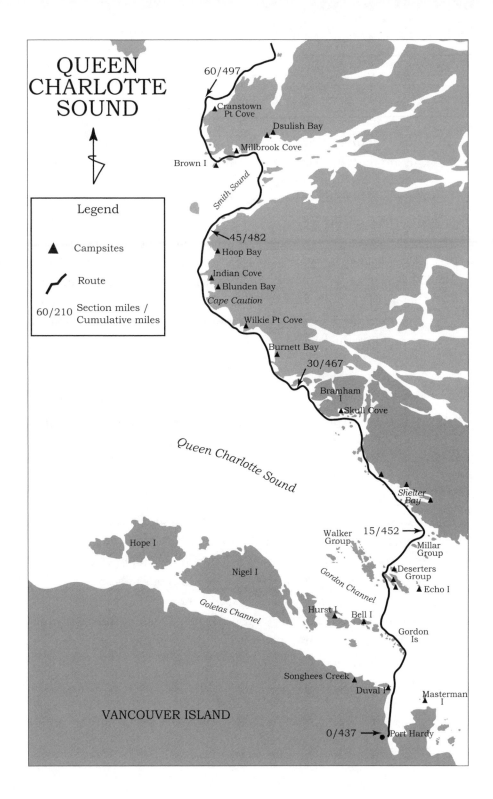

QUEEN CHARLOTTE SOUND

60/497

Cranstown
Pt Cove

Dsulish Bay

Millbrook Cove

Brown I

Smith Sound

Legend

▲ Campsites

Route

60/210 Section miles /
Cumulative miles

45/482

▲ Hoop Bay

Indian Cove
▲ Blunden Bay

Cape Caution

Wilkie Pt Cove ▲

Burnett Bay
▲

30/467

Bramham
I
▲ Skull Cove

Queen Charlotte Sound

▲

*Shelter
Bay* ▲

15/452 →

Millar
Group

Walker
Group

Hope I

▲ Deserters
Group

Nigel I

Gordon Channel

▲
▲ Echo I

Goletas Channel

Hurst I
▲

Bell I
▲

Gordon
Is

Songhees Creek ▲

Duval I ▲

Masterman
I ▲

0/437 → ● Port Hardy

VANCOUVER ISLAND

with the Northshore Inn (corner of Market Street and Highway 19), less than a two-minute walk away, for parking.

At the bottom of Hardy Bay is the Sunny Sanctuary Campground (250-949-6753) near the south end of town, at 8080 Goodspeed Road, just off the transisland highway. Although located on the water, Sunny Sanctuary is, unfortunately, not the best spot to launch unless you're willing to time the tides exactly. The estuary inundates only briefly at high tide, and there's a bit of a carry. Additionally, the exposed mud flats make for a messy and buggy launch. Sunny Sanctuary charges about $50 Canadian for vehicle storage. If launching from Tsulquate Park or the public docks, but opting to store your vehicle at Sunny Sanctuary, before calling for a taxi, walking, or hitchhiking, ask the campground host for a ride. The owners are very helpful, and if time and pocketbook permit they can be quite accommodating.

The Queen Charlotte Sound portion of central British Columbia focuses on the corridor where the open Pacific funnels into and out of Queen Charlotte Strait. The water is fresh, clear, cold, and fast. It has to be to get all the way behind Vancouver Island, in and out, twice a day. And it accelerates as the entry narrows and is further constricted by the many little island groups at the mouth of the strait. Tidal exchanges carry an astounding volume of nutrients that sustain dense invertebrate populations. Conspicuous in the 100-foot-visibility water are anemones and sea stars of all sizes and colors, often piled in promiscuous mounds of teeming activity. Keep an eye below and another ahead.

Knowledge, good planning, speed, and endurance are essential to crossing Queen Charlotte Strait, heading up Queen Charlotte Sound, and reaching fully protected waters again. As when eating an elephant, each morsel is cut, chewed, and digested one bite at a time. If you don't already have them, invest a few bucks on Canadian Hydrographic detail charts #3548 and #3549, so that each island and passage between Port Hardy and the mainland is crystal clear. Get a reliable weather report, set a date, and get an early start to take advantage of the best conditions.

Between Port Hardy and Duval Point is a 2-mile warm-up paddle to the mouth of Hardy Bay. Duval Point is on Duval Island; Strawberry Pass (mile 2/**439**) separates Duval from Vancouver Island. Inside is a scenic little channel with a fishing lodge and campsite—in case of any last-minute doubts. Another fine campsite just before committing to the crossing is Songhees Creek (mile 2/**439**), 2 miles west up the coast.

Two miles across Goletas Channel lie the Gordon Islands, the first stepping-stones in a series of many. The Tatnall Reefs and Nahwitti Bar secretly protect Goletas Channel from Pacific swells. One of four subsidiary channels that lead from Queen Charlotte Strait to Queen Charlotte Sound, Goletas Channel's currents, when present, are moderate and laminar. Head for the eastern end of the Gordon Group, near Doyle Island, turn the corner, and head up the north shore of the group. Many landing spots and a small cove midway up the north side of Doyle offer

respite. Doyle and Heard, as well as upcoming Hurst, all have fish farms. As you course northwest toward Heard Island, study conditions in Gordon Channel in anticipation of the crossing to the Deserters Group, and keep an eye out for the Port Hardy–Prince Rupert ferry.

God's Pocket Provincial Marine Park: Just to the west-northwest of Heard Island lies God's Pocket Provincial Marine Park. The park showcases some of the spectacular invertebrate biomass along the Queen Charlotte Strait littoral and so is a popular diving destination. The park includes Bell Island (mile 8/**445**, and about

Unnamed cove, Gordon Islands, Queen Charlotte Sound

a mile off route) and Hurst Island (mile 8/**445**, and about 3 miles off route). Traditionally, God's Pocket, a small cove on the west side of Hurst Island, has been a sailor's haven for the crossing of the strait and has a resort. Bell has a remarkable campsite in a protected little cove hidden behind the Lucan Islands. The campsite itself is on top of a shell midden about 16 feet higher than the beach. Minimize your impact; middens are archaeological sites.

Harlequin Bay, deeply indenting the east side of Hurst Island (mile 8/**445**), has a campsite at its head. The long beach dries at low tide, so time your arrival on the higher part of the tide. Water is seasonally available at various sources. A trail crosses the island to the resort, where water is certainly available.

Gordon Channel, too, in spite of its width, is somewhat protected both by flanking Nigei Island and an underwater sill that runs from Bell to Staples Island. Currents are not a concern. From Heard Island, nip across another 2 miles to the congested southern edge of the Deserters Group and into Shelter Passage. The Deserters are replete with protected bights, accessible landings, and a fish farm off the west-central coast of Wishart Island (mile 12/**449**). Wishart has a couple of nice campsites, one on the tombolo off its south end and another on the east side opposite Deserters Island.

Go around either end of McLoud Island (mile 13/**450**), check the tide tables, and position yourself for the 1.5-mile crossing of Ripple Passage. Tidal streams, in springs under full current, can attain 4 knots, with rips and eddies in places. If the tide is flooding, head straight for the Millar Group; if it's ebbing, work your way down the Deserters Island coast and plunge across near Echo Island. If you need to wait, McLoud has a campsite on its north shore and Echo has one on its south shore. The Millars, like the other groups, are strikingly beautiful and accessible. Most are rounded, bare rock with sparse vegetation reminiscent of a Japanese Zen garden.

Richards Channel separates the Millar Group from the Jeanette Islands adjacent to the mainland. Ghost Island splits Richards Channel's

1-mile width. At the narrowest point at the worst of times, currents can reach 3 knots. Once across, take a minute to savor the accomplishment, but if time and conditions allow, crank out the miles.

Shelter Bay (mile 18/**455**) is the first best camping opportunity on the mainland. The cove east of Westcott Point has a surf-free white sand beach just behind the brace of islands protecting the foreshore. A tad off route is another campsite at the end of the south branch, in the east end of Shelter Bay.

Two miles on, the Southgate Island Group offers some protection. There is a nice campsite on the mainland in the semi-lagoon behind Arm Island (mile 20/**457**). Log booms are often stored behind Knight Island.

For a few more miles along, in the vicinity of Bramham Island, the coastal topography affords some nicks and crannies before the starkly exposed shores of the Cape Caution region. Unfortunately, we did not linger long in this area, taking advantage of good conditions to round Cape Caution into Smith Inlet. The Coast Ranges' pediment here is extensive and low lying, creating a landing- and campsite-friendly area, barring surf activity. But even this last negative aspect has its positive side: sandy beaches with broad foreshores.

The Deloraine Islands and Murray Labyrinth are replete with low islands and foreshores, implying many camping possibilities. Gradual foreshores are good indicators of shallow waters offshore and this happens to be the case here, making for good shellfish habitat. Aboriginal shell middens abound. Inside Skull Cove (mile 26/**463**) there is a protected camp. The entire easternmost island is a shell midden!

Miles Inlet (mile 28/**465**), halfway up Bramham Island, is the last secure port south of Cape Caution. It is popular with small cruisers. With a following sea, entry into its 75-foot channel can be a bit unnerving. Old-growth cedars line the banks. Again, my apologies. We did not explore it. With a little bit of luck, you might find a campsite, if needed, within.

Slingsby Channel and the Fox Islands are two other spots I know nothing about (as good a reason as any to write about them). Because they face nearly due west, swells from that direction are funneled and compressed at the entrance. Not a good spot to seek shelter. Furthermore, tidal floods can reach 7 knots and ebbs 9 knots.

Heading north past the Fox Islands and Lascelles Point, the relatively featureless Cape Caution headland dominates. South of the cape a series of broad and shallow bays and coves with white sandy beaches beckon: Burnett, Wilkie, and Silvester. The natives knew Burnett Bay as "Place to Dance on Beach." But beware, these bays are pounded by surf, and the only dance you might indulge in is the dance of success and survival at landing. More than one kayak expedition has been tested in these waters. The cove just north of Wilkie Point (mile 36/**473**), due to its horizontal depth and protective fore island (extending underwater as a shelf), does, however, offer a somewhat protected landing on the sandy beach, with pleasant camping and a stream nearby.

Cape Caution: Known to the native people as "Forehead," Cape Caution (mile 39/**476**) was so named by Vancouver after nearly losing the *Discovery* in the vicinity. Between Slingsby Channel and Smith Sound lie nearly 20 miles of bluntly exposed waterfront capped by the glabella of Cape Caution. The full might of the North Pacific can and does crash into this brow. Confused sea conditions caused by reflected swells, ebb tides, and freshwater runoff flowing due west, and further exacerbated by shallow water directly off the cape extend for at least a mile to seaward. Even the bonsailike vegetation, like kinesic meteorological records, reflects the violence. A lighthouse crowns the cape. North of it, safe harbors become more common, at least for the kayaker.

Rounding Cape Caution requires some strategy. From Wilkie Point Cove to the first protected inlet north of the cape lie 6 choppy miles, or a 90-minute to two-hour determined paddle. Stay well offshore. One mile west of the cape draws only 7 fathoms (42 feet) of depth, while within a half mile, depth sounds at only 29 feet. Such shallows affect swell. With accompanying clapotis, be prepared for a turbulent ride. Not to belabor the point, but get an early start so as to pass the cape during the morning hours. Monitor both the evening and daybreak weather forecasts. If you have a VHF radio, you can get a personalized, custom, up-to-the-minute weather and sea state report from the Egg Island meteorological station located 6 miles northwest of the cape and about 2.5 miles off the headland. Though conventional reports always include the Egg Island data, the lightkeepers volunteer updated weather information on Channels 82A and 09 with the call sign "Egg Yolk."

Once past Cape Caution, three or four small bays and coves offer some protection to the desperate paddler. The north and south extremities of Blunden Bay (mile 41/**478**), looking like the pincers of a giant crab's claw, extend some shelter with attendant camping on the sandy beaches. Adjacent Indian Cove—named for its popularity as a rendezvous for natives traveling between Fitz Hugh and Queen Charlotte Sounds—is a bit more protected but has a narrower entrance.

North of Neck Ness, Alexandra Passage protects the southern approach to Smith Sound. At first glance, Alexandra Passage seems an imaginary designation. However, Hoop Reef, guarding Hoop Bay (mile 43/**480**), marks the start of a series of reefs and offshore islands that create Alexandra Passage. Slip behind the reefs for access to the bay and good, sandy camping. Protection Cove, close east of Milthorp Point, is also good for kayaks. Round Macnicol Point, and by the time you reach Jones Cove you'll have entered Smith Sound and will be past the Cape Caution difficulties.

Smith Sound: Coast along the shore to the Search Islands and island-hop across Smith Sound's opening to the Barrier Group and on to Smith's north shore. Dsulish Bay (mile 53/**490**), a tad off course eastward, has two good campsites with sandy beaches. The Millbrook Cove area (mile 54/**491**) has a few camp prospects, some on shell middens (which, if at all possible, ought to be avoided due to archaeological concerns). Beware camping on the mainland, as this is prime grizzly country. If possible, opt for any one of the numerous islands dotting the sound. Our favorite was Brown Island (mile 56/**493**) at the northern, outermost extremity of Smith Sound.

Brown is an excellent spot for an isolated layover day after the rigors of Cape Caution. Far enough from the mainland to discourage curious bears, its protected east side has a blindingly white sand beach subdivided by rock outcrops and intertidal shelves into individual

Brown Island campsite CREDIT: *T. COBOS*

campsites. The views east up the sound and onward north are incomparable, photogenic, and transcendent. Strategically scattered drift logs make for convenient and aesthetic clotheslines and kitchen counters. A complete circumambulation of the island is a half day well spent. After our dinner, during the gloaming, a small pod of orcas appropriated an onshore rock outcrop for a good scratch. What a treat after a long, eventful day!

The run to Rivers Inlet around Kelp Head is the last bit of Queen Charlotte Sound that must be negotiated. It is nothing like Cape Caution. For one, the 5-mile distance is short, and outlying reefs and islands break much of the swell. The angle too is slightly off. Calvert Island's protective influence starts to play a role, especially in north and northwesterly blows. Expect to see exceptional populations and varieties of wildlife where this last bit of open Pacific meets the inland corridor of

Rivers Inlet. Past Kelp Head and around Cranstown Point (mile 60/**497**) lies a beautiful, protected beach with excellent beachcombing and camping. There is even a 40-yard-long, primitive trail connecting the protected cove with the Queen's Pond. The contrast is remarkable. Welcome to Rivers Inlet.

Fitz Hugh Sound: Rivers Inlet (mile 60/497) to Bella Bella (mile 130/567)

Compared to the run around Cape Caution, this section, Rivers Inlet and the cruise up Fitz Hugh Sound to Bella Bella, is a paddle in the park. Tidal currents are not a concern. At 2 knots maximum, even these become negligible during runoffs as fresh water pouring into the sound neutralizes floods. Winds are quite predictable: calm in the morning with afternoon breezes that taper off in the evening, unless a low-pressure system threatens or just after one passes and high pressure reasserts itself. Fog can sometimes hamper visibility. Commercial traffic, having given Cape Caution a wide berth outside, funnels inside into Fitz Hugh. Don't get in the way of large boats and tugs with loads at the entrance to narrow Lama Passage. They must execute a wide but tight turn.

This is the traditional land of the Heiltsuk (Bella Bella) people. Namu, the only settlement en route, is one of the oldest native habitation sites along the entire Inside Passage. Archaeological excavations have rendered radiocarbon dates of 8,000 BC. Penrose Island Marine Park, on the north side of Rivers Inlet, encompasses much of Penrose Island and the adjacent archipelago to the south and west. Once out of Rivers Inlet, the foreshore steepens and campsites again become scarce. Much of Fitz Hugh Sound's west coast is protected by inclusion in the 304,000 acre Hakai Provincial Recreation Area, one of B.C.'s largest marine parks.

Rivers Inlet: Rivers Inlet extends deeply into the Coast Mountains and, as its name implies, it is a catchment basin for an inordinate number of streams, each with heretofore relatively undepleted salmon populations. From spring to fall, each species-specific salmon run attracts

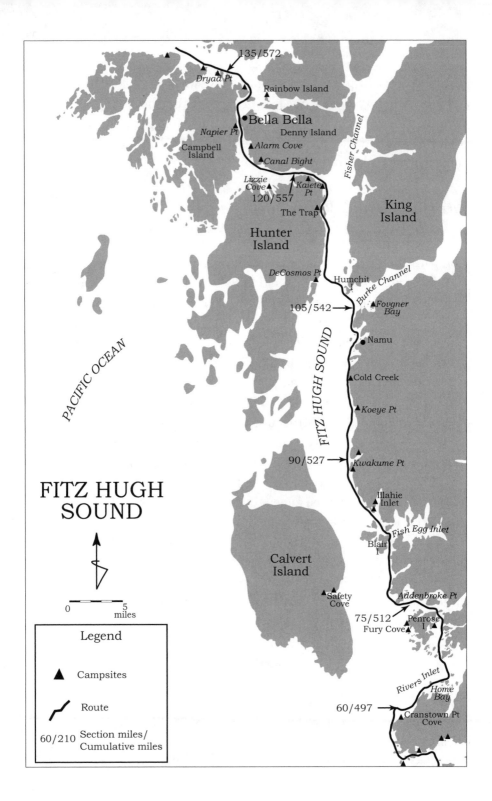

FITZ HUGH SOUND

PACIFIC OCEAN

135/572

Dryad Pt

Rainbow Island

Bella Bella

Napier Pt

Denny Island

Campbell Island

Alarm Cove

Canal Bight

Lizzie Cove

Kaiete Pt

120/557

The Trap

Hunter Island

King Island

Fisher Channel

DeCosmos Pt

Humchit

Burke Channel

Fovgner Bay

105/542

Namu

Cold Creek

Koeye Pt

FITZ HUGH SOUND

90/527

Kwakume Pt

Illahie Inlet

Fish Egg Inlet

Calvert Island

Blair I

Safety Cove

Addenbroke Pt

75/512

Penrose I

Fury Cove

Rivers Inlet

Home Bay

60/497

Cranstown Pt Cove

0   5
    miles

Legend

▲ Campsites

⋏ Route

60/210 Section miles/
        Cumulative miles

predators of all shapes and sizes. Since salmon are the foundation upon which this biotic edifice is built, every living thing congregates to get a piece of the action. The inlet's protrusion into the mountains is a highway to the coast for grizzlies. Additionally, its contiguity with the open Pacific at Kelp Head attracts species usually found at a greater distance from shore: Dall's porpoise; minke, northern right, and humpback whales; along with orcas, sea lions, and sea otters.

Man, the ultimate predator, has no permanent presence here, but the seasonal visitors are target-fixated on only one thing: salmon. Anglers' outposts, sometimes quietly fading, reincarnating, or relocating, cater to the annual fish frenzy. Drop by Big Spring Fishing Lodge, Rivers Inlet Sporting Lodge, Black Gold Fishing Lodge, Goose Bay, Bucks Camp, Friendly Finn Bay Retreat, or Rivers Lodge for water or an emergency. Not that these folks are unfriendly, but they are definitely preoccupied. In 1951, sport fisherman Frank Piscatelli (yes, the name is for real) bagged a chinook weighing 82 pounds. The commercial canneries that once peppered Rivers Inlet—as many as 17 at one time—are all closed now. Most employed native or, prior to WWII, Japanese labor. Only pilings and brick ruins remain. Overfishing has lately become a problem, but environmental groups are now working to restore the inlet's productivity.

Beyond Cranstown Point the shore rises to steep cliffs, an area known as "The Wall" and considered one of the top fish producers within Rivers Inlet. Head northeast toward Sharbau Island to position yourself for the inlet's crossing. Just south of Sharbau, in Home Bay, is the Big Spring Fishing Lodge, built on a recycled rail car ferry barge. (No services are available here, other than water.) Graze by the archipelago guarding the entrance to Duncanby Landing and Goose Bay on the way to Bull Island. Water, showers, laundry, liquor, and limited groceries are available at Duncanby Landing. From Bull Island to Bilton Island on the north shore of Rivers Inlet is a scant 1.5-mile crossing.

Klaquaek Channel: Enter Penrose Island Provincial Park through protected Klaquaek Channel heading due north. The shallow verges of

Big Frypan Bay (mile 70/**507**), just east of Quoin Hill and midway up Penrose Island, plus the many islands dotting Klaquaek, contain a handful of campsites, some on shell middens. Most of Penrose's goodies (including campsites on Fury Island and Fury Cove) lie in the small island group on the Fitz Hugh side of Penrose, a viable alternative route up into Fitz Hugh Sound. On the Walbran Island side of Klaquaek Channel, Sunshine Bay nestles a small floating itinerant community (no services). At the top end of the channel, a small island (with Rivers Lodge on its north shore) straddles the junction of Klaquaek with Darby Channel.

Turn west into Darby Channel toward Fitz Hugh Sound. Pass Finn Bay at the top end of Penrose Island, home to Friendly Finn Bay Retreat and Bucks Camp, last of the Rivers Inlet fishing resorts. Pierce Bay, the last bay on the north shore before Addenbroke Point, might yield a campsite on one of its many islets or coves. There is an active logging operation at the north end. Once round Addenbroke Point in Fitz Hugh Sound, campsites become much scarcer.

From Addenbroke Point, head north to Arthur Point, coasting along the mainland shore of Fitz Hugh Sound. Across the Sound—albeit 5 miles off route—on Calvert Island lies Safety Cove (mile 77/**514**), where Vancouver wrapped up the 1792 surveying season. *Coastal Waters Recreation Maps* indicates a campsite at its head alongside Outsoatie Creek. Tim Lydon, in *Passage to Alaska,* notes a small, sandy camp along the north shore. Pass by Phillip Inlet into Convoy Passage and head north between Blair Island and the mainland. Cross Patrol Passage to the west and Fish Egg Inlet to the east, over to Salvage Island and into Fairmile Passage. Fish Egg Inlet is extensive and very wild, with isolated lagoons protected by overfalls. It is full of intertidal critters and the wildlife that scrabble a livelihood from them.

North of Salvage Island, Illahie Inlet, fronted by the Green Island Group (mile 85/**522**), cuts into the mainland. The Green Island Group has a couple of campsites. One, shown in *Coastal Waters Recreation Maps,* we did not persevere enough to find. It is located on Green Island itself, north of the giant midden site on the west side. The other covers a small, bare rock islet just off the northwest corner of the largest island at the entrance to Illahie Inlet. If you can hold out, there is a much nicer campsite 4 miles farther north.

About 0.5 mile south of Kwakume Point (mile 89/**526**), two treed islets are connected to shore by a white sand beach. Overnight accommodations just don't get any better than this. Kwakume Point itself has a light. Another 0.5 mile or so north, Kwakume Inlet (mile 90/**527**) cleaves the mainland. Just 0.75 mile inside the inlet, along the north shore, there is another campsite. Remember that the entire mainland coast south of Namu is grizzly country; camp defensively.

Koeye River: The Koeye River (mile 95/**532**; pronounced "Kwy") has significance disproportionate to the modest watershed it drains. In 2001 the Raincoast Conservation Society, Ecotrust Canada, and the Land Conservancy of B.C. deeded a 183-acre parcel and lodge at the mouth of the river to the Heiltsuk and Owikeeno First Nations, original stewards of the Koeye. On August 11 of that year, more than 300 members of those tribes, invited guests, and chance visitors gathered at the Koeye to celebrate the transfer of ownership. Additionally, much of the moss-draped, old-growth forest lining the river is now protected from further logging. Just inside the mouth, along the south shore, are some good campsites. About a mile up the channel, the ruins of the Koeye

Orcas cavorting in Fitz Hugh Sound

Lime Company line the north shore, upstream of which the river widens into a grassy plain with stunning views of snow-capped peaks to the east. Wildlife abounds.

Three miles north of the Koeye and just below Uganda Point, the Cold Creek (mile 98/**535**) delta has a good camp on a long pebble beach, perhaps—in terms of bears—a safer alternative to the Koeye. Head north past Ontario Point into the small channel between Lapwing Island and the mainland and into Namu Harbour.

Namu: Namu (mile 102/**539**) does not present a lovely first impression. Paddling up in a kayak, the industrial conglomerate, extended over the water on giant piers, overwhelms the natural beauty of Whirlwind Bay. Out of the corner of your eye, however, you can spot its outlying extremities: old white clapboard buildings connected by an intricate system of wooden walkways and piers ingeniously wending their way through the contours of the landscape, subtle hints of the delights hiding behind the dreary facade. Namu (meaning whirlwind) is a 10,000-year-old Heiltsuk settlement that has been continuously occupied to the present. Six thousand years ago, with growth sluggish and GDP flat, Namu's citizens launched a radically new economic development scheme: salmon exploitation. Ever since, salmon have been the economic mainstay of the area. In 1893 Robert Draney, a European-Canadian, opened the first fish cannery in the village. The enterprise thrived and grew, adding a sawmill in 1909. British Columbia Packers Ltd. bought out and consolidated all the Namu operations in 1928. For more than 50 years, under the benevolent company town regimen of B.C. Packers, Namu supported a population of Heiltsuk, other First Nations, European-Canadians, Japanese, and Chinese, of up to 400 personnel and their families.

The cannery shut down in 1980. Processed fish were then shipped south to Vancouver and west to Japan. In the early 1990s, the processing plant discontinued operation and B.C. Packers sold out. Attempts to resuscitate Namu as a fishing resort have required frequent intervention and intensive care. Namu, though barely holding on to life, has good prospects. The Heiltsuk are currently seeking to regain this property and have it designated a Canadian and World Heritage Site.

A multitalented family of caretakers keeps the central core of the old town spruced up and is slowly increasing the variety of services available. They sell gas, run a limited-services machine shop (a godsend when one of our rudders broke), maintain a few dwellings for "bed & shower" rentals, mow the lawn, and even offer tours (run by an industrious daughter for a nominal "donation"). There are plans to reopen the café and store. At the time of our visit, the old store still had quite a selection of leftover dry goods from which the caretakers kindly let us reprovision, gratis.

You can camp on Clam Island just offshore. A better bet is to ask permission to pitch a tent on the spacious mowed lawn behind the mooring docks (there may be a charge). Use of the bathrooms, a not-negligible environmental concern, is included. Spend a day touring the town and hiking up the boardwalk to Namu Lake, source of the generator's power. The elevated walkways are surrounded by berry bushes and are so high up that bears can harvest the berries below, undisturbed by human traffic. Many of the buildings are well preserved and evoke nostalgia for an era long past. At night, with the generator lighting up the entire place, the walkabout is particularly eerie and rewarding. Don't miss the historic native community and Asian compound on the south side of the Namu River. A stone fish trap at its mouth is one of the few visible reminders of the prehistoric occupation of Namu.

One summer morning in 1965, salmon fisherman Bill Lechkobit found two killer whales, a bull and a calf, caught in his net near the Namu cannery. Sensing an opportunity, instead of setting them free, he offered them to Ted Griffin, owner of a Seattle aquarium. Griffin promised Lechkobit a handsome profit for the whales' safe delivery. By the time the fisherman had built a floating pen for the long tow down the windy waterways to Seattle, the calf had escaped. Still, Lechkobit was lucky. On the way down, the pen held, Cape Caution and the weather cooperated, and the remaining whale survived the indignities of the passage. In Seattle, the orca was installed in a pen named for where he was captured: Namu. He became a celebrity, which fostered a new appreciation for orcas and whales generally.

North of Namu, the route up the Inside Passage zigzags west and north, following channels laid out along geographic weaknesses. At some point, Fitz Hugh Sound must be crossed. But where? South of its intersection with Burke Channel, Fitz Hugh is broad and subject to the squamish (katabatic) winds that blow down Burke, a steep, glacier-cut inlet snaking deep into the Coast Ranges. North of Burke, Fitz Hugh narrows considerably and becomes Fisher Channel.

Depart Namu early. Burke's winds don't usually kick up until after 10 AM. Time the crossing—if possible—of Burke's mouth with a waning flood and stay out where the entrance is widest. Strong tidal currents bedevil Burke. Before Edmund Point (mile 105/**542**), angle out toward Humchitt Island. Just inside Burke Channel, on the south cove of the largest island in Fougner Bay and about 1 mile east of Edmund Point, there is a campsite. From Humchitt Island, cross Fisher Channel, still on a waning flood or slack and early in the morning, to De Cosmos Point on Hunter Island.

Just 0.5 mile below the point, the entrance to De Cosmos Lagoon (mile 110/**547**) beckons. The lagoon is nearly landlocked and its entrance is choked with kelp and overhanging tree branches. Strong currents enter and exit. But just inside, on the north shore where a creek disgorges, is a small campsite.

Head up Fisher Channel along Hunter's east shore into the passage between Clayton Island and Hunter. A broad alluvial plain, nicknamed "The Trap" (mile 115/**552**), opens up on Hunter's shore. Camping is possible, though not particularly aesthetic. Continue north past Long Point and Long Point Cove to Pointer Island and Kaiete Point.

Kaiete Point (mile 117/**554**), the entrance to Lama Passage, once had a manned lighthouse. Today only a helipad remains. If you can negotiate a landing, there is no better campsite. With powerful views up and down Fisher Channel and into Lama Passage, a night on the helipad is like camping out inside a symphony.

Sir Alexander Mackenzie Provincial Park: Thirty miles farther up Fisher Channel from Lama Passage (after Fisher becomes Dean Channel)

Sir Alexander Mackenzie Provincial Park commemorates the first recorded transcontinental trek across then-unmapped North America. Mackenzie's feat in 1793 was one of the most phenomenal exploratory ventures ever accomplished. Though a bit distant from the Inside Passage route for a side trip (unless you're as ambitious as Mackenzie) and outside the scope of this guide, the park is accessible by float plane or powerboat from Bella Bella.

When Alex Mackenzie (the knighthood came later) set out to find the Pacific in 1789, the United States had not yet fully ratified its new Constitution, and Lewis and Clark were mere teens. Mackenzie did not ask for and did not get any government support. Though keenly aware of imperial concerns and the expansion of geographic knowledge (Lewis and Clark were later to rely on and carry Mackenzie's *Voyages from Montreal*), Mackenzie's primary aims were commercial: market advantage for his North West Company. He was an intelligent, determined, patient, linguistically gifted, and extremely diplomatic Scotsman. Traveling mostly with native companions employed along the way, it is a testament to his talents that Mackenzie survived and prevailed over extraordinary circumstances.

Mackenzie reasoned that beyond the Continental Divide streams would flow into the Pacific. His strategy was inferentially simple but realistically complex. On his first try he descended the unexplored Mackenzie River, second only in size to the Mississippi-Missouri watershed in North America, and followed it to the sea, which turned out to be the Arctic instead of the Pacific Ocean. Lesser men would have been satisfied. Unflummoxed and undeterred, Mackenzie retraced his steps and turned west. But his companions had had enough: Not one accompanied him.

Thoroughly committed and inured to hardship, he recrossed the plains, surmounted the Rocky Mountains, and ran headfirst into the Coast Range and the animosities separating the interior from the coastal tribes. Finally, under extreme danger to his life from distrustful and bellicose Bella Coola and Bella Bella natives, he reached the Pacific at Dean Channel and there inscribed on a rock: "Alex Mackenzie from Canada by land 22 July 1793," The inscription, now incised into Mackenzie's

Rock, is the centerpiece of the park. Camping, though not much else, is available.

Outbound, Mackenzie had averaged a phenomenal 20 miles a day; on the return, he picked up the pace to 25. Ironically, through a chance meeting with a Bella Bella (now Heiltsuk) native, he found out that he had missed Captain Vancouver, busy mapping Dean Channel on his first expedition, by only a few weeks.

Lama Passage, the southernmost of three channels leading west to Bella Bella, is the most popular and shortest route up the Inside Passage. Be aware of traffic. Two miles in, on the east side of Serpent Point Light (mile 119/**556**), there is another campable spot. The remaining north shore of Hunter Island along Lama Passage is indented by at least five coves with outlying islands. Many have camping possibilities. We camped on one of the islands in Lizzie Cove, also known as Cooper Inlet (mile 123/**560**), site of an old native village.

A better bet is to course along the Denny Island shore. There is a camp on Canal Bight's (mile 125/**562**) outermost cove. Another mile up the coast, behind Walker Island (mile 126/**563**), which has a light, lies another campsite. Alarm Cove's (mile 126.5/**563.5**) southern incut also has camping.

After Napier Point, in Lama Passage's narrowest section, you enter the Bella Bella conurbation: Waglisla, Bella Bella, and Shearwater. Inside McLoughlin Bay (mile 129/**566**) the B.C. Ferry terminal services the area. Immediately afterward, SeeQuest Adventures' headquarters—a kayak tour outfit—line the shore. They can provide, among other services, a campsite and taxi service into New Bella Bella. There is no camping inside Bella Bella proper, except at slightly out-of-the-way Rainbow Island (see below), and the nearest campsite afterward is 3 miles beyond the towns, so plan your stopover with these camping details in mind.

Bella Bella: Bella Bella, New Bella Bella (Waglisla), and Shearwater (mile 130/**567**) are the three more or less contiguous settlements that sprang up around the Hudson's Bay Company's Fort McLoughlin since 1833. Bella Bella and Waglisla were (and primarily remain) native settlements established to facilitate trade with the fort. Shearwater is the most recent addition. What started out as a resort has expanded into a town. The three combined are the largest outpost of civilization between Port Hardy and Prince Rupert, with a combined population of about 2,000. All services are available. Groceries, liquor, charts, post office, water, and RCMP are best accessed from the Waglisla government dock near the north end of New Bella Bella. Don't miss the Heiltsuk Cultural Centre, located in the Bella Bella Community School just up from the wharf, for information on Heiltsuk history, language, and culture. Camping is available at the already mentioned SeeQuest Adventure headquarters and on the

Camp on unnamed island, Lizzie Cove, Lama Passage, British Columbia

north end of Rainbow Island just northwest of the three towns. There are also B&Bs and hotels.

The Heiltsuk have a reputation for hostility. Alexander Mackenzie, a model of tact and understatement, after being belligerently accosted by the informant who relayed a not-too-friendly encounter with the Vancouver expedition, states: "I do not doubt he well deserved the treatment which he described." More recent visitors, including a few kayakers, sometimes describe ominous exchanges. Perhaps first impressions can be deceiving. The Bella Bella whom Mackenzie encountered had a strong martial tradition. They assumed all visitors were warriors bent on personal glory, so a challenge was the best greeting to extend.

Heiltsuk chauvinism was built on a foundation of tenacious self-reliance and independence. To themselves, they were second to none. Ever prickly but ingenious, the Heiltsuk coped with contact resiliently. Fort McLoughlin was supplied by the *Beaver,* a side paddle-wheeler and the first steam-powered vessel on the Northwest Coast. For more than 50 years the *Beaver* plied the Inside Passage, a floating mercantile and often the only source of external contact for the inhabitants. After the decline of the sea otter, other furs such as beaver, river otter, mink, and marten were traded for woolen and cotton clothing, axes, gunpowder and shot, blunderbusses, muskets, sugar, molasses, tobacco, rice, vermilion, iron, Indigo blue blankets, scissors, butcher knives, looking glasses, needles, and pea jackets. With smoke bellowing from her stacks, a large woodcutting crew to feed her engines, and four brass cannons, she was an impressive sight made more so, to the natives, by the mystery that she had no visible means of propulsion. John Dunn, trader and interpreter stationed at Fort McLoughlin in the mid-1830s, relates the following incident:

> They (the natives) promised to construct a steamship on the model of the Beaver. We listened and shook our heads incredulously: but in a short time we found they had felled a large tree and were making the hull out of its scooped trunk. Some time after, this rude steamer appeared. She was... thirty feet long, all in one piece... resembling the model of our steamer. She was black, with painted ports; decked over... the steersman was not seen. She was floated triumphantly... They thought they had nearly come up to the point of external structure; but the enginery baffled them; this, however, they thought they could imitate in time by perseverance and the helping illumination of the Great Spirit. (Dunn, History of the Oregon Territory, 1844)

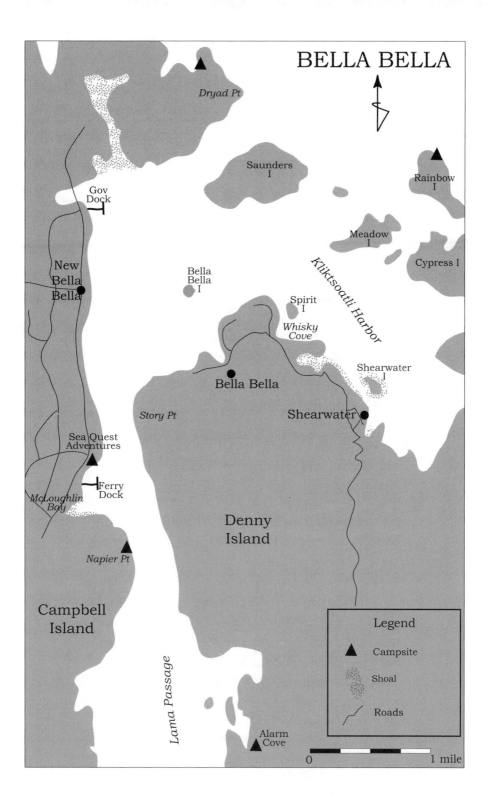

BELLA BELLA

Dryad Pt

Saunders
I

Rainbow
I

Gov
Dock

Meadow
I

Cypress I

New
Bella
Bella

Bella
Bella
I

Kliktsoatli Harbor

Spirit
I

*Whisky
Cove*

Shearwater
I

Bella Bella

Story Pt

Shearwater

Sea Quest
Adventures

Ferry
Dock

*McLoughlin
Bay*

Denny
Island

Napier Pt

Campbell
Island

Lama Passage

Alarm
Cove

Legend

▲ Campsite

Shoal

Roads

0   1 mile

In later years the Heilsuk have bent over backward to improve their image and attract more tourism. With the recent opening of the Discovery Coast Ferry, this entire area has become more accessible. Our own experience was very friendly—we were off-handedly offered an outlying cabin—but otherwise uneventful.

Princess Royal Channel: Bella Bella (mile 130/567) to Butedale (mile 214/651)

The third portion of the central coast begins with a couple of long zigzags that access three alternate approaches, more or less of equal length, into Princess Royal Channel, which separates Princess Royal Island from the mainland. It is wild and steep, subject to strong currents and very isolated. Klemtu and Butedale are the only outposts of civilization with Butedale only just. Campsites are scarce, and not just due to harsh terrain. Klemtu is Kitasoo First Nations territory. In the past, the Kitasoo, lacking a tourism policy, had asked that their area not be promoted in paddling guides—though they welcomed visitors. Now, visitors are asked to register with the Klemtu tourism office (see appendix B) before conducting any activities in the area. All my research notes on this area were lost in a car accident, so I rely on my ever fading memory for campsite locations. Lack of marked sites on the accompanying maps does not indicate their absence, only of their paucity and the author's inadequacy.

Seaforth, Mathieson, Finlayson, Tolmie, and Princess Royal Channels are the primary traffic routes up and down the Inside Passage along this section. Winds freshen in the afternoons, and—in the long, narrow sections—can be funneled with alarming velocity. The main route, after Seaforth Channel, goes up Mathieson Channel, across Jackson Passage to Finlayson Channel, and straight up into Heikish Narrows where it joins Princess Royal's Graham Reach.

The two alternates offer, on the one hand, more of the same or, on the other, a stark choice. Alternate #1 curves over to Klemtu, where it rejoins the ferry route up Sarah Pass and Tolmie Channel into Graham Reach, a tad longer than the main route. Alternate #2 skips Jackson Passage and goes straight up through uncharted Griffin Passage, a

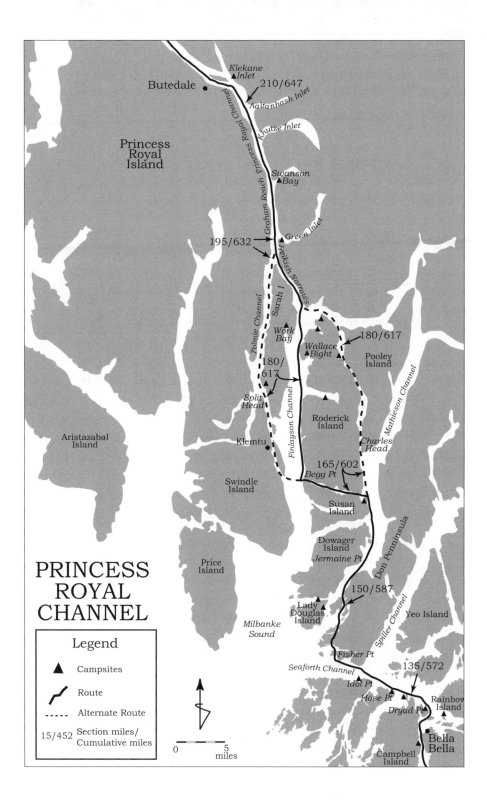

Butedale •

Klekane
▲*Inlet*

210/647

Aaltanhash Inlet

Princess
Royal
Island

Knutze Inlet

Swanson
▲*Bay*

Green Inlet

195/632

Tolmie Channel

Sarah I

Work
Bay

Wallace
▲*Bight*

180/617

Pooley
Island

180/
617

Heikish Narrows

Mathieson Channel

Split
Head

Finlayson Channel

Roderick
Island

Charles
Head

Klemtu •

165/602

Begg Pt

Aristazabal
Island

Swindle
Island

Susan
Island

Dowager
Island

Jermaine Pt

Don Penninsula

Price
Island

150/587

Lady ▲
Douglas
Island

Yeo Island

Spiller Channel

Milbanke
Sound

Fisher Pt

Seaforth Channel

135/572

Idol Pt

Hose Pt

Rainbow
Island

Dryad Pt

Bella
Bella •

Campbell
Island

PRINCESS
ROYAL
CHANNEL

Legend

▲ Campsites

⌇ Route

- - - - Alternate Route

15/452 Section miles/
         Cumulative miles

0   5
    miles

narrow and rapid-strewn wilderness adventure, actually a tad bit shorter than the main route. The two alternate routes are described immediately following their point of convergence with the main route.

Nearly abandoned Butedale separates Princess Royal Channel's length into Graham and Fraser Reaches. The old cannery is a welcome haven and offers a convenient respite and terminus for this portion.

Seaforth Channel: Exit Bella Bella and round Dryad Point, with its exceptionally attractive lighthouse and homestead, to enter Seaforth Channel. Almost all north- and southbound traffic converges in Seaforth Channel. Sea conditions tend to be calm with currents not a concern. The Heiltsuk have long inhabited these shores. There are many archaeological sites, including petroglyphs, some totem poles, and abandoned villages. The first campsite, only 3 miles from Bella Bella, is just inside Ardmillan Bay (mile 133/**570**) around Dryad Point. Continue west past Thorburne Island, and pass the Waglisla Float Plane fuel dock deep in Ormidale Harbour. Around Defeat Point lies Kynumpt Harbour (mile 135/**572**), locally known as Strom Bay. The picturesque inlet has a couple of campsites and a 2-mile-long trail into Bella Bella.

The Kintail Point Peninsula dominates the northwest extremity of Campbell Island and separates Seaforth Channel from Raymond Passage, which must now be crossed over to Horsfall Island. Just around Hose Point (mile 137/**574**), on Horsfall's northeastern tip, there is a small cove with a gravel beach and two small streams. Inside the forest a couple of tent pads have been cleared to create a discreet campsite. From McGown Point, at the northwestern tip of Horsfall, cross Joassa Channel's entrance over to Dufferin Island, and head for Idol Point, launching spot for the crossing of Seaforth Channel.

Before crossing Seaforth, there is one more campsite with a stream 1 mile off route and west of Idol Point in a small bay just before Denniston Point (mile 136/**573**). Angle northwest to the southeast corner of the Don Penninsula. Spiller Channel joins Seaforth from the northeast.

Yeo Island: About 4 miles up Spiller (and 4 miles off route) lies Yeo Island. The Kokyet Indian Reserve encompasses the southwest corner of Yeo Island and all of offshore Grief Island. Prior to the establishment of Fort McLoughlin, Kilkite Village, largest of the Heilsuk settlements, was located on Yeo's extremity. The ferocity of the villagers kept Hudson's Bay traders away. The village is long since abandoned. Spiller Channel and its environs, before the publication of Chart #3940 in 1996, was the largest uncharted area of the British Columbia coast.

Course along the south shore of the Don Penninsula to Fisher Point, home to two totems known locally as the Watchmen. They are located high up on the granite face. Slip through Baldony Pass between Watch Island and the mainland and into Reid Passage. Reid is the favored small-craft route that avoids the exposed waters of Milbanke Sound. Oddly, tidal currents always flow north. Reid Passage disgorges into wider Port Blackney, at whose south end sits Oliver Cove Marine Park on the east side, and Boat Inlet on the Cecilia Island side. Oliver Cove, with its sand/mud beach and the ruins of two cabins deep in the overgrowth, is popular with sailboats but does not offer reasonable camping.

Oliver Cove, Reid Passage, British Columbia

Heading north from Port Blackney the shorter, easier, and more interesting route is up through Lady Trutch Passage. There may be a campsite among its many coves and islands. On the other hand, veering west of Lake Island into Mathieson Channel's Perceval Narrows opens up a couple of camping possibilities. Cockle Bay (mile 150/**587**), on the east side of Lady Douglas Island, with its long, sandy beach, has good camping. Just north, Moss Passage (mile 151/**588**, and a tad off route) also has some small sandy beaches suitable for camping. During spring tides, currents can run 5 knots in Perceval.

Beyond Moss Passage and Lake Island, head up Mathieson Channel to Jermaine Point. If you're not already on the Dowager Island side of Mathieson, cross over. Pass Arthur Island and the three coves behind it, which offer possible campsites, especially in the upper coves. Oscar Passage, not quite as popular or scenic a route to Klemtu as upcoming Jackson Passage, separates Dowager Island from Susan Island.

Jackson Narrows, at Jackson Passage's east end and now a B.C. marine park, is barely 600 feet wide. Rescue Bay (mile 163/**300**), a popular sailboat anchorage, guards the entrance. Chances are good that there may be a campsite within its shallow confines (Jennifer Hahn, in her book *Spirited Waters,* reports camping in the vicinity.) At this point, the adventurous Griffin Passage alternate route, heading due north, diverges. (This is described later.) The main route and its twin alternate (also described later) traverse west through Jackson Passage to Finlayson Channel. Tidal currents in Jackson are generally moderate (1–3 knots). About halfway through the 7-mile-long passage, Lochalsh Bay is home to a large salmon farm.

Begg Point (mile 170/**607**) marks Jackson's juncture with Finlayson Channel and the point of divergence for the alternate route via Klemtu (described later). The main route follows upper Finlayson Channel into Heikish Narrows. Since most commercial traffic heads up Tolmie Channel, the upper reaches of Finlayson bask in solitude.

Upper Finlayson Channel is steep-to. Spring tides can attain 3 knots. Camping is very scarce, though some possibilities exist within the many inlets indenting the northern shore of Roderick Island and wherever streams hit the coast. Head up Roderick Island's steep west coast. Near mile 174/**611** two streams join Finlayson. The first drains Roderick and two subsidiary lakes; the second flows into Mary Cove. Either might provide a flat spot, though the head of Mary Cove is shallow—probably muddy—and dries for a distance. Watson Bay (mile 179/**616**), about 3 miles deep, also has possibilities. Two streams flow into its head, and Bolt Point, three-quarters of the way in, is connected to the north shore by a tombolo—always a good prospect. Bottleneck Inlet (mile 182/**619**) is not a good camping prospect. The walls are steep and, although a stream flows into its end, it dries shallow and muddy with tidal fluctuations.

Next up is Wallace Bight (mile 183/**620**), a better possibility. Three streams flow into it, and two subsidiary bays indent its extremities. The better bet is the upper bay, which has drying sand flats (not extensive), small islets, peninsulas, and an isthmus.

Before Finlayson Channel joins Sheep Passage and Heikish Narrows, three more bays with possible camping potential indent both sides of the channel. Work Bay (mile 184/**621**), on the Sarah Island shore, has four streams entering, one in a beautiful 200-foot cascade. Goat Cove (mile 186/**623**) and Kid Bay (mile187/**624**), on the Roderick Island side, are slightly out of the way. Goat Cove has a creek, old-growth forest, and drying flats that are not extensive. The Griffin Pass alternate route joins the main route at the entrance to Heikish Narrows.

Heikish Narrows: Six-mile-long Heikish Narrows is best transited with the tide. Maximum floods and ebbs peak at about 4 knots. Fortunately, flow is laminar. There may be a flat spot along the Sarah Island shore, perhaps behind Hewitt Island. The alternate route via Klemtu rejoins the main route at the top of Sarah Island, where Heikish Narrows and Princess Royal Channel converge.

Alternate Route #1: Begg Point (mile 170/607) to Sarah Point (mile 195/632) via Klemtu

The alternate route via Klemtu is very similar in character to the main route but less isolated. Nearly the identical length and no more difficult, it is the primary north-south trafficway. Klemtu village and picturesque

Boat Bluff lighthouse—probably the most photographed lighthouse along the Inside Passage—are highlights. Mountains rise directly out of the sea with impunity. Barring the crossing of Finlayson Channel, the route is cloistered by the soaring coastlines of the flanking shores.

From Begg Point (mile 170/**607**), at the junction of Jackson Passage with Finlayson Channel, head almost due west across 2-mile-wide Finlayson Channel to Freeman Point at the southern tip of Cone Island and enter Klemtu Passage. Currents in Klemtu Passage are weaker than in Finlayson, which here, at its midriff, might reach 1 knot but then only on spring tides.

Klemtu: Klemtu village (mile 175/612) has about 400 residents and is the capital of the Kitasoo First Nation. There are two grocery stores (one with banking services), a post office, medical clinic, showers, a commercial campground, and a B&B. Dock at the rocky beach next to the ferry ramp at the north end of Trout Bay. North of Klemtu, flat ground for camping is nearly nonexistent. Inquire locally—at the

Boat Bluff Lighthouse, Sarah Island, Tolmie Channel, British Columbia

tourism office—or at Boat Bluff lighthouse, 4 miles north, for additional information concerning camping possibilities.

Continue north out of Klemtu along the east coast of Swindle Island and pass by Jane Island and adjoining Jane and Sarah Passages. Boat Bluff, with its colorful and elegantly designed light station, dominates the southern tip of Sarah Island and marks the entrance to Tolmie Channel.

Tolmie Channel: Tolmie's currents are a bit odd. Tidal streams flood north and ebb south. The flood stream is weaker than in Finlayson but the ebb is not only stronger, it runs for an hour and a half longer. At springs, currents peak at 3 knots in the narrower portions of Tolmie, but barely reach 1 knot in the broader parts. Between Split Head at the northern tip of Swindle Island and Sarah Island, favor the Sarah side. There can be tide rips and turbulence south of Parry Patch. Directly north of Split Head, on Sarah Island, there is an unnamed bay (mile 182/**619**) behind a small island that offers a campsite. There are three tent sites in the forest above the gently sloping rocky beach and a creek just east. Tolmie runs for the 17-mile length of Sarah Island's west coast where, at the top, it joins Heikish Narrows to become Princess Royal Channel's Graham Reach beyond Sarah Point (mile 195/**632**), where this alternate rejoins the main route.

Alternate Route #2: Rescue Bay *(mile 163/300)* to Finlayson Head *(mile 187/624)* via Griffin Passage

Griffin Passage separates Roderick Island from Pooley Island and runs north-south. The traverse of Griffin Passage ranks as an exceptional experience in a region where the extraordinary abounds, and it is slightly shorter than the main route and its twin alternate. The Canadian *Sailing Directions* indicates that the passage is "unsurveyed." Skeptical of the claim, we decided to see for ourselves and headed straight for Griffin.

In 1995, Don and Reanne Douglass, authors of a very detailed and comprehensive series of cruising guides to the Inside Passage, attempted a full transit in their 40-foot diesel trawler *Baidarka*. They failed. Resorting to a high-powered inflatable tender, Don was able to explore and record multiple depth soundings while Reanne monitored tidal fluctuations from *Baidarka*. Their conclusion was that Griffin is not suitable for most craft. It remains an adventure for a traverse by kayak.

In an area bordering the Fjordlands, where most shores are vertical, Griffin Passage's are surprisingly accessible. Black bears are very common. We saw five in its 13-mile length. Seals abound. Pooley Island is home to many wolves and, so far, one of the most extensive stands of intact coastal temperate rain forest. Though the northern extremities of both sides of the pass are being clear-cut, the central and lower portions are untouched and unvisited. Two sets of saltwater rapids keep the meek—and expensive boats—at bay. And the tides, and their resulting currents, are confusing and counterintuitive.

Tidal currents appear to flow south at all times. Between the two sets of rapids lies a 6-mile-long "lake" whose level never seems to fluctuate. Though the rapids never disappear, high water reduces the gradient and quiets the rapids' tempo. It is only at or near high water that it is possible to traverse each rapid against the current. And even then the upstream paddle requires a strongly determined effort.

From Rescue Bay (mile 163/**300**) where the main route enters Jackson Passage, head due north 5 miles to Charles Head and the entrance to Griffin. The foot of South Rapid lies 2 miles within. The rapid arcs slightly and favors the steep eastern shore. Head for the eddy on the inside bend of the western shore. Although this side of the channel is not steep and landings are possible, the terrain is so rugged—rocky with deep pools, slippery seaweed, thick kelp, and even thicker trees above the high-water line—that lining or a portage are not practical. Prepare for an upstream run and enjoy the myriad starfish and anemones that thickly populate the intertidal zone while you scope a line or await a better tidal level. At the top, a midchannel rock serves as a seal haul-out.

Our strategy had a series of components—some of them last-minute, desperate expedients. Wait for high water. Start the approach in the relatively calm water at the base of the eddy. Get in the eddy's upstream flow adjacent to the rapid, and work the paddle as if you were fending off two rattlesnakes with one hoe. Maintain a line and enough speed to break through the headfall. A rudder is invaluable for keeping a course. Unfortunately, at some point, the kelp becomes too thick for purchase. No problem. Drop the paddle (a paddle park is useful), and grab the kelp (don't worry, it won't break) so as not to lose ground. Like a legless beggar on a wheeled platform, use the kelp to pull yourself upstream. It took us two tries to gain calmer water above the rapid.

The second rapid, 6 miles on at the north end of the midsection lake, is, tactically, a smaller version of the first rapid. Approach on the west side. Though a bit steeper, the rapid is shorter. Lining and portaging are impractical. Hug the shore, work up speed, pull on kelp, and break over the headfall. Soon thereafter Griffin opens up with grassy, campable shores on the west side (mile 179/**616**). Lime Point and the logging operation's headquarters on the west shore bound Griffin Passage's north entrance, where it joins Sheep Passage, on the east. Exit into Sheep Passage.

Sheep Passage's shores are steep-to and the peaks rise to 3,000 feet all around. Turn northwest toward Fawn Point and cross over to Finlayson Head. Carter Bay, to the north, preserves the 1909 wreck of the SS *Ohio* in the northeast corner. The bow section is exposed. Finlayson Head marks the south entrance to Heikish Narrows, where this alternate rejoins the main route at mile 187/**624**. Traverse Heikish Narrows (see description above) to Princess Royal Channel, where the alternate route through Klemtu joins the main route at Sarah Point (mile 195/**632**).

Main Route: Continued . . .

Princess Royal Channel: Princess Royal Channel separates Princess Royal Island from the mainland. It is 38 miles long and divided, in the main, into two parts, Graham Reach and Fraser Reach. Work Island, near Princess Royal's midpoint—and flanked by short and parallel Butedale and Malcolm Passages—further separates the two reaches. Just what is a "reach"? Perhaps the channel is subdivided into reaches because tidal streams, just like those behind Vancouver Island, reach (flood/ebb) around the north and south ends, meet in the middle at Aaltanhash Inlet, and then reverse their flow when the tides reverse. Current velocity varies according to how far tidal incursion has advanced.

And that velocity, at its greatest, is no inconsequential matter. The trick, for a kayak, is to go up Graham Reach during a flood and exit Fraser Reach on the ebb.

Princess Royal's shores are mostly perpendicular precipices. Landings—much less campsites—are few, tenuous, and impractical. Most are located adjacent to stream outflows or bays and inlets. The channel funnels winds, which, when contrary to currents, can cause an unnerving midsize chop. Winds, in steady conditions, tend to freshen after noon. Get an early start for any transit.

About a mile up Graham Reach, on the mainland side, Green Inlet (mile 196/**633**) breaks the coastal barrier. Netherby Point, on the south side of the inlet, has a campsite carved out of the forest by a pair of enterprising Germans. Fronting the south side of the point is a bare patch of granite good for disembarking, cooking, and watching the world go by. Enter the forest toward the point for the cleared tent area. Some gardening may be required.

Swanson Bay (mile 200/**637**), also on Graham's east shore and about 4 miles north of Green, has the ruins of an old sawmill and cannery. The red brick chimney stands out. Certainly a campsite can be found or hacked out of the brush near the stream.

Cruise up Graham past Khutze and Aaltanhash Inlets (where the tides meet) to Redcliff Point. Steep-to Work (probably once Wark) Island dominates the view. Tim Lydon camped at a short beach (mile 212/**649**) near a valley, 0.5 mile from Work Island, probably on the mainland side of Princess Royal Channel at the mouth of Klekane Inlet. Butedale lies 2 miles farther along on the Princess Royal Island shore.

Butedale: Butedale (mile 214/**651**) has seen better times. The 1891 *Coast Pilot* reports an Indian summer village at the head of the bight. By 1923, when the Canadian Fishing Company bought the site, a processing plant and cannery had already been established. The company harnessed the power of Butedale Creek's near-vertical descent from enormous overhead Butedale Lake with a giant Pelton wheel turbine hooked up to a wooden penstock. Butedale was only one of more than 20 Canfisco operations along the Inside Passage that thrived until overfishing depleted the salmon runs. By 1973, canning had ceased; the

Butedale, Princess Royal Channel, British Columbia

lights were kept on to maintain a load on the generator. Only a caretaker remained to run the store, provide moorage, and sell fuel. Butedale must have seemed like an apparition out of *The Twilight Zone* to mariners coming upon it after leagues of dark monochrome wilderness. To then dock and find only a custodian must have been doubly startling. Butedale changed hands several times, each new owner trying to make something of the place, but the graceful settlement slowly deteriorated. "In the mid-1980s," according to Joe Upton, "the turbine failed, the lights went out, and the place was abandoned to the forest."

Increasing vandalism and a change of hands in the mid-1990s brought back a caretaker. Big plans to reopen the store and fuel dock, restore the town, and attract cruise clientele have waxed and waned. When we were first there in 1999, there was no ramp. Access was via a rickety, precarious vertical ladder more than 20 feet tall. Disclaimer warning signs and the barking of the caretaker's dogs discouraged visitors. Heavy snows that winter had collapsed several key buildings. By

2000, Butedale's resurrection had made some progress. The pier sported a new access ramp and a welcome sign.

For the kayaker, Butedale is a must stop. Approach from the new ramp and avoid everything else; many of the waterfront improvements are in imminent danger of collapse. The caretakers are friendly (and so are their dogs) and welcome company. Water and a flat spot to pitch a tent (the concrete helipad works fine) are always available. There is a trail up to the lake, where the fishing is said to be excellent and the mosquitoes voracious. But the real prize is the view. From such a commanding perspective, the curving penstock plunges your eyeballs down into the miniature town, waterfall, bay, Work Island, and curving channel ramparts, instantly blurring the distinction between foreground and panorama. Breathtaking.

Grenville Channel: Butedale *(mile 214/651)* to Prince Rupert *(mile 335/768)*

The last portion of the central British Columbia coast very nearly parallels the 315-degree trend of the mainland coastline. The route takes in the second half of Princess Royal Channel (Fraser Reach), successive McKay Reach (which leads into Wright Sound), and laser-straight Grenville Channel, then skirts the Skeena River delta before arriving at Prince Rupert. The wilderness and isolation continue. Hartley Bay, a Tsimshian settlement, and Oona River—both slightly off route—are civilization's only outposts. Treeline noticeably descends, and snow-capped ridges atop bald, soaring batholiths seem only an arm's length away.

While Fraser Reach retains the vertical character—in spades—of the previous portion's shorelines, the topography beyond McKay Reach eases up. Landings and possible campsites are more common, though that isn't saying much. The Skeena River, one of B.C.'s major drainages, cuts a wide swath through the Coastal Ranges, such a wide swath that a railroad and a major Al-Can Highway spur have allowed Prince Rupert to become second only to Vancouver in Canadian–Pacific Rim commerce. Both the highway and ferry service intimately connect Prince Rupert with the rest of Canada, Alaska, and the Lower 48 states,

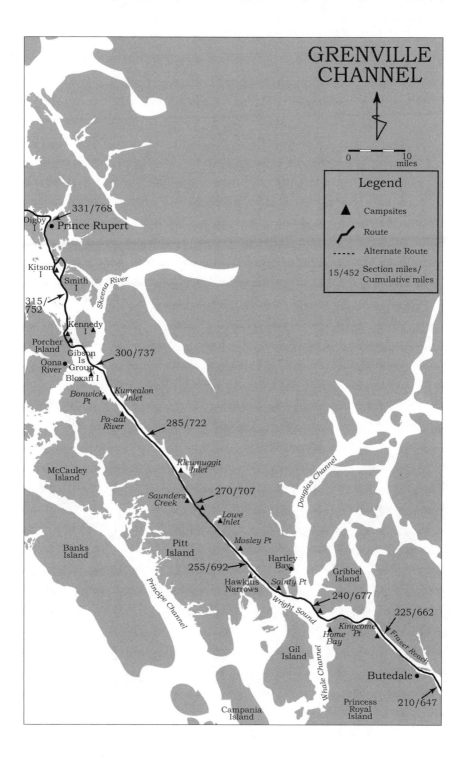

GRENVILLE CHANNEL

Legend

▲ Campsites

⌁ Route

- - - - Alternate Route

15/452 Section miles/
Cumulative miles

0   10
       miles

331/768

Digby I

Prince Rupert

Kitson I

Smith I

Skeena River

315/752

Kennedy I

Porcher Island

Gibson Is Group

Oona River

300/737

Bloxam I

Bonwick Pt

Kumealon Inlet

Pa-aat River

285/722

McCauley Island

Klewnuggit Inlet

270/707

Saunders Creek

Lowe Inlet

Banks Island

Pitt Island

Mosley Pt

255/692

Hartley Bay

Douglas Channel

Gribbel Island

Hawkins Narrows

Sainty Pt

Wright Sound

240/677

225/662

Principe Channel

Kingcome Pt

Home Bay

Fraser Reach

Gil Island

Whale Channel

Butedale

Campania Island

Princess Royal Island

210/647

making for relatively simple Inside Passage expedition logistics. In a kayak, however, the entire Skeena delta is best skirted.

Leave Butedale on an ebb tide, early in the morning. Thirteen miles of Fraser Reach separate Butedale from Kingcome Point, Princess Royal Channel's juncture with McKay Reach. Except for one stunning campsite, the walls are perpendicular with absolutely no landings. At about mile 226/**663**, where a short but spectacular and voluminous waterfall plunges from the Princess Royal Island side, there is a bare granite shelf adjacent to the stream's north shore. When we passed, it had a temporary wattle shelter, missing only one of those ubiquitous blue tarps. There is no more spectacular night's lodging.

At Kingcome Point, turn west into McKay Reach, where the shores open up to some farther-ranging views. Eight-mile-long McKay, due to its relative broadness, does not constrict tide or wind and so, generally, remains calm. Round Trivett Point, the northernmost extension of Princess Royal Island, and continue on to McKay's junction with Whale

Orca working the shore, Wright Sound, British Columbia

Channel and Wright Sound. Whale Channel lived up to its name—three orcas cruised by us, working the shore for hidden morsels.

Just around Nelly Point (mile 237/**674**) lies Home Bay, a broad indentation lined with white sand and giant drift logs. Except for the extensive drying sand flats, Home Bay makes an excellent, sunset-graced overnight stop. Alternatively, the bare rock shelf between Nelly Point and Home Bay's mouth yields at least one campsite. Camping by Nelly puts one in an excellent position for an early morning crossing of Wright Sound.

Wright Sound: From Nelly Point, cross McKay's mouth to Point Cumming (mile 238/**675**), at the southwest corner of Gribbell Island. A sandy beach on the south shore offers a welcoming camp. Position yourself for the crossing of Wright Sound/Douglas Channel. Wright Sound is the junction of seven separate channels. It is intimidatingly broad, more so after the narrow confines of the previous days. Tidal currents come and go from so many directions, and the influx of fresh water is so extensive at times that, in the aggregate, they all cancel each other out and are of no concern.

Weather systems, however, are another story. Douglas Channel is subject to extreme winds. So extreme that it has its own marine weather forecast Area. Inflow and outflow winds gather speed over vast areas of fetch and create rising seas of 4, 6, or even 8 feet. When Pacific depressions approach (or depart), southeast (or northwest) winds pick up, meet the Douglas Channel blows in Wright Sound, and mate like a pair of depraved badgers, creating total confusion. Again, cross early. From Point Cumming, coast up the shore for about 2 miles and cross over the 3.5 miles of Wright Sound/Douglas Channel to Promise Island. The entire 8-mile paddle from Nelly Point to Point Cumming to Promise Island's Cape Farewell should take no longer than 3 hours.

Hartley Bay: Hartley Bay, also known as Gitga'at, is only 5 miles off route from mile point 244/**681**, and is a Tsimshian First Nations village located on the mainland at the mouth of the Kukayu River facing Promise Island. There are only 180 year-round inhabitants—although

638 are registered as residents—whose primary livelihood is fishing. Water, groceries, and some provisions are available. Also present are a post office, medical clinic, store, fish hatchery, and Tsimshian carving shed. Hartley Bay is a dry community—that means no recreational alcohol. Camping might be available either in the village or on the white gravel beach in adjacent Coghlan Anchorage.

Grenville Channel: Grenville Channel is 45 miles long, straight as an arrow, and 0.25 mile wide at its narrowest. After Princess Royal, one look at Grenville on the chart will evoke ghosts, like vague apprehensions suspended in neural time, of vertiginously impenetrable shores without campsites or landings, of harrowing winds buffeting strong, opposing currents, and of anxious preparations. Many a kayaker has detoured into Principe Channel. Nothing could be further from the truth.

Tidal streams in the narrow portion attain 2 knots during flood and up to 4 knots on the ebb. Ebb streams continue to run for an hour and a half after low water along the shore. According to the Canadian *Sailing Directions,* "Strong eddies can be encountered abreast Lowe Inlet with the ebb stream." The Douglasses have clocked 6-knot ebb currents off James Point at Lowe Inlet. This little bit can be simply avoided by hugging the shore. Pitt Island, like Princess Royal and Vancouver Islands, obstructs the tides and causes them to split, do an end run, and meet in the middle of the posterior channel. In Grenville, currents meet and reverse at Evening Point near Klewnuggit Inlet. Although the Countess of Dufferin and Burnaby Ranges that channel Grenville rise steeply, the shores are not precipitous, and campsites are reasonably spaced.

Just north of Camp Point, in the small cove below Sainty Point (mile 247/**684**), is a campsite and a good spot to wait out a contrary current in Grenville Channel. From Sainty Point Cove, a favorable current— and wind—can assist you up to Lowe Inlet in as little as half a day.

For the more adventurous, the entrance to Union Passage (mile 252/**689**), on the west side of Grenville, holds a seldom-used campsite fronting old-growth forest. However, Hawkins Narrows, the entrance to Union Passage, must be negotiated. Here, tidal streams can attain a maximum of 8 knots. Slack water in Hawkins occurs 15 minutes before

Grenville Channel, British Columbia

high and low water at Prince Rupert and lasts about 5 minutes. But this is only an extreme during spring tides; at neaps the window of opportunity is much wider. The campsite is located barely 0.5 mile in from Grenville, just around the point defining the south entrance of Hawkins Narrows on the Pitt Island side.

Mosley Point (mile 256/**283**), 9 miles up Grenville from Sainty Point and often unlabeled, has a good campsite with a nearby stream that drains Belowe Lake.

Lowe Inlet: A prominent offshore island indicates the location, from many miles away, of Lowe Inlet (mile 264/**701**). The inlet pierces the Countess of Dufferin Range 17 miles up Grenville Channel on the mainland coast. Nettle Basin, the bay at the head of the inlet—with much of its foreshore low-lying—is 2 miles from the mouth and is separated from the rest of Lowe by a narrow, intrusive peninsula. The Kuwowdah River drains sizable Simpson and Lowe Lakes, cataracting into Nettle Basin via two-tiered Verney Falls. During tidal fluctuations, First Verney

Falls doubles in height. Adjacent to the north side of the Kuwowdah River's mouth, a small bight indents the shore. In its shallow depths, an aboriginal fish weir survives; from its shore, a primitive trail leads to Lowe Lake.

During the salmon runs, spawning females pepper the air at the base of the falls like shrapnel during an artillery barrage. Bears, both blacks and grizzlies, are common. In 1999, the Canadian government built a small warden's cabin with appurtenant outhouse, in the forest near the neck of the peninsula that defines the southern edge of Nettle Basin. The cabin is not obvious from a kayaker's perspective on the water. Due to the abundance of bears, find the cabin, and—at least—camp on the cleared ground adjacent to it, follow bear camping procedures rigorously, use the outhouse, and leave no trace.

The maps and charts show little indication of it, but, ever so gently and slowly, both shores of Grenville Channel north of Lowe Inlet ease up, allowing many more camping opportunities. Near mile 269/**706**, on the east shore, are a couple of consecutive camp spots. Saunders Creek (mile 272/**709**), on Grenville's western shore and below a high waterfall—according to the Douglasses—has a good haul-out beach and campsite. Nabannah Bay (mile 277/**714**) also has some campsites.

Twelve miles north of Lowe Inlet, at Klewnuggit Inlet (where the tides meet), Grenville widens considerably. Give Morning Point a wide berth. The tides' point of convergence seems to have accumulated a great deal of sediment and has built up a reef with shoals, breaking waves (in adverse conditions), and extensive shallows. Klewnuggit Inlet Marine Park, one of B.C.'s newest provincial parks, encompasses East Inlet and Brodie and Freda Lakes in the far reaches of the inlet.

Past Kxngeal Inlet, Baker Inlet comes in from the east. On the Pitt Island side of Grenville Channel, across from Baker, the Pa-aat River (mile 290/**727**) enters. Camping is possible at its mouth where, along the south bank, the remains of a white building stand out.

Four miles farther on, two large logging complexes operate out of Kumealon Inlet, one on the north shore inside the entrance, the other in Kumealon Island Cove. On the west side of Grenville Channel, Bonwick Point (mile 294/**731**) caps a small peninsula with a cluster of coves about it. The head of the northwesternmost cove is grassy, with suitable ground for camping. Cross over to Gibson and Bloxam Islands (mile 300/**737**), which mark the end of Grenville Channel. Gunboat Harbour, with drying flats at its head, separates the two islands and might yield a flat spot. (Tim Lydon reports camping somewhere on the group.)

The Gibson Island Group, including Bloxam, Bedford, and Marrack Islands form the axis for the convergence of four major channels: Grenville and Ogden from the south, and Arthur and Telegraph Passages from the north. The map is deceptive. Telegraph Passage is schizophrenic, but the opaque beige water near Gibson Island hints at its true nature: Sometimes it looks and acts like any other littoral passage, but more often it is actually a continuation of the Skeena River.

Skeena River: The name comes from a corruption of a Tsimshian word meaning "water from the clouds." Though only about 350 miles long, the Skeena River is the second largest river system in British Columbia and one of the world's largest undammed rivers. With good reason. The Skeena would be tough to tame. While providing a wide transmontane valley that connects interior British Columbia with Prince Rupert and the Pacific Ocean via both highway and railroad, it has exceptionally swift currents, exceptionally heavy sediment loads that create constantly shifting sand deposits, and exceptionally violent floods. Great conditions for supporting big populations of smelt, oolichan, and one of the largest runs of wild steelhead—the seagoing or anadromous version of rainbow trout—in the world.

As one of the very few corridors through the Coast Mountains, the Skeena has always been an important conduit for commerce. Prior to contact, coastal and interior natives would gather to fish and trade along the river each autumn as far as 180 miles inland from the coast. When the Hudson's Bay Company's traders first reached the area, they capitalized on the location and built the first of many trading forts along the Skeena near present-day Hazelton. By the 1850s, railroad surveyors were eyeing the practicality of a line to the sea and the opening of Canada's northernmost ice-free port on the Pacific. The first white settlement at the mouth of the river, Port Essington, grew around a mercantile opened in 1871. It soon bustled with salmon canneries and several thousand inhabitants. Unfortunately, when Prince Rupert, an excellent and natural deep-water harbor, was chosen as the terminus of the new railroad on the coast, Port Essington went into decline. After two catastrophic fires in the early 1960s it gave up the ghost.

Do not be tempted to hug the mainland coast, nipping into and across the Skeena River mouth in hopes of cutting a few miles. Not a good idea. We did and nearly came to grief. The Skeena is a big river with a tremendous outflow augmented by the Ecstall River right at its mouth. De Horsey Island diverts the entire combined flow of both rivers down Telegraph Passage between Kennedy Island and the mainland. Stay well away from Telegraph! Although the *Sailing Directions* reports only a 4-knot, south-flowing ebb, it adds, almost as an afterthought, that river runoff *greatly accelerates* the ebb. With understated self-assurance it declares the north-going flood to attain 3 knots, but fails to mention that the flood and the river's flow are like ants and termites—totally incompatible. Where they meet head-on, the turbulence is doubly disconcerting because the clash is mostly invisible. Where they don't meet head-on, each current separates and hugs opposite sides of the channel—river on the Kennedy Island side, flood tide adjacent to the mainland—like passersby in a crowded aisle. Making headway against the main flow, which would have to be crossed, is nearly impossible.

Even testing the waters is out of the question. The eddy line is 50 feet wide, very turbulent, and chaotic with giant whirlpools. No place to crisscross, especially during unfavorable winds. The resulting 1.5-mile ferry glide is a Sisyphean epic toward a nearly unlandable shore on Kennedy Island. (We were lucky. Thanks to the not infrequent loggers, who had bulldozed a landing spot halfway up Kennedy's east shore, we were able to disembark and camp.) Furthermore, exiting the Skeena's main current involves negotiating drying tidal flats. Consequently, beyond Grenville, this route goes outside Kennedy and Smith Islands in a wide flanking arc, along with the big boats, to Prince Rupert.

From the Gibson Island Group, the route heads northwest into Arthur Passage, the main traffic route up the Inside Passage. Aim for the southern tip of Kennedy Island via Marrack Island or Porcher Island, which defines the west flank of Arthur Passage.

Oona River: At the top of Ogden Passage and before the entrance into Arthur, Oona River (mile 301/**738**), a small village on its namesake's stream, lies 4 miles due west—and off route by as many miles—of Gibson on Porcher Island. Scandinavian immigrants established the town in 1917. At one time, its shipyard built and launched more than 100 boats. The log schoolhouse, built in 1920, is still in use. Only 35 residents remain. A proposed paddler's B&B may already be open and still operating. Porcher Island appears to be bear-free; not one bear has ever been sighted.

At this point, Porcher Island and the mainland funnel the southern end of Chatham Sound. Nearly all south- or northbound traffic must pass through Arthur Passage. During the 1990s this location was strategic territory in the US-Canada Salmon Wars. According to Joe Upton:

> *During the Fish War of 1994, Canadian patrol boats waited in this area to capture American fish boats that had not paid a $1,500 transit fee to use the Inside Passage. The fee was imposed as a political move when Canadian officials became frustrated at the reluctance of Alaskans to agree to a treaty allocating fish that swam the border waters between the two countries.*

Arthur Passage is best negotiated along the Porcher Island side. The Kennedy Island shore is steep with few landings. Flood tides, which come in from the north, attain 2.5 knots. Kelp Passage, between Lewis and Porcher Islands, is the more interesting route—for a kayak. Lewis Island has some gravel beaches with room for a few tents. At the north end of Lewis, veer right into Bloxam Passage, and cut back south into Lawson Harbour (mile 308/**745**), protected by outlying Break Island.

An abandoned Lewis Island settlement hugs the south shore beach, where a flat spot for a tent can certainly be found.

North of Lewis, head up to the east side of Elliot Island and over to Hanmer Island. Then make a beeline for Genn and Little Genn Islands. Don't be tempted to head due north to Smith Island or, even worse, into the pass between Smith and De Horsey Islands. Drying sand flats from the Skeena River outflow extend northwest from Kennedy Island nearly to Little Genn Island and block the pass between Smith and De Horsey at low tide.

From the Genns head north, crossing the entrance to Marcus Passage. Stay well out of Marcus where its entry funnel is at its widest. Flood streams can reach 3.5 knots, while ebbs top out at 5 knots. (Note that these figures are for the narrowest section of Marcus.) Streams turn (slack) 1 hour after high water. Aim either for Smith or Kitson Island (mile 319/**756**). Both are attractive choices with very different route consequences. A broad drying sand flat, the Flora Bank, reefs the area between Kitson and Lelu Island about a mile to the northeast, forcing northbound traffic either east of and around Lelu or west of Kitson. First the east route.

Aim for the gap between Smith and Lelu Islands, straight for Phelan, where the remains of the Caspaco and North Pacific canneries jut out from the grassy shores. The North Pacific Cannery, the oldest standing cannery on the West Coast, was in operation from 1889 to 1968. It has been converted into the North Pacific Cannery Museum with demonstrations and tours, while the mess hall now boasts a restaurant, and the bunkhouse is a B&B.

Round Lelu Island counterclockwise, first up Inverness Passage from the museum, then slip west into Porpoise Channel between Lelu and Ridley Islands. Tidal currents in Porpoise can reach 2 knots. Head for Prince Rupert along the west shore of Ridley Island. Don't be tempted to approach Prince Rupert up the backside of Ridley. A backfilling operation has connected Ridley to Kaien Island, and the passage no longer exists. Farther up the east side of Kaien, tidal constrictions at Wainright Basin, Morse Basin, and Fern Passages cause strong currents that are impractical to transit.

If, from the Genn Islands, you head directly for Kitson Island (mile 319/**756**), you'll miss the cannery museum, while opting for the around-Lelu-Island route still allows for a visit to Kitson Island Marine Park. There is a sandy beach on the east shore with camping both on the beach and behind. A trail from the far eastern end of the beach leads to an outdoor toilet. There is no water.

The approach to Prince Rupert is heralded by lots of marine hubbub. Port Edward in Porpoise Harbour is a major fish market and processing center. Fishing boats converge on wholesale buyers with suitcases full of cash and big signs advertising "Cash Buyer." Along the southwest coast of Kaien Island giant conveyor piers, ethereal and spindly (for such a grand scale), like spider's legs, reach tentatively out to Asia. Some convey grain, some coal or pulp, some more voluminous items. In the fog, the approach to Rupert seems to take forever with one mega pier appearing before the last one fades, separated only by the ample room necessary for giant trans-Pacific freighters, gargantuan exemplars of humankind's interconnectedness, to maneuver.

Prince Rupert: By Inside Passage standards, Prince Rupert is a big city with a population of 16,000. It is the secondary base of the Canadian Coast Guard–Western Region, responsible for the area between Cape Caution and Alaska. The primary base, in Victoria, covers Cape Caution to Washington State. The fleet has 15 vessels, a half dozen helicopters, and three hovercraft, plus about a hundred auxiliary vessels and small craft.

Prince Rupert was founded soon after the turn of the 20th century by Charles Hays (who drowned in the sinking of the *Titanic*) to service the Pacific terminus of the Grand Trunk Railway. He named it after the first governor of the Hudson's Bay Company, Prince Rupert of the Rhine, cousin of Charles II, the lucky heir to the then newly restored English throne. It is the Skeena River, with its broad and massive channel providing reasonable transit through the B.C. Coast Ranges, that makes possible the very existence of Prince Rupert. Construction of the railway began simultaneously from both ends, Rupert and Winnipeg, in 1907. It took seven years to complete. The connecting highway was completed during WWII as part of the Al-Can project. Hays's prescience

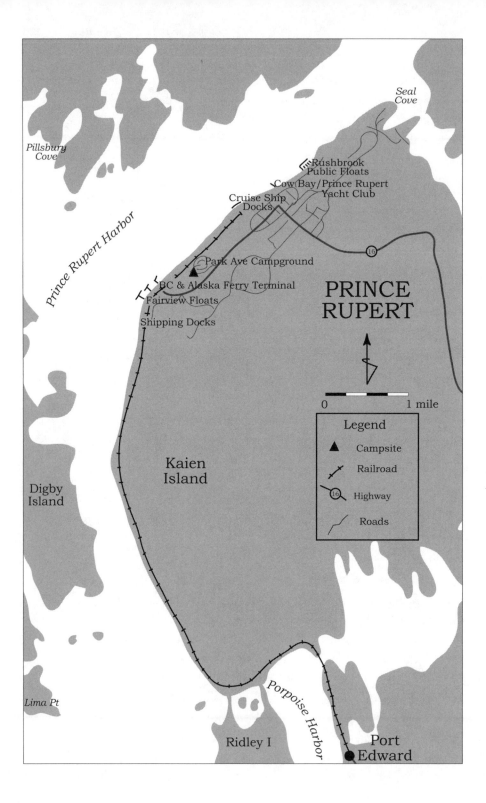

Seal Cove

Pillsbury Cove

Rushbrook Public Floats

Cow Bay/Prince Rupert Yacht Club

Cruise Ship Docks

Prince Rupert Harbor

Park Ave Campground

BC & Alaska Ferry Terminal

Fairview Floats

Shipping Docks

PRINCE RUPERT

16

0   1 mile

Legend

▲   Campsite

⊬   Railroad

16   Highway

Roads

Kaien Island

Digby Island

Lima Pt

Ridley I

Porpoise Harbor

Port Edward

and Rupert's geographic exclusivity ensured the city's success and continuing prosperity. Every service imaginable is available but not, from a kayaker's point of view, suitably condensed.

Paddlers terminating their trip here and shuttling back to Port Hardy via the B.C. ferry should take out next to the Alaska and B.C. Ferry dual terminals at the south end of the city, about halfway up Kaien Island. Kayak wheels might be handy but not essential. Fairview floats, docking facility for Rupert's fishing fleet and likely put-in for the next leg of the journey, are next door. The municipal campground (250-624-5861) at 1750 Park Avenue (Park Avenue is the extension of the ferry ramp into town) is close by—at about a half mile, arguably within walking distance—but not on the water. Right next to the campground is the Anchor Inn, at 1600 Park Avenue (250-627-8522). There are also two or three B&Bs in the vicinity, who may provide a pickup and drop-off at the ferry terminal for you and your gear. The Pineridge (250-627-4419) and Mountainside (250-627-1000) B&Bs are on Sloan Avenue. For additional Prince Rupert services, see the next chapter.

Inquire at the ferry terminal or call 1-888-223-3779 for sailing times to Port Hardy, price—there is a surcharge for kayaks—and to make reservations, suggested but not required. The voyage back to Port Hardy, all 331 miles, goes by in a trice and from quite a different perspective. Taxis are available at the Port Hardy ferry terminal for transport to the Sunny Sanctuary Campground and your vehicle.

One additional possible strategy is to store your kayak for your return at a marina, your overnight accommodations, or one of five vehicle storage depots in Prince Rupert: Northcoast Pacific Mini Storage (Seal Cove, 624-5879); Park Avenue Corner Store; FAS Gas (1665 Park Avenue, 250-624-3201); Rupert Towing and Lowbed Dispatch (101 Shawatlans Road, 250-624-2722); Totem Lodge Motel (1335 Park Avenue, 250-624-2273); or Parkside Resort Motel (#101, 11th Avenue East, 250-624-9131). Just remember that you'll need to get your kayak back home somehow, or sell it, after the trip.

6
Alaska Panhandle

Prince Rupert to Juneau

382 miles

> The frontiers are not East or West,
> North or South,
> but wherever a man fronts a fact.
> —Henry David Thoreau

The last frontier. Alaska hangs off the shoulder of the North American continent like the proverbial carrot-on-a-stick and attracts a diverse assortment of characters with peculiar predilections. Dreamers, cranks, end-of-the-roaders, all manner of people make their way north or, having had the blessing of Alaskan birth, remain. Many are back-to-the-landers: wannabe trappers, homesteaders, or pot farmers; some are angst-ridden Greens. A few are fed-up militia misfits, Libertarian idealists, or just run-of-the-mill misanthropes; most are insufferably self-reliant—and competent—egoists. Soldiers, petty bureaucrats, and resource extractors, drawn by big bucks to endure 2-year stints in the bush, commit, endure, and often burn out. All have found a welcome niche in Alaska. That is, for as long as they can abide the dark, the damp, and the cold. Not a few are socially inept, given to non sequiturs and conversational spurts and lapses reminiscent of communication on time-delayed satellite radios complete with bad reception. Most are vulnerable sorts, often overly friendly, open, and honest, yet suspicious and quick to anger. All are eccentric to a fault. It is truly a quaff of fine ale. To a special sort of woman, these are MEN, *real* men.

Chuck La Queue (his real alias) is a *real* man. Tall, hirsute—handsome, in spite of his thick Barry Goldwater glasses—and slightly lordotic,

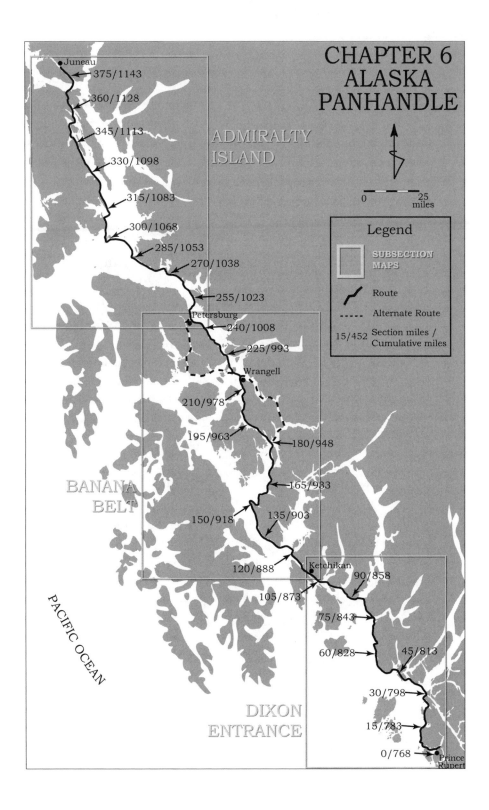

CHAPTER 6
ALASKA
PANHANDLE

ADMIRALTY
ISLAND

BANANA
BELT

PACIFIC OCEAN

DIXON
ENTRANCE

Juneau
375/1143
360/1128
345/1113
330/1098
315/1083
300/1068
285/1053
270/1038
255/1023
Petersburg
240/1008
225/993
Wrangell
210/978
195/963
180/948
165/933
150/918
135/903
120/888
105/873
Ketchikan
90/858
75/843
60/828
45/813
30/798
15/783
0/768
Prince Rupert

0   25
        miles

Legend

	SUBSECTION MAPS
	Route
	Alternate Route
15/452	Section miles / Cumulative miles

Chuck drove his VW microbus to Alaska to prospect a job with the newly approved Trans-Alaska Pipeline project in 1973. Accosted at the border by overly enthusiastic INS agents, he fought back with a full, double-barreled arsenal of a cappella Irish rebel songs at high volume and in a full-throated, resonant baritone. Chuck is a world-class kayaker. He was fresh off a first descent of the headwaters of the Amazon and needed a change. Unable to sign on with the Alyeska Consortium immediately, he joined the commercial crab fishing fleet for a stint in the frigid waters of the Gulf of Alaska. He survived one season. Chuck wasn't—and isn't—a team player. Once, when planning a kayak expedition and short on funds, he tried a new approach to victualing. He'd heard that strapped inner-city senior citizens in New York City were resorting to subsisting on pet food for its value-to-volume efficiency, so he packed a month's supply of Gaines Burgers. When they turned out to taste like lard-laced sawdust with just a hint of offal, he tried cooking them. Though they were still inedible, he nonetheless ate them. To his grumbling teammate, a redhead with a limp whom he'd enlisted during a night of excess at the Red Dog Saloon in Fairbanks, he declared, like a disgruntled prospector (a profession he pursues intermittently), that if she didn't like the way things had turned out, he'd "buy her out!"

Chuck is particular. Once, passing the time at a local watering hole, he befriended an attractive off-duty Tongass National Forest rangerette from the Ketchikan district. Passing time soon became making time. Since he'd been considering an Inside Passage paddle, he asked her in what direction the predominant winds blew. She responded that she hadn't noticed. All of a sudden, Chuck visibly lost interest and left. Puzzled—they'd already locked eyeballs and were sniffing each other like dogs—I asked why he walked away from a sure prospect. "She's unobservant," he tersely declared with not a little contempt for her, her competence, the Forest Service, the question, and even me—for prying. Today, Chuck splits his time between working winters for the pipeline in Prudhoe Bay and doing construction in summertime Phoenix, Arizona. To do otherwise, he quietly avers, would be unAlaskan.

Markle, another *real* man, is Chuck's neighbor. In Detroit, before he moved to Alaska, he sold used cars. He lives in a mini-Quonset hut, uninsulated except for the stacks of books, clothes, and outdoor gear along the outside walls. An oversize wood-burning stove dominates the Quonset. Unlike Chuck, Markle has running water, phone, and electricity from a utility. Now he lives his passions: kayaking and mountaineering, at both of which he's notably accomplished. When the outdoor season dawns, an intricate—and predictable—minuet ensues. Markle requests a sabbatical from his job. Invariably, he's turned down. So he quits and goes off chasing what's important to him. Upon his return, his old boss invariably rehires him. Seems his skills are indispensable. To supplement his income he sequesters himself with a phone for extended commodities-futures trading sessions. Markle, like Chuck, is unmarried and lives alone.

We met Kristin on the water. She was kayaking to Alaska to find a *real* man. At 24, she was becomingly steatopygous with a strong upper torso to match. Since she was barefoot, unkempt, and underdressed, with a shotgun slung from her shoulder, few men could resist her. Her eyes were pools of mystery; she was quiet and verbally shy. Pouty, everted lips shielded oversized and bunny-toothed incisors that hinted of prognathy. She had a perfectly rounded, dolichocephalic skull with a high forehead. A hint of lanugo caressed her cheeks. She was quite compelling in an untraditional sense. An assayer by trade, Kristin hailed from Dawson in the Yukon Territory and was traveling light—no stove, a simple tarp, no brand-name gear. She was obsessively focused on her quest, and no single man got away from her. She was literally testing every available male on her route, fishermen first. When we last heard of her—she was a minor legend by then—she'd taken up with a part-time fisherman and log salvager living at the edge of a small waterfront community.

Log salvaging, or beach logging, like gathering aluminum cans along rights-of-way in the Lower 48, is a handy source of pocket money and a not uncommon sight along the Inside Passage. The log salvager, one man working with a small skiff or inboard, often with his son, will scour sounds, inlets, passages, and beaches for escaped logs on the lam.

On a bad day, suitable driftwood will suffice. Spotting a likely mark, the salvager will typically nose the boat up to the beach, jump out with a choke cable while the boat idles, hawse it around the log, jump back in, and hope his engine and skill can refloat it for a bounty. A sawmill will pay, depending on the species, upwards of $500 for a 50-foot-long, 18-inch-diameter log. The same size log, prime construction-grade Douglas fir, dressed—with little or no taper—might retail for $1,500.

The welcome sign in the park next to the chamber of commerce in Port Hardy encapsulates a particular view of the Northwest Coast: "Port Hardy: Logging, Fishing & Mining." The sign is incomplete; "Tourism" is missing. These pursuits are as intricately intertwined with the Northwest Coast as Guinness, sheep, and music are with Ireland. All four are pursued at industrial proportions; as family enterprises; and as individual efforts that supplement fluctuating and seasonal incomes.

Perhaps Alaska attracts its fair share of eccentric opportunists because, perceiving itself a tough sell, it has resorted to offering particularly attractive packages—thong-clad, some might say—of its resources. Allotted on an individual basis, some of these packages are outright giveaways. The 1862 Homestead Act, repealed in 1976, was resuscitated in Alaska in 1984 for an encore. Before the state act was terminated in 1991, 1,600 Alaskans were awarded homestead permits. It was still a tough sell. Only 12 percent proved up their land. In step with the generous land allotments, logging, fishing, mining, and tourism followed suit. During the early years, individuals could appropriate up to 25,000 board feet of lumber and 25 cords of wood from the Tongass National Forest. Trap fishing, outlawed virtually everywhere along the Inside Passage at a very early date, was outlawed in Alaska only at the time of statehood in 1959. The controversial—and still extant—Mining Act of 1872 allows mineral claims on public land without payment of royalties and with allowances for patenting. The most innovative mineral giveaway has to be the Alaska Permanent Fund, established in 1976. Funded by oil revenues, the Fund pays a dividend to every resident who has lived in Alaska for at least six months. The 2002 check totaled

$1,540.76. For a time, the United States Forest Service (USFS) allowed special use permits for recreational cabins in the Tongass. Today, the Forest Service maintains recreational cabins for public use, at a nominal fee.

Logging

Along the Inside Passage, the trees are tightly spaced, the branches almost touch, and undergrowth clogs the understory, but the timber industry is as ever present as rain. Clear-cuts, abandoned roads to nowhere, booming grounds, tug-towed booms, pulp mills, solitary log salvagers, deadheads, helicopter skidders, log freighters, and lumber barges are each a visible component of an intricate and complex operation that we tried to accurately fit and sequence—like a puzzle—and then comprehend to keep our minds entertained while paddling. From the water, the forest seems impenetrable.

One day, in Sunderland Channel, the lateness of the hour and the absence of beaches forced us to broach the forest battlements, enter, and—improbably but desperately—look for a clear, flat spot. We were stunned. Inside, the forest opened up somewhat and little undergrowth grew. But the slash piles, oil spills, and garbage—the stink and detritus of loggers long (and not so long) past, dominated the scene and shocked us. Trained as an archaeologist, I must have been the only one of our group who found anything redeeming in the tableau. I looked for some diagnostic sign that might date the depredation. It was right there in front of us, invisible—a case of being unable to see the trees for the forest—giant stumps like spectral headstones commemorating a vanished world, 5 to 8 feet high and 6 to 8 feet in diameter; pockmarked with two to four incongruous, ax-hewn niches, always 2 or 3 feet below the flat top; and widely spaced among the spindly second- and third-growth saplings that had regenerated a mere 3 to 10 feet apart. So widely spaced were the big fellows that the scale of that extinct and unimaginable prehistoric forest must have been Brobdingnagian. We wanted to see—what in our mind's eye we pictured as a Tolkien-like copse—such a forest.

A surprising number of locales along the Inside Passage, even in Puget Sound, are touted as being "old-growth" or, as is now more common, first-growth. In a nutshell, an old-growth forest is one that has never been logged. So we made a point of seeking out vestigial old-growth sanctuaries such as the Brothers Islands, just south of Admiralty Island. We were underwhelmed. True, there was gardenlike under-growth—gorgeous moss and ferns—no stumps, and no sign of man. These islands had never been logged. But the trees were a humdrum 1 to 2 feet in diameter. We'd been expecting to see the old giants. We felt cheated.

The definition of old-growth can be a bit slippery. Up to 15 to 20 percent of a stand can be logged and still be considered old-growth; an entire forest can be clear-cut and also be considered old-growth if the event occurred more than 125 years ago. And tree size is not a factor. Local microclimatic conditions determine whether a particular stand of trees achieves its full genetic potential or not. And potential they do have. The largest trees were the Douglas fir, the Sitka spruce, and the western red cedar. Botanists theorize that the tendency toward gigantism is a function of millennia of genetic evolution uninter-rupted by the glacial episodes of past ice ages. The Inside Passage was generally ice-free when much of the rest of North America was covered with ice. Certain arboreal genetic lineages advanced and retreated in step with the glacial advances, along the ice-free corridor, adapting and surviving. What to our imagination are true old-growth forests—with trees averaging 8 feet in diameter, exceeding 200 feet in height, and more than 300 years old—are now rare and remote. Most have been logged.

At first, the Northwest Coast forests were perceived as an obstacle to be cleared. But the exceptional size and straightness of the timber won shipbuilders' praise and proved better than Baltic stands for masts and spars. With the passing of the Age of Sail and increased settlement, lumber demand for terrestrial uses exploded. The first sawmills along the Inside Passage were built at Olympia and Victoria in 1848. Their lumber built San Francisco, Seattle, and Victoria. Alaska's first sawmills were built by the Russians in Sitka and by the Americans in 1879 near Wrangell. During WWI and WWII, demand for Sitka spruce to build fighter planes and British Mosquito bombers soared.

All logs now end up at mills. Giant pulp mills—in Tacoma, Port Townsend, Nanaimo, Powell River, and Ketchikan (along our route)—predominate. Pulp mills are not picky; they'll accept any tree, turn it into pulp, and make paper; 13 tons of wood yield 1 ton of paper. Some mills specialize in dissolving pulp—mostly from hemlock—which is further processed into rayon, cellophane, and plastics. Pulp mills even process wood chips and sawdust, sawmill by-products once burned as scrap, but now in demand. Tugboats towing giant wood-chip barges from sawmills to pulp mills are a common sight along the Inside Passage. Although sawmills—many mom-and-pop operations—still eke out a decent livelihood, they play a lesser role. Exceptionally prime timber makes its way into lumber, particularly for Asian markets and for specialty uses such as plywood. On the one hand, dwindling timber resources and increasing populations have driven up demand and timber prices; on the other hand, engineered wood products (wafer board, glue-lam beams, particle board, etc.), steel, and concrete have replaced dearer lumber. While pulp mills are certainly an efficient way to use sawmill waste, demand for paper has also mushroomed, particularly since the advent of the computer and the "paperless office," and no simple substitute has jumped into the breach.

Logging mostly starts out as a one-to one, mano-a-mano affair, one man vs. one tree; after all, man hasn't yet devised a combine to harvest timber. Lumberjacks, kited up like medieval knights—helmets, face guards, ear muffs, gloves, ballistic cloth chaps, steel-toed boots, and a whirring lance of a chain saw with bars up to 4 feet in length—don't cry "timber!" Individual sounds can't penetrate the armor, just the aggregate hum of chain saws and skidders. One man can size up, notch, fell, and trim a 100-foot-tall, 18-inch-diameter (without the bark) tree in well under half an hour. It wasn't always so.

During the 19th century, Douglas firs along the Northwest Coast could reach 300 feet in height and 15 feet in diameter. No saw could span such girth; no one man could fell such a leviathan. To complicate matters, a tree's foundation—its root system—funnels up into the

*Hand-logged, old-growth stump.
Note springboard notch on right.*

trunk, forming an acutely tapering pediment that buttresses the tree and impedes its downfall. This area, sometimes reaching 6 feet above the ground, is cull when the tree is rendered into lumber, so loggers always severed the tree well above its roots, where the taper became more uniform. To reach this height, a temporary scaffold consisting of a single plank called a springboard, like a diving board to nowhere, was wedged—without additional fasteners—into an ax-cut notch about 3 feet below the proposed cut line. The weight of the logger—and not a little faith—kept the plank from slipping out. Two planks, on opposite sides of a tree, provided minimal platforms for two well-balanced saw cutters.

First, the directional notch on the downhill side of the tree was cut about one-quarter to one-third through the tree. Then the loggers would switch to the opposite, uphill side of the tree and begin the felling cut, always noticeably above the directional notch. The sawyers would seesaw all the way to the saw's capacity, usually no greater than 10 feet. The tree's heartwood was then tackled with broadaxes measuring 16 inches at the face, until the tree's weight gave way along the remaining thin hinge. At this point, nimble choppers executed a well-timed leap off the planks. Cutting one tree could consume an entire day. Then as now, a particularly prime tree's landing would be cushioned by a bed of smaller trees and branches, to prevent splintering and kickback.

In the early days, steep topography was an asset. All trees would fell downhill. If they needed help getting to the water after the branches had been trimmed, a series of smaller logs placed perpendicularly, sometimes notched to keep the aim true, and often greased—sometimes with whale oil ("greasing the skids")—would aid the skidding process, getting the log to a common transport depot. At first, gravity was often sufficient to get a tree to the water; if not, trees were harnessed to horse and ox teams. "Donkey engines," stationary steam or diesel motors with giant drums and cables, soon replaced the livestock. Today, giant bulldozers skid the timber.

Or, sometimes, helicopters. Expensive though it might seem, as both the distance from prime timber to the sea and the cost of extending access roads into increasingly rugged terrain have increased, heli-logging has come into its own. Without extensive logging roads, impact and erosion are minimized or eliminated. In some areas, under some resource management regimens, helicopters are the only viable skidders. But beware if you find yourself under their flight path. Newly guillotined and choked by a single cable, heli-logs rain down a constant shower of bark, branches, and detritus. In many cases, these prime logs are deposited directly onto a log-carrying barge for transport to a sawmill.

Self-loading log barges, 200 to 400 feet in length with crews of two to four, and log freighters—bigger still—are often seen in the distance cruising outside waters. Empty, they resemble castle moat bridge supports with buttressing towers and cranes at the fore and aft ends. At a distance, empty or full, these squat castles unexpectedly puzzle. The logs are stacked crosswise on the decks and are unloaded by flooding water compartments on one side of the ship. The resulting list, or tilt, slides the logs off. Log ships transport unmilled logs over long distances or rough water, often to Asian markets. US regulations require Alaskan timber to undergo "primary processing" prior to export, usually into squared-off logs called cants. (Native-owned timber, according to the Alaska Native Claims Settlement Act, is exempt; most of the high-quality Native timber is shipped as raw logs to Japan.)

Logs are stockpiled at "booming" areas, the nearest protected waters adjacent to the cutting site or, at the receiving end, the lumber or pulp mill. Booming areas are defined by and subdivided into holding pens by perimeter logs strung together by cables and marked into lots for easy identification. At the Powell River pulp mill, exposed to the full fetch of the Strait of Georgia, the anchored, rusting hulls of surplus WWII merchant marine ships create the booming ground.

Transit between booming grounds is a tedious, labor-intensive, low-tech affair with long reaction times and minor episodes of tragic farce not unlike herding sheep, complete with maverick escapees. Transport holding pens, as above, sometimes and seemingly absurdly strung together in lengths as long as three, are hitched to a single tug for tow. Tugboats are not the most nimble wranglers. Basically gargantuan, seaworthy diesel engines, they are long on raw power but short on balletic grace. The log bundles are not hydrodynamic, immeasurably resist organization, and retain oodles of inertia. Kayaks often outpace tugged log bundles. Avoid them like drunken mendicants. Their reaction times are measured in increments of an hour, and current, wind, and sea conditions can discombobulate the entire jury-rigged affair. Getting started and docking a load are tests of patience and seamanship. For longer voyages and before the introduction of self-loading log barges and ships, the log bundles—with a great deal of pressure—were chained together into a cigar-shaped, single towable mass called a Davis raft, measuring 280 feet long by 60 feet wide and 30 feet deep.

Various entities own—and manage quite differently—different portions of the Inside Passage forests. In the state of Washington, besides National Forests, Parks, and various other federal, state, and local entities, a great deal of forested land is privately owned. Tacoma-based Weyerhaeuser owns much of its resource thanks to government subsidies, in the form of undeveloped acreage, granted the railroads after the Civil War as a quid pro quo for building line extensions. In 1900 Frederick Weyerhaeuser bought 900,000 of these acres from the Northern Pacific Railroad. Weyerhaeuser, Georgia-Pacific, and others now primarily manage "tree farms" on their deeded land.

British Columbia's government owns 95 percent of the province's forests and manages them through the B.C. Forest Service. Far from affording a venue for conservation, government ownership sometimes seems a detriment. Canada has always been imbued with an interventionist economic philosophy, in the belief that nothing gets done unless government lends a helping hand. Consequently, government takes an active part in growth and development by subsidizing resource exploitation. Leases to timber corporations such as MacMillan-Bloedel, B.C. Forest Products, Crown Pacific, and Western Forest Products—at exceptionally good terms—are the norm. "Dumping!" cry the Americans, and in May 2002 the United States imposed duties averaging 27 percent on Canadian imports. "It's the biggest trade battle on the planet," says Pierre Pettigrew, Canada's trade minister.

On the other hand, government has lately been intervening more and more for conservation, setting aside more land for parks and removing acreage from consideration for timber leases. In 1997, under the Forest Practices Code, the Inside Passage (in the stricter sense, not the entire North Coast) was declared a scenic area, a designation that means scenic integrity, and not timber production, will be the paramount planning guideline. According to the B.C. Forest Service, now only 16 percent of the North Coast forest is considered available and suitable for logging.

The Tongass National Forest—the largest national forest in the US—started life in 1902 as the Alexander Archipelago Forest Reserve. In 1907, Teddy Roosevelt substantially increased the reserve to create today's Tongass National Forest, which encompasses 80 percent of all the land in Alaska's southeast. Back then, "reserve" and "national" didn't quite mean what they mean today.

As a timber resource, the great forests of the Lower 48 were quickly disappearing. So it seemed logical that the vast forests of newly acquired Alaska would continue to supply demand. At one time, laissez-faire market forces would have been allowed to operate unhindered. But in 1873, Karl Marx, in the first volume of *Das Kapital,* argued that a brain was needed behind Adam Smith's "invisible hand" to control and guide it so it would make better choices: government. With policies developed centrally, at the national level, by disinterested experts, instead of the anarchy of self-interest of countless citizens, exploitation and extraction of the new resource could be maximized with greater efficiency. "Reserve" meant "reserved for exploitation" and "national" meant "officially nationalized for exploitation." The National Forest Service was the entity of experts created to manage and promote economic exploitation of forest resources. From the beginning, they tried to bring economic development to southeast Alaska by offering cheap timber to companies willing to build local mills.

But that now-handcuffed invisible hand was proving hard to direct. Even with subsidies, the distance, rugged terrain of Alaska, and cheapness of other timber sources attracted only local hand loggers and mom-and-pop sawmills to the Tongass. World War II and the postwar economic boom increased exploitation, but apparently not enough for the economic planers in Washington, D.C. In 1947, Congress passed the Tongass Timber Act, which not only authorized the Forest Service to offer generous incentives to timber companies, but also guaranteed that the subsidies would not deplete the agency's annual funding. In one stroke of the economic planning pen, large-scale logging was now truly viable in Alaska.

Two takers stepped up to the trough: the soon-to-be Louisiana Pacific Paper Company and the Alaska Pulp Company, a newly formed Japanese consortium incorporated in Juneau. The 50-year contracts that each were awarded built pulp mills in Ketchikan and Sitka and brought growth and economic development to the panhandle. So as not to completely eliminate competition, the Forest Service reserved one-third of its "crop" for smaller operators. But free government money and a guaranteed majority stake are hard to resist, and corrupt completely. By the 1970s both Louisiana Pacific and APC had conspired to corner the market by buying out or forcing from business all competitors, then used the no-longer-competing competitors to manipulate federal timber auctions and thereby artificially depress the pulp market price. With an intricate but fraudulent shell game, both companies reshuffled vast profits to parent corporations to make the mills appear barely profitable and thereby secure lower timber prices. Since lower prices encourage consumption, panhandle forests suffered.

To make matters worse, the Alaska Native Claims Settlement Act awarded half a million acres of prime forest in southeast Alaska to local native corporations. They soon set out to substantiate the fears that were the original impetus for the establishment of the failed reservation system: They logged with a vengeance in an attempt to make their corporations profitable. Within 10 years they clear-cut as much as Louisiana Pacific and APC combined had razed since the 1950s.

But the tide was turning. During the late 1950s and early 1960s, people were beginning to value pristine forests not just as sources of timber and jobs but also for recreation, biodiversity, *un*development, and just for their own sake. These nouveau values were exemplified by the Sierra Club, which now attracted legions of conservation-minded folk. The organization, founded in 1898 for hikers and climbers, had become a political powerhouse by 1960. Using a combination of lawsuits and lobbying, the Sierra Club was instrumental in beginning to reverse the status quo. In 1964, Congress passed the first Wilderness Act.

The conservationists' unlikely ally was an independent logger whose 1981 lawsuit against the pulp mills exposed both the economic inequities in the Forest Service's system and the fraud and corruption in Louisiana Pacific and APC. As more people learned that the Forest Service was losing millions of dollars on the Tongass timber program, taxpayers joined conservationists, hunters, fishermen, and small businesses in demanding reform. In 1984, Congress designated 5.4 million acres of southeast Alaska as wilderness and turned the 2-million-acre Glacier Bay National Monument into a national park. But the real victory came in 1990 with the Tongass Timber Reform Act, which designated a further 1 million acres as wilderness, abolished the $40 million timber fund, and decreased the target cut. By 1997, Forest Service reforms, the burden of unresolved lawsuits, and accumulated pollution fines forced both companies to close their Alaskan pulp mill operations.

In 1999, a new Tongass Land Management Plan extended a broad panoply of protections to panhandle forests. Once spreading to more than 2,000 acres, today the average size of a Tongass clear-cut is 80 acres, and only 10 percent of the Tongass is scheduled for harvesting over the next 100 years.

Fishing

For a kayaker, fishing for fish that don't eat is a true challenge. The most effective method for bagging a salmon along the Inside Passage is to beg, buy, flirt, or somehow talk your way into a salmon from a passing commercial fishing boat. Most will proudly offer a token of their catch. Gillnetters reeling in and clearing their nets are excellent prospects. Sometimes they snag out-of-season species that must be released. Most of the time the unfortunate fish is so damaged it can't survive and, hating to waste an otherwise fine fish, the skipper is more than happy to see it somehow end up in a paddler's larder. Keep a supply of plastic garbage bags handy in which to pack the salmon so as not to contaminate the kayak with fish smell. One hour or more before camping, stop at a handy beach to clean, fillet, cut up, and pack the meat in a small plastic bag. Discard the offal responsibly and burn the plastic garbage bag. Though it's hard to beat barbecued salmon, you don't want to attract uninvited ursine guests. Try boiling, er, poaching. Cleanup is a cinch, and the salmon is every bit as delicious. Season with salt, lemon, and pepper.

Commercial salmon fishing is strictly regulated according to political jurisdiction, season, fish stocks, salmon species (see chapter 1 and appendix D for habits and identifying features of each salmon variety), and methods of fishing. Three methods are commonly employed along Inside waters: trolling, gillnetting, and purse seining. Each type of boat is quite distinctive, but all are extremely common. They vary in length from 30 to 50 feet, with purse seiners sometimes reaching 100 feet.

Trolling is the simplest method. Two to four tall trolling poles, lowered to 45 degrees for fishing, distinguish salmon trollers. Each pole deploys a weighted line with multiple lures. Although salmon don't normally eat during the spawn, they retain a strong instinct to snap. The lines are hauled periodically, either by hand or with power winches—*gurdies*—and fish removed. Unlike netters, salmon trollers are not restricted to a certain area and range far and wide, with a crew

The most effective way to catch a salmon from a kayak. CREDIT: T. COBOS

of one or two for up to a week. An Alaskan hand-trolling license is relatively cheap and easy to acquire, allowing almost anyone to become a commercial fisherman. Elderly pioneers supplementing retirement income, well-off suburbanites writing off expensive cruisers as a business expense, aging hippies in rotting hulks, and men undergoing midlife crises all contribute to Alaska's colorful cast of independent fishermen.

Gillnetters fish with a fine nylon rectangular net about 1,000 feet long by 20 wide. These are deployed in a straight line, across a likely salmon travel path, to snag the commuting fish by their gills. Floats—with a large, distinctive orange one supporting the end—hold the net up. Every one to four hours, the nets are hauled up by a giant power drum—the gillnetter's distinctive identifying feature (see photo above)—and picked clean. Many are outfitted with trolling gear as well. Gillnetters often work in concert. Prior to the adoption of gasoline engines, oar and sail propelled trollers and gillnetters.

Purse seiners are more complicated, crewed by three to seven, and aided by a tubby skiff tender. Each fishing episode is a frenetic affair. When a school is located, the trap—a net about 1,200 feet long by

70 feet deep, supported by movable booms and shaped like an old-fashioned net purse (or scrotal sac) when closed—must be quickly set. The tender circles the prey widely with one end of the net and closes the circle, returning the net's end to the seiner's boom. The net is supported by floats and held vertically by weights at the bottom. If the set is successful, a line channeled through metal rings then draws the bottom of the purse tight. The purse is then hauled in and the catch sorted. No matter what the weather, seining crews work in complete foul-weather gear. Nets always capture jellyfish that, inevitably, end up cascading gelatinous, stinging slime onto the crew. Purse seiners, easily identified by their nets aloft and pendant (or adjoining) tender, account for the largest proportion of commercially harvested wild salmon.

Some fishermen work independently, and others are on contract to commercial fish companies; all deliver their catch to fish-buying tenders and, in more remote areas, scows, whose crews often set their own lures: beer, liquor, cheap groceries, hot showers, whatever the market calls for. We ran into two competing fish-buying scows in Foggy Bay, halfway between Prince Rupert and Ketchikan. Though they may not retail fish, when not busy buying they might sell a kayaker some groceries or a shower.

Salmon are retailed fresh, smoked, frozen, or canned depending on their quality. One outfit, kind enough to invite us in for a bed and a feed, specialized in smoked, spicy teriyaki king (chinook) salmon. I couldn't get enough of it. After dinner, a corporate floatplane landed at the dock and disembarked two formally suited and smiling Japanese, one with an attaché bag handcuffed to his wrist. "Our client," whispered our generous host. Best smoked salmon I'll ever taste.

In Alaska, the number of commercial fishing permits is limited. Someone wanting to enter the trade must buy an existing license from someone else. Prices reflect current demand. Twenty years ago, power-trolling permits cost about $20,000. Catches are further limited by a complex schedule of openings and closings for different areas, different fishing methods, and different species, translating into long hours of intense work followed by extended periods of costly inactivity.

Since 1980, salmon farms have become a common sight along the B.C. coast. Salmon aquaculture was first developed in Norway, and—when worldwide wild stocks began to shrink—spread to the UK, Chile, and Canada, where the helping hand of government provided generous subsidies. The fish are raised in net pens supported by rafts and are fed pellets just like fish in a home aquarium. When natural populations made a comeback in the 1990s (see below), B.C.'s salmon farms experienced serious consolidation. Today there are only 80, but they supply a disproportionate majority of commercially marketed salmon. By 1993, farmed salmon harvests reached 24 million tons with a value of $75 million. Though controversial, Atlantic salmon are the favorite fish species for farming due to their docility in tight quarters, larger size, and resistance to disease. As an artificially introduced species on the Pacific coast, escaped Atlantic salmon pose the dangers of predation, competition, displacement, and increased risk of disease to the native populations. Consequently, Alaska bans finfish aquaculture, and Washington very stringently regulates it. In 1999, sea lice were reported on wild salmon near Vancouver Island fish farms; Atlantic salmon are the suspected culprits. This is one more point of contention in the ongoing US-Canada fish wars.

The commercial salmon industry along the Inside Passage dates back to the 1820s, when the Hudson's Bay Company shipped salted salmon to markets in Hawaii, China, Australia, England, and America's eastern seaboard. The salmon, more often than not, arrived in less than prime condition. Although Nicolas Appert had invented the canning process in 1809 under the funding and direction of France's war department, the technology spread slowly. For one thing, Napoleonic France was not known for sharing much of anything other than grief and subversion; additionally, the strange new process was suspect. It would be another 50 years before Louis Pasteur was able to explain why the process worked.

The first salmon cannery in British Columbia opened for business in 1870 near Vancouver. Canneries in Puget Sound—at Mukilteo in

1877—and Alaska—at Sitka and Klawock in 1878—soon followed. By 1901 there were 70 canneries along B.C.'s coast, and Alaska wasn't far behind. Haines, Wrangell, and Petersburg all had canneries. At one time, during the 1920s, 25 canneries were operating on Prince of Wales Island alone. In 1940, Ketchikan had 13 canneries. Today, few active canneries survive, while the rest, haunted carapaces of an abandoned industry, are succumbing to fecund decay and encroaching salal, alder, and berry bushes.

By the end of WWII, overfishing was taking its toll and stocks began a gradual, determined, and ultimately precipitous decline. Fishermen and canneries went bust. Salmon prices soared. Governments and private interests poured money into research. Finally, in the 1970s, hatcheries succeeded in producing viable salmon that could be reintroduced successfully. By the 1990s, many stocks were well on their way to recovery. But the canneries never came back. By and large, modern refrigeration and freezing have superseded Appert's invention. You can tour the Deer Mountain Hatchery in Ketchikan and the Douglas Island pink and chum hatchery in Juneau.

Oyster and, to a lesser degree, mussel farms are found all the way from Puget Sound to the Wrangell area. Because they need warmer water, most of the farms are south of Port Hardy. Alaskan oyster farming began near Ketchikan in 1930 from imported Japanese spat (baby oysters); today, Alaskan-reared Pacific oysters are grown from spat imported from the Lower 48. The farms are modest affairs, invariably marked if the critters are raised on the bottom, or recognizable as floating rafts.

Finally, probably the most ubiquitous, albeit humble, landmarks (seamarks?) along the entire paddle are shrimp and crab pots. You can spot these by their telltale floats, sometimes in the unlikeliest of places, which mark their location and anchor the trap. Shaped like big cheese wheels, the traps are crafted of wire mesh and baited. A funneled one-way opening secures the catch.

Mining

When Ginger and Dana Lamb set out to kayak from San Diego to Panama (see the introduction) during the Great Depression, they supplemented their meager resources with a .22 caliber rifle for hunting, and a gold pan for spending money. Today's kayakers—some, at least—are not quite so penurious.

However, walking-around money is always a welcome addition to any excursion. You too, in the time-honored tradition of the Lambs and the hundreds of thousands of prospectors who made their way up the Inside Passage, can supplement your pocket money by placer-mining for gold. All you need is a pan and a small, folding army surplus shovel—or the sturdy blade of a paddle.

Placer-mining is the oldest method of recovering gold from alluvial deposits. Gold, locked in strata high up in the mountains, is freed through erosion and wends its way down creeks and rivers. The more turbulent the water, the heavier the material it can carry. As the stream slows, the heaviest particles settle out first. Placer-mining takes advantage of this principle. Panning employs a pan or a batea (a pan or basin with radial corrugations) in which a few handfuls—or a shovelful or paddleful—of dirt and a large amount of water are placed. By swirling the contents of the pan—as if aggressively panhandling—the miner washes the siliceous material over the side, leaving the gold and other heavy materials behind.

The first gold strike along the Inside Passage, in 1850, was at Gold Harbour in the Queen Charlotte Islands. It was short-lived. Only the original discovery panned out. Six years later, Indians discovered gold along the Fraser River and set off a gold rush that brought nearly 30,000 prospectors in one summer to the present-day Vancouver area. Many were disillusioned forty-niners. Most remained disillusioned.

Wrangell was originally founded by the Russians, as a tiny outpost of empire, to strengthen their claim against Hudson's Bay Company incursions. It was immediately—and diplomatically—leased to the Brits. Gold strikes up the Stikine River and in the Cassiar Mountains in 1861, and again in 1873, ballooned it into a tent city of 15,000. During the last half of the 1860s and through the 1870s, there were many more gold discoveries along the B.C. coast, but none compared to the 1880 strike in Juneau, Alaska. In October of that year, a Tlingit guide led Sitka prospectors Richard Harris and Joe Juneau to the mouth of soon-to-be-named Gold Creek. It was a fabulous strike, and Harris and Juneau staked their claims along with a 160-acre townsite for the expected rush. That first year yielded $2.5 million in today's dollars.

Juneau's mother lode, the gold-bearing strata that fed the placer deposits, were the mountains immediately backing the new town: Gold Creek's entire watershed, plus several adjoining watersheds. When placer-mining's easy pickings ran out, prospectors tackled underground lode mining, a much more time-consuming and capital-intensive affair. The extra effort afforded the necessary time for the development of a substantial settlement. Ironically, the first big underground mine was not behind Juneau but in front of it, across Gastineau Channel, on Douglas Island. Big underground mines on Mount Roberts, behind Juneau, soon followed. The not-so-pure gold ore required purification. So, in 1889, the Tacoma Smelting and Refining Company set up shop in Puget Sound to refine at first gold, and later, as those deposits became depleted, silver, lead, and copper from the Juneau-Douglas mines. Mining in Juneau continued for 64 years, until it ceased in 1944. Paddling into Alaska's capital, one of the first sights you'll encounter is the ruin of the Alaska Juneau Mining Company, along with countless adits, looming vertiginously over the city.

We made a beeline for Gold Creek to see where all the commotion had started. What a grand disappointment! I suppose it was inevitable that the stream suffered during the gold rush, but the solution almost seems worse. One sorry little sign commemorates Juneau's founding. The channel has been unelaborately and inartfully lined with concrete, without a thought for the poor salmon. We watched the pathetically heartbreaking attempts of a dozen superpiscine salmon fighting to make their way upstream. There wasn't enough water in the wide channel for the fish to gain a fin- or tailhold. With Juneau's receptivity to tourism, it's a wonder no restoration has been attempted. Amazingly, one local paddler told us that the city had been offered a grant for just such a project but inexplicably turned it down.

The biggest gold rush of all burst upon the world in 1897, but did not take place anywhere near the Inside Passage's protected waters. The previous year, when "Lying" George Carmack and his sidekicks, Skookum Jim and Tagish Charley, boasted of striking pay dirt at a small creek just east of Dawson City, Yukon, no one believed them. Until, that is, Carmack showed off a thumb-sized nugget of pure gold he'd picked off a protruding bit of bedrock. Local prospectors, working at Fortymile just west of Dawson, rushed to stake out the best claims. But it would take nearly a year and a 1,700-mile voyage down the Yukon River, plus the passage to San Francisco and Seattle, before news of the strike hit the press. The dispatch came in the form of suitcases, carpetbags, packing cases, bottles, cans, and every other type of container imaginable filled to bursting with two tons of pure gold unloaded at the San Francisco docks. The stampede was on.

Dawson City was not the most accessible destination. The simplest route was up the Pacific to Skagway or Dyea, then 20 miles up and across the Coast Mountains through Chilkoot or White Pass, and another 450 miles north down the Yukon River to Dawson. Regular steamship service, inaugurated during the Juneau rush, quickly reached capacity.

So more vessels provided passage. More than 100,000 treasure seekers set out for the Klondike; maybe 40,000 reached Dawson City. As more and more ships—some barely meriting the designation—plied their way north, those sailing in winter, and particularly those not fully up to the rigors of sailing Outside, rediscovered the protected waters Inside. Thus was the truly greatest bonanza of all unearthed—Inside Passage tourism.

Though seemingly much more mundane than gold, the discovery of coal along the Inside Passage in some ways had a greater and more lasting impact. Welsh coal, at tremendous expense, fed all the metallurgical industries in the nascent colony. In 1849, one year before the first gold strike in the Queen Charlottes, a Heiltsuk native at Bella Bella's Fort McLaughlin observed a blacksmith impose his will on a piece of iron with the help of black rocks. When the native found out that the coal came from halfway around the world, he told the smith that there were black rocks a lot closer, near his home by present-day Port Hardy.

The Hudson's Bay Company confirmed the find, established Fort Rupert to protect the site, and imported English miners, as they doubted that the natives would make good coal miners. Both the *Beaver* and the newer trading vessel, the *Otter,* were immediately converted from wood to coal. One small step in the conservation of the B.C. forests.

Three years later, a much higher-quality coal was discovered at Nanaimo, so the HBC built a fortification, the Bastion (still there), and transferred the miners down from Fort Rupert. The Nanaimo seam proved extensive and very productive well into the 20th century. Nanaimo coal was exported to Puget Sound and San Francisco. Kayakers can visit some of the preserved adits—one tunnel is reputed to lead all the way across Newcastle Island Passage to Nanaimo—on Newcastle Island, named after the miners' hometown in England. Coal was also later discovered at Bellingham, in Puget Sound.

For such a small place, Newcastle Island was a cornucopia of mineral goodies. The search for flawless quarry stone for the newly proposed San Francisco mint ended in 1869 with the discovery of perfect sandstone on Newcastle. The quarry supplied large monolithic blocks for much of the Northwest's grandiose public architecture—including the towers of Christ Church Cathedral in Victoria—up until 1932, by which time the coal mining and stone quarrying had totally trashed the island. In 1931, the Canadian Pacific Steamship Company bought what was left of the little island and developed it into a park resort. The sandstone quarry exhibit on the park's perimeter walk is very impressive.

The largest and most visible mining operation that a paddler will see along the Inside Passage is on the approach to Texada Island. We joked that from a distance it looked like the largest kitty litter quarry in the world. Since 1887, Texada has yielded huge amounts of high-quality limestone. Today it ships 3 million tons a year to the B.C. market for use in the pulp mills, agriculture, and the construction industry—for quicklime, cement, quarry rock, and even marble (due to part of the limestone strata adjoining an igneous lens), limestone's metamorphic reincarnation.

The region's most controversial open-pit mining operation—which an Inside Passage paddler is unlikely to encounter—is located deep in Misty Fjords National Monument. In 1974, the US Borax Corporation patented what was later identified as the largest molybdenum deposit in the world—perhaps 10 percent of known reserves—at Quartz Hill, about halfway between Behm Canal and the Canadian border. Molybdenum is used to harden and retard the corrosion of steel and other alloys. The claim remains valid since it predates the National Monument designation. As of this writing, market prices preclude any mining activity.

The Coast Mountain ranges and offshore islands—of which they are a part—have been heavily mineralized due to tectonic forces at the Pacific–North American Plate interface. In addition to gold, molybdenum, and coal, large deposits of silver, copper, lead, iron, zinc, uranium, asbestos, and jade have, in most cases, been mined and exhausted. Presently there is very little mining going on along the coast, with the notable exception of Texada Island, and a potash mine on Ridley Island outside Prince Rupert.

Tourism

> *Tourist: One that travels from place to place*
> *for pleasure or culture.*
> —*Webster's Third New International Dictionary*

Arguably, one of the earliest and most famous self-described tourists to visit the Inside Passage was John Muir. Muir steamed to Wrangell and canoed to Glacier Bay in 1879, when the Alaska Purchase was only 12 years old. Many more were soon to follow, albeit not in quite his frugal style. Muir's account of his visit proved so inspiring that steamship companies began to offer summer tours up the Inside Passage. The first was the steamer *Idaho*, which came north in 1883. The tourism industry was launched. By 1889, 5,000 tourists a year were making the trip up the Inside Passage. According to Tourism Vancouver, more than a million cruise ships visit the Inside Passage annually. Mind you, that is cruise ship with a small "c"—anything from the gargantuan liners of the Royal Norwegian Line to, yes, solitary kayaks, and every imaginable craft in between.

Cruise ships come in many categories. The behemoths—many painted an imperious and dazzling white—dominate, if not in numbers, at least in sheer size. British Columbia and Alaska ferries qualify—and they can barely keep up with demand. Were it not for the sheer number of do-it-yourself, boatless summer visitors, ferry bookings would not require advance notice. A variety of smaller-scale cruises cater to the educational, ecotourism, and mother-ship kayak touring markets. An increasing number of kayak tour companies find a way to scratch out a living. A few offer land-and-water tour combos. Finally, in sheer numbers, private boats—from elaborate sailing rigs and luxurious yachts and ambitious, modest-sized inboard and outboard vessels occasionally testing their limits, to trans–Inside Passage kayakers, rowers, and canoeists—fill out the flotilla.

In spite of the clarification, the numbers are still staggering. Some 680,000 cruise ship (with a capital "C") passengers toured the Inside Passage in 2001. Princess Line alone had 104 departures in 1999. On a typical summer day, 45,000 passengers (about 2,000 per ship with another 1,000 as crew) are sailing through on self-contained floating cities more than 700 feet long and 20 stories tall. Cruise companies claim to pump $719 million a year into Alaska's economy alone. The impact is enormous. Juneau, a town of 30,000, can host up to 10,000 visitors on as many as five ships on some summer days. When several vessels are in port simultaneously, they dwarf the capital city's buildings. The resident population of most towns along the Inside Passage doubles during the tourist season to accommodate the influx. Docking facilities in many towns, which once accommodated both ferries and cruise ships, have had to be rebuilt with separate berths. Plenty of Alaskans are grateful for the visits; others have mixed views of the cruise ship crowds.

With good reason. The sheer numbers are starting to sully the very beauty that brings visitors north in the first place. A typical cruise ship generates about 210,000 gallons of raw sewage a week, lesser amounts of oil, assorted hazardous wastes, and more than a million gallons of gray water. Not all ships are as fully self-contained as they ought to be. In 1998, Holland America pleaded guilty to two felony counts of illegal dumping in the waters near Juneau. The next year, Royal Caribbean pleaded guilty to seven felony charges for dumping oily bilge water and toxic chemicals into southeast Alaska's waters. The company had rigged ships with secret piping systems to bypass oily water separators, and then falsified records to conceal the dumping. In 2000, 79 water samples from 80 cruise ships' wastewater storage tanks—stuff normally expelled into the ocean—exceeded federal minimum standards for suspended solids and fecal coliform bacteria. Some samples exceeded the criteria by 50,000 times! But, to most Alaskans, the very worst, the truly ultimate tragedy, occurred when a cruise ship struck and killed a 45-foot pregnant humpback whale near the entrance to Glacier Bay National Park.

In 1996, the National Park Service, reacting to increased demand, made plans to increase the number of cruise ships allowed into Glacier Bay National Park by 30 percent, from 107 to 139 per season. Fearful that the consequences could be dire, the National Parks Conservation Association, a public interest group, filed suit on the grounds that no environmental impact study had been done. In 2001, the Ninth Circuit Court of Appeals agreed. The NPS had to roll back cruise ship visits and complete an environmental impact study. The state of Alaska also stepped in.

In June 2001, Governor Tony Knowles convened a special session of the state legislature for the express purpose of addressing water pollution, air pollution, and trash disposal from cruise ships. The legislation passed and immediately went into effect. Now an even tougher measure, based on a 1999 $5 per-passenger tax levied by the city of Juneau, is being proposed through a statewide ballot initiative. As much as a $50 per-head tax would be imposed on tourists entering Alaska on cruise ships. The Northwest Cruise Ship Association believes such a tax would deter visitors. With cruise ship traffic increasing at the rate of about 10 percent per year, many voters don't seem to think so.

When a cruise ship sails past, most kayakers are struck by the contrast between themselves and the passengers. Though both share the same purpose, the methods differ—vastly. Cruise ship tourists generally admire kayakers but think they're a tad crazy. Kayakers' attitudes toward cruisers range from dismissive to contemptuous. What's it like to trade places?

A typical cruise lasts one week, makes six stops of eight to ten hours, and averages, at the moderate end, about $800. According to Peter Schmit, a passenger in 2002:

> *Our ship, built in late 1999, was home to 2,000 passengers, with a crew of 950. It is literally a city at sea. It has its own sewage treatment and water desalination plants, eight restaurants, 12 bars and lounges, two swimming pools, a spa, a beautiful fitness center, running track around the perimeter (3.5 laps made a mile), a library, gambling casino, a 1000-seat theater, and way too many shops. The 80,000-ton ship cruised at about 22 miles per hour.*

Most cruise ship tourists rave about their experience and would highly recommend it. Though it's definitely not my idea of a good time, it's no wonder the industry is growing so fast. Even my 70-year-old mother cruised to Alaska. More amazingly, some kayakers are even extending cruisers the hand of friendship. Lately, scuttlebutt has it that one Alaskan Inside Passage kayaker has taken to promoting his book with slide and lecture presentations on cruise ships.

Natural History

The Alaska Panhandle has always seemed an odd extension of Alaskan territorial integrity. More a historical accident than an integral part of the main Alaskan landmass, at one time it *was* Alaska. It was the rest of Alaska, the landmass west of 141 degrees longitude and north of the panhandle—in effect, Seward's Icebox—that, pretty much by default, was lumped together with the rich southeast. Southeast was hospitable. It was home to as many salmon as the mainland had mosquitoes, it nurtured forests that made the rest of Alaska look like it was on chemotherapy, and it was home to the sea otter, that little floating gold mine that brought the Russians over in the first place.

Although the Russians made inroads north of Southeast, there was little to attract or keep them there. And they never ventured east of the panhandle. Not only were the Coast Mountains impenetrable, but British westward expansion put paid to that notion. The brewing controversy was negotiated in 1825 under the auspices of the Convention of February, when the Russians and British settled on a serpentine border that addressed each power's concerns. Russia wanted the entire littoral for fishing and whaling, and marine access to native communities for trading; Britain was little interested in the coastline, but wanted as much of the inland terrain as possible to maintain its fur trade. The new border had only been cursorily confirmed at the time of the Alaska Purchase. When gold was discovered in the Klondike and thousands invaded the panhandle, a serious border dispute arose. There was even talk of war.

When Britain rejected war out of hand and offered to arbitrate, Canadians took up the offer, because they thought Britain was on their side. The US also agreed because they had not rejected war as an option, and had in fact just won a war that added Hawaii, the Philippines, Puerto Rico, and Cuba, and had a new president, Theodore Roosevelt, who carried a "big stick" in foreign policy. Canada, wanting sea access for the Yukon, claimed the heads of the major inlets; the US wanted the Russo-British line honored. Negotiations were further complicated by the fact that Canada, at this time, still lacked full treaty negotiating power. Britain, in 1903, sided with the US. However the boundary survey was not completed until 1914.

Dixon Entrance, the second, and smaller of the two main bodies of open water to be crossed on the Inside Passage, roughly marks the US–Canada boundary. North of it, a very dense maze of islands sets the panhandle apart from Canada. According to the National Forest Service, there are 2,000 islands along Alaska's southeast coast. The Alexander Archipelago, as they are collectively known, is striking in its cohesiveness, extent, and the size of the major islands. Prince of Wales Island, at 2,770 square miles, is the largest. Not far behind are the ABC's—Admiralty, Baranof, and Chichagof Islands. After central British Columbia, the panhandle section might seem overpopulated. Fortunately, nearly all the people are concentrated in relatively large towns; along our route—Prince Rupert, Metlakatla, Port Simpson, Saxman, Ketchikan, Meyers Chuck, Wrangell, Petersburg, Juneau, and Douglas. Campsites are not as scarce as in B.C., but neither are they as plentiful as in the Gulf Islands.

Southeast Alaska is different—and not just in contrast to the main part of the state, as previously noted. Latitudinal changes, subtle in quality and degree—none quite so striking as the disappearance of the madrona north of Desolation Sound—have been accruing during our progress north. The "land of the midnight sun" effect is striking. On June 21—the longest day of the year—the sun rises about 4 AM and sets

Large expanses of white sand beach are common near Dixon Entrance, B.C.–Alaska, where the open Pacific pounds the coastline.

about 10 PM. Because the sun is circling just below the horizon, most of the few nighttime hours are in twilight. No need for a flashlight. At the other end of the year, midwinter Juneau has only about six hours of daylight, with sunrise at about 8:45 AM and sunset at about 3 PM.

Alaska weather is just a tad brusquer. Rain and fog are more frequent. Low-pressure fronts, which in summer break through the Pacific High about every two to six weeks along the lower Inside Passage, occur at intervals of one to three weeks in Southeast. Although these fronts usually last only a day or two, in Southeast they can stall out and linger longer. Accompanying winds are commensurately stronger. In lower B.C., low-pressure fronts typically generate winds of 20–25 knots; in Southeast, the same fronts blow harder, around 30 knots, with occasional summertime gale-force blows. Watch out for these.

The Alexander Archipelago is very protected, particularly along our route, which courses as far east as possible. However, many of the channels and passages are quite wide and long. The accompanying fetch and exposure to the force of storm winds can create rough seas. Crossings of Portland and Behm Canals, Frederick Sound, and Stephens Passage are long enough for conditions to change during a crossing. Always be aware of diurnal and atmospheric wind changes.

With a handy wrist barometer, such as the Suunto, you can monitor atmospheric wind. Wind velocity is directly proportional to the rate of barometric pressure change—up or down. Falling pressure of 1 millibar per hour equals a 20- to 30-knot wind; 2 millibars per hour equals 35- to 45-knot winds, while 3 millibars per hour translates to 50- to 60-knot storm winds. On the rising scale, 1 millibar per hour generates gale winds of 25–40 knots.

After cruising in B.C. and listening to Environment Canada's marine weather forecasts, Alaskan forecasts might be slightly disappointing. The Pacific Weather Centre in Vancouver prepares forecasts several times a day and broadcasts continuously on VHF weather channels. Lots of repeater stations provide adequate coverage all the way up to Ketchikan. In contrast, the National Weather Service in Juneau issues only one forecast a day, at 5 AM, and repeats it every 5 minutes on Weather Channel 1 or 2. Transmitters are located only in Haines, Juneau,

Sitka, Wrangell, Ketchikan, and Craig, and repeater stations are few, so the effective range of the broadcast stations is only about 20 to 40 miles.

The observant will notice other subtle changes. Timberline drops, sometimes to only 2,000 feet, and the boreal mix changes. While the more southern forests are primarily composed of Douglas fir, the dominant species in Alaska are western hemlock and Sitka spruce with a scattering of red cedar, Alaska cedar, and mountain hemlock. Climax forests—old-growth, where these can still be found—have smaller trees: only 200 feet tall and 5 to 8 feet in diameter. There are lots of salmonberries (similar to blackberries but colored orange to dark red), elderberries (bitter), and several varieties of blueberries and huckleberries, all in impenetrable thickets. Southeast's forests have no poison oak or poison ivy.

Campsites in Southeast are a tad more abundant. Though vegetation remains a barrier and much of the ground is rough, the steepness of the topography eases. In a pinch, bivy spots are plentiful. In this chapter, many potential camps are not marked—there are just too many. Some possibilities will be indicated in the text, but only definite campsites are marked on the accompanying maps.

The panhandle is proud Tlingit country. Strong and bold enough to hold their own against most invaders, they nonetheless suffered some incursions. Oral tradition holds that, aboriginally, the Cape Fox people, of Tsimshian origin, used much of Revillagigedo Island during summers. In the late 17th or early 18th century, the Haida invaded the south end of Prince of Wales Island and successfully retained it. The Russians were even more successful, establishing settlements first at Sitka—after many setbacks and constant vigilance, a state of détente emerged in due time—and then at Wrangell. In 1887, a Tsimshian settlement, New Metlakatla, was founded on Annette Island. Eight hundred twenty-five Tsimshian, under the leadership of the Reverend William Duncan and with permission from the new US government, relocated in Alaska. They had come from Old Metlakatla, just north of present-day Prince Rupert, to escape liquor and other unhealthy influences, including—in particular—doctrinal differences with the dominant Church of England.

The Route: Overview

In keeping with the spirit of the oversized scale of Alaska, the panhandle section, at 382 miles, is the longest segment of this Inside Passage route. It is also, by far, the most varied. It is divided into three equal portions: Dixon Entrance, the Banana Belt, and Admiralty Island. Each one begins and ends at a major town. Only the Wrangell portion, a.k.a. the Banana Belt, has any alternate routes; one up the east side of Wrangell Island—the main route goes up the west side—and another, farther up, through Wrangell Narrows instead of across the Stikine River delta at Dry Strait.

Dixon Entrance is not Queen Charlotte Sound; for one thing, it is only one-third as long. Outlying islands protect the route out of Prince Rupert as far as Portland Canal, the first major obstacle and the US–Canada border. At more than 3 miles in width, with only a partially—and distantly, at that—protected mouth, and a 100-mile length that funnels wind and tide, the Portland Canal crossing must be carefully negotiated. Once across, the route courses up the last bit of exposed Dixon Entrance into Revillagigedo Channel and Misty Fjords National Monument, finishing up in protected waters with a clear shot at Ketchikan. Highlights include Port Tongass on Sitklan Island (an abandoned Tlingit village); Tongass Island, with the ruins of an old customs fort; and Saxman Village, a suburb of Ketchikan with a magnificent display of Tlingit life, totem poles, and a longhouse.

From Ketchikan, the route joins Clarence Strait and heads north to Meyers Chuck, an endearing and welcoming tiny homesteader settlement. At Deer Island, the first of two possible alternates diverges. The main route cuts due north to Zimovia Strait and up along the west coast of Wrangell Island to Wrangell, the last Russian settlement in Alaska and home of the legendary Chief Kah Shakes. The alternate route, about 5 to 7 miles longer, courses the narrow channels between Wrangell Island and the mainland, visiting the Anan Bay Bear Observatory.

Wrangell sits at the southern extremity of the Stikine River delta. Although most major river deltas along the Inside Passage cause difficulties best avoided, the Stikine obstructs with little more than mostly

Longhouse and totems at Saxman Village, Alaska

negotiable mud and sand flats. The main route takes the shortest distance, up Dry Strait and through the barely navigable deltaic flats into Frederick Sound. The next alternate, up Wrangell Narrows, skirts the sediment flats but adds another 11 miles and follows the ferry route. Both converge on Petersburg.

Near Petersburg and up Frederick Sound, you'll encounter the first bergy bits, calved from the Le Conte Glacier. Crossing the 15-mile-wide junction of Frederick Sound and Stephens Passage to Admiralty Island is the second crux of this leg. Fortunately, the Five Finger Island Group and the Brothers Islands provide handy stepping-stones.

Admiralty Island, Kootznoowoo (Fortress of the Bears), with a bear density approaching one bear per square mile, will give a kayaker a moment's pause. Nonetheless, with a little bit of forethought and safe camping practices, encounters can be mitigated. A cursory glance at the map would route you up Stephens Passage. The route, however, marches up Seymour Canal. At its head some thoughtful soul has engineered and built a portage rail tramcar that artfully connects what would otherwise be a grueling 1-mile-long portage to the northern end of Stephens Passage. The Pack Creek bear viewing observatory, about halfway up Seymour Canal, is a definite objective, albeit with not a few logistical entanglements.

A final and relatively uneventful 3-mile crossing of Stephens Passage puts you at the mouth of Gastineau Channel and the outskirts of Juneau, Alaska's state capital.

Dixon Entrance: Prince Rupert *(mile 0/768)* to Ketchikan *(mile 110/883)*

Unless you're paddling straight through from the last section, you'll likely arrive at Prince Rupert via car, ferry, or plane to attempt the Alaska Panhandle. If coming by plane (commercial airlines serve Prince Rupert), you'll need to carry a collapsible kayak or have made arrangements to store your boat at the end of the last section's trip. If you're arriving by ferry from the south, both the B.C. ferry, out of Port Hardy, and the Alaska Marine Highway Ferry, stop at Prince Rupert. By car, an excellent highway connects central British Columbia with Rupert.

There are three docking facilities in Prince Rupert, each one suitable for a different strategy: from southwest to northeast, Fairview Floats, Cow Bay (Prince Rupert Yacht Club), and Rushbrook Floats. Rushbrook has the only boat ramp. Arriving and paddling on through by kayak pretty much requires an overnight layover. The Cow Bay facilities may be the best alternative. Cow Bay is picturesquely and centrally located with at least a couple of B&Bs and within walking distance of a grocery, liquor store, nautical supplies, good eats, the museum, and a native cultural center. Eco-Treks Kayak Adventures (250-624-8311) is headquartered at Cow Bay and may help you get your bearings.

If you are arriving by ferry, Fairview Floats are right next door to the terminal. In spite of berthing the Prince Rupert fishing fleet, Fairview is fairly kayak friendly—just stay out of the way. Half a mile up the road are the municipal Park Avenue Campground, the Anchor

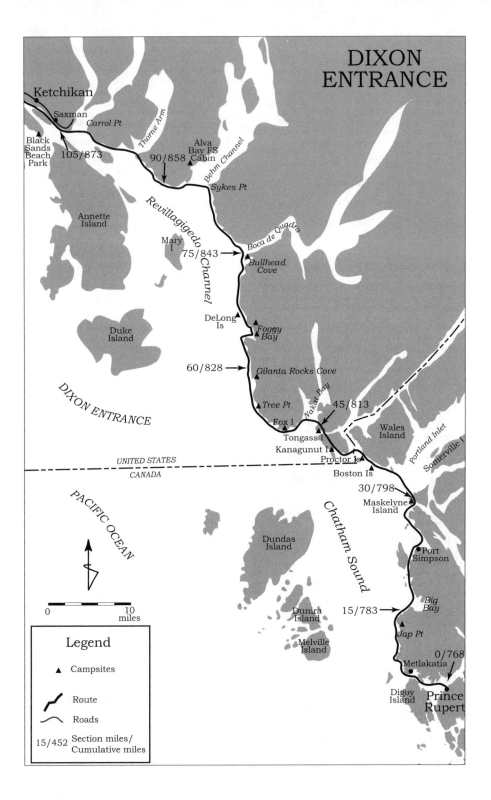

DIXON ENTRANCE

Ketchikan

Saxman

Carrol Pt

Thorne Arm

Black
Sands
Beach
Park

105/873

90/858

Alva
Bay FS
Cabin

Behm Channel

Sykes Pt

Annette
Island

Revillagigedo Channel

Mary
I

Boca de Quadra

75/843

*Bullhead
Cove*

Duke
Island

DeLong
Is

*Foggy
Bay*

DIXON ENTRANCE

60/828

Gilanta Rocks Cove

Tree Pt

Fox I

Nakat Bay

45/813

Wales
Island

Portland Inlet

Tongass I

Kanagunut I

Proctor Is

Somerville I

UNITED STATES

CANADA

Boston Is

PACIFIC OCEAN

30/798

Maskelyne
Island

Chatham Sound

Port
Simpson

Dundas
Island

Dunira
Island

15/783

*Big
Bay*

0
10
miles

Melville
Island

Jap Pt

0/768

Legend

▲ Campsites

Route

Roads

15/452 Section miles/
Cumulative miles

Metlakatla

Digby
Island

Prince
Rupert

Inn, and at least two B&Bs. Groceries, restaurants, and cultural activities will require a taxi ride into the downtown area.

If you're coming by car, Fairview is also probably your best bet, with nearby vehicle storage at the Park Avenue Corner Store (FAS Gas) and the Totem Lodge Motel, both across from the campground. Considerably cheaper for long-term parking, however, is the Parkside Resort Motel, near Rushbrook at #101 11th Avenue East.

Prince Rupert is somewhat spread out and will probably require some driving from any of the docking facilities to get this leg of the expedition up to snuff. A large Safeway and government liquor store are downtown, nearest Cow Bay, as is Smile's Seafood—great fish and chips. Also located nearby are chart and navigational supply stores with Canadian government-approved capsicum bear spray for sale. Don't miss the Museum of Northern B.C. and the First Nations Carving Shed, where you're likely to observe a tree trunk metamorphose into a stunning totem at the hands of an insouciant but expert carver. Both are near the Safeway.

Mileage tabulation for this section begins at the Fairview Floats. Head out of Prince Rupert toward Venn Passage, the favored route for small craft heading north. Venn Passage is subject to 3-knot currents. The stream turns about one hour before high water, so try to leave Rupert near high-water slack for a favorable current. Just before Venn Passage narrows, Fallen Human Bay, or Pillsbury Cove, indents the Tsimshian Peninsula coast. Near Robertson Point, close to the high-water line, a petroglyph known as "The Man Who Fell from Heaven" has been bas-reliefed on the shore rock. Pass "Old" Metlakatla, a Tsimshian village on the north shore, at the end of Venn Passage. The Reverend William Duncan and some Fort Simpson area native converts founded Metlakatla in 1862. Later, Duncan and some of the natives were to relocate again in Alaska, at "New" Metlakatla. Round Observation Point and enter Chatham Sound.

Head up the mainland coast. North of Jap Point and in the vicinity of Tree Bluff (mile 12/**780**), sandy shores afford some camping. Pass

Big Bay and enter Cunningham Passage, where currents never exceed 1 knot. Stay close to shore and pass through tiny Dodd Passage for entry into Port Simpson at Stumaun Bay.

Port Simpson: Also known as Lax' Kw' Alaams, Port Simpson is a busy native village with water and a small grocery store. A longhouse and craft shop are visible from the floats but are not in operation. A local gillnetter informed us they'd been built for the tourist trade; however, cruise ships refuse to stop at Port Simpson.

Exit Port Simpson up into Rushbrook Passage and bear right through the small pass (Dudevoir) separating Maskelyne Island from the tip of the Tsimshian Peninsula. The southeast tip of Maskelyne Island (mile 30/**798**) has an excellent campsite with an abandoned cabin, a good spot from which to tackle the crossing of Portland Inlet in the early morning.

Portland Canal: Portland Canal and Inlet, 100 miles in length, is the longest fjord on the entire North American continent. For most of its course it delineates the boundary between Canada and the US, the one exception being close to its mouth, where a few of the islands seem to be apportioned haphazardly. At Manzanita Cove on the west side of Wales Island stands one of four US Customs House cabins built in 1896 for the initial surveys of the Alaska border. When the border was determined to jog just north, through Pearse Canal, the Customs House ended up on Canadian soil. About 10 miles up the inlet, behind Somerville Island, lies Khutzeymateen Inlet, Canada's only grizzly sanctuary. The twin towns of Hyder, AK, and Stewart, B.C., connected to the Al-Can by the Cassiar Highway, mark the head of Portland Canal.

Portland Inlet is a productive fishing ground, usually worked by many commercial and sport fishing boats. The crossing of Portland Inlet, from either Maskelyne or Hogan Island to Tracy Island, is about 3.5 miles, or about 1 hour. Much of its mouth is open to Dixon Entrance, and the inlet can be both choppy and subject to swell. Get an early start. Since Portland Canal trends northeastwardly, some protection is afforded by crossing farther up the canal. Tidal currents can ebb at 3 knots and flood at 2 knots, though weaken somewhat at the inlet as the fjord widens. From the Maskelyne Island camp, approach the crossing up (north) Paradise Passage. If the tidal streams oppose—they can attain 3 knots—approach Portland from the west side of Maskelyne.

From Tracy Island head for the small, well-protected channel between Boston (mile 38/**806**) and Procter (mile 39/**807**) Islands. Both sets of islands have beautiful sandy beaches with good campsites, the last ones in Canada. The border runs up Tongass Passage between Wales (Canada) and Sitklan (US) Islands.

US Border Crossing: US Customs regulations require that all boats entering US waters report to the nearest Customs facility prior to any landing. The nearest Customs office is in Ketchikan, about 70 miles farther along this route. What to do? Don't be anarchists like us and just ignore the whole procedure. On the other hand, don't be overly conscientious. One hapless group of Inside Passage kayakers working their way north pitched camp two or three times after entering US waters and before arriving at Ketchikan. Being all good citizens, they headed for the Customs office to report their arrival. During the entry interrogation the paddlers admitted to multiple landings prior to Customs clearance. Officers confiscated their boats and gear. Only after an embarrassing newspaper publicity campaign did Customs relent. Don't incriminate yourself. Probably the best approach for clearing US Customs is to call ahead (1-800-562-5943 or 907-225-2254), preferably from a reliable landline in Prince Rupert. Failing that, use a VHF radio via a marine operator (if you can get coverage) to communicate with either the US Coast Guard or US Customs to announce your arrival.

Misty Fjords National Monument: Once across the border and nearly all the way to Ketchikan, you will be paddling in Misty Fjords National Monument. The Monument was created by President Jimmy Carter in 1978 and encompasses nearly 3,570 square miles (2.2 million acres). In 1980, Congress further designated nearly the entire Monument a wilderness area.

From the Procter Islands, cross the imaginary border to Island Point at the south end of Sitklan Island and enter narrow Lincoln Channel. According to the Douglasses, the southernmost bight (mile 42/**810**) on the Kanagunut Island shore has a suitable kayak campsite. The northern bight on the Sitklan Island side is the site of the abandoned Port Tongass native village.

Tongass Island: Exit Lincoln Channel headed for Dark Point on the mainland. Just north and offshore lies Tongass Island (mile 45/**813**). Not to be confused with Port Tongass village, the passage separating Tongass Island from the mainland is also known as Port Tongass for its protected situation. Even more confusing, the south side of Tongass Island was once the site of a Tlingit village also known as Port Tongass. This Port Tongass was abandoned in the early 1900s when the inhabitants relocated to Saxman. Around 1920, a handful of ex-residents returned to find that a Seattle-bound vessel had stolen one of their totems. Incensed, they set out for Seattle, 600 miles away, to retrieve their pole, which was eventually erected in downtown Pioneer Square. Unable to recover it, they sued for theft and won monetary compensation. By the 1970s the rest of the poles had been moved to Ketchikan/ Saxman, although Joe Upton reports several rotting pole remnants among the underbrush as late as 1982.

Tongass Island's east shore, about halfway up where the small bay is located, was the site of Fort Tongass. In 1868, the US government established the fort—manned by 60 men, billeted mostly in tents—to prevent smuggling and keep the peace. It was abandoned two years later. Not much is left. The site has been overgrown with berry bushes and is nearly impenetrable. A few bricks and metal parts are scattered about. Without a machete, it is not a suitable campsite. The best campsites are located on either of the two tiny islands fronting the village bay or in the bay itself. Sandy beaches, the specter of Port Tongass village, and views out to the Lord Islands make for an incomparable overnight stay. The shore around Katakwa Point, connecting the fort and the village, has extensive reefs and rocks full of shellfish and critters—perfect for beachcombing. If you're lucky enough to spot a trade bead, leave it for the next visitor.

Depart Tongass Island either due west or up Port Tongass Channel and then west across 2-mile-wide Nakat Bay to Cape Fox, and begin working your way up around Peninsula Ridge. Fox Island Cove (mile 50/**818**) has a decent campsite. Although not really a cove, it is the protected area between Cape Fox and Fox Island. Until Foggy Bay, about 15 miles away, the shores are fully exposed to Dixon Entrance. Pacific swells can make for an exciting transit.

Tree Point Light (mile 55/**823**) is the first in US waters. Peter McGee reports a possible campsite here, though with breaking swells and many offshore rocks, we did not explore. Before it was automated in the 1970s, the crews lived in four beautifully crafted houses set in the woods near the cove south of the light. Three miles north of Tree Point Light, Gilanta Rocks (mile 58/**826**) guard the entrance to an intriguing little cove ringed with a sandy beach and old-growth forest. Above the beach you might find the remnants of an old Tlingit village where, as recently as 1936, a few totems still stood.

Revillagigedo Channel: Foggy Point marks the entrance to Revillagigedo Channel. Vancouver named Revillagigedo Channel and Revillagigedo Island, the location of Ketchikan, after Don Juan Vicente de Guemes Pacheco de Pedilla, Count of Revillagigedo and Viceroy of Mexico. The spelling and pronunciation of the name have confounded many an English speaker over the years. In 1920, Ketchikan adopted a resolution asking the US Board of Geographic Names to change the name to Revilla. The petition was denied, and people still fumble with the syllables and spelling. Let's give it a shot. The initial R is hard, like a double RR in Spanish; the double LL is pronounced like the English Y; the successive Gs are soft, like the English Hs: Rheh-vee-ya-hee-hey-dough. Actually, not so difficult. Currents are not a concern.

Foggy Bay: Foggy Bay is a wide indentation on the mainland coast divided into four distinct areas: Outer Cove, Inner Cove, Very Inlet, and the De Long Islands. Foggy Bay, true to its name, tends to be foggy when surrounding areas are clear. There are at least three campsites of varying quality. The first, on a small peninsula on the west side of Outer Cove (mile 65/**833**) is tolerable. The nearby anchorage often hosts a fish-buying tender. Inner Cove (mile 66/**834**) lies behind the largest island in Foggy Bay. A state trooper's cabin, though not available for a layover, is next to a small creek and affords water and a flat spot. Very Inlet is truly wild rain forest teeming with rapids, bears, and martens.

Worth a visit if you have the time. The best campsites are on the De Long Islands (mile 68/**836**). Tending to less fog and oppressiveness, they harbor some starkly beautiful white sand beaches visible on route. Kirk Point marks the northern limit of Foggy Bay. It was once the site of a native village, the residents of which formed part of the founding population of Saxman.

North of Foggy Bay, continue along the mainland shore. Just before Boca de Quadra Inlet, two small bays indent the shore. Kah Shakes Cove is named after a series of famous chiefs from the Ketchikan/ Wrangell area, all named Kah Shakes. It too is the site of an abandoned native settlement. Bullhead Cove immediately follows, bounded on the north by Kah Shakes Point (mile 74/**842**). The point has a fine beach suitable for camping on the south side.

Cross the mile-wide mouth of Boca de Quadra. The flanks of North Quadra Mountain, on the other side, afford no landing. Continue up the mainland coast to Sykes Point at the entrance to Behm Canal. Point Alava (mile 88/**856**), on the Revillagigedo Island shore, is about 2 miles away. Two miles off route to the north, Alava Bay hosts a 12 x 14 public Forest Service cabin. Though reservations and a fee are required for use, the cabin's foreground has good, flat camping next to a stream.

From Point Alava, coast up the shore of Revillagigedo Island's southernmost peninsula, passing Lucky Cove, to Cone Point and cross the mouth of Thorne Arm. Round Revillagigedo's second peninsula, passing Coho Cove, to Carroll Point. The small bight on the south side of the point, Icehouse Cove, is the tidewater terminus of the 1.2-mile-long Black Mountain USFS Trail. The trail was built by the Civilian Conservation Corps (CCC) in the late 1930s, traverses muskeg, and terminates at a pond.

Cross the combined heads of Carroll and George Inlets, about 2 miles, to Mountain Point, an unincorporated suburb of Ketchikan. Another 2 miles brings you to the end of Revillagigedo Channel and its junction with Nichols Passage and Tongass Narrows, which is divided into two subsidiary channels at its southeast end by Pennock Island. The Tlingit buried their dead on the southern end of Pennock. After the founding of Ketchikan, residents continued the practice until the 1930s.

The last campsite before Ketchikan is 2 miles off route to the south. Black Sands Beach State Marine Park (mile 106/**874**) lies 0.6 mile south of Gravina Point on Gravina Island. Black Sand Cove has crystal clear waters, unusually warm due to the black sand and dotted with sea stars and anemones. There is a state-maintained shelter at the head of the cove. Since 1915, the cove has been a favorite picnic site for local residents.

On August 9, 1994, at 6:20 AM, the 704-foot cruise ship *Nieuw Amsterdam,* pride of the Holland America Line–Westours, ran aground in heavy fog at Gravina Point. Rocks ripped the ship's hull near the port bow and tore a blade off the port propeller. Tugs were deployed for a rescue. None of the 1,225 passengers or 500 crew was injured.

Saxman: Incongruously and unexpectedly—particularly if you're paddling close to shore—a paved avenue lined with totems and leading to a longhouse will break through the trees. The urge to stop and explore is irresistible. This is Saxman, a native village 2.5 miles south of Ketchikan, and best explored from Ketchikan as a layover day activity. Saxman was founded in 1894 by Cape Fox and Tongass Island natives who wanted to combine into one village at a place suitable for a school. It is named in memory of Samuel Saxman, a Pennsylvania schoolteacher at Tongass, who drowned while searching for the new village site.

The 24 totems were brought to Saxman during the 1930s under a combined CCC and USFS project from abandoned villages on Tongass, Cat, Pennock, and Village Islands and Kirk Point. Some are original, some restored, and some are replicas—a process that continues today at the carving shed, next to the Beaver Tribal House and gift shop. Notable poles include the Lincoln Pole, carved in 1883 from a photograph of the president to commemorate the clan's first sighting of a white man many years previously; and the Seward Pole, a plain shaft with a single seated figure wearing a potlatch hat. The pole commemorates Secretary of State William Seward's visit to Tongass Island in 1869.

Ketchikan: Ketchikan and its suburbs (almost too harsh a word) are spread along the waterfront nearly continuously from Mountain Point to Point Higgins (and beyond) and across Tongass Narrows from Clam Cove to the airport. There are about 14,000 people in the city proper. Creek Street, a liquid avenue complete with stilted buildings and boardwalk sidewalks—a bit of an Old West Venice, "where the men and the fish came to spawn"—marks the center of town. It has always boasted an independent, freewheeling reputation. A 1926 newspaper report disclosed that there were more than 200 prostitutes, considerable bootlegging, and drug trafficking in the town.

Absolutely nothing beats the long-haul kayaker's stylin' entrance up Creek Street, amid the picturesque shops, dwellings, historic red light district, and pedestrian bustle. Moor in Thomas Basin right at Creek Street's mouth at the Ketchikan Yacht Club or at the City Floats, another 0.5 mile west on the other side of the cruise ship docks. There is no camping. Right adjacent to Thomas Basin, however, on waterfront Steadman Street, is the New York Hotel, a reconditioned turn-of-the-20th-century boardinghouse that provides lodging and breakfast for about $90 per double. Just south is Tatsuda's IGA for groceries and a nearby laundromat. An alternate, albeit not as centrally located dock is Bar Harbor, another mile north up the waterfront, with slightly cheaper nearby accommodations. Shop at either Alaskan & Proud to Be, three blocks south of the Airport Ferry Terminal, or the hypermarket one block south of Bar Harbor Basin.

Ketchikan started out as a Tlingit summer fishing camp, "Kitsch-khin," meaning "spread wings of a prostrate eagle." White settlers established first a salmon saltery and then a cannery in the 1880s. By 1900, Ketchikan was incorporated and exporting so much salmon that it was nicknamed the Salmon Capital of the World; by the 1940s, 13 canneries were operating. Logging developed as an adjunct to the fishing. The Ketchikan Spruce Mill produced lumber for the canneries' packing boxes. Later on it switched to exporting cants (sawed logs) to Japan. Another sawmill turns out dimensional lumber. In 1954 Louisiana–Pacific built a pulp mill at Ward Cove for the production of dissolving pulp, used in the manufacture of plastics and synthetics. The Cape Fox Native Corporation logs native lands around Ketchikan as well.

Ketchikan is second only to Juneau as Southeast's governmental administrative center. It is the headquarters of Misty Fjords National Monument and the Tongass National Forest's regional headquarters. A new USFS complex, the Southeast Alaska Visitor Information Center,

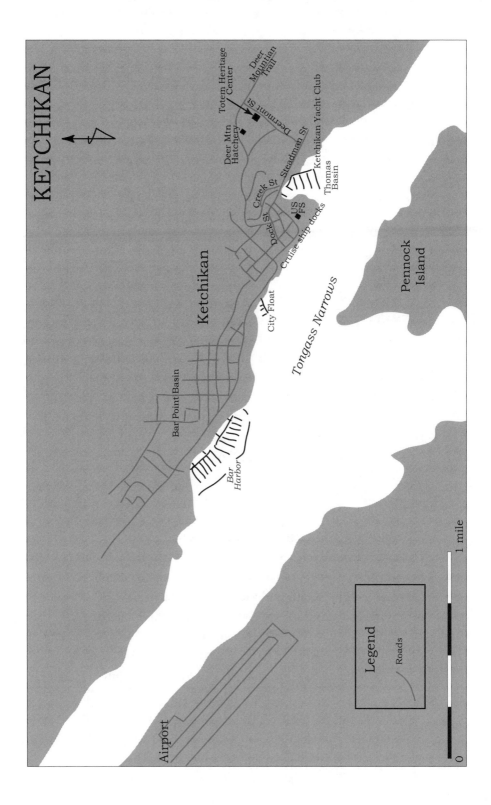

or SEAVIC, has taken over or expanded on many duties previously administered from Juneau. And, of course, considering itself a border town, Ketchikan has a strong US Customs, Immigration and Naturalization Service, and US Coast Guard contingents.

Salmon is no longer king, increasingly playing second fiddle to tourism. Downtown redevelopment is centered around the new Thomas Basin cruise ship docks and business hours, even days, revolve around cruise ship visits and schedules. But tourism has not spoiled Ketchikan's character, only broadened it. Ketchikan is not a dying town saved by tourism; it is full of energy and bustle. Besides drying wet gear, washing laundry, and resupplying, there is much to see and do.

For a good leg workout and views of the harbor and city, hike the 3-mile Deer Mountain Trail that starts just south of Creek Street. With more than 160 inches of rain a year, never venture out without a slicker. Explore the Creek Street Historical District teetering on pilings with its focus on the 20-odd brothels that were closed as recently as 1953. The Tongass Historical Society Museum at 629 Dock Street has a little bit of everything: local history, native culture, timber, fishing, and mining. The Deer Mountain Hatchery, on Ketchikan Creek, spawns 400,000 salmon and 35,000 steelhead annually and offers tours. The new USFS Southeast Alaska Visitor Information Center, built on the site of a former spruce mill and adjacent to Thomas Basin, has elaborate interpretive exhibits about public lands, resources, and recreational opportunities throughout the Tongass. In Ketchikan, totem poles rule. The Totem Heritage Center at 601 Deermount Street displays original, unrestored totem poles retrieved from the abandoned Tlingit communities of Tongass and Village Islands and the Haida village of Old Kasaan. Lastly, don't forget to backtrack on land and visit Saxman Village.

Every visitor to Alaska's panhandle wonders about the viability of communities unconnected to the outside world by conventional roads. So do Alaskans. A road from Ketchikan to Canada's interior highway system has been proposed but tabled, so far. It would include a road across Revillagigedo Island to Behm Canal, a shuttle ferry across Behm, and a connector along the Unuk River Valley to the Cassiar Highway: all told, 86 miles of roadbed in Alaska and 67 miles in Canada.

Creek Street, Ketchikan, Alaska

Banana Belt: Ketchikan (mile 110/883) to Petersburg (mile 249/1,017)

The middle portion of the panhandle section is 139 miles long. Locals refer to it as the Banana Belt for its high precipitation, unusually mild summer temperatures, and stable wind and sea conditions compared to farther north. No single body of water dominates; instead the route exits Tongass Narrows to Clarence Strait, thence into Ernest Sound, Zimovia Strait, Dry Strait, and finally Frederick Sound. Three communities are visited: Meyers Chuck, Wrangell, and Petersburg. The entire course is well protected, and tidal currents are not much of a concern. The 5-mile crossing of Behm Canal soon after Ketchikan is more tedium than hazard.

There are two route alternates. The first goes up the east side of Wrangell Island and visits the Anan Creek Bear Observatory. It is 5–7 miles longer than the main route, which courses up the western side of

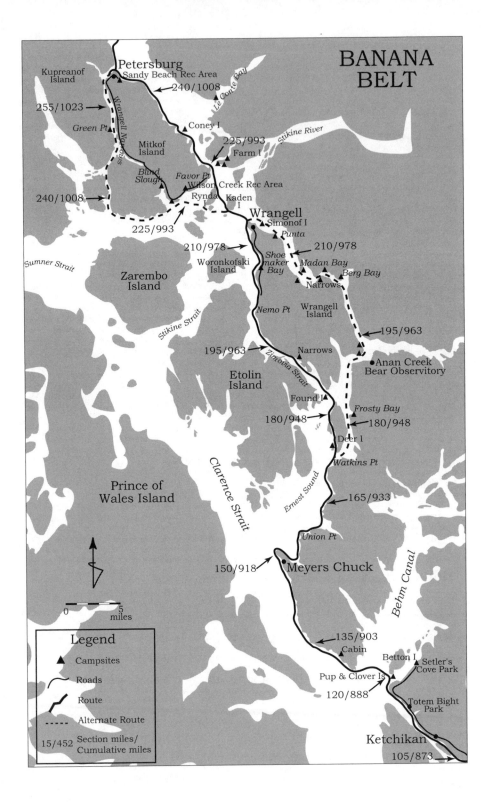

BANANA
BELT

Kupreanof
Island

Petersburg
Sandy Beach Rec Area
240/1008

Le Cone Bay

255/1023 →

Green Pt

Wrangell Narrows

Coney I

Stikine River

225/993
Farm I

Mitkof
Island

*Blind
Slough*

Favor Pt
Wilson Creek Rec Area

240/1008 →

Rynda
I   Kaden
I

225/993

Wrangell
Simonof I
Punta

210/978 →

210/978

*Shoe
maker
Bay*

Madan Bay

Berg Bay

Woronkofski
Island

Narrows

Sumner Strait

Zarembo
Island

Nemo Pt

Wrangell
Island

195/963 →

Stikine Strait

195/963

Zimovia Strait

Narrows

● Anan Creek
Bear Observatory

Etolin
Island

Found I

Frosty Bay

180/948

180/948

Deer I

Prince of
Wales Island

Clarence Strait

Watkins Pt

Ernest Sound

165/933

Union Pt

Behm Canal

150/918 →
● Meyers Chuck

0   5
miles

135/903
Cabin

Betton I
Setler's
Cove Park

Pup & Clover Is

120/888

Totem Bight
Park

Legend

▲ Campsites

    Roads

    Route

---- Alternate Route

15/452 Section miles/
       Cumulative miles

Ketchikan

105/873 →

Wrangell Island. After Wrangell, the second alternate route diverges and goes up Wrangell Narrows, the main Inside Passage traffic route. This one is 11 miles longer than the main route, which hugs the mainland coast going directly north, across the Stikine River delta.

Shallow deltaic flats requiring precise tide timing (and probably some dragging) are the only obstacles. Each will be described immediately following its point of convergence with the main route.

The leaving of Ketchikan is a drawn-out affair. Past Thomas Basin and Pennock Island, Tongass Narrows squeezes down to its narrowest point. The airport and industrial development line the shores. A small bight, Port Gravina, indents the coast near the north end of the airport runway. Now a ghost town, in the 1890s Port Gravina was a small town centered around a sawmill. A group of Tsimshians from Metlakatla who had attended the Sitka Industrial Training School started the settlement and sawmill in 1892. It was the first business to be capitalized, built, managed, and operated entirely by Alaskan Indians. Port Gravina burned to the ground in 1904 during a Fourth of July celebration and was never rebuilt.

Past Lewis Point (on Gravina Island) and Peninsula Point (on Revillagigedo Island), Tongass Narrows open up. Pass by Ward Cove, site of the Ketchikan Pulp Company's giant pulp mill and booming grounds and the mouth of one of Revillagigedo Island's major drainage valleys. Just beyond lie a group of islands protecting Refuge Cove, site of a marina with some supplies.

Totem Bight State Historic Park: Just before Mud Bay, emerging from the mists, two tall totems mark Totem Bight. Don't miss it. The park is a curious combination of landscaped, manicured lawns and gardens with an elaborately decorated clan house and totems. The site, next to a salmon stream, was a Tlingit summer campsite. The Civilian Conservation Corps, working with master native carvers, completed the park in 1941. Though there is no camping, shelter from the rain is available, and a gift shop/snack bar combo is located where the road meets the park.

Point Higgins: Point Higgins, not much more than a rounded change in the coast's direction, is the northwest corner of Revillagigedo Island. The 1869 *Coast Pilot* reports the native village of "Tilhnach" on or near the point. The point's name is illustrative of one of Vancouver's charting procedures. Vancouver did not know Ambrose Higgins of Ballengh, Ireland at the time he passed the point. On his way home to England, he stopped in Valparaiso, Chile, where he met Higgins, by then governor and captain general of Chile, who proved amicable and hospitable. This indicates that a good many of the places Vancouver charted were christened some time after the survey, probably during the final preparation of the charts.

How does an Irishman become governor of a Spanish province? Higgins immigrated to South America, joined the Spanish Army at a young age, and changed his name (actually baldly transliterated it and added an O) to Ambrosio O'Higgins de Vallenar. He performed well and worked his way up to the rank of Captain of Cavalry, after which he was titled a marquis before being appointed governor. In 1796, he was promoted to Viceroy of Peru until his death in 1801. Higgins is notable for fathering (illegitimately) Bernardo O'Higgins, War of Independence

Reconstructed longhouse, Totem Bight State Historic Park, Alaska

liberator and first President of the Republic of Chile. Vallenar Point, Gravina Island's northern and corresponding terminus of Tongass Narrows also honors Higgins, as the transliterated version of Ballengh.

Round Point Higgins to Survey Point, in preparation for the 5-mile crossing of Behm Canal's western entrance. Just around the corner from Survey Point, the Clover Pass Resort and Knudson Cove Marina operate a variety of services. The closest developed campground is Settler's Cove State Park, about 5 miles up Clover Passage on the Revillagigedo side of the channel. Pup and Clover Islands (mile 122/**869**), at the start of the Behm Canal crossing, may offer camping opportunities. Clover has the ruins of a structure, while Pup was homesteaded and patented in the 1930s. Modern maps of the Tongass National Forest indicate both as public land.

Clarence Strait: Caamano Point, the target on the other side of Behm Canal, marks the southern extremity of the mainland's Cleveland Peninsula and this route's junction with Clarence Strait. Clarence Strait is big. More than a hundred miles long and relatively wide, it separates Prince of Wales Island from the rest of the archipelago. However, strong currents and nasty seas do not bedevil it—at least from a kayaker's point of view. Out in the middle, spring tides can attain 4 knots; summertime seas tend to be calm. Vancouver named the strait after the king of England. You don't remember a King Clarence? He was born William Henry, third son of George III, who was king during the American Revolution. (For a more sympathetic portrayal of this tragic sovereign's life, check out the excellent, award-winning movie *The Madness of King George* with Nigel Hawthorne.) William Henry held the title Duke of Clarence. Serving in the Royal Navy at that time, he was nearly captured by Washington's forces. George III was succeeded by his elder son, George IV, who died in 1830. Clarence followed him as William IV for a scant seven years. Queen Victoria then ascended the throne for a long and stable reign.

Prince of Wales Island: While he was at it, Vancouver named Prince of Wales Island after the eldest son of George III. Prince of Wales is the largest island in southeast Alaska and the second largest island in the state, after Kodiak. Human bones close to 10,000 years old have been discovered here. The island is geologically unique, in that much of its bedrock is porous limestone, otherwise rare in southeastern Alaska. The limestone drains well, creating ideal conditions for tree growth, particularly for Sitka spruce in low-lying river valleys. Consequently, some of the biggest spruce trees along Inside grew on Prince of Wales. There are a few still left, measuring more than 6 feet across and 200 feet tall. Otherwise, most of the island was extensively logged prior to 1990, with the exception of a cosmetic seashore fringe.

The bight on the Clarence Strait side of Caamano Point is the site of southeastern Alaska's only (abandoned) antimony mine. The claims are held, but undeveloped, by the Duval Corporation of Tucson, Arizona.

Up from Caamano Point, the shore trends in a northwesterly direction, with few landmarks for a good 20 miles. Many tiny inlets, none discernible on the 1:250,000 scale topo map, indent the coast. One (about mile 130/**898**), not clearly visible from the water, has a double bight with a shingle beach and private cabin in the woods. It is an excellent campsite in an area not particularly devoid of them. Keep a lookout between the minor points labeled Jay and Pen prior to Niblack Point.

Meyers Chuck: Meyers Chuck (mile 149/**917**) is a tiny, old, terminally cute, and fortuitously located settlement and harbor. The name is one of the few remaining examples of Chinook, a trade language (like Swahili) developed by Northwest Coast natives and white traders to facilitate commerce between the two cultures and among the different native language groups. A chuck is a saltwater body that dries at low tide. Other Chinook jargon geographic names include tatoosh (breast), chickamin (metal or mineral), and skookum (strong; combined with chuck, as in Skookum Chuck, this renders the word for tidal rapids). By the late 1800s, white settlers began living year-round at Meyers Chuck. The town developed around fishing, and by 1922, soon after nearby Union Bay Cannery opened, it boasted a post office, general store, machine shop, barber shop, bakery, and bar. By 1939, 107 residents lived in Meyers Chuck.

The 1940s decimated the chuck's population. Many residents left to join the armed forces or wartime production in the Lower 48. Declining salmon stocks made fishing less profitable. When the Union Bay Cannery burned down in 1947 and no one attempted to rebuild it, jobs disappeared. Atop all this, land titles were in legal limbo. When the land was finally patented between 1965 and 1969 and the community was withdrawn from the Tongass National Forest, Meyers Chuck stabilized, for a while. A state-of-the-art school was built in 1983. However, two major fires that year consumed much of the town and the enthusiasm of the Chuckers. The school is no longer staffed. A state land-disposal sale was offered in 1986 but did not precipitate a land rush. A new air float and docking facility graces the harbor and immeasurably improves the community's infrastructure. Still, the present population hovers at 37. There has recently been talk of combining Meyers Chuck in the same borough with Hyder, but, due to conflicting visions, residents are reticent.

Meyers Chuck, Alaska

Enter Meyers Chuck through the foul passage just south of Meyers Island, dock at the new pier, and inquire from the locals as to the lay of the land. Though there is no handy camping in the village, kayakers have often been provided shelter in the inoperative school. If offered this hospitality, minimize your impact. Camp in the covered gymnasium, and flush the toilets with a bucket of water, as there is no running water in the building. One absolutely incongruous public telephone—complete with urban-style phone booth—stands at the head of the dock trail next to the community bulletin board. The post office is open on Tuesday from 11 AM to 2 PM and on Wednesday for one hour after the mail plane arrives. One attractive restaurant is open whenever demand and the whims of the owners coincide. A small art gallery operates on and off.

Beyond Meyers Chuck, turn Lemesurier Point and enter Ernest Sound. The ruins of the Union Bay Cannery mark the middle of Union Bay's east shore. There may be camping in Union Bay, though we did not explore. Currents in Ernest Sound flood and ebb at about 2 knots. The Ernest Sound route is the most popular cruising course between Ketchikan and Wrangell.

Cross Union Bay to Union Point, flanked by Magnetic Cove, on the south, and Vixen Harbor, on the north. Both inlets may have possible campsites. Cross Vixen Inlet to Vixen Point and continue up the coast, passing Emerald Bay and Eaton Point to Watkins Point.

At Watkins Point, this section's first alternate route diverges from the main route. While the primary route crosses due north to Deer Island and then goes up Wrangell Island's west side, through Zimovia Strait, the alternate follows a series of channels and passages up Wrangell's east side. The alternate route is described immediately following the main route's arrival at Wrangell.

From Watkins Point, cross Seward Passage to Point Peters (mile 175/**943**) on the southern tip of Deer Island. Just around the west side of the point, a very attractive and tree-clear high bench beckons as a potential campsite. Our own experience, however, was disturbing. Checking out the campsite, we were astounded at the abundance of bear scat. Every 5 to 6 feet, in every direction, lay fresh, huge piles of black excrement. Very disappointed, we headed for the small islands off the west side of the point, where we found an adequate campsite. Wherever you choose to camp, be aware that the Anan Creek Bear Observatory is nearby, and this entire area has a very high and concentrated bear population. (As of 2004, a seasonal youth camp has been established on Deer Island.)

Make your way up the west side of Deer Island through the intriguing archipelago just offshore to Deer's northern tip. Cross over to Found Island.

Found Island: In 1923 Found Island (mile 183/**951**) was home to a fox farm operated by Louis Scribner. It is one of a select type of island—smallish, topographically accessible, somewhat isolated from other land masses—that flourished as fox farms during the 1920s and is the first of many encountered along this route. Enterprising Russians, aware of diminishing trap line returns, probably started the practice. According to historian Patricia Roppel:

> *Island fox farming developed in the Aleutian Islands and spread to most suitable islands in Southeastern Alaska by the early 1920s. A man, a married couple, or a syndicate which hired a watchman would apply to the USFS for a lease on a specific island. By 1923 over 150 island leases were issued in the Tongass National Forest. The farmer built a cabin to live in, a shed for his gear and feed, feeding troughs, and sometimes pens, and then imported pairs of blue foxes. Live foxes were purchased from farmers in the Interior of Alaska, and as farms became established, from other Southeastern Alaska fox farms. In 1922, a pair of breeding blue foxes cost between $350 to $400, and litters averaged from six to nine kits. It took about three years before the fur could be harvested . . . a blue fox pelt sold in Tacoma for $166.50.*

*Fox farmers believed that using small islands and stocking them
to capacity, and hiring reliable caretakers to cover every portion
of the daily needs gave the best results... A great deal of
experimentation with different foods, housing, breeding, and
marketing pelts took place. Fox farmers tended to feed salmon
and other fish, fish offal from the canneries, seals, grains and
meals, and anything handy. Manufacturers of prepared feed
had just started researching proper diets. In later years a more
scientific diet improved survival rates.*

*By the time Dr. E. F. Graves, Territorial veterinarian, evaluated
the success of fox farms in Alaska in 1928, he found many fox
farmers had failed. Large losses occurred from internal and
external parasites, faulty breeding, digestive disturbances,
killing by wolves and eagles, and poaching... Graves thought the
average island-run ranch was conducted by methods which were
wasteful and extravagant and run by people totally unsuited to
their task of handling and raising foxes.*

One Fish & Wildlife officer, during Southeast's fox farming heyday,
commented that "the only fox men that were going to make money
were those who could double the capacity of their stills." By 1932, the
Great Depression reduced pelt prices to about $10, bankrupting most
farmers. Few farms remained by the 1940s. Fox farm islands nearly always afford a camping opportunity.

Enter Zimovia Strait, separating Wrangell Island from Etolin Island.
Tidal currents running at about 1.5 knots enter and exit the strait from
both the north and south ends and meet near Village Islands.

Thoms Place, a cove on the Wrangell side of the channel, is an undeveloped park. A creek flows into drying flats at its head.

The Narrows: Beyond Thoms Place, enter the Narrows of Zimovia
Strait, a particularly attractive area. Much of the Narrows all the way to
Village Islands is the site of an abandoned Tlingit village, whose center
was on the point due east of the more southern of the two main Village

Islands. You can still see signs of cleared landing places on the beaches for the big canoes. The village was called Kots-lit-na (Willow Town), though it is sometimes referred to as "Old Wrangell." The Narrows is the last dependable at-large camping prior to Wrangell, still 20 or so miles north of the last Village Island. The first likely camp, on Wrangell Island, is due east of the Zimovia Islets (mile 191/**959**), where the topo map indicates a couple of cabins. According to the local *Wrangell Guide*, one of the cabins is a state-owned public recreation site. Other likely campsites dot the Narrows/village area.

Round Nemo Point. Four miles farther up the Wrangell Island coast, the Petersburg, Alaska-Canada USGS 1:250,000 topo map indicates a campground at the end of the Wrangell highway. This campground no longer exists. A small offshore island just before and another just opposite the nonexistent campground will accommodate a tent or two in a pinch.

North of Chichagof Peak, Shoemaker Bay (208/**976**) gives the first indication of approaching Wrangell. The impressive buildings of the Wrangell Institute, a boarding school for native children built in the 1930s, contrast elegantly with the green fields of the grounds. The school was closed in 1987 due to the use of asbestos during construction and is scheduled for demolition. Though part of the bay is used to store log booms, Shoemaker Bay accommodates a boat harbor and some services for sport fishing boats. There is an RV and tent campground and the adjacent, 3.5-mile-long Rainbow Falls–Institute Creek Trail. The Shoemaker Bay RV Park is about 5 miles from Wrangell.

Wrangell: Cruise on by Wrangell Harbor and continue to the city dock (also known as the cruise ship dock, though *big* cruise ships don't often stop at Wrangell) or the ferry terminal, both at least another 0.5 mile on, depending on your destination and plans. Wrangell Harbor is crowded and not particularly centrally located. The uncrowded city dock offers out-of-the-way kayak parking, particularly under the pier. There is no parking at the ferry dock (a tad farther), but Fennimore's Bed, Breakfast & Bikes is immediately adjacent.

Although there is no handy public campground for kayakers in Wrangell, a variety of lodging options are relatively close at hand. Right at the top of the city dock, the Stikine Inn, charging about $110, is the handiest alternative. About two blocks away to the south, at 223 Front Street next door to the Diamond C Café, is the Thunderbird Hotel and Laundra-mat. The Thunderbird runs about $75 for two. At $18 per person, the thriftiest alternative is the Wrangell Hostel in the first Presbyterian Church up the hill at 220 Church Street. Couples' rooms are available, though bath, toilets, and a great kitchen are shared.

There are a half dozen B&Bs; all will provide transportation. I'll only mention Fennimore's because of its location right next to the ferry terminal. Two giant breakwaters on the north side of the terminal create a square beach that makes for a suitable landing. It runs about $70 for two.

City Market is located on Front Street, about a block south of the Thunderbird Hotel, while Bob's IGA Supermarket is virtually outside the Thunderbird's back door. Both sell liquor.

Wrangell, with a population of only 2,500, is the smallest major city along Alaska's panhandle. It does not owe its existence to logging, mining, fishing, or tourism but rather to its strategic location at the mouth of the Stikine River, a major artery connecting interior B.C. with the coastal archipelago. Old Wrangell, the Tlingit village in the Narrows, gained importance and reputation when Gush-klin, chief of the Stikine Tlingits, decisively defeated We-Shakes, a Nisga'a chief after a long-running contest for hegemony over the region. As a token of respect and submission, the Nisga'a chief conferred the prestigious title of We-Shakes, meaning, "splash of a killer whale's fluke," on Gush-klin. It was the beginning of a powerful dynasty that lasted until 1944, at the death of Chief Shakes VII.

During the late 1700s, when European explorers and traders began visiting the area, Chief Shakes could see the handwriting on the wall. So he established a village at the site of present-day Wrangell (on Shustaak Point and Shakes Island) to better control trade with the interior tribes. By 1811, the Stikine Tlingits were conducting a profitable beaver and otter pelt trade with the Russians. Meanwhile, the Hudson's Bay Company, expanding ever westward, was eyeing the Stikine River delta as a possible outpost site to coordinate trade with the interior. When the Russians got wind of the plan, they dispatched Captain-Lieutenant

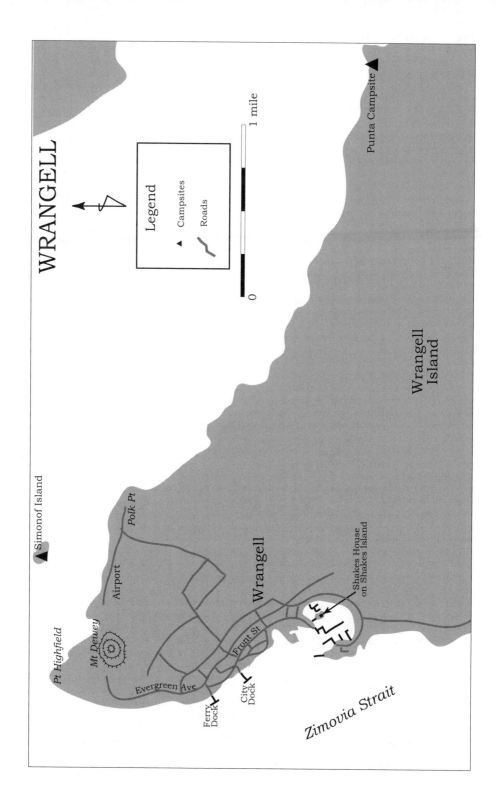

Dionysi Zarembo in 1833 to preempt the British by building their own fort at the delta. Stephen Hilson relates:

> *When the Russians first arrived at the harbor presently called Wrangell, they met a family... (who) was pursuing their summer fishing activities. The Russians made it known to the head of the family that they wanted to speak to the local chief (Shakes IV) and sent the Indian to Old Wrangell to get the leader. When the fisherman paddled into Old Wrangell he gave a whoop to announce big news. He told Shakes IV that the Russian ship was anchored near his fish camp and the commander expected Chief Shakes to paddle up there for a meeting. The chief instructed his man to return to the Russian and inform him that since he was certainly no more important than the chief, he would have to come down to Old Wrangell to conduct his discussions.*
>
> *Some time later the Indian paddled back to Old Wrangell to tell Shakes that the Russian claimed he could not sail his ships down the narrow and uncharted Zimovia Strait, therefore the chief must come to him.*
>
> *Undaunted, Shakes sent 200 canoes to the Russian and towed him (and his ship) to Old Wrangell where the conference regarding the construction of the fort was held.*

In 1834, the Russian fort at Wrangell was christened Redoubt Saint Dionysius and soon intercepted the first Hudson's Bay Company trading expedition. The ensuing crisis was settled by Shakes, who reminded both parties that the Stikine Tlingits controlled interior trade with the Athabaskans, not the Russians or British. The British withdrew.

But the Russians weren't really interested in expanding their empire (after all, they were already overextended), only in keeping the British from expanding *theirs*. Once the British submitted to Russian jurisdiction at the Stikine delta, the Russians offered to lease the new settlement to the Hudson's Bay Company for 2,000 otter pelts annually, plus a quantity of wheat and salt beef. In 1840, Redoubt Saint Dionysius became Fort Stikine. In spite of the booming commerce with the natives, the British abandoned Fort Stikine in 1849, and the settlement languished until the 1861 Stikine gold strike, when a minor boom revived the town.

In 1867, when the United States purchased Alaska, the US Army took control of Fort Stikine, built a new fort, and renamed it Fort Wrangell after Baron Ferdinand Wrangell, last manager of the Russian-American Company. Wrangell briefly ballooned to 15,000 (albeit temporary) residents during the Cassiar gold rush in interior B.C., when it was used as the gateway to the goldfields up the Stikine. The settlement was almost abandoned after the Cassiar rush. In 1888 the US Army transferred the reins of government to a civilian US commissioner and abandoned Fort Wrangell. When steamers transporting the 1898 Klondikers used Wrangell as a stopover, the town revived and then grew slowly around fishing and logging.

Wrangell is small enough that you can walk to all the major attractions. The old downtown—what is left of it after two major fires—proudly preserves many old wooden false-fronted buildings. The harbor berths an extremely active fishing fleet. Right in the middle of it is Shakes Island with Chief Shakes's tribal house and totems. The entire compound was built by the Civilian Conservation Corps in 1939 and 1940 with direction from the Stikine Tlingit and is meant to be a faithful reproduction of the original work. More than 1,500 mostly native visitors conducted the last great potlatch of the local Tlingit people at its dedication in 1940. The event was crowned by the investiture of Chief Shakes VII, last of the Shakes chiefs. (Shakes VI died in 1916.) If the clan house is closed, call 907-874-3747 for a tour. A donation is requested for admission.

For a good leg workout and stunning views of the town and surrounding seascape, hike the improved trail up Mt. Dewey, between Wranglell and the airport. Petroglyph Beach, a 15-minute walk north of the ferry terminal or city dock on Evergreen Avenue, lies below the high-tide line at the end of a signed trail and wooden boardwalk. Lastly, if you arrived at Wrangell via the main route, you will have missed the Anan Creek Bear Observatory (described along the alternate route, immediately following), about 30 miles south of Wrangell on the mainland. Many local outfitters (see Appendix B for a handful) offer day and overnight tours to the Observatory or up the Stikine River.

Alternate Route #1: Watkins Point (near southern tip of Deer Island; mile 175/943) to Point Highfield (mile 215/983) via the east coast of Wrangell Island

The Seward Passage/Blake Channel/Eastern Passage alternate route is 5–7 miles longer than the main route and includes the Anan Creek Bear Observatory. (Backtracking south to Wrangell is an additional 2 miles, hence the 7 miles.) Many consider it the more scenic of the two choices. South of The Narrows, vertical cliffs line the shores for much of its length.

From Watkins Point, follow the mainland coast past Sunny Bay and Point Santa Anna. Santa Anna Inlet has a quarter-mile-long creek at its head flowing out of Lake Helen. USGS topo maps indicate a cabin there, so camping ought to be possible. There is a 3-mile overland trail across the Cleveland Peninsula to Yes Bay in Behm Canal. Five miles farther up Seward Passage lies scenic Frosty Bay (mile 182/**950**). About half as deep as Santa Ana Inlet, Frosty Bay's mouth is protected by a resident colony of seals off its west entrance. According to the Douglasses: "A logger's cabin on the southwest shore near the log transfer site has been renovated by the USFS for use as a recreational cabin," so, one way or another, there's probably a spot to spread a sleeping bag.

Continue north to the top of Ernest Sound. The entire Cleveland Peninsula shore from Frosty Bay to Anan Creek is precipitous, but for one notable exception. In a small bight just below Point Warde stand the few remains of an abandoned cannery, another possible campsite. At the junction of Ernest Sound, Bradfield Canal, and Blake Channel (mile 192/**960**), Anan Bay indents the Cleveland Peninsula's northwest corner while directly opposite, a beautiful campsite graces the southeast tip of Wrangell Island: a perfect base for a visit to the Anan Creek Wildlife Observatory.

Anan Creek Wildlife Observatory: Until 2004, access to the Observatory was lightly regulated. Due to phenomenally increased demand, the US Forest Service established a permit system in that year to regulate the number of visitors at any one time. Permits are for a specific date and must be obtained in advance from the Tongass National Forest, Wrangell Ranger District, P.O. Box 51, Wrangell, AK, 99929; phone 907-874-2323. For an Inside Passage kayaker who may not be able to plan his arrival precisely, this could prove daunting. However, the ranger in charge has assured me that he'll make every effort to accommodate visiting through-kayakers.

Failing that, there is always the more conventional approach: an outfitter. Most folks visit the observatory guided by an outfitter from Wrangell at a cost of about $200. The day trip consists of a prior or even last-minute arrangement through an outfitter's kiosk at the Wrangell city dock. The 90-minute jet boat shuttle is comfortable, includes an orientation, and provides 4–6 hours of viewing at the observatory. Breakaway Adventures offers a bare-bones trip for $150 and guarantees a bear sighting (during July and August) or your money back.

During July and August, the waterfalls of Anan Creek abound with salmon, drawing bears, eagles, and seals. There are some 40 to 60 black bears and 15 to 20 brown bears in the area. The Forest Service has built a roofed observatory overlooking the falls half a mile from the bay and accessible via a planked boardwalk. Regulations require that you stay on the boardwalk and carry no food. While on the boardwalk, talk loudly or make noise to broadcast your presence. Bear repellent, to deter the overly curious, is not a bad idea.

Why does Anan Creek, not a large drainage, attract so many bears? Let's look at it from the perspective of a salmon and its hunters. The configuration of the last mile of the stream is peculiarly unique. The mouth of the creek is constricted by a Gibraltar-like set of tall, narrow rock gates, behind which is a broad, shallow tidal flat—a natural weir that traps fish during tidal fluctuations. A couple of hundred yards upstream of the lagoon, the creek narrows down at a declivity above a series of small pools, where the fish must regroup and reconsider their strategy. The falls are not easy. It is here that they are most vulnerable to bear predation; and it is here where the decks and blinds of the observatory have been elegantly constructed.

Bears are not the only predators to have taken advantage of Anan Creek's unique topography. Bifurcating the tidal lagoon is a broad, flat, round peninsula—a perfect location for a Tlingit summer village. Their use was so intense—and ancient—that the spit remains their property. Even small children could wander out into the muddy flats and collect salmon by hand. Myriad drying racks with strips of phosphorescent flesh, like pennants at a used car lot, must have highlighted all the activity. When white men arrived, the inevitable cannery was built on the site. By the early 1900s, the salmon had nearly disappeared. Today, there is no sign left of the incursion, though the fish have come back with a vengeance.

Dances with Bears: V

The photographers' blind at Anan Creek is limited to five observers for half an hour. There is a sign-up sheet on the upper decks. I thought I was prepared: five rolls of ASA 200 slide film—36 exposures each—and a 160mm telephoto lens. I crouched on a tiny stool behind a slit opening. In less than half an hour a fat black bear waddled down to the upper pool, quickly scanned the situation, and snatched a big salmon with a slice of the paw and a snatch of his jaw. He paused on his perch, the flopping of the fish forcing his head to wobble comically from side to side, like a bobble-head doll, obviously pleased with himself. Out of the forest, a big old black sow casually approached the pool, ignoring the rotting remains of five salmon carcasses. Clearly, like a corpulent Roman at an orgy, she was forcing herself to eat. From another quadrant, a diffident youngster cautiously surveyed the scene and waited for an opportunity to approach a pool.

As of yet I hadn't taken one shot. Conditions—the deep forest, overcast skies, long lens, not-fast-enough film and, surprisingly, light-sucking black fur—conspired to render my attempts useless. I despaired.

Suddenly, a murmur alerted me. From downstream, a self-conscious, nonchalant, big, blonde brown bear with an oversized head zigzagged his way up. Every black bear froze in its tracks and watched the brown's every move. He stopped about 50 yards away to inspect a floater—an old, dead salmon. After a nibble or two, he climbed on a rock and set out to cast his paw. What a treat! Now we'll see a true virtuoso at the top of his game, we thought. But try as he might, he was unable to land even one fish. Instead, this blonde turned out to be totally inept. Still, his impressive presence intimidated the other bears and, lucky for me, his light blonde fur reflected plenty of light for a few good shots.

From the observatory, aim north for Blake Island at the mouth of Blake Channel. Floods run north, and ebbs run south, both with a velocity of 2–3 knots. Blake is narrow, cliff-lined, and moderately swift of current so plan to go with the flow. Two-thirds of the way up the west side of Blake Island, a small bay (mile 194/**962**) breaks the shoreline: a good campsite if the one nearest Anan is occupied. Berg Bay (mile 202/**970**), named after the Berg Mine and the abandoned community of Berg (not the presence of icebergs) has a Forest Service cabin at its head with a USFS float. Camping is possible in this stunning alpine setting, where permanent snowfields grace the 5,000- to 6,000-foot peaks less than 10 miles to the north.

Blake Channel then turns northwest and sharply constricts at the Narrows, a 250-yard-wide, 1.5-mile-long mini-channel that bends a farther 90 degrees to the southwest. There are at least two campsites each along both the Wrangell Island shore and on outlying islands along the mainland shore through this stretch. In spite of its narrowness, the Narrows does not present a current obstacle. Tidal flows around Wrangell Island enter and exit from the island's extremities and meet at the Narrows, where currents tread water. Eastern Passage—where the shore's steepness eases considerably—leads from the Narrows to the top of Wrangell Island. Being much wider, Eastern Passage's tidal flows attain only a 1.8-knot velocity. The passage floods south and ebbs north.

At the end of the Narrows, on the extreme southeast tip of Madan Bay (207/**975**), there are more campsites. Additionally, across the channel in the crotch below Channel Island, at the terminus of an old logging road (and where the 1:250,000 map indicates a cabin), there is another good campsite. Pass Channel Island and Point Madan en route to Wrangell Island's northern tip. Halfway up, just below the "Punta" triangle (mile 216/**984**) there is a campsite on the Wrangell Island shore. Just prior to Point Highfield, Wrangell's busy airport breaks the quiet. Directly offshore, Simonof Island (mile 221/**989**) provides the last camp before Wrangell. Immediately behind Point Highfield, you'll notice a giant avulsion on the crowding mount. Bulldozers, draglines, Euclid dump trucks, and barges are consuming the hill to expand the airport and transporting the fill to build a new breakwater for a bigger harbor. Round Point Highfield and rejoin the main route. Wrangell lies about 1 mile south.

Main Route: Continued . . .

The departure from Wrangell confronts the paddler with the whole reason for the town's existence, the delta of the mighty Stikine River. Its broad sedimentary fan extends 20 miles north from Wrangell. From the Stikine's mouth it reaches west about 15 miles out, nearly grabbing Mitkof Island's toe and almost making it part of the mainland. Unlike other major river deltas along the Inside Passage, the Stikine delta is quite negotiable by kayak. The route through it, Dry Strait, is protected, relatively short, and—because it traverses the delta's outside verge— hardly subject to the brunt of the river's current. The main obstacles are drying mud flats and tidal currents. Most cruising, ferry, and commercial traffic avoids the delta entirely, traversing the well-maintained, albeit narrow, Wrangell Narrows as the preferred route to Petersburg. Although 11 miles longer, this second alternate route will be described immediately following the main route's arrival at Petersburg.

Dry Strait: Traversing the delta's 20-mile breadth requires about a six-hour paddle coupled with a route and timing strategy. Dry Strait mostly dries at or near low water. Tidal currents up Sumner Strait can attain 2 knots. Where they meet and oppose the river's flow, they weaken considerably. Ebbs, when both river and tide flow in the same direction, can attain 5 knots around Blaquiere Point. Passage north should be attempted on the upper half of a rising tide, or three to four hours from Wrangell before high tide. With this strategy, high tide should find you somewhere in the middle of Dry Strait with plenty of water underthwarts and ready to meet and ride Frederick Sound's ebbing tide north. According to the *Coast Pilot,* Dry Strait is "extensively used by fishing boats and towboats." We saw no one.

With sufficient water, any compass course from Wrangell to Dry Strait is theoretically possible, especially for a kayak. There is, however, a preferred transit channel for craft with any draught and it is this channel that is here described. From Wrangell, head for the south shore of Kadin Island. Then make your way to Rynda Island. About halfway up its east coast the high-water boat passage through Dry Strait commences. Aim for Blaquiere Point (a.k.a. Favor Point) and hug the Mitkof

Dry Strait, Stikine River delta, Alaska

Island shore. There is an old boat ramp just past the point. On the opposite shore, in the marshes at the western tip of Farm Island (mile 225/**993**) are three USFS recreational cabins, where camping may be possible. But beware: The Dry Strait area is notoriously buggy. If for some unfortunate reason you run aground, get out, line the boat, and persevere. Adequate depth is just a few yards away. Once past Dry Island—and the navigational light just opposite on Mitkof—the permanent water of Frederick Sound begins.

For the next 60 miles, wide Frederick Sound will be our highway north. Currents can reach 1.5 to 2 knots. Pass Cosmos Point and Ideal Cove. Much of Mitkof Island's east coast is low-lying, with many possible campsites. Notable is steep-to Coney Island (mile 232/**1,000**), an old fox farm site. Immediately opposite on the mainland shore and guarded by the Stikine delta's mud flats lies Le Conte Bay.

Le Conte Bay: Deep within Le Conte Bay (mile 232/**1,000**), North America's southernmost tidewater glacier descends from the mountains into the sea. The Le Conte Glacier calves a constant parade of icebergs that usually line Frederick Sound's north shore below the Horn Cliffs. From a distance some look like luxury yachts. Sometimes they reach Petersburg. At this point Frederick Sound is 6 miles wide, putting the bay that many miles off route, while the glacier itself is another 10 miles inside the bay. Further impeding access, the Stikine delta's northern edge obstructs the entrance to the bay. For some, however, a visit to this frigid kingdom and notable landmark is irresistible. This is remote and rugged country. Cruising boats seldom enter due to the multiple obstacles of icebergs, tidal flats, and rocky shoals.

If you decide to visit, from Coney Island head due north toward the mainland, skirting the mud flats of the Stikine delta. Just past Camp Island, turn east for Indian Point and Le Conte Bay's entrance. Air temperature noticeably drops. There are numerous campsites around Indian Point. Within the bay, shores steepen, so choose a campsite at or prior to Thunder Point.

The Le Conte Glacier's mile-wide face is very active. Some 2,000 harbor seals live in the bay and rear their pups on the bergs. Do not approach nurseries. Be aware that since icebergs float with two-thirds of their mass below waterline, they can unexpectedly flip as they melt. Do not approach the face of a tidewater glacier too closely; bergs can calve at any time. Not that one of these spalls is likely to land right on a kayak. The real danger lies in the percussion wave—sometimes unexpectedly large—that can swamp or flip nearby small craft.

Iceberg from Le Conte Bay, Frederick Sound, Alaska CREDIT: T. COBOS

From Coney Island, 15 mostly uneventful miles remain to Petersburg. Camping is not particularly scarce. Around Frederick Point, the shore becomes rocky and steep. A small bight about a mile before the northern tip of Mitkof Island shelters Sandy Beach Recreation Area (mile 245/**1,013**) at the northern end of the Mitkof highway and still about 2 miles from downtown Petersburg.

Petersburg: Sandy Beach includes Tent City, a tents-only camping area that is a good staging point for a visit to or layover in Petersburg. The facility has 50 wooden tent platforms, rest rooms, showers, phone, and cooking area. Although no reservations are required, a permit is. It is open May 1 through September 30. In spite of the 2-mile distance to town, do not preclude Tent City as your Petersburg accommodations. Petersburg is small (population 3,600) but very busy—it is the home port of more than 300 commercial fishing boats—with a small harbor. Lodging is often full and dear. The other available campsite is the Le Conte RV Park, on 4th and Haugen Drive, downtown but about five blocks from the docks. Additionally, there is the Petersburg Bunk & Breakfast Hostel at 805 Gjoa Street. Though not near the water, at $25 per person per night, it's a bargain.

Paddling into Petersburg harbor is a fine experience. Continue up to the tip of Wrangell Island and enter the north end of Wrangell Narrows. If the tide is contrary—and it can be strong within the narrows—hug the shore; it's only 1 mile or so to the very busy harbor. Medium-sized vessels of every sort are continuously coming and going and vying for berthing space. Exactly where to head for? If equipped with VHF, call the harbormaster on Channel 16 at least 30 minutes before your arrival, then switch to Channel 9 to receive a mooring assignment. With the kayaks safely berthed, you can seek accommodation at the Le Conte RV Park or upgrade to one of the many hotels or B&Bs in town. The Scandia House, running $90–$175, is only about a block and a half from North or Middle Harbor at 110 North Nordic Drive. All services are available in this tidy town within short walking distances, including a kayaking outfitter, Tongass Kayak Adventures. Call them at 907-772-4600.

Petersburg, in spite of its seemingly Russian name, was founded in 1891 by Peter Buschman, a Norwegian immigrant, and named after him. Buschman built a salmon cannery and sawmill and laid out the town's neat grid. Other Norwegians soon followed and developed a well-planned, Scandinavian-style community. Petersburg still honors and celebrates its Norwegian heritage on May 17th (Norwegian Independence Day) during the Little Norway Festival. What set Petersburg apart from other Southeast towns was the nearby location of the Le Conte Glacier's ice. Although the salmon cannery was successful, the endless source of ice allowed Petersburg to become the halibut capital of Alaska. Packed in glacier ice, the delicate and flaky, fine white fish was shipped by steamer to Seattle and forwarded to eager East Coast markets.

The town remains the major fish-processing community in the panhandle. Petersburg Fisheries, Buschman's old company, is now a subsidiary of Icicle Seafoods. Besides the salmon and halibut industries, Petersburg has diversified into crab, herring, prawns, and the delicate Petersburg shrimp, fished within a 25-mile radius of town.

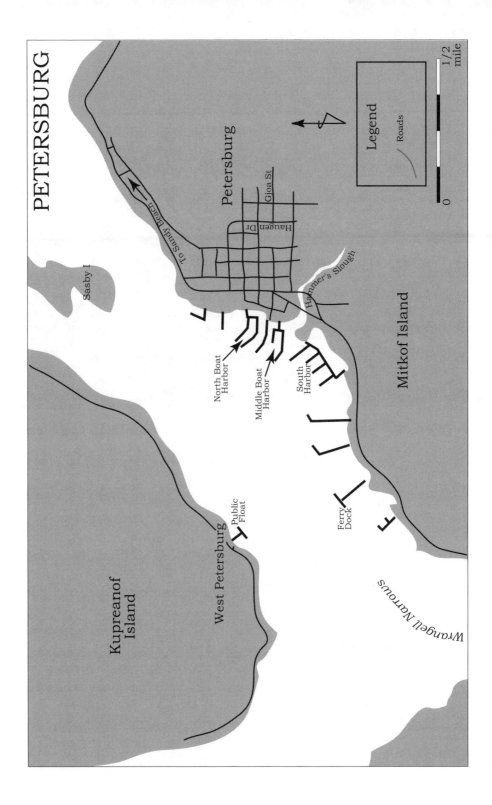

PETERSBURG

Kupreanof Island

West Petersburg

Public Float

Sasby I

To Sandy Beach

Petersburg

Haugen Dr

Gioa St

North Boat Harbor

Middle Boat Harbor

South Harbor

Hammer's Slough

Ferry Dock

Mitkof Island

Wrangell Narrows

Legend

Roads

0   1/2 mile

Petersburg, Alaska, with Devil's Thumb in the background

On a clear day, Petersburg is framed by the ice fields and naked rock peaks of the Coast Range. Devil's Thumb rises agonizingly close. Because it lacks a deepwater port, large cruise ships do not call at Petersburg. It is not a kitschy town. Walk south to Hammer's Slough, where stilt houses and wood-planked streets line South Harbor. Next to the Sons of Norway Hall stands a bronze commemorative statue of a fisherman, mute reminder that fishing is serious business. Close by is Sing Lee Alley Books, one of the Inside Passage's best bookstores.

Alternate Route #2: Wrangell (mile 213/981) to Petersburg (mile 249/1,017) via Wrangell Narrows

Note that the Wrangell-Petersburg distance via the main route is 36 miles, while along the alternate it is 47 miles, 11 miles longer than the main route. It entirely avoids the Stikine River delta and approaches Petersburg with the big boys up Wrangell Narrows. A navigationally challenging adventure for most craft, it is far less so for kayaks, which need only time their passage in concert with the tides.

From Wrangell, head towards the passage between Liesnoi and Kadin Islands. Tidal currents flood Sumner Strait from the west at a maximum of 2 knots but diminish considerably where they meet the Stikine's outflow. Ebb tides are much stronger. If you leave Wrangell at or near high tide, you can ride the ebb the full 26 miles to Point Alexander, entry to Wrangell Narrows. Instead of heading for the Dry Strait boat passage, stay south and west of the delta, skirting Greys Island round the south. Aim northwest for Wilson Island off Mitkof Island's shore.

On Mitkof Island, a road from Petersburg follows the shore east of Blind Slough. Nearby, the Wilson Creek Recreation Area (mile 225/**993**), near the Banana Point boat ramp, has good camping with picnic tables and an outhouse. Another 2 miles brings you to Blind Slough, one of twin sloughs that, with a connecting river valley and low depression, nearly cut Mitkof into two islands. Green Point (mile 227/**995**), the northeastern entrance to Blind Slough, has good camping. Ohmer Creek Campground, at the head of the slough, is well developed with improved tent and RV sites, picnic tables, bathrooms, and drinking water. A small fee is required.

Wrangell Narrows: Wrangell Narrows separates Kupreanof and Woewodski Islands from Mitkof Island. Vancouver found a nearly unnavigable slough. During the 1940s, enterprising locals dredged themselves a waterway with a controlling depth of 19 feet and width of 300 feet. Still, the really big cruise ships don't fit. Were it not for its existence, most Inside Passage vessels would have to go 200 miles around Kuiu Island and through Chatham Strait. According to the *Coast Pilot:*

> *Wrangell Narrows extends ... for 21 miles ... The channel is narrow and intricate in places, between dangerous ledges and flats, and the tidal currents are strong. It is marked by an extensive system of lights, lighted ranges, daybeacons, and buoys ... Waterborne traffic through the Narrows consists of cruise ships, state ferries, barges, and freight boats carrying lumber*

products, petroleum products, fish and fish products, provisions, and general cargo.

The strongest currents occur off Turn Point and off Spike Rock and South Ledge Light. The velocity of the current at times of strength at these points is between 4 and 5 knots. During spring and tropic tides, velocities of 6 to 7 knots may occur.

The tides meet just south of Green Point between lights #44 and #48, 12 miles up from the south entrance and about 8 miles down from the north entrance. Plan on rounding Point Alexander and entering the Narrows on the last three hours of a flood tide, so that high-water slack finds you at Green Point. Tidal changes at the southern end and in the center are about 20 minutes (or longer) behind Petersburg. Watch for rips that form off Point Alexander on the flood. You can then ride the 8 miles north to Petersburg on the ebb.

The Wrangell Narrows terrain is mostly shallow—hence the dredging—below the surface and continues low-lying inland beyond the shore. Keep an eye out for ferries and other heavy traffic, whose wakes can be disastrous in shallow water at close range. Terrain-wise, camp-sites are abundant, with cabin density increasing the closer one gets to Petersburg. Most of the upper Mitkof Island shore is, if not private, not part of the Tongass National Forest like the Kupreanof and Woewodski side. Camping is mostly tolerated, however, be sensitive and respect cabin sites, particularly in Keene Channel and near Petersburg.

Midway Rock marks the beginning of the narrows and strong currents. At the junction with Beecher Pass, favor the Mitkof Island side as cross currents impinge. Pass Papkes Landing, a lumber company bulkhead pier, and wait for the ebb tide at Green Point. Scow Bay is the site of the Beachcomber Inn, a waterfront hotel and restaurant that occupies a former cannery. Local seafood is the specialty of the house. Another 3 increasingly developed miles remain until Petersburg. See the description of the main route for access, camping, and lodging at Petersburg.

Admiralty Island: Petersburg (mile 249/1,017) to Juneau (mile 382/1,150)

Admiralty Island, second largest in the Alexander Archipelago, and Frederick Sound/Stephens Passage, dauntingly broad and second to none in size and consequence, dominate the last third of the Alaska Panhandle section. Reaching the south bastion of Admiralty across the junction of the two waterways is the crux of this section, and many a paddler has paused thoughtfully with trepidation. Although the 15-mile distance is broken by island stops, the five-hour paddle is long enough for conditions to impose their own agenda. Some turn back in defeat. More than a few endure an unexpected spanking. Once committed, cross with perseverance, tenacity, and a willingness to reassess strategy as conditions evolve.

There are no human settlements along the route. On Admiralty, brown bears outnumber humans two to one, and there are more bald eagles than in all the other states combined. Still, the hand of man is artfully and hospitably evident along the entire route. Five Finger lighthouse, NFS cabins and shelters, the Pack Creek bear observatory tower, and the Oliver Inlet portage tramway are far from unwelcome intrusions. Campsites are plentiful, including one on muskeg. Juneau, the accidental capital of Alaska, is a fitting and dramatic conclusion to a nearly complete Inside Passage quest.

Leave the bustle of Petersburg and cast yourself into the mists and sighs of Frederick Sound. Currents reach only 1.5 to 2 knots, and diminish as the sound widens in a northward trend. The ever-increasing distance between Kupreanof Island and the mainland dictates a choice of shores in anticipation of the crossing to Admiralty Island. Favoring the Kupreanof shore forces a longer and more exposed crossing than coasting along the mainland, where no portion of the crossing is longer than 4 miles.

Head for the Sukoi Islets (mile 252/**1,020**) for the shortest crossing of the lower reaches of Frederick Sound. The Sukois were once the site

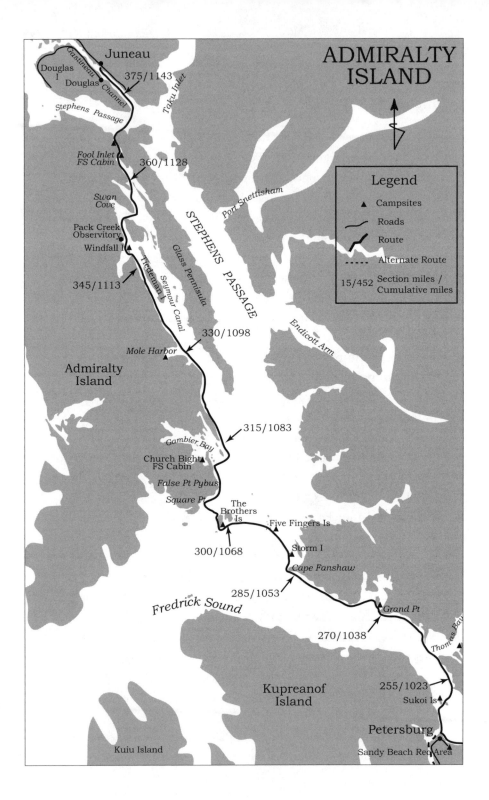

of a fox farm, so camping ought to be possible. Aim for Point Agassiz on the mainland and, once across, work your way up to Wood Point and the entrance to Thomas Bay.

Thomas Bay: Thomas Bay (mile 259/**1,027**) is the home port of two glaciers, the Baird and the Patterson. Although neither is a tidewater glacier, there is much of interest in this complex and variegated bay. Camping is possible at a number of spots. Counterclockwise past Wood Point, seaweed-choked Bock Bight is the first feature. Just past is Ruth Island, which guards the delta of the Patterson River, the Patterson Glacier's outflow stream. The glacier has receded more than 5 miles from tidewater and is not visible without a good, long hike. An old network of logging roads brackets the delta and extends some way toward the glacier. A few cabins stand on the western shore. On the eastern shore of the delta, the logging road extends as far north as Cascade Creek, where another cabin sits by the beach just opposite the bight created by Spray Island.

Six miles farther north, at the head of Thomas Bay, spectacular and sheer-sided Scenery Cove indents the shore. The Baird Glacier mud flats separate tidewater from the glacier. It is a fair walk to the pool at the snout of Baird Glacier, but a rewarding one.

Long, low, and shoaly Point Vandeput protects the north entrance to Thomas Bay. Skirt it widely. In October of 1879, when John Muir, led by a group of Tlingit, canoed from Wrangell to Glacier Bay, his Point Vandeput camp was the scene of a macho drama. According to Stephen Hilson:

> *Upon leaving in the morning they're confronted by heavy seas pounding the encircling reef. Because of obvious dangers, the Indian chief and guide advise an immediate return to camp. Muir infers the chief is a coward and goads him into attempting to cross the pounding surf. After barely escaping destruction in the waves and rocks they succeed in crossing the reef. All aboard have been thoroughly frightened... except the chief. Once out of danger he calls Muir back to his section of the canoe and delivers a reprimand that went something like this: "You know many*

things . . . I do not. You can tell us about the sun and the stars and the great world outside; you have traveled on the steam horse to many lands, but you do not know Alaska and her waters. Many times on this trip you have acted like a silly child. If we had listened to you we would not be alive now. You forced us to cross that reef when we were taking our lives in our hands. Perhaps you, Charlie, John and Kadishan might have swum ashore if our canoe had been smashed, but Mr. Young and I are not strong, and I am old, and we would have been drowned. Would you be happy now on the shore with us lying among the breakers? Hereafter, let me manage this canoe. Don't act like a fool anymore!" There was no forthcoming rebuttal.

Around Point Vandeput, Pacific storms can wend their way up wide Chatham Strait and into still-broad Frederick Sound, as the above anecdote tellingly recounts. Be defensive. Coast up the shore to Grand Point and the entrance to Farragut Bay (mile 270/**1,038**). Farragut has two arms, a big mouth, and an island—Read Island—that was once, during the 1920s, a fox farm. We camped on an islet off Read Island, but other possibilities abound.

Continue westward past Cat Creek and Point Highland to Cape Fanshaw, about a day's paddle from Farragut Bay. Cape Fanshaw separates Frederick Sound from Stephens Passage and, as if to underscore the point, turbulent shoal water extends more than 600 yards off the light on the point. When Vancouver named the cape, he found the remains of an abandoned village in the immediate area. Fanshaw Bay scallops the coast on the north side of the cape with a handful of islands that protect the otherwise exposed waters. Again, there are many camping choices.

Storm Island (mile 288/**1,056**) once had a fox farm with a cabin near the southwest tip. Unfortunately, the improvements have deteriorated to such a degree that camping is impractical near the old cabin site. The opposite end, at the northeast corner, affords flatter, lower, and more open ground with a good view of Five Finger Islands. Deeper in Fanshaw Bay lies the abandoned outpost of Cape Fanshaw on the mainland side of Cleveland Passage, while on the Whitney Island side a few more cabin sites dot the shore.

Wherever you camp, try to get a site with a view of Five Finger Islands, the first of two stepping-stones on the crossing to Admiralty Island. Since both Frederick Sound and Stephens Passage are susceptible to morning fog, and daybreak conditions are most propitious for a crossing, a good visual compass bearing is a must for such an undertaking.

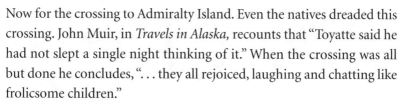

Now for the crossing to Admiralty Island. Even the natives dreaded this crossing. John Muir, in *Travels in Alaska,* recounts that "Toyatte said he had not slept a single night thinking of it." When the crossing was all but done he concludes, ". . . they all rejoiced, laughing and chatting like frolicsome children."

Currents in Stephens Passage vary between 0.5 and 2 knots, depending on the stage and cycle of the tide, and on the width of the channel. The distance from Storm Island to Five Finger Islands is approximately 4.5 miles, while from Bill Point at the north end of Whitney Island the distance is about 0.5 mile less. If going on a compass bearing, current and wind drift must be taken into account. Luckily, the Five Finger Island group has about a 3-mile spread, and winds tend to channel up or down the Passage, as does the current.

If conditions, or confidence, are not forthcoming, going up to Juneau via the eastern shore of Stephens Passage is a good alternative. The shore is always close by, campsites are plentiful, and the views of the Sumdum Glacier up Holkam Bay and up Taku Inlet are spectacular, with majestic mountains so close you can smell the ice-ground rock.

But back to the crossing. Get a weather report, a compass bearing, and an early start, and then paddle defensively like hell for Five Finger Islands.

Five Finger Islands: Five Finger Light (mile 293/**1,061**) was the first manned lighthouse in Alaska and the last one automated, in 1983. While we were there, it was still partially manned. Landing is steep and tricky in a tiny bight at the west end. A short trail leads to the lighthouse

Five Finger Islands lighthouse, Clarence Strait, Alaska

grounds. Many warnings deter entry. There is plenty of room to camp outside the buildings. An automated weather station reports continuously to the weather channel. Some of the Fingers are home to seals. The views are lofty and royal, a fine place to take stock of the next leg of the crossing: west to the Brothers.

From the lighthouse to "Little" Brother is about 7 miles. Hopscotching across some of the Fingers reduces the distance to about 4.5 miles. The very center of Stephens Passage is a feeding ground for humpback whales. At different times, on separate trips, we counted more than 30 flukes and spouts ranged in a 230-degree arc. Highly variable—and deep—midchannel topography, with its proximity to the open Pacific and twice-daily tidal exchange create a particularly euphausid-rich environment with attendant bounties of small schooling fish.

The Brothers: Reaching the Brothers (mile 300/**1,068**) generates a somewhat premature sense of relief. Only one 3-mile crossing left to Admiralty Island. Sunset magazine has reported that the islands are covered with old-growth forest. While this is true, they are not an ideal locale for the legendary giants associated with the precontact Inside Passage. While there are no bears on the Brothers, the resident deer population leaves a particularly large and cohesive spoor. There are many places to camp. One particularly nice spot, in a small copse on a tiny hill, lies on the west side of the south end of West Brother.

In some respects the 3-mile crossing to Admiralty Island is the most serious portion of the entire crossing. Naturally, you would be tempted to head due north for False Point Pybus. Don't! Currents rounding Admiralty's southeast corner create turbulent eddies, which combine with the tidal rips associated with prominent points—which this emphatically is, in spite of its misleading "False" appendage—and result in very dangerous conditions over a broad area. This danger zone shifts location depending on whether the tide is incoming or outgoing. Additionally, the constriction of the channel created by the Brothers causes the currents to accelerate significantly beyond a kayak's top speed. Aim for minor Square Point, midway between Point Pybus and False Point Pybus, and then proceed toward False Point Pybus, hugging the shore.

Admiralty Island: The Tlingits know Admiralty Island as Xutsnu:wu— Fortress of the Bears. An apt name, as it is home to some 1,700 brown bears, or about one bear for every square mile. The bears are a distinct population noted for their spectacular heft and size. It is also particularly dense with eagles: Researchers have counted nearly 1,000 bald eagle nests along the island's perimeter and estimate the total population at around 2,500. In 1978, President Jimmy Carter declared more than 90 percent of the 100-mile-long island a national monument, thereby preserving southeastern Alaska's largest intact expanse of old-growth rain forest. Two years later, Congress designated most of Admiralty Island National Monument as wilderness.

Nonetheless, the Tlingit retain a strong presence at the village of Angoon on the west coast. Xutsnu:wu, rendered in English as Kootznoo-woo or Hootznahoo, was also the name of Admiralty Island Tlingit. It inauspiciously became the source of another English word. As S. E. Hilson recounts:

> *During the 1800's, the Indians of the Angoon area were referred to as "Hootchenoo" Indians—one of many derivations from the Hootznahoo name. They were reportedly the first to learn the process of distilling rum from molasses as taught by American soldiers. Home-brew product was first called "Hootchenoo" and then shortened to "Hootch."*

In 1879, when John Muir paddled past the village on his way to Glacier Bay, he heard "... a storm of strange howls, yells and screams rising from a base of gasping, bellowing grunts and groans... This was the first time in my life that I learned the meaning of the phrase 'a howling drunk.' "

In October 1882, Angoon was the site of an unfortunate tragedy precipitated when the harpoon gun of a whaling boat accidentally exploded, killing a shaman. In retaliation, the village took hostage a steam launch with two crewmen and demanded the customary compensation of 200 blankets. Not only did the US government deny the claim, but they also sent the navy to exact 400 blankets as a punitive fine from the village for the fracas. Failing payment, the navy threatened the destruction of Angoon. The boat and crew were released a short time later, but the villagers decided to call the navy's bluff by not paying the fine. The following day, the navy shelled Angoon, killing several children and destroying homes, canoes, and winter stores. Starvation followed in the long winter.

But the Tlingit, even at this early time, displayed a surprising sophistication: They filed suit in federal court. After almost 100 years, in 1973, the US government finally paid $90,000 in compensation for the incident.

A few scattered abandoned mines and canneries, private holdings, public docks, seaplane bases, Forest Service cabins, shelters, and outposts round out Admiralty's contribution to civilization, with the Pack Creek Bear Observatory a notable attraction.

Hug the shore rounding indistinct False Point Pybus, and sneak northward between the offshore rips and beach bights. Landing sites abound. Conditions ease as you progress behind the lees of Admiralty's east coast and the Gambier Bay archipelago.

Gambier Bay (mile 312/**1,080**) is a strikingly beautiful, multitentacled, and island-doted haven for transients of all sorts. The USFS keeps a public-use A-frame cabin about 3 miles from the entrance in subsidiary Church Bight. The structure is plainly visible only from up close, has bunk space for five, and is supplied with a woodstove and split logs. There is room outside to pitch a tent. Alternatively, there are many potential campsites throughout the bay. Just beware drying fore flats. Exit from the bay requires rounding Point Gambier at all but high, or nearly high, tide levels.

Progress north from Gambier Island leads into Seymour Canal, bounded on the east by the Glass Peninsula. Fully protected waters.

Mole Harbor: Past Pleasant Bay, Mole Harbor (mile 330/**1,098**) opens on the western shore. Mole Harbor, in spite of extensive drying flats, has a USFS Shelter at its head that makes a good campsite. No reservations are required. Be aware that the term shelter, in this case, refers to protection from wind and rain, not bears. The shelter is open on one side. A 2-mile trail leads through the rain forest to Beaver Lake.

Deep inside, by the Mole River, lie the remains of the old Hasselborg homestead. For 35 years, Allen Hasselborg worked as a big-game guide and prospector, personally killing nearly 200 brown bears before becoming an ardent conservationist. He survived two bear maulings and died at 79. The Pack Creek Observatory was his vision.

It is a relatively easy day's paddle up Seymour Canal and past Tiedeman Island to Windfall Island, headquarters and campground for the Pack Creek Bear Observatory.

Dances with Rangers: III

It would be only a slight exaggeration to say that we set out to paddle the Inside Passage in order to visit the Pack Creek Bear Observatory. To arrive by kayak would be elegance beyond compare. With more than 1,100 miles behind us, we were intoxicated with accomplishment and saturated with a serene sense of fulfillment. It just didn't get any better than this.

Dieter, the solo German paddler with whom we'd been playing tag for the last 300 miles, felt the same way. Outfitted in Sitka slippers, a sou'wester, cagoule, and skimpy Speedo, he couldn't sit still. His exuberance rendered an idiosyncratic paddling strategy: multiple marathon days alternated with extended bivouacs, which, in turn, were punctuated by impulsive exploratory excursions, often in the wee hours of night. Dieter had bagged Windfall Island's best campsite.

"Have you seen the bears yet?" we asked.

"Verboten." For some unintelligible reason he had failed to visit the observatory. We assured him that we'd sort things out and see the bears together.

The Pack Creek ranger station sits offshore on Windfall Island. It is a modest affair: a couple of serviceable corrugated fiberglass and canvas shacks logistically supported by an aluminum outboard and radio. Animated discussion emanated from the main building. We approached quietly but confidently. It was late. The weather was socked in. We surprised the rangers.

Our research had indicated that permits and reservations, both for a specific date—especially during prime season—were required. However, unable to pinpoint the exact date of our arrival six months in advance, we decided to throw ourselves at the mercy and discretion of the resident ranger; not an unreasonable option, according to the Juneau dispatch office. We knocked on the door. The room went quiet and a young, curly-haired, out-of-uniform ranger opened the door.

"What do you want?" she asked, as if we were the umpteenth petitioners at the end of a long and tiresome day.

We introduced ourselves and told our tale. We asked about camping. We asked about seeing the bears. Did we have a permit and reservation? We explained our situation, conveyed our willingness to comply in any possible manner with the intent of the regulations, and beseeched their indulgence.

Brown bears outnumber humans two to one on Admiralty Island.

No luck. So we groveled from every angle imaginable, but the rangers remained uncompromising in their vigilance. No exceptions. Tina tried to make a human connection, asking their names, where they were from, and about possible common acquaintances. Indicating that such a line of inquiry was irrelevant to our request, the taller ranger said her name was of no concern and declared that "Annapurna" would suffice. She exuded misanthropy as if it were a proud badge of dedication to her task.

My disappointment didn't squelch my resolve, and I tried one last ploy. I asked what would happen if we visited without a pass. Bad move. The question went over like hairy armpits at a fashion show. It was a personal affront—to the rangers, to the USFS, and to the bears. I was told that Juneau law enforcement would be called in to arrest us, and we'd be hauled before a judge and fined an unlimited amount.

It was time to retreat. I hadn't come to Pack Creek for—as in the Monty Python skit—abuse and an argument. We slept fitfully that night and launched at 4 AM, hoping to avoid the rangers and start the new day with a different perspective. As we passed by Pack Creek's broad alluvial fan, a mama grizzly with two curious cubs came out to dig for grubs and clams. One cub stood up to get a better view of us. We snapped photographs. It was going to be a great day.

Pack Creek: Pack Creek (mile 349/**1,117**) enters Seymour Canal at the north end of Windfall Harbor. Windfall Island, the ranger station and campsite location, is less than 0.5 mile offshore, fronting the harbor and creek delta. Do not land anywhere near Pack Creek. There are two designated free campsites, one on the southern tip in the forest and one on the east shore near the north end. There is room for more than one party. The ranger station is in a small bight directly opposite the Pack Creek delta.

The observation tower is about 1 mile up the creek along a well-developed trail accessed from the south end of the alluvial fan. Pack Creek bears are people-accustomed and not hunted, so dangerous confrontations are rare. Stay on the trail, follow all the regulations, and bring no food. Most visitors arrive by air charter and are escorted. The observatory is open from 9 AM to 9 PM. Between June 1 and September 10, a fee permit is required. Bear activity climaxes during July and August. Permits may be obtained from the Forest Service Information Center at Centennial Hall, 101 Egan Drive, Juneau, AK 99801, and the Admiralty Monument office in Juneau. Apply in person, by mail, or by phone at 907-588-8790. Permits are available March 1 each year, and they are good for up to three days. Make reservations well in advance. Pack Creek is extremely popular, and the rangers are unlikely to make exceptions.

Absent a valid permit, there are other likely bear-viewing opportunities inside Windfall Harbor or, farther up Seymour Canal, in Swan Cove. The Seymour Canal Eagle Management Area centers primarily on Swan and Tiedeman Islands, so enjoy the unrestricted viewing opportunities.

From Pack Creek, head up the channel between Swan Island and the bulk of Admiralty Island toward Swan Cove, where there is a better than even chance of spotting a bear. Hang a sharp right and then a left around King Salmon Bay's southern peninsula. A series of reefs, small islands, and peninsulas obstruct entry into Fool Inlet, Seymour Canal's head of navigation. Entry is best during favorable tides.

The head of Fool Inlet (mile 364/**1,132**) dries foul, though a deeper channel leads most of the way in. Frantic paddling, lining, or knuckling upstream are viable options during low tides. The Alaska State Parks Department maintains a visitor cabin, nestled against the hill on the east side of the low-lying area, that sleeps six and has both an oil and wood stove. A fee of $25 and reservation are required. Very limited camping is adjacent.

A narrow sliver of land, barely a mile wide, and bracketed by Seymour Canal on the south and Oliver Inlet to the north, attaches the Glass Peninsula to the rest of Admiralty Island. The isthmus is slightly humped with a long, gradual slope on the Seymour Canal side and a short, steep incline descending into Oliver Inlet from its high point. Away from the water, the shoreline vegetation gives way to taiga interspersed with open muskeg. It is a portage route in long use prior to contact. The state has built a roller-coaster tramway to facilitate and modernize the portage. If in working condition, it's a hoot to use.

The southern terminus of the tramway is just north of the cabin. If the tram cart is absent, you'll have to walk to the Oliver Inlet side to retrieve it. The cart easily carries two kayaks and two people's gear. A towline may or may not be attached. Verify that the brakes work well.

Tramway portage, Fool Inlet to Oliver Inlet, Admiralty Island, Alaska

Maintain complete control even on the mildest of descents. Just prior to the steep Oliver Inlet descent, the rails have been disconnected to prevent accidents. At this point (mile 365/**1,133**), you must unload the tram cart and complete the portage by hand, on foot. A wooden platform with an Alaska State Parks skiff provides a novel campsite on the muskeg. There is no adequate flat ground at the Oliver Inlet end of the tramway for camping.

Oliver Inlet is narrow and 3 miles long. Time stands still here, and the merest sound seemingly reverberates for minutes. Moss-covered trees and the complete absence of wind and chop add to the spooky quality. Rapids separate the inlet from northern Stephens Passage. Best to exit near high-water slack or during ebb. The rapids are at their worst during spring tidal exchanges. Neap tides, on the other hand, render mild riffles.

Oliver Inlet debouches into northern Stephens Passage, where tidal currents vary from 0.5 to 2 knots. Work your way eastward along the northern shore of the Glass Peninsula to an advantageous position for the 3-mile crossing to Douglas Island's Tantallon Point. About a third of the way across, you will enter the jurisdiction of the City and Borough of Juneau. What the hell is a borough?

Borough: Traditionally, a borough was the smallest English and Scottish political entity. The concept survived a move to New York City, where it serves the same purpose, but hardly anywhere else. Delegates to Alaska's constitutional convention were painfully aware of the territory's scant population and its eccentric distribution: maybe two cities, a handful of towns, a brace of villages, and vast empty areas devoid of conventional rural inhabitants, often owned by the federal government. At best, growth would be fitful. So they designed a simple, flexible system of local government that allowed a maximum of local self-government with a minimum number of local government units to prevent duplication of tax-levying jurisdictions.

Instead of being subdivided into counties (or parishes, in Louisiana) like other states, Alaska was divided into a new entity—boroughs. Boroughs are ruled by mayors and councils if "organized" or directly by the state if "unorganized." Ideally, there is no municipal government level below the borough. If the major feature of a borough is a city, then the borough is called "city and borough," and the entire borough is run by the "city."

Gastineau Channel: Gastineau Channel separates Douglas Island from the mainland and extends about 16 miles, connecting upper Stephens Passage with Saginaw Channel. Juneau, Alaska's capital, lies about halfway up the channel. Tantallon Point marks the west side of its south entry. The east side of the channel is defined by the mainland's Point Salisbury, where, just a couple of miles to the east at Grindstone Creek, the Taku Tlingit had a village. When Vancouver entered Gastineau Channel in August 1794, it was so choked with ice from the Taku and Mendenhall Glaciers that he was unable to complete his investigations. Currents in the lower portion are of no particular concern until the vicinity of Juneau where, near the Douglas-Juneau Bridge (including the Harris and Aurora Harbors), they can become quite strong. Gastineau Channel is narrow and carries a great deal of traffic and shipping, particularly huge cruise ships.

Immediately round Point Tantallon, Juneau exurbs are evident and increase in density as you progress north. Look for frantic salmon runs along the mainland-side watersheds, and beware of traffic.

Juneau: The Juneau metropolitan area is large, with a population exceeding 30,000 and more choices than I could reasonably outline here. Where to head for? Seven miles up Gastineau Channel and 2 miles before the Douglas–Juneau Bridge, the Douglas Boat Harbor—on the Douglas Island side and protected by Juneau Island and two breakwaters—provides a public boat ramp and handy disembarkation point. Right next door is the Savikko Park RV Camping facility (907-586-5255), unfortunately with only four RV parking spots and no amenities. By land, Douglas Boat Harbor is 4 miles from downtown Juneau; but by kayak, across the channel, only 1 mile.

Farther on, immediately past the bridge in Juneau proper is the Harris Boat Harbor, the only other launch ramp (at its northern end) near downtown Juneau. Just across Egan Drive and slightly kiddy-corner from the harbor is the Breakwater Inn, with reasonably priced and accessible lodging catering to seafaring folk from the Aurora and Harris

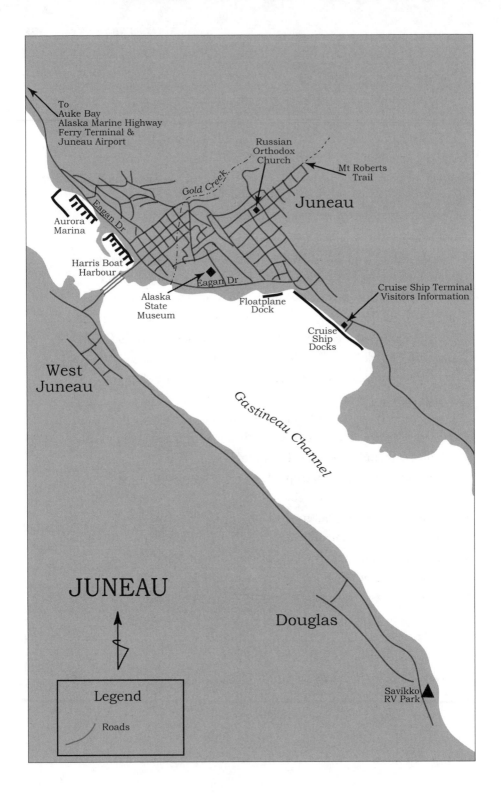

marinas. It includes a decent restaurant. But getting there from Douglas requires some strategy.

Juneau Harbor is very busy, and made more so because, for all intents and purposes, Gastineau Channel dead-ends at Juneau, and shipping must U-turn to exit. As if multiple cruise ships of all sizes, commercial shipping, and private boats were not enough of an obstacle, the Seadrome Dock is also downtown and, during passable weather, the source and destination of interminable seaplane traffic. The prudent will approach Juneau up the Douglas Island side of the channel and cross over (if heading for Harris Marina) under the bridge. But where is the fun in that?

Going up the Juneau side of Gastineau is much more exciting and puts the paddler in the thick of things. Stay close to shore to avoid docking, launching, and maneuvering craft of all sizes. You may have to pass up to six giant cruise ships, sometimes double-parked. Stay close but not too close; make sure they're not about to move; and don't go near the business end. Past the seaplane dock, traffic eases up. Still, don't interfere with operations at the Coast Guard dock, the last of the obstacles to watch out for.

The unprepossessing, concrete-lined watercourse coming in at the top of the bay and just beyond downtown proper is historic Gold Creek, maternity ward and wet nurse for infant Juneau. Adjacent to the east bank but not visible from the water is a well-stocked grocery and liquor store. Nearby, and visible, is the Prospector Lodge, a more-or-less handy alternative to The Breakwater Inn if the latter has no vacancies.

Although Juneau was founded and built on mining, today tourism and government are the mainstays. In seasonal respects, they're complementary. Legislative sessions convene during the winter, when Juneau swarms with representatives and lobbyists. The much larger tourist run swarms the capital in summer. Juneau would probably be much larger were it not for its isolation. Although engineering proposals have been drawn up to extend Juneau's roads to connect with the Al-Can Highway, residents invariably vote the initiatives down in fears that, with the influx of unsavory transients, they'll lose their small-town atmosphere. The proposed road would traverse the pristine Taku River Valley, already threatened by the reopening of the Tulsequah Chief mine.

There is much to see and do in Juneau. The city lies along a narrow strip of land between Gastineau Channel and a sharply abutting salient of the Coast Mountains. There are many improved day-hike (or shorter) trails that depart right from downtown. One of the best starts out at the end of Sixth Street and goes up to the terminus of the Mount Roberts aerial tramway. Views of the city and surrounding area—including a true perspective of the gargantuan size of cruise ships—are incomparable. You can descend via the tramway. If nothing else, venture up for a reconnaissance of Mendenhall Bar, the northern half of Gastineau Channel and the next portion of the Inside Passage. A shorter but more popular hike is the Perseverance Trail, accessed from Basin Road at the intersection of Sixth and East Streets. It parallels the upper reaches of Gold Creek.

Douglass-Juneau, Alaska and Gastineau Channel

Juneau is a walking town. Don't miss the old residential districts nestled up against the mountains, where much of the walking takes place along wooden boardwalks lined with historic clapboards, shanties, toeholds, and newer homesteads. Up here you can visit the tiny, octagonal Saint Nicholas Russian Orthodox Church. Although built in 1894, nearly 30 years after Russia sold the Alaska colony, Saint Nicholas is the oldest original Russian church in Alaska. Nearby is the Wickersham State Historic Site, home of Judge James Wickersham. Wickersham came to Alaska in 1900 and was instrumental in converting military rule to civilian government and subsequent territorial status. He became Alaska's voteless delegate to Congress and a strong advocate of statehood, which he failed to realize, dying 20 years before the 49th state was admitted.

St. Nicholas Russian Orthodox Church, Juneau, Alaska

Juneau's downtown caters to the tourist trade. Among the many curio shops are some fine native art galleries and numerous eateries. Merchant's Wharf, adjacent to the seaplane float, hosts the Hangar, a medium-priced restaurant overlooking the harbor with excellent food and a seemingly limitless selection of draught and bottled specialty beers. Next door is a fast-food, fish-and-chips purveyor whose halibut and salmon are second to none. The Alaska State Museum, on Whittier Street, covers all aspects of Alaskan history in a vibrant, up-to-date manner with rare and insightful Native Alaskan displays.

If you drove up to Prince Rupert to paddle this section of the Inside Passage with a hard-shelled boat, you must now catch the Alaska ferry back to Prince Rupert. Unfortunately, the ferry terminal is 14 miles away in Auke Bay, and conventional taxis are ill equipped for the task. Contact either Alaska Boat & Kayak at 101 Dock Street in Douglas (907-586-8220), or Auke Bay Landing Craft in Auke Bay (907-790-4591) for help or suggestions. We took a more entrepreneurial approach, keeping a sharp eye out for vehicles with kayak racks. (There are many.) We focused on rattletraps, or at least vehicles that indicated their drivers would probably welcome a modest supplementary honorarium, and approached the mark with a generous offer. Our very first target accepted.

Alternatively, you could paddle the 14 miles to Auke Bay, either after a visit to Juneau or as the destination point for this portion of the Inside Passage. Take out at the Auke Bay Marina about 2 miles east of the ferry terminal at the head of Auke Bay. Paddling upper Gastineau Channel, called Mendenhall Bar, requires some preparation. See the next chapter for details.

Another approach is to store the kayaks in Juneau until the next leg of the Inside Passage. Use the same strategy as above, but focus on storage instead of transport. Ferry or fly back to Prince Rupert. Juneau's airport is 9 miles west of downtown. If you arrived in Juneau via folding kayak, logistics are much simpler.

7

Glacier Bay

Juneau to Head of Muir Inlet

130 miles

> *He who does not want to live forever*
> *has not lived at all.*
> —*Wallace Miller*

Asia and America, like Siamese twins, were once joined together. Siberia–Beringia–Alaska; Alaska–Beringia–Siberia: They were all of one piece. The same life circulated throughout their river valleys and swarmed over their plains. None of the inhabitants—plant or animal— could distinguish where one ended and the other began. This lack of discrimination also dogged man, whose random wanderings populated Alaska and, ultimately, all of the Americas.

When the scalpel of climatic change separated the bodies (discarding Beringia, like some vestigial prosthesis, to the depths of the sea), subconscious atavistic links remained. Circumpolar communities, mimicking formenkreis populations, retained genetic and cultural ties that have waxed and waned with climatic variation, imperial fortunes, and the passage of time—including that anomaly in the space-time continuum, the International Dateline: Today in Alaska is tomorrow in Siberia. Lapps, Samoyeds, Tungus, Yukaghirs, Chukchis, and Koryaks have always been aware of and retained nebulous ties with the Greenland, Polar, Baffin Island, Labrador, Iglulik, Aivilik, Netsilik, Copper River, Mackenzie, North Alaskan, and Bering Sea Inuit. Not even the ham-fisted quarantine imposed by the 70-year Soviet regime could sever the yearnings of one, albeit divided, people. In any case, Soviet-

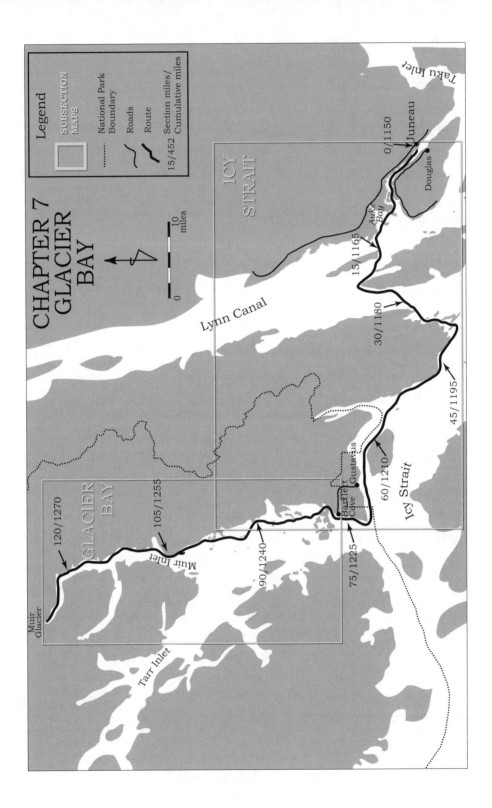

Legend

SUBSECTION MAPS

National Park Boundary

Roads

Route

15/452 Section miles/Cumulative miles

CHAPTER 7
GLACIER
BAY

0   10
miles

Taku Inlet

Juneau

0/1150

Douglas

ICY
STRAIT

Auke Bay

15/1165

Lynn Canal

30/1180

45/1195

60/1210

Gustavus

Bartlett
Cove

Icy Strait

75/1225

90/1240

Muir Inlet

105/1255

GLACIER
BAY

120/1270

Muir
Glacier

Tarr Inlet

imposed isolation ultimately proved transitory and was even partially overcome by the sanctioned legitimacy of an official title: the quadrennial Inuit Circumpolar Conference, which in the mid-1980s convened in Kotzebue, Alaska. Even Mother Nature feels the tug. Every year, in a vain attempt to reconnect the twins, she freezes solid 4 or 5 feet of the Bering Strait's surface.

During the European Age of Exploration, Western Europe and Russia undertook uncoordinated flanking maneuvers, expanding west and east, respectively. Because the world is round, they ultimately collided in Alaska. The clash not only reconfigured relationships between the conquering powers, but also—in spite of being disruptive to the aboriginal inhabitants—forged new ties between conquerors and conquered. In some cases the new ties were of a subtle continuity. The Russians who went to Alaska were, by and large, physically indistinguishable from native Alaskans. Most were *promyshlenniki*, Siberian freelance traders whose physiognomy was the result of centuries of European and Siberian interbreeding. Why did Russia spread east into Siberia and, as if Beringia still existed, continue into Alaska?

The Eurasian landmass is an incomprehensibly large (it is *never*, ever accurately depicted on any map all at once), amorphously sprawling blob with few distinctive protuberances—Scandinavia, Iberia, Italy, Arabia, India, Malaysia, Korea, and Kamchatka are the few that come to mind—much less any natural borders immediately evident from a cursory glance at a map. Nonetheless, Western convention has stubbornly—but with a nod to history and tradition—insisted on classifying this blob as two separate continents: Europe and Asia. Just exactly where does one end and the other begin? Most people know that France is in Europe and Burma is in Asia, but on which continent is Armenia, the Aral Sea, the Caspian Sea, Chechnya, or Turkmenistan? The upper portion of the western boundary between the two continents has always been the Ural Mountains, a 1,200-mile-long, north-south range trending along 60 degrees of longitude. South of the range, down to the Caspian Sea, the Ural River continues the boundary. West of the Urals lies Russia proper; Siberia lies to the east. Curiously, at only 6,000 feet elevation at its highest point, and with vast, accessible lowlands on both sides of the range and the river, this "boundary" is pretty porous.

Columbus went west to reach the East. Ivan the Terrible went east to exact revenge and seek security—revenge for 250 years of Mongol and Tatar (or Tartar—Muslims from Turkestan) domination, and security (from those self-same Siberians) in the form of defensible borders. Back in the winter of 1237, Batu Khan, grandson of Genghis Khan, riding at the head of a disciplined horde of 120,000 men, had swept like the wind across the frozen expanses of Siberia and conquered all of Russia, penetrating as far west as present-day Hungary. The Siberians were cruel and ruthless, wreaking death and destruction and exacting tribute. Survivors—those who were caught—were roasted or flayed alive. As trophies of war, the Mongols cut off ears.

Russian resurgence was slow and disorganized. Asia had left a deep imprint. In order to beat the Easterners, Russians adopted many of their customs, not least a proclivity for absolute, cruel, and despotic rule. By 1480, Moscow's power was secure enough that it stopped paying tribute to Siberia. In the parry and counterthrust of the Russian reconquest, many refugees fled south, out of the clutches of either Siberian or newly assertive Russian satraps. These Cossacks (from the Turkish *kazak,* meaning "rebel" or "freeman"), as they came to be known, retained their independence through a strict, majority-vote democracy and a warrior cult forged in self-defense and honed as freelance mercenaries.

In 1547, an extraordinary youth of 17 by the name of Ivan was crowned prince of Moscow. With the help of the Cossacks, Ivan the Terrible (his new nickname was a compliment) united all the lands of Russia east of the Urals and adopted the title Czar, Russian for Caesar. But peace was not good for the Cossack economy. Possessing only the skills of war, the independent-minded southerners took to piracy on the Volga and more ambitious, entrepreneurial conquests. Under Vasily (Yermak) Timofeivich, 840 Cossacks set out in 1581 to attack Isker, the Mongol/Tatar capital of western Siberia (from *sibir,* Tatar for "sleeping land" or *siber,* Mongolian for "beautiful," "wonderful," or "pure"). Czar

Ivan was furious. He did not want to reawaken the dormant Mongol/Tatar Empire.

But the Mongols had gone to seed and proved no match for the Cossacks. Yermak took Isker within two years. In a shrewd move, he sent 10 percent of all the plunder—more than 100,000 rubles worth, a fabulous sum in those days—as a personal gift to Ivan. Much of the booty was in furs—sable, ermine, bear, and other peltry. At the time, Russian sable commanded a prince's ransom in Western Europe; in Russia, a single pelt could buy a 50-acre farm. The Czar responded by pardoning the Cossacks for all their crimes, decorating Yermak, promising reinforcements for further conquest, and creating a special, privileged regiment, the Siberian Cossacks. To keep the riches flowing, he also guaranteed the *promyshlenniki* unfettered access to Siberian resources in return for a 10 percent portion. The Russian conquest of Siberia had begun.

Czar Boris Godunov, who succeeded Ivan in 1584, continued the eastward expansion. In 20 years, western Siberia was held by a line of forts stretching from the Arctic to the highlands bordering the northern verges of the Manchu Empire. Furs, plunder, revenge, and expediency drove the onslaught, with no small part played by the decline of Mongol/Tatar power. Finally, 405 years after his forebears had conquered Russia, Altyn Khan, heir to the throne of Ghengis, announced that he was ready to submit to the Czar and become a vassal of Moscow.

By 1632 Russians reached the Lena River and established a redoubt at Yakutsk. Yakutsk's commander soon dispatched a 20-man mounted regiment under Ivan Moskvitin to see what lay beyond the Stanovoi Mountains to the east. In 1639, Moskvitin—the Cossack Balboa—reached the Sea of Okhost, the northern terminus of Asia's Inside Passage, a much less protected waterway between Japan, the Kuril Islands, and the Kamchatka Peninsula. Siberia, a distance of 5,800 miles, had been conquered in 60 years.

Russian expansion was not just due east. Cossack adventurers soon set their sights on Mongolia, China, and Manchuria. Success bred overconfidence and arrogance. In 1658, Russia reached for China. For the first time since their arrival in Asia, the Russians met thorough defeat at the hands of a Manchu army that numbered 10,000. But China had no wish to arouse a permanent enemy. In a shrewd move that neutralized any further military adventurism, China opened its markets to Russian furs and introduced the would-be conquerors to a new addiction: tea. The policy proved admirable: peace and commerce broke out along Siberia's southern border.

Although Russians had reached the Pacific, no one knew—or seemed to care—whether Asia and America were connected. Not even the man entrusted to ascertain the facts, Vitus Bering—a plodding and incurious but brave and determined (*and* tactful and kindly to boot; qualities that kept this and subsequent expeditions from total meltdown) Dane—cared much about the mission entrusted to him by the one man who did care, and mattered. In 1689, a 17-year-old, 7-foot giant of a man with a will and a vision to match had ascended to the throne of Muscovy. Peter the Great weaned himself on the acquisition of knowledge and was consumed with pushing the frontiers of science. In 1719 he had dispatched a two-man expedition to settle the question. The modest enterprise fell short of the challenge. Five years later, on the advice of his admiralty, he commissioned Bering to settle the matter once and for all. Unfortunately, Peter died the following year and was succeeded by his widow, Catherine I.

Bering had his hands full. Russia's single Pacific port, Okhost (built by Moskvitin's Cossacks), wasn't much more than a handful of log buildings with a wharf, ice-locked for six months and fog- or storm-bound the rest of the time. To reach Okhost, Bering first had to get to Irkustk—in itself no mean feat—when setting out from St. Petersburg. Out of Irkustk, the first 1,500 miles down the Lena River to Yakustk was traversed by boat or horse, depending on the season. Next came the difficult part: 700 miles and multiple 4,000- to 5,000-foot climbs across the Stanovoi Mountains. Reindeer were drafted. Since iron was scarce, dozens of horses had to haul the anchors and metal rigging for the boats that still had to be built.

In the fall of 1727, after a year and a half of traversing Siberia, Bering arrived at Okhost, where he spent the winter preparing for the next leg of the journey. The following year he sailed 600 miles across the Sea of Okhost to the Kamchatka Peninsula. There he dismantled necessary supplies for the trek across that God-forsaken appendage— about the size of Italy—to the side facing America, where he founded Petropavlosk, his forward base of operations. In July 1728, he finally launched the *Saint Gabriel.* It was a short mission. Although he determined that Asia was not connected to America, in the process lending his name to that buffer of water, he never saw America. Bering's 1730 report to the Moscow Academy of Sciences served only to whet the appetites of the Admiralty, Czarina Catherine, and Bering himself. At its conclusion he proposed another expedition.

Three years later he found himself leading 900 people in "the largest expedition of its kind ever undertaken by any European government for the purpose of scientific and geographical research up to that time." Its remit was staggering. First, small subsidiary salients were to explore and map the entire arctic coast from St. Petersburg to the Bering Strait; ditto for the Pacific shore from the Bering Strait down to the Amur River. Third, another subsidiary command was to explore the archipelago south of Kamchatka (the Kurile and Sakhalin Islands) to Japan, claim everything that it could, and establish trading relations with the Japanese.

Bering himself led the fourth contingent of the Great Northern Expedition, as the entire enterprise came to be called. This was to establish Russian sovereignty on the American Northwest Coast. To conceal its true purpose from rival powers, the expedition was cast as a follow-up attempt to determine whether Asia and America were joined—the first attempt having failed. Expedition members were under special instructions "for public display" to that effect, and had been sworn to secrecy. Bering had been under no misgivings about the nearness of America during his first voyage. When he turned back, in spite of not actually seeing America, he knew it was there. The signs were all evident: shorebirds, coastal fog, shallow waters, green driftwood and grasses, littoral echoes, and continental shelf currents. The last objective of the

Great Northern Expedition—led by a 600-man-strong contingent from the Academy of Sciences—was to catalogue the plants, animals, minerals, and ethnic tribes of the new lands.

After eight years of preparation and travel across Siberia, Bering once again found himself in Petropavlosk. This time he embarked in two newly built boats, the *Saint Peter,* under his command, and the *Saint Paul* under Aleksei Chirikov. On 16 July 1741, after weeks of wandering in the fog and losing Chirikov, Bering finally saw the mainland of America. The clouds parted dramatically, and there, bathed in god-light, stood the awesome peaks of the Saint Elias Range. His work, he prematurely concluded, was done. Tired, burnt out, and worried no end about food, safety, and the weather, Bering was ready to go home. Georg Steller, the expedition naturalist, however, prevailed on him to make landfall at least to fill water casks, collect specimens, and contact the inhabitants.

But bad weather kept the *Saint Peter* offshore. Attempting both to make homeward headway and make landfall in the new land, Bering ended up zigzagging back along the Aleutians where, on Bird Island, he finally met Americans. The meeting was anticlimactic and was characterized by misunderstanding and hurt feelings—on both sides. Bering never reunited with Chirikov. Only 115 miles short of Kamchatka, her crew weakened by constant storms and scurvy, the hapless *Saint Peter* shipwrecked on an uninhabited island that was to bear Bering's name and become his final resting place.

Meanwhile Chirikov, commanding the *Saint Paul,* beat Bering to the punch by discovering Alaska—in the form of Prince of Wales Island—on July 15, 1741, one day before Bering's sighting. A few days later, he dispatched 11 armed men with a Koryak interpreter and trade trinkets in the ship's longboat up Lisyansky Inlet, near modern-day Pelican on Chichagof Island, to contact the natives. Both the men and the boat disappeared. Chirikov waited five days, but saw none of the prearranged, agreed-upon distress signals—only a blaze that grew bigger. Thinking that the longboat had perhaps been damaged, he sent the boatswain in the one remaining yawl with a carpenter, a caulker, and a sailor. The second boat also disappeared, followed by another bonfire.

Later on, two natives paddled out from the bay, shouted something twice—while still at a considerable distance—and paddled back to shore. Chirikov tried to entice them back and lingered for another day. But without shore boats to replenish dwindling supplies and water, Chirikov reluctantly weighed anchor and headed for home, abandoning his missing men to their fate. To this day, Tlingit lore in the Pelican area proudly boasts of this ruse.

The *Saint Paul* also worked its way back to Kamchatka along the Aleutians, successfully trading with the Aleuts and even getting them to convey fresh water in bladders. They arrived at Petropavlovsk on the 10th of October.

Russia went to Alaska to insure that no part of Asia was overlooked and even—in a final blaze of hubris—to take its place among the world's powers by staking an American claim. Time, distance, arctic waters, and the final containment of the Mongols; scurvy, starvation, and disorganization; and the death of the driving forces behind eastward expansion, Peter and Catherine, finally stopped the Russian advance. Bering's death prior to his return and the loss—in typical Russian fashion—of his logbooks, charts, and reports into the abyss of provincial archives put the final nails in the coffin of the entire enterprise. Czarina Elizabeth, Peter's beautiful but intellectually challenged daughter— who wanted no part of statecraft—succeeded Catherine and, through active neglect, terminated all further official eastward progress. Russia was whole; America no longer fit neatly into the picture. So why did Alaska still end up in the Russian embrace? Other, more fundamental forces— greed and opportunity—were already at work, unfolding an entirely new scenario.

Parallel to official history, unofficial history was also taking place. For example, the Bering Sea ought to have been called the Dezhnev Sea. True to traditional Russian bureaucracy and disorganization, the question of whether Asia and America were connected had already been settled as far back as 1648, 80 years before Vitus Bering. Only no one had as yet bothered to formulate, much less ask, such a question. A band of Cossacks under Semyon Dezhnev—investigating possible commercial prospects, of course—had sailed down (north) the Kolyma River in willow boats into the Arctic Ocean and rounded Siberia's eastern tip to the mouth of the Anadyr River, a voyage of 2,000 miles. Their report, however, never made it to St. Petersburg, having been buried in the local files at Yakutsk. Dezhnev, after retiring to Moscow, was himself unaware of the import of his discovery. Today, Siberia's easternmost salient is named Cape Dezhnev to commemorate the Cossack. Never mind: in Russia, scuttlebutt ruled. On that venture, the Cossacks had encountered wonderful new creatures—fur seals and sea otters—the latter with pelts that outshone even the sable for richness and beauty. *Promyshlenniki* swarmed to exploit the new commodity—prematurely. Neither animal was common off Siberia, and no bonanza was realized. But a few pelts found their way to China, where they commanded exorbitant prices. A seed had been planted.

Likewise it was neither Bering nor his subordinate Chirikov who "discovered" Alaska. In a classic example of one hand being unaware of the doings of the other, the Supreme Privy Council had authorized a military expedition, under Afanasy Shestakov and Dmitry Pavlutsky, to consolidate Russia's hold over the entire northeast salient of Siberia by pacifying the rebellious Koryaks and Kamchadals. After much cruel slaughter—including the death of Shestakov—and a series of face-saving treaties, Pavlutsky decided to do a little exploring and search for the "Great Land," rumored to lie close off the Chukchi Peninsula. He appropriated Bering's *Saint Gabriel*—after all, it was between voyages and unemployed—for the task. In command he placed Mikhail Gvozdev with a crew of 39 men. According to Benson Bobrick, in *East of the Sun: The Epic Conquest and Tragic History of Siberia:*

> *Sailing from the mouth of the Anadyr in July 1732, they paused briefly at one of the Diomede Islands, and then continued eastward, apparently coming within sight of Cape Prince of Wales, Alaska. Drawing near, they saw that it was quite large*

and covered with forests of poplar, spruce, and larch. After skirting the coast for several days, they found "no end in sight." At one point, "a naked native paddled out to the vessel from shore on an inflated bladder," and through their interpreter asked them who they were and where they were going. They replied that they were lost at sea and were looking for Kamchatka. The native promptly pointed in the direction from which they had come. They did not make a landing, however, and because after their return they failed to collate their notes and make an adequate map, their voyage did not come to official attention until a decade later, in 1743. By then the priority of their discovery had become a technicality . . .

So there you have it: Vitus Bering discovered neither Bering Strait nor Alaska. But he did put them on the map.

From Bering's second voyage, Chirikov had returned without incident; Bering, on the other hand, weakened by scurvy and early winter storms, shipwrecked on Bering Island, part of the Commander Group, in 1741. Bering never recovered. The survivors subsisted through the winter on the abundant wildlife. The following year, they built a boat from the wreckage and sailed into Petropavlosk wretchedly but triumphantly gowned in blue fox, seal, and otter furs. The 900 sea otter pelts they managed to bring back proved more than enough to have paid for a quarter of the cost of the entire expedition from the time it left St. Petersburg. The fur rush was on.

Frenzy gripped the Kamchatka garrisons. Yemelian Basov, Sergeant of Cossacks at Nizhnekamchatsk, was possessed. He immediately raised capital for a fur hunting venture, rounded up a crew of 30 *promyshlenniki*—working on shares—built a flat-bottomed river scow called the *Kapiton,* and set off for Bering Island in the fall of 1743. He succeeded beyond his wildest dreams and returned for a second, third, and fourth winters. The number of skins from the second year alone totaled 1,600 sea otters, 2,000 fur seals, and 2,000 blue fox.

In no time, the little Commander Group's fur-bearing population was close to exhaustion, so the Russians sailed farther east, to the Aleutians. On September 25, 1745, the *promyshlenniki* landed on Agattu and encountered Americans for the first time. One hundred dancing Aleuts greeted the Russians. The meeting did not go well. Misunderstanding led to overreaction, and at least one native was shot dead. A separate encounter, on Attu, took place at Massacre Bay, where the Russians took advantage of Aleut hospitality by raping a number of women and slaughtering the men who came to their aid. Unofficial Russia had arrived in Alaska, though it would take another 18 years for them to methodically work their way up the Aleutian chain.

For the next 122 years, Russia continued its eastward expansion into Bolshaya Zemlya, the Great Land, as they had renamed the Aleuts' Alaxsxag, which means "the object toward which the action of the sea is directed." As a colonial venture, the entire enterprise was without parallel. For one, it was the world's most distant colony, at 9,000 miles from St. Petersburg to its first "capital" at Three Saints Bay, on Kodiak Island. Alaska had no strategic significance; it was not a refuge for dissidents; there was no scramble for empire; religious conversion was not a factor; riches for state coffers played no part. Government offered no support, and even washed its hands of the whole matter. Ragtag individual and undercapitalized collective entrepreneurs, impervious to hardship, unsophisticated—often psychopathic—yet maudlin, wild-eyed, and superstitious with traces of mysticism pushed into the new land with only one objective: furs for the Chinese market, which they forced the Aleuts to hunt.

It would be years before St. Petersburg recognized its illegitimate offspring. And the response would always be too late, usually inadequate, and lacking in proper supervision. A few lucky twists of fate tempered and redeemed the entire undertaking. The eventual depletion of sea otters, uncooperative geography, and Tlingit resistance contained the Russians. De facto Governor Alexander Baranov's able administration transformed a potential *Lord of the Flies* nightmare into a passable colony.

But true civilization was absent until the arrival of Reverend Ivan Veniaminov, later to become head of the Russian Orthodox Church and canonized St. Innocent in 1979. The prelate singlehandedly transformed Russian-native relations from adversarial to cooperative, introduced the norms of civil society to the hintermost frontier, and recorded more scientific data—in ethnology, linguistics, meteorology, and the natural sciences—than all previous attempts.

Even so, Alaska remained a bastard child. The colony was indefensible, counted fewer than 800 Russians, and was a drain on the treasury. If prospectors from the California gold fields or Mormons fleeing persecution were to invade Alaska, St. Petersburg risked losing all control. After Russia's 1857 defeat at the hands of the British in the Crimean War, the Ministry of Foreign Affairs floated the possibility of the colony's sale. The sale would help to pay war debts; consolidate Far Eastern territories; cock a snook at the British by nearly doubling the landmass of the United States—Britain's rival in North America; and forge an alliance with that promising, up-and-coming power. The American Civil War, however, put the deal into deep escrow.

Confederate raids on American whaling ships in the Bering Sea convinced Secretary of State William H. Seward that a US Navy presence in the region was imperative. Emperor Alexander II and President Andrew Johnson had both come round to favoring the deal. Russian and American popular sentiment however, were both against the transaction. Alaska was soon referred to as Seward's Icebox, and a skeptical Congress was loath to consider or approve it. Nonetheless, when Eduard Stoeckl—the Russian diplomat empowered to pursue negotiations—and Seward met in March of 1867 to discuss trading rights, Seward popped the question: Would Russia consider selling Alaska outright?

Stoeckl had been authorized to accept $5 million. But the cagey negotiator played his cards well and responded noncommittally. When Seward offered $5 million, Stoeckl countered $10 million. They soon settled on $7.2 million. The formal transfer took place at Sitka on October 18, 1867.

There are striking geographic and developmental similarities between the two twin landmasses. Dual river systems—the Kolyma and Indigirka watersheds in eastern Siberia, and the Yukon and Kuskokwim rivers in Alaska—drain their central vastnesses. And both face off nose-to-nose at the Chukchi and Seward Peninsulas. Developmentally, Siberia's fur rush overflowed logically and directly into Alaska. But by the time of the sale, both Siberia's and Alaska's fur resources were running short, and a new mother lode displayed bright potential: gold.

The discovery and exploitation of the yellow ore unfolded in radically different ways along the river valleys of the now even more separated twin landmasses. Gold had been discovered at Nerchinsk and along the Lena and Yenisey river valleys in the early 1800s. It was at first a state monopoly, but by 1836 private prospecting and mining operations became legal. The gold, however, could only be sold to the state. In contrast, neither the US nor the Canadian governments placed any constraints on the Inside Passage's gold strikes. Every prospector could keep all of his sweat-gotten gains.

Predictably, the mines developed at different times—this time Siberia lagging behind Alaska—and along somewhat different philosophies. By 1904, the last big strike, at Fairbanks, had played out and although gold mining continues today, it plays a decreasing role in Alaska's economy. Siberia's geologically analogous gold deposits were exhumed at much greater cost. Never a populous place, far eastern Siberia was peopled by a handful of indigenous natives, adventurous Cossacks, opportunistic freelance traders, and—after 1825—political convicts and exiles. During the 1917 Russian Revolution and the Civil War that followed it, anti-Bolsheviks of all stripes went to Siberia to escape persecution. Many surreptitiously took up prospecting. After the Civil War, Lenin, to rebuild the country and nurture the shattered economy, legalized free enterprise and declared an amnesty.

Prospectors poured in. In 1910, gold was discovered along the Kolyma River but, due to political and social upheavals, nothing much came of it. By the late 1920s, substantial quantities of gold were being mined, and, in conjunction with the new mother lode along the Indigirka River, the Kolyma fields were proving to be the equivalent of a Soviet Alaska. Inevitably, the new government was soon on the horns of a dilemma. It could either continue tolerating free enterprise and miss out on the bonanza, or nationalize the resource and invest a great amount of capital in the development of the area. The first option was anathema for political reasons—after all, the Bolsheviks were trying to establish Communism. Only nationalization was left. However, there was no capital available. Josef Stalin, Lenin's successor, decided to "invest" the one resource the government could dispose of—human beings.

In 1931, the Far Northern Construction Trust, Dalstroy—an early subsidiary of the *Glavnoe Upravlenie ispravitel'no trudovykh lagerei,* or Gulag (Chief Administration for Corrective Labor Camps)—was set up and began preparations for a major gold mining enterprise. Soviet propaganda even depicted the basin as a sort of Russian Klondike. Dalstroy's first miners were excess peasants from the Ukraine, victims of the collectivization of Soviet agriculture. Lots more miners would follow. During the mid-1930s, Trotskyists, Social Democrats, Mensheviks, Anarchists, and members of other left-wing organizations were shipped east to take up pick and shovel. In 1937, purged Communist Party members were reassigned from their desks to gold mining in the Kolyma and Indigirka fields. Two years later, when the USSR and Germany invaded Poland and the Baltics, most prisoners of war were redeployed to mine gold. When Hitler turned on Stalin in 1941, all Russians of German extraction were relocated to Siberia. Some ended up mining gold. But the cruelest, most ironic gold mining assignment came after the war. To cleanse all possible ideological contamination, every Russian soldier who had spent time as a POW of the Nazis made the obligatory trek east for reeducation through gold mining.

At first, the policy was to produce gold efficiently; after 1937, the policy was to eliminate prisoners—through exposure, disease, exhaustion, and starvation. More than 3 million perished in the Kolyma-Indigirka gold mines alone. The Kolyma fields, a total of about 80 mines, produced 3,300 tons of gold over the course of 22 years. By comparison, Alaska's gold rush era—from 1880 to 1904—lasted 24 years. One conservative estimate is that every kilogram of gold cost one human life. With Stalin's death in 1953, conditions slowly improved. After the fall of Communism and breakup of the Soviet Empire, the remnants of Kolyma and its capital, Magadan, were preserved in memorials, museums, and restorations—like some grotesque cross between Auschwitz and Skagway—to bear witness for future generations.

Natural History

George Vancouver did not encounter Russians until his survey of the Northwest Coast was nearly complete. Following the strategy espoused by this book, Vancouver undertook the survey over the course of more than one season, wintering in the Hawaiian Islands between charting explorations. In the first year, 1792, he got as far north as Bella Bella, British Columbia. The following year he reached a point near present-day Petersburg, Alaska. In 1794 he took a different tack. Starting in Cook Inlet, Vancouver decided to work his way south to his previous point of completion. Straightaway he ran into Russians. Vancouver noted that they were thoroughly absorbed in the fur trade. The Russians had not yet founded Sitka and had settled only as far east as Kodiak Island. Hoping to meet and pay his respects to the Russian American Company's new manager, Vancouver paid a courtesy visit. Unfortunately he missed him. Alexander Baranov, who had arrived a scant three years earlier, was off consolidating his new charge.

Vancouver reentered protected waters at ice-choked Icy Strait, the northernmost entrance to the Inside Passage. He never saw Glacier Bay. Not that he missed it: Glacier Bay did not exist. Although the entrance—a 6-mile bight backed by a several-hundred- feet-thick glacier reaching back into the mountains—was there, in 1794 the rest of the bay lay entombed under a mile-thick shroud of ice.

Therein lies the wonder of Glacier Bay National Park. In the first 120 years since Vancouver's visit, Glacier Bay's ice cap retreated 65 miles, uncovering a new land. The rate of recession was phenomenal and unprecedented. Never in recorded history has a glacier retreated as fast as the one that filled Glacier Bay. Then all of a sudden, the glaciers stopped. By 1916, the Grand Pacific Glacier at the head of Tarr Inlet settled more or less where it holds court today. Though some glaciers still recede and some grow—and exactly what they will do is the subject of much study and speculation—nature suddenly imposed a rough equilibrium. The glaciers' maximum 2-miles-per-year retreat during the bay's formative years had ceased. It was during this time, in 1879, that John Muir "discovered" Glacier Bay. Only 85 years had elapsed since Vancouver's passing. In that short time the ice had retreated nearly 50 miles. Muir was spellbound. He built a cabin at Muir Point near the glacier that now bears his name, returned for three more visits, and added his efforts to the preservation of the bay.

Glacier Bay hasn't always been covered with ice. Tlingit oral tradition recounts a time when the invasion of the glaciers drove the inhabitants out. At times, that glacial advance was almost but not quite as phenomenally fast as the later historical retreat. A variety of evidence indicates that prior to 2,000 BC, Glacier Bay looked much as it does today. Then, during the Little Ice Age, the ice girded its loins and rumbled south. A thousand years later, it trapped remnants of the old forest in graveyards of ghostly deep freeze. These copses of interglacial wood are still visible along Muir Inlet. During the reign of Peter the Great, Glacier Bay's Tlingit were under siege. They cut their losses, retreated, and relocated across Icy Strait at present-day Hoonah. By the mid-18th century, the wall of ice was 20 miles wide, a mile thick, extended more than 100 miles back to its source in the St. Elias Range, and protruded into Icy Strait.

Glacial advances and retreats did not begin 4,000 years ago. Prior to the Little Ice Age, many advance and retreat episodes punctuated Alaska's—and the entire world's—history interminably back into the fog of time. Besides the four major Pleistocene ice ages, glaciologists have indications that the earlier Pliocene was also peppered with glacial epochs. Barring unforeseen circumstances, the cycle will continue. As of 1990, most of the park's tidewater glaciers were stable or advancing, not retreating—particularly along the west arm and the outer coast.

When a fat man rises from a water bed, the mattress rebounds to its old shape. So it is with the land. During the years of the last glacial retreat, when the enormous weight of the ice was lifted from Glacier Bay, the land—depressed for so long—immediately began to rise. The rate of rebound—isostatic compensation—is astonishing. In the Bartlett Cove area, the land rises 1.5 inches per year. Kayakers navigating with USGS topographic maps soon discover that some waterways are now blocked, or at least require a high tide for passage, or even a short portage.

As the glaciers retreat and the land rises, it also reawakens. Algae are the first colonizers of the bare rock, gravel, and glacial till exposed by the ice. Mosses, sedges, grasses, dwarf fireweed, and dryas, with its ability to fix nitrogen, then get a toehold. In 30 to 40 years' time, willows and Sitka alder take over, reaching heights of 10 feet and thoroughly blocking human access. Where there's enough nitrogen and sun, cottonwoods and willows set down roots. But the alder thicket is so effective at blocking sunlight that it keeps most seedlings—including its own—from propagating and prevailing. The exception is Sitka spruce, which thrives in the shaded conditions. Eventually the spruce take over and create a true forest. Finally, the plant succession cycle reaches a climax—a more or less balanced and self-sustaining population of final species—when western hemlock predominates.

Bartlett Cove, ice-free for 200 years, nestles in a mature hemlock and spruce forest community. To travel up bay from the park headquarters is to travel back in time through the plant succession cycle. North of Bartlett Cove, hemlocks progressively thin. Beyond Mount Wright, spruce become rare; alder and willow thickets prevail. At the heads of the distal bays and inlets, glacial snouts root into morainal troughs devoid of any plant life.

Glacier Bay exuberates with animal life. Humpback—and, to a lesser degree, minke—whales are common. Luckily for the pinnipeds, orcas don't often wander in too far. Around the Marble Islands in mid-bay, the cacophony of endangered Steller sea lions is audible for miles. Curious to a fault, they will investigate kayakers. Harbor seals concentrate on ice floes off the face of glaciers in the spring to bear pups. Don't spook them.

More than 200 species of birds have been sighted in the park. Besides the more common ravens, eagles, gulls, grebes, loons, terns, and cormorants, you're likely to see busybody pigeon guillemots; comical oystercatchers with their distinctive orange bills; murres and murrelets; kittiwakes; sometimes-confused phalaropes, sandpipers, and yellowlegs; tentative plovers and turnstones; and elegant tufted puffins and harlequin ducks, kabuki characters in a maritime pageant. Many of these species have communal nesting sites on islands and in the upper reaches of the park. Don't freak the birds. Ptarmigan, dim-witted as they seem to be, are not uncommon.

Moose entered the park in the 1940s and can usually be spotted along the eastern shore, particularly in the Beardsley Islands. Mountain goats and marmots populate the more recently unglaciated areas, feeding on grasses, shrubs, and buds. Black bears are common in the vegetated areas; grizzlies, less so. Within the park, bear management is exceptionally effective. Park regulations require backcountry users to store all food in bear canisters. These are provided free of charge. Observe all food storage and preparation guidelines to ensure both the safety of the bears and that of future visitors. Firearms are not allowed. Respect the areas that are closed due to exceptional bear activity. Bears that acquire bad habits are soon banished; visitors responsible for those bad habits are held accountable.

Much of Glacier Bay National Park is true wilderness, although within the park along this route, you'll probably encounter more kayakers than in any other portion of the Inside Passage save for the Robson Bight, San Juan, and Gulf Islands sections. Private motorized vessels are strictly limited; more common are tour boats, including the park concessionaire's *Executive Explorer* and *Wilderness Explorer.*

Even outside the park, glaciers are never far away. To the north and east, the ice caps of the St. Elias and Coast Ranges encircle the straits and inlets of the upper Inside Passage. No doubt this contributes to the sense of community that predominates among giant Juneau and its smaller neighbors nearby: Douglas, Mendenhall, Auke Bay, Haines, Skagway, Hoonah, Gustavus, and Elfin Cove, all held together by ferry services, float planes, and fishing and cruising craft, as well as two road connections to the outside world. With all the traffic, cabins, and evidence of logging, you never feel you're too far off the beaten path.

The Route: Overview

The last—and, at 130 miles, shortest—section of the Inside Passage is subdivided into two portions, Icy Strait and Glacier Bay. The first portion, out of Juneau, uncharacteristically runs 77 miles due west and courses along private land, more of Admiralty Island National Monument, and lots more of the Tongass National Forest. Juneau and its suburbs, along tricky Gastineau Channel, dominate the first 15 miles. Another 20 miles up Stephens Passage and down Lynn Canal—around the northern tip of Admiralty Island—puts you at the eastern end of Icy Strait. Just before the entrance to Glacier Bay National Park, you pass Gustavus, the only town along the route. The first portion ends at Bartlett Cove, park headquarters.

The last portion, entirely within the park, heads due north, the final 53 miles of the Inside Passage—up Glacier Bay and all the way to the head of Muir Inlet. Unfortunately—or fortunately, depending on your perspective—you must then retrace your paddle to get back to Bartlett Cove and connect with public transportation to return home. No alternate routes are offered.

There are many logistical choices, and travel plans should be roughly sketched out before heading out. These will be affected by your choice of kayak: hard-shelled or collapsible. Alaska State Ferries and commercial airlines service Juneau. Arriving by ferry from your point of departure—Bellingham, Prince Rupert, or even Haines—you can take any type of kayak. If you choose to fly, you'll be limited to a collapsible boat unless you stored your hard-shell boat in Juneau at the end of the last leg. You can even rent a kayak in Juneau. (See appendix B.)

From the head of Muir Inlet, the return to Juneau can require at most two transportation connections, depending on your ambitions. Logistically, the simplest is to paddle back to Bartlett Cove and make arrangements there for a shuttle to Juneau. Two options are available. The Auk Nu Ferry, a giant catamaran that will carry hard-shelled kayaks, runs daily between Gustavus and Juneau. Arrange the transportation for you and your kit from Bartlett Cove to Gustavus at Bartlett Cove. With a collapsible kayak, you can return to Juneau on the Auk Nu Ferry or fly back from Gustavus. Again, vehicular taxi services are available between Bartlett Cove and Gustavus. All of these options can be arranged at the last minute from the information desk inside the Glacier Bay Park Lodge.

If an additional 53-mile paddle from the head of Muir Inlet back to Bartlett Cove—after kayaking the entire Inside Passage—is more than you can stomach, take heart. The Glacier Bay Park tour concessionaire makes daily runs to the mouth of Muir Inlet and, with advance reservations, will conveniently pick you up and shuttle kayaks and kayakers back to park headquarters. But you'll still have to paddle 25 miles back from the head of Muir Inlet to the Mount Wright pickup location. This option must be prearranged at the Glacier Park Lodge and has little flexibility.

Icy Strait: Juneau (mile 0/1,150) to Bartlett Cove (mile 77/1,227)

Whichever way you arrive in Juneau, you must now prepare to launch from your previous point of completion—Douglas Boat Harbor, the Harris/Aurora marina complex, or Auke Bay. This route description begins where it left off, at the Harris Boat Harbor. The launch ramp at Harris Boat Harbor is adjacent to the south side of a blue storage building and separated from it by a strip of grass, where gear can be organized and stockpiled. It gets plenty of sun, offers some wind protection, and sees little traffic.

Pack enough provisions for this entire section—the 130 miles to Muir Glacier and the 53-mile return paddle to Bartlett Cove. Gustavus, the only town (with all services) along the route, is very spread out, is

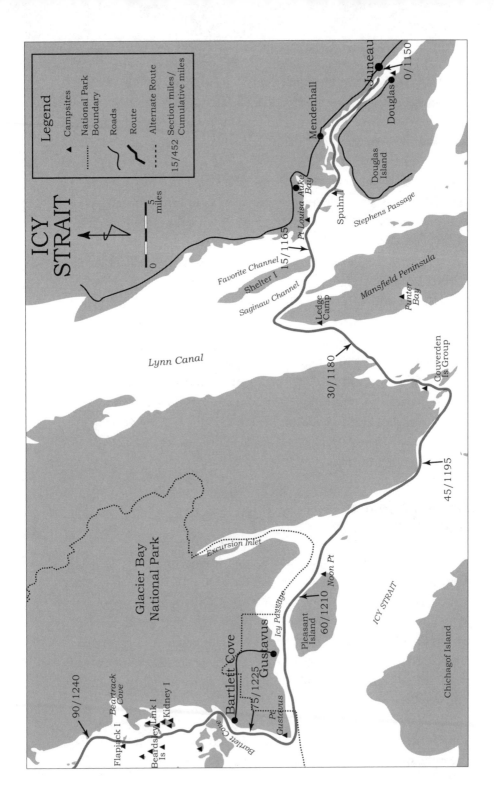

Legend

- ▲ Campsites
- ⋯⋯ National Park Boundary
- Roads
- Route
- Alternate Route
- 15/452 Section miles / Cumulative miles

ICY STRAIT

0 ⟋ 5 miles

Juneau

0/1150

Douglas

Douglas Island

Mendenhall

Stephens Passage

Pt Louisa Auke Bay

Spuhn I

15/1165

Favorite Channel

Shelter I

Saginaw Channel

Ledge Camp

Mansfield Peninsula

Funter Bay

Lynn Canal

30/1180

Couverden Is Group

45/1195

Glacier Bay National Park

Excursion Inlet

Noon Pt

Icy Passage

60/1210

Pleasant Island

ICY STRAIT

Chichagof Island

90/1240

Beartrack Cove

Flapjack I

Beardslee Link I

Kidney I

Is

Bartlett Cove

Gustavus

Pt Gustavus

75/1225

Bartlett Cove

not really a waterfront community, and has no harbor other than a long access pier spanning the tidal flats that front the town. Though you could resupply there, it may be simpler not to. Bartlett Cove relies on a road connection with Gustavus, 10 miles distant, for supplies.

Mendenhall Bar: Mendenhall Bar is the upper half of Gastineau Channel. Specifically, it is the drying sand and mud flat between Juneau and Auke Bay. Plan well your departure from Juneau and traverse of the bar to avoid lining and dragging your boat unnecessarily. Set out from Juneau on a flooding tide, an hour or so after low tide. The center of the bar dries at a 10-foot tide or lower; any tide above 10 feet will float a kayak. Be aware, however, that actual high tide levels are frequently lower than the predicted levels. If you run out of water (provided that you launched on a rising tide), just wait for the tide to raise your boat. If you must line or drag, the footing is usually good and clean.

The Mendenhall Bar deepwater channel is well marked. You can pick up a diagram of the channel at the harbormaster's office in the marina complex. Nine red buoys—on the right-hand side going north—and 14 green buoys on the left demarcate the navigation channel. There is little traffic up or down the bar, and currents are not difficult to deal with, as the total volume of water is not great.

Egan Drive/Glacier Highway parallels Gastineau Channel, but

Gastineau Channel at low tide, with Juneau in the background the sedimentary flats are so broad that the kayaker is left in comparative isolation. The Mendenhall Wetlands State Game Refuge encompasses much of the saltwater marsh area along the channel. Juneau proper soon gives way to the suburb of Lemon Creek. Due north lies the Mendenhall Glacier, Juneau's ice tiara. The glacier is a small salient of the vast, 1,500-square-mile Coast Range ice field and drains a good portion of it via the Mendenhall River. The Mendenhall Glacier has retreated only 2.5 miles in the last 230 years. The community of Mendenhall sits on its east bank. Broad alluvial fans at the mouth of the river constrict Gastineau Channel and create Mendenhall Bar, the only flat area large enough to accommodate Juneau's airport. The channel then opens up into Fritz Cove, with Auke Bay to its north.

Slip north between the Mendenhall Peninsula and Spuhn Island (mile 9/**1,159**) to enter Auke Bay. Spuhn Island is mostly private, though uninhabited. It has a variety of good campsites. An old homestead—now in ruins—lies inland. An orchard and several buildings, with a Model T Ford pickup in the barn, evoke the fox farming era.

Head for Point Louisa (mile 13/**1,163**) where the Auke Village Campground, a commercial facility, offers fully developed camping for a fee at the south end of Fairhaven. For centuries, Auke Village was the site of an Auk Tlingit winter village. The Yax-te totem pole commemorates the site. Inside Auke Bay are the Juneau Alaska Ferry terminal and the Auke Bay Public Float Facility. All services are available.

From Point Louisa the route crosses the junction of Lynn Canal with Stephens Passage and Chatham Strait by island-hopping to Shelter Island and Admiralty Island's Mansfield Peninsula. Lynn Canal joins Stephens Passage via Favorite and Saginaw Channels. Currents at the south end of Lynn Canal average 0.3 to 1 knot. A 2-mile crossing of Favorite Channel separates Fairhaven from Adams Anchorage at the south end of Shelter Island. Another 2-mile crossing, this time of Saginaw Channel, attains tiny Barlow Point on Admiralty Island. Currents at this transect can be tricky. Ebb currents, flowing north, are about twice as strong as floods and can attain 2 knots. When the moon is in quadrature (90 degrees to the sun), the current frequently ebbs throughout the day. Slip between Barlow Point and the Barlow Islands into Barlow Cove, a popular local small-craft anchorage.

The northern tip of Admiralty Island is capped by beautiful Point Retreat Light. Landing is not particularly easy. Turn south along the Mansfield Peninsula until a suitable opportunity for crossing Lynn Canal over to the Chilkat Range peninsula presents itself. Between Point Retreat and Funter Bay, a 10- to 20-foot-high granite shelf lines the coast. Some sections are wide enough for a clean, scenic, and commanding camp, particularly near mile 27/**1,177**—shelf camp (see photo on p. 75). Though the crossing of Lynn Canal is only 3 miles wide, and currents rarely exceed 1 knot, a camp along this ledge is ideal for an early morning crossing to Point Howard. Alternatively, Funter Bay—as much as 5 miles off route, depending from where exactly you choose to cross—has extensive beaches at the head of Coot Cove. The bay has two state maintained public floats, some cabins at the head of Crab Cove and the ruins of the Funter Bay Cannery.

Couverden Islands, Icy Strait, Alaska

Couverden Island Group: South of Point Howard, a scallop indents the mainland shore, giving entry to a delightful group of islands with protected waters. Many of the islands in the Couverden Group (mile 37/**1,187**) are campable. Stephen Hilson reports an abandoned Tlingit village and an abandoned cannery in the bight just due north of Ansley Island. At high water, a marked passage connects Lynn Canal with Icy Strait along the mainland shore. At most other times, passage is possible just north of the northwest tip of Couverden Island. A public float in Swanson Harbor faces Ansley Island. At low water, this transit requires a short portage. There is a good campsite on the Couverden Island side. In the late 1800s, Couverden Island was the site of an Anglo village and a wood depot for early steamboats.

Round the southern tip of the Chilkat Range peninsula and enter Icy Strait. Two miles up the coast, where the 1:250,000 Juneau quadrangle indicates a cabin, Hilson locates historic Grouse Fort, an abandoned native village. The coast turns north into Excursion Inlet, and the Chilkat Range looms precipitously right out of the water. This section is known as the "home shore" and traditionally is reported to be a good fishing area.

Excursion Inlet: About 3.5 miles inside Excursion Inlet lies the small settlement of Excursion Inlet, comprised mostly of a cannery with support services. During WWII the settlement was the site of a major military base built to supply Aleutian operations. It could accommodate 5,000 men and 5 Liberty Ships. Unfortunately, it became obsolete before completion. So the base was converted to a POW camp, and 1,200 captured German soldiers were shipped in to dismantle it. Escapes were discouraged by a presentation that included a detailed map of the area that indicated they were a long way from nowhere in the middle of a wilderness and that they were surrounded by ferocious bears and Indians who had never been conquered by white men. Only two prisoners escaped. They soon returned voluntarily, after having been eaten by mosquitoes, treed by a bear, and scared by Indian fishing boats in the area.

Before heading into Excursion Inlet, cross westward to the Porpoise Islands, site of Steve Kane's 1923 fox farm, and on to Pleasant Island.

Pleasant Island: Noon Point (mile 57/**1,207**), Pleasant Island's eastern point, is a particularly attractive campsite: a scattering of white sandy foyers nestled among rocky outcrops. Most of Pleasant Island's north shore also offers good camping. On October 24, 1879, John Muir, his companion (Presbyterian missionary S. Hall Young), and their Indian guides camped on the western shore of Pleasant Island en route to Glacier Bay. After stocking up on firewood in anticipation of camping on ice, Young christened the place Pleasant Island because "...it gave us such an impression of welcome and comfort."

Enter Icy Passage. Normally one would be tempted to almost bypass Pleasant Island and course along the mainland's south coast. In this case however, the island's camping and welcoming shores offer an attractive route, while extensive—sometimes mile-wide—drying sandy flats befoul Icy Passage's north shore. Somewhere past Pleasant Island's northernmost tip, angle across Icy Passage to the Gustavus pier.

Gustavus: Gustavus (pop. 260) is the town that serves Glacier Bay National Park. The town was founded in the early 1920s by the Matson family as a homestead with the encouragement of federal agencies to help develop the area. Located along the mouth of the Salmon River, the village is an atypical Inside Passage settlement, in that it is spread out over flat and fertile deltaic terrain with difficult shoreline access. (It is more than a mile from the head of the pier to Gustavus.) The Matsons developed a farming community that provided meat, garden produce, and, especially, strawberries to a growing regional economy. All services are available. From a kayak, sampling Gustavus's riches is not easy and probably best left to a post–Inside Passage visit by road from Bartlett Cove. A handful of historic lodges, inns, and bed-and-breakfasts dot the community and would make a delightful penultimate celebratory stay before embarking back to Juneau.

Continue on to Point Gustavus (mile 72/**1,222**) staying as far from shore as tidal conditions warrant. At the point, currents—which can attain 6 knots entering and exiting Glacier Bay all the way up to Willoughby Island—minimize sand deposition, and the shore offers attractive camping possibilities without long carries. Turn north into

Glacier Bay National Park and paddle another 5 miles to Bartlett Cove (mile 77/**1,227**), the park's headquarters. Head for the boat launch between the breakwater and fuel dock and the large National Park Service public use dock. The Park's visitor information kiosk is located at the foot of the pier. A variety of accommodations from free camping to luxury lodge suites are available.

Glacier Bay: Bartlett Cove (mile 77/1,227) to Muir Glacier (mile 130/1,280)

Glacier Bay National Park: Much to the consternation of the Matson family and several of the local native residents, President Calvin Coolidge created Glacier Bay National Monument in 1925, limiting commercial activity and preserving about half the present park area. The monument was increased in size in 1939, and made a national park in 1980, at which time it was enlarged again to its present size of 3.3 million acres with the addition of the Alsek River estuary. In 1986 UNESCO designated the park a Biosphere Reserve, and in 1992 it became a World Heritage Site.

Bartlett Cove has limited services. White gas and bear canisters are available. Gustavus, 10 miles distant, has groceries and a hardware store, but transportation between the town and the cove is expensive and often slow. The national park campground is just west of the landing pier. It is well protected, well developed—including free firewood, picnic tables, rain shelters, and warming stoves—and is absolutely free, though you must register at the park check-in kiosk. Laundromat and showers are available. Glacier Bay Lodge has rooms for about $130 and cheaper dormitory-style accommodations. The lodge restaurant is excellent, with reasonably priced breakfasts and lunches. Dinner can be expensive.

Kayaking is very popular in the park. If it gets too popular, the Park Service may consider implementing a quota system similar to the one in place for motorized vessels. Before undertaking a paddling trip, you must register and attend a video orientation. There is a kayak transport concessionaire that offers drop-off and pick-up service, both of which

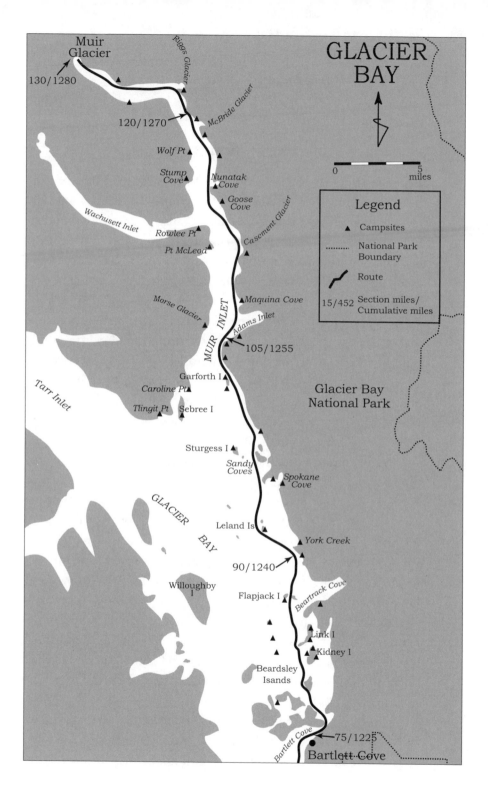

GLACIER BAY

Legend

▲ Campsites

⋯⋯ National Park Boundary

⌇ Route

15/452 Section miles/ Cumulative miles

0 — 5 miles

Muir Glacier

130/1280

Riggs Glacier

120/1270

McBride Glacier

Wolf Pt ▲

Stump Cove ▲

Nunatak Cove

Goose Cove

Wachusett Inlet

Casement Glacier

Rowlee Pt ▲

Pt McLeod ▲

Morse Glacier

Maquina Cove ▲

MUIR INLET

Adams Inlet

105/1255

Garforth I

Caroline Pt ▲

Tlingit Pt ▲

Sebree I

Tarr Inlet

Glacier Bay National Park

Sturgess I ▲

Sandy Coves

Spokane Cove

GLACIER BAY

Leland Is

York Creek

90/1240

Willoughby I

Flapjack I

Beartrack Cove

Link I

Kidney I

Beardsley Isands

Bartlett Cove

75/1225

Bartlett Cove

must be arranged in advance if you plan to make use of one of these options. You are now ready to complete the last portion of the Inside Passage.

Beardslee Islands: The best route north to Muir Inlet traverses the Beardslee Islands. These islands are low-lying—the tallest is only 200 feet high—protected, ringed by shallow waters, dense with greenery, full of wildlife, and closed to motorized travel from May 15 to September 15. They are a maze to navigate. With the Beardslees isostatically rising 1.8 to 2 inches a year, interisland channels disappear and new islands appear with surprising rapidity. Chart makers can barely keep up. Additionally, with so many tiny landforms and few unambiguous landmarks, chart scale—the chart's ability to display minimal features—must be taken into account. In the Beardslees, your map may actually be wrong—in spite of a lousy map reader's first instinct, namely to question the map instead of his skill. Get the highest resolution and most up-to-date chart available, and don't lose track of your location. There is no fresh water in the Beardslees.

To enter the archipelago, round the east end of Lester Island, southernmost and largest of the Beardslee Islands and the north shore of Bartlett Cove. This passage dries at low tide and is passable only near high tide. Depart Bartlett Cove one to two hours before high tide. Leaving after high water exposes the paddler to contrary currents, often strong enough to impede relaxed progress. Alternatively, (and this will be the route in the not-too-distant future) exit Bartlett Cove around Lester Island's west end. Strong currents—up to 6 knots—dominate Glacier Bay's main channel, so slip into Secret Bay through the channel between Young and Lester Islands. Exit Secret Bay through the channel that separates the northern tip of Young Island from the newly attached northern peninsula of Lester Island. The western shore of this peninsula (mile 81/**1,231**) has a good campsite.

Directly north of the main mass of Lester Island, two unnamed islands—the first about 0.5 mile long; the second, ham-shaped and twice as long—lie offshore of the mainland. Round either side. A slightly north-by-northwest, long reach separates the Eastern Beardslees from the Western Beardslees. Continue up this channel. Many campsites dot both groups.

In the eastern group, Kidney Island (mile 84/**1,234**), has three campsites, all near the north end: one each on the west and east (Hutchins Bay) sides, and one on the northern tip. Link Island (mile 85/**1,235**) has two campsites, one on each side of the island about halfway up.

The western isles tend to bareness, which makes them excellent bird nesting sites. Some are off limits, but those that are available offer campsites with glorious sunset views over the Fairweather Range. Three separate camp spots (between miles 84–85/**1,234–1,235**) on different unnamed islets are marked on the accompanying map. The largest, northernmost island of the Western Beardslees was once a Beardslee family fox farm. Some remains can still be seen, though camping is not particularly good, except on the newly attached island just to the north.

Exit the Beardslee Islands through whatever channel is open. Trend toward Flapjack Island, where deeper water predominates. The last island (mile 88/**1,217**) on the mainland side (not for long) has a campsite on its fouling east shore.

North of the Beardslees, the full splendor of Glacier Bay opens up—a panorama of ice interspersed with protruding rocky tors. The open waters have a calming effect on currents, but just the opposite on winds. Cross Beartrack Cove's 2-mile-wide mouth. There is another campsite—shingle beach—on Beartrack's southern shore, off mile 88/**1,238**. Head toward York Creek (mile 90/**1,240**) where two campsites bracket each side of the bight. North of Beartrack Cove, the mainland coast is steep-to and mountainous, with few camping or landing spots. Much of this shore is often closed due to aggressive bear activity. Note well on your map the exact limits of the annual closures. The prudent paddler will coast near the shore—the better to spot bears—but will plan to camp on the offshore islands. We once watched a hapless black bear that, after ending up on an unlikely and exposed ledge while haphazardly tracking fresh shoots, could find no way out of his vertiginous predicament.

He finally free-fell down to a steep scree slope, upon which he glissaded uncontrollably for perhaps 100 feet. Gaining solid footing, he ran off, annoyed and no doubt surprised at his good fortune.

Offshore lie the Leland Islands (mile 93/**1,243**) with a cobble campsite on the southwestern shore of the larger island. From here you'll be treated to the ongoing drama of life at the sea lion haul-out on South Marble Island (The island's southern half is closed year-round.) Dive-bombing birds add their chorus, but the production is not complete until the minkes and humpbacks join in—breaching, spyhopping, and lobtailing.

Sandy Coves: North of Leland Island, the precipitous mainland shore is broken by the Sandy Coves island and peninsula grouping. Although much of the shore will probably be closed to landings, the area is delightful to paddle through. Had you been paddling the Inside Passage in 1857, this would have been the end of the trip: the Muir Glacier reached to Sandy Coves. Spokane Cove (mile 95/**1,245**) has extensive sand flats at its head but offers up at least two campsites, one by the south entrance and more along the peninsula jutting out from its north side. Sturgess Island (mile 99/**1,249**) has a good campsite at its northern tip from which to explore the Sandy Coves group. The passage between the mainland and the largest island (unnamed) is navigable only at high tide. Sheer cliffs and muddy little bights are a paddlers' paradise. Hidden nooks, overhangs, and ledges nurture wildlife. Puffins, pigeon guillemots, and gulls nest on the walls, while oystercatchers ply their trade; bears frequent the estuaries. Near the northern end of North Sandy Cove (mile 100/**1,250**) there is another campsite.

At this point Glacier Bay divides into its two arms, with Muir Inlet beckoning north. Currents in Muir Inlet never exceed 1 knot. Three good campsites dot the western shores, one at Tlingit Point, another on the south end of Sebree Island (mile 100/**1,250**), and one on the spit at Caroline Point. The mainland's eastern shore is dominated by hulking Mount Wright. Watch for mountain goats on its flanks. Garforth Island (mile 102/**1,252**) lies close offshore. There is camping at both the south and north ends. Do not be seduced by the relative safety of island

Crested puffins, Glacier Bay National Park, Alaska

camping. In 1982, an enterprising black bear swam over to Garforth and brazenly raided campers' tents. Just beyond Garforth Island, Mount Wright recedes, and a gently sloping cobbled shore stretches around Muir Point (mile 104/**1,254**) into Adams Inlet. There is plenty of camping, but remember that this is the drop-off and pick-up area for kayak shuttles. Across Muir Inlet, on the western shore, there is a campsite at the Morse Glacier outwash (mile 105/**1,255**). Muir Point was the terminus of Muir Glacier at the time of John Muir's visit. It was here that he built a cabin as a base camp for his explorations.

Cross the 1.5-mile-wide mouth of Adams Inlet into a land almost devoid of conifers. Maquina Cove (mile 108/**1,258**), 0.5 mile north of Point George, has a landing beach and possible campsite. Past a point labeled Cush on topographic maps, the huge Casement Glacier comes into view. The outflow (mile 111/**1,261**)—and shore—is flat for about 7 miles up to Goose Cove (mile 114/**1,264**) and provides good camping. The glacier itself has receded about 4 miles from shore. Hike up Forest Creek for a closer view. Goose Cove dries to mud at its head; the campsite is at the entrance on the east shore, where a backcountry ranger station once sat.

Due west of Casement Glacier, across Muir Inlet, Wachusett Inlet curves in. There is camping at Point McLeod and Rowlee Point (mile 111/**1,261**).

Round the headland separating Goose Cove from Nunatak Cove (mile 116/**1,266**). Nunatak Cove also dries to mud; the best campsite is on the south shore near the mouth. A distinctive hill called the Nunatak (a hill completely surrounded by glacial ice) dominates the north shore and once saved John Muir's life. After 10 days of glacier exploration in 1890, nearly snowblind and exhausted on the way back to his cabin, he fell into a crevasse and was swept down by the current. He managed to save himself and his sled and crawl up onto the Nunatak's bare ground, where he warmed himself and made a dry camp. The 1,205-foot-high knob once made a neat hike with commanding views of upper Muir Inlet. Though you can still hike up—approach from the south up a creek—alders and willows dominate and impede progress. From the north, there is less brush but the route is steeper and rockier.

Stump Cove (mile 116/**1,266**) on Muir Inlet's western shore has good camping and very accessible nearby interstadial stumps. Just north of Westdahl Point, stumps project from the bank above the high-water shelf. Some are 10 or 15 feet tall, some have fallen, and some, undoubtedly, still lie buried. Don't miss a chance to see and touch 3,000-year-old wood. At least consider going up one side of Muir Inlet and returning down the other.

North of Nunatak Cove, a 3-mile-long crescent (mile 117/**1,267**) indents the eastern shore. Its low beaches offer many camps. Across the inlet, Wolf Point (mile 117/**1,267**) has a good camp, the last before impressive White Thunder Ridge.

McBride Glacier: McBride Glacier (mile 119/**1,269**), still a true tidewater glacier, is slowly retreating. The river of ice is hidden between

McBride Glacier, Glacier Bay National Park, Alaska

the Van Horn and McConnell Ridges and is not visible until the last bit of the approach. There is camping on both the south and north shores of the outwash, among stranded bergy bits. Unfortunately, air temperature is nearly 10 degrees colder within the outwash corridor. Tidal currents entering and exiting the lagoon are impressive as they promenade bergs in and out the mouth. If you paddle into the lagoon, remember not to approach nesting seals or the face of the glacier. Not that calving bergs might get you, but their compression waves can easily swamp a kayak.

About 2.5 miles north of McBride, at its junction with Riggs Glacier, Muir Inlet arcs westward. There are few landing spots along the base of McConnell Ridge.

Riggs Glacier: Riggs Glacier (mile 121/**1,271**) can't seem to make up its mind. A 1987 guidebook reported it as retreating. Three years later the USGS announced that "the glacier has shown signs of advancing."

Riggs Glacier, Glacier Bay National Park, Alaska

Since the late 1960s, the glacier has temporized at its present location. This is enough time for a little greenery to sprout and create some wonderful campsites at its outwash moraine. There are great views up and down the channels—watch for mountain goats on the incredible flanks of Mount Brock—and of the glacier itself. With only 8 miles to go, the Riggs Glacier campsite makes an excellent up-and-back base camp to conclude the Inside Passage.

Prepare yourself for the climax of the most magnificent trip of your lifetime. If going up and back, empty your boat and cruise lightly. This last bit is particularly spectacular, not only because the walls of Muir Inlet narrow and rise precipitously in swaths of bare rock to incredible heights, home to many nesting bird species, but also because—due to the arcing curve of the channel—the panorama unfolds slowly. During the summer, motor restrictions usually apply for upper Muir Inlet. There are few campsites.

Carved walls and glacial silt, upper Muir Inlet, Glacier Bay National Park, Alaska

About 2 miles up from Riggs Glacier is a small campable site (mile 123/**1,273**) on the south shore. Another mile farther, on the north shore along its most prominent salient, there is another campsite (mile 124/**1,274**).

Muir Glacier: Muir Glacier (mile 130/**1,280**) has been retreating for 200 years, sometimes hastily, sometimes lackadaisically. According to Muir's accounts, the retreat was relatively slow between 1880 and 1890, the decade of his visits. For years after the turn of the 20th century, the glacier gained worldwide fame as the first cruise ships brought doughty tourists right up to its face. Then, all of a sudden, the retreat became a rout: So much ice decomposed so fast that the inlet became totally clogged with bergs and no vessel could approach within sight of the snout. As recently as 1960, upper Muir Inlet—beyond Riggs Glacier—was still covered in solid ice. Between 1972 and 1982 the rate of recession accelerated: more than 3 miles of inlet were uncovered. Since

Muir Glacier snout, top of Inside Passage, Glacier Bay National Park, Alaska

then the retreat has slowed noticeably. The ever-changing nature of the glacier's snout and terminal moraine sometimes provides a campsite.

Approach the glacier up the bed of its outflow stream or along the more gravelly areas to avoid the fine, silty, ever present mud. Congratulations. Take a picture, take a pee, never forget this moment, and have a safe journey home.

Acknowledgments

When the facts change,
I change my mind.
What do you do, sir?
—John Maynard Keynes

Putting together a guidebook takes little talent. It's basically a compilation of data already in the public domain. Still, writing a book is a voyage of discovery. I've never written a book before. Frankly, it's overwhelming. To learn the conventions, I looked at how other books are put together; what other people have done, particularly with the more formulaic parts such as the table of contents, index, and acknowledgments. Where appropriate, I end up imitating. Indices are the toughest; there really isn't much of a shortcut. Acknowledgments are where the author thanks people without whom the work would not be what it is, or might not even exist. Does anyone read the acknowledgments? I always do, though rather perfunctorily.

Some acknowledgments begin by diluting responsibility for the book: "It takes a community to write a book..." or "I have depended upon others...," etc. Unfortunately, for me this did not ring true. I was the only one paralyzed before the computer screen agonizing about just what to say and how to say it, and wondering if it was worth saying. No one but me struggled to find just the right word and analyzed it for suitability, scope, and nuance. I am the only one responsible for the veracity of what I've presented.

Just how many creative ways are there to thank someone for help? Even my thesaurus is at a loss for words: "much obliged," "indebted to,"

Acknowledgments

"appreciative of," "praise," "hymn," "paean to," et al. Unbelievably, it then emigrates overseas to: *gracias, merci, danke, grazie,* etc. Thanks, but no thanks. Some writers left me chuckling and, finally, slack-jawed at their bold-spirited but cornily convoluted steps into untrod appreciative territory: "Oceans of thanks to..." "Applause for..." "Three cheers for..." "Infinite blessings to..." "A ball of sun to..." "High fives to..." "Mucho kudos for..." "Wildflowers to..." "I must uplift those who..." "Beer and kinky sex to..." "Jelly-filled donuts to..."and my favorite of all, "Puddle stomps to..."

There is absolutely no way I can compete against this lineup. So I'll just capitulate and thank—some profoundly—the following people, in no particular order, noting their contributions:

Tina Cobos, my lover and consort, for her unconditional support, boundless enthusiasm, and unedited honesty. As my editor of first resort, she nipped some of my extravagant flights of fancy (and aborted takeoffs) and eased the burden on subsequent editors. As a paddling companion, she turned trouble into fun and fun into ecstasy.

Howard Miller, my late father, for living a life full of reason, adventure, and accomplishment (writing included) as if there were no other choice. He was an inspiration in the realization that we are each of us in the driver's seat of life and can go anywhere we choose.

Ana Maria Miller, my late mother, for her encouragement, if not in my adventures, at least in my attempts to write, and for her endowment of roots and wings. I must also, perversely, give thanks for her timely death—it was expected, drawn out, and wrenching—during the fourth leg of this hegira. It galvanized my commitment to write this guide.

Anita Hatch-Miller, my sister, for bearing the brunt of my mother's daily care.

Ann-Lawrie Aisa, my undergraduate Spanish literature professor and friend, for her technical editorial skills, unstinting help, and enthusiastic encouragement.

Pedro Aisa, also my undergraduate Spanish literature professor and lifelong friend, for existing.

Catherine Moody, once a protégé, ever a friend and confidante, for nudging this Luddite into the computer era, taking time out of her graduate studies to provide thoughtful feedback, illustrating this book with superb maps, and paddling the Vancouver Island portion with us.

Roy Smith, mentor, inspiration, hero, sometime writer, fellow climber, and kayaker, for deigning to read and comment on the manuscript.

Chris and Kathy Grace, friends and fellow kayakers—with a boat collection exceeding 20—for sharing their food, wine, graciousness, conviviality, and home in Port Townsend, Washington, which we used as a staging point for many of the Inside Passage legs. To Chris, fellow bibliophile, in particular, for essential research and outrageous opinions; and to Kathy for reading much of the manuscript and finding no fault with it.

Martha Reinke, ex-lover, talented hack, animating spirit, and co-expeditionist, for getting me started writing, and under whose aegis I published my first paying article.

Dave and Beth Scalia, Inside Passage companions on the panhandle portion, for sharing the experience, making the trip legs safer and more fun, and providing valuable feedback on the manuscript.

Lance Moody and Wendy Ballas, Inside Passage companions on diverse sections of the trip, for their company and support.

Wallace Miller, my late uncle, for his poetry and unconventionality.

Zack Zdinak, longtime associate and talented artist, for taking a chance on this whole uncertain venture and gracing the book with his art.

Todd Balf and Bill Bradford, editors at *Canoe* and *Liberty* magazines, respectively, for finding enough merit in my writing to publish me nationally.

The Kelty Company, for contributing their Sunshade.

The crew of the *Grizzly Bear*, Kent and Joannie, for a delightful visit, invitation to kit down in the newly completed ranger's cabin at bear-thick Lowe Inlet, and invaluable leads and information.

The caretakers at Namu and Butedale for their hospitality, help with repairs, laundry, and showers.

Mark R. McCaughan, MD, for the kind use of his cabin.

Julie Rowe, Information Assistant for the Southeast Alaska Discovery Center, for going above and beyond the call of duty by hand-copying out-of-print information that was essential for this book.

Reed Waite, executive director of the Cascadia Marine Trail, for advice, help, and for gracing this venture with the kind thoughts in his foreword.

Jennifer Hahn, Dorcas Miller, and John Dowd, accomplished kayakers and authors and the 2002 West Coast Sea Kayak Symposium presenters for help, advice, and encouragement.

Chuck Carpenter for independent research and support; and Steve Booth for critical feedback.

The owners and crews of Arizona Fiberglass and Boat Repair, Inc., and The Graphic Center and Stanley Lumber Company for help, patience, and information.

And lastly, thanks to Bill Bowers, my editor. I've heard—and experienced—horror stories of editors butchering writers' prose beyond recognition; of excisions so extensive they're really amputations. Bill paid me the finest compliment an author can expect to get: He let my work be. For that I will forever respect, cherish, and remember him. Thank you, Bill.

Appendix A: Maps

Maps are to reality as
bumper stickers are to philosophy.
—R. H. M.

1:250,000 SCALE TOPO MAPS required for the Inside Passage for both recommended and alternate routes:

United States
Seattle, Washington
Ketchikan, Alaska-Canada
Craig, Alaska
Bradfield Canal, Alaska-Canada
Petersburg, Alaska-Canada
Sumdum, Alaska-Canada
Sitka, Alaska
Juneau, Alaska-Canada
Mt. Fairweather, Alaska-Canada
Skagway, Alaska-Canada

Canada
Victoria—92 B
Vancouver—92 G
Port Alberni—92 F
Bute Inlet—92 K
Alert Bay—92 L
Rivers Inlet—92 M
Bella Coola—93 D
Laredo Sound—103 A
Hecate Strait—103 G
Douglass Channel—103 H
Prince Rupert—103 J

Appendix B: Resources

*Every mystery solved
brings us to the threshold
of a greater one.*
—Rachel Carson

General

U.S. Coast Guard

Tel. (206) 217-6000 or 220-7000

Emergencies: (206) 286-5400

Bellingham, WA: Tel. (360) 734-1692

Everett, WA: Tel. (425) 252-5281

Port Angeles, WA: Tel. (360) 452-2342 or 457-2226/2200

Ketchikan, AK: Tel. (907) 228-0260

Juneau, AK: Tel. (907) 463-2065

Cellular: *CG; VHF: 16 or 12 or 22A

Canadian Coast Guard, Pacific Region

350-555 W. Hastings St., Vancouver, B.C. V6B 5G3

Tel. 604-631-3702; (250) 363-2333

(250) 627-3081/3074 (Prince Rupert)

Web site: www.ccg-gcc.gc.ca/main.htm

Emergency: 1-800-567-5111 or cellular, #311

US Customs
648 Mission Sreet, Suite 101, Federal Building & Courthouse,
    Ketchikan, AK
Tel. (907) 225-2254 or 1-800-526-5943
San Juan Islands, WA: (360) 378-2080

Canada Customs (Revenue Canada)
Tel. 1-800-222-4919 or 1-888-226-7277 (from U.S.)
Web site: www.ccra-adrc.gc.ca

US Forest Service, Tongass National Forest
Information Center, 101 Egan Drive, Juneau, AK 99801
    Tel. (907) 586-8751
Ketchikan: Southeast Alaska Visitor Center, 50 Main Street,
    Ketchikan, AK 99901
    Tel. (907) 228-6214
Wrangell: District Office, 525 Bennet Street, P.O. Box 51,
    Wrangell, AK 99929
    Tel. (907) 874-2323
Petersburg: Petersburg Ranger District, P.O. Box 1328,
    Petersburg, AK 99833
    Tel. (907) 772-3871
Web site: www.fs.fed.us/r10

Washington Water Trails Association
4649 Sunnyside Avenue North, Room #305, Seattle, WA 98103
Tel. (206) 545-9161
Web site: www.wwta.org

British Columbia Marine Trails Association
c/o Ecomarine
1668 Duranleau Street, Granville Island, Vancouver, B.C. V6H 3SA
Web site: www.bcmarinetrail.com

Weather

U.S. National Weather Service
Olympia, WA
Tel. (360) 357-6453
VHF: Channel 1 or 3
Ketchikan: WXJ-26 (162.55MHz)
Wrangell: WXJ-83 (162.40MHz)
Petersburg: WXJ-82 (162.55MHz)
Juneau: WXJ-25 (162.55MHz)

Environment Canada Weather
Tel. (604) 664-9010
VHF: WX1 (162.55 MHz)
        WX2 (162.40 MHz)
        WX3 (162.475 MHz)
        21B & WX4 (161.65 MHz)

Weather One-on-One
Tel. 1-900-565-5555
Cellular: 0-955-656-5555
Talk directly to a weather forecaster for a per-minute charge,
    2-minute minimum. Credit card required.

Charts, Maps, Tide Tables & Books

National Ocean Service
Distribution Branch, Riverdale, MD 20737
Tel. (301) 436-6990

Canadian Hydrographic Service, Chart Sales and Distribution, Institute of Ocean Sciences
9860 West Saanich Rd., P.O. Box 6000, Sidney, B.C. V8L 4B2
Tel. (250) 363-6358
Web site: www.charts.gc.ca

Crown Publications Inc.

521 Fort St., Victoria, B.C. V8W 1H9

Tel. (250) 386-4636

Web site: www.com/crownpub

Source for all Canadian government publications including nautical
charts, topographical maps, marine books, history and natural
history books, First Nations books, etc.

Nanaimo Maps and Charts

8 Church St., Nanaimo, B.C. V9R 5H4

Tel. (250) 754-2513 or 1-800-665-2513

Source for Canadian and American maps and charts.

World Wide Books and Maps

736A Granville St., Vancouver, B.C. V6Z 1G3

Tel. (604) 687-3320

Source for Canadian and American maps and charts.

Armchair Sailor

2110 Westlake Ave. N., Seattle, WA 98109

Tel. (206) 283-0858 or 1-800-875-0852

Web site: www.armchairsailorseattle.com

Source for American and Canadian charts, pilots, and nautical books.

Canada Map Office

Department of Energy, Mines & Resources, 615 Booth Street,
Ottawa, Ontario K1A 0E9

Tel. (613) 952-7000

United States Geological Survey

Information Services, Box 25286, Denver, CO 80225

Tel. 1-800-USA-MAPS or 1-888-ASK-USGS

Web site: www.usgs.gov

USDA Forest Service
Information Center, 101 Egan Drive, Juneau, AK 99801
Tel. (907) 586-8751
Web site: www.fs.fed.us/r10

International Sailing Supply
320 Cross Street, Punta Gorda, FL 33950
Tel. (813) 639-7626 or 1-800-423-9026
Specialty waterproof charts for Puget Sound and San Juan Islands.

Coastal Waters Recreation
Suite 547, 185-911 Yates St., Victoria, B.C. V8V 4Y9
Tel. (250) 383-5555
Web site: www.coastalwatersrec.com

Ferries

Washington State Ferries
801 Alaskan Way, Seattle, WA 98104
Tel. (206) 464-6400 (Seattle)
(250) 381-1551 (Victoria)
(250) 656-1531 (Sidney)
Toll free, 1-800-84-FERRY (within WA)
Web site: www.wsdot.wa.gov

B.C. Ferries
1112 Fort St., Victoria, B.C. V8V 4V2
Tel. (250) 386-3431
In Vancouver, (604) 669-1211
For prerecorded schedule information,
(250) 381-5335 (in Victoria or outside BC)
Toll free, 1-888-223-3779 (within BC)
Web site: www.bcferries.bc.ca

Alaska Marine Highway
P.O. Box 25535, Juneau, AK 99802
Tel. (907) 465-3940/3941 or 1-800-382-9229 or 1-800-642-0066;
    from WA, 1-800-585-8445; from Canada, 1-800-665-6414
Bellingham: (360) 676-8445
Prince Rupert: (604) 627-1744/1745
Ketchikan: (907) 225-6182/6183
Wrangell: (907) 874-2021
Petersburg: (907) 772-3855/3856
Web site: www.akferry.com

Puget Sound Express
Tel. (360) 385-5288
Web site: www.pugetsoundexpress.com

Victoria Clipper
2701 Alaska Way, Pier 69, Seattle, WA 98121
Tel. (206) 448-5000 (reservations) or 443-2560 (administration)
Toll free, (outside Seattle or Victoria) 1-800-888-2535
Web site: www.victoriaclipper.com

MV Coho
Black Ball Transport, Inc.
1077 Main Street, Suite 106, Bellevue, WA 98004
Tel. (425) 622-2222
Port Angeles: 101 E. Railroad Ave., Port Angeles, WA 98362
Tel. (360) 457-4491

Auk Nu Ferry
Tel. 1-800-820-2628
Web site: www.glacierbaytravel.com

The following sites consolidate all ferry information: www.youra.com
    and www.ferrytravel.com

Supplies & Outfitters

Roll-Aid Safety, Inc.
P.O. Box 72005, Vancouver, B.C. V6R 4P2
Tel. (604) 224-4010
Web site: www.roll-aid.com

Rapid Products, Inc.
Tel. (303) 761-9600
Web site: www.rapidair.net

Kokatat
5350 Ericson Way, Arcata, CA 95521
Tel. (707) 822-7621 or 1-800-225-9749
Web site: www.kokatat.com

Gaia
PI Outdoors, 215 Rocky Mount Road, P.O. Box 1067,
    Athens, TN 37371
Tel. 1-888/746-1313
Web site: www.pi-outdoors.com

Watershed
Tel. 1-800-811-8607
Web site: www.drybags.com

Chota Outdoor Gear
P.O. Box 31137, Knoxville, TN 37930
Tel. (423) 690-1814

Sea Kayaker
P.O. Box 17029, Seattle, WA 98107
Tel. (206) 789-9536
Web site: www.seakayakermag.com
Source for hydrophones and other neat stuff.

Ecomarine Ocean Kayak Centre
1668 Durenleau Street, Vancouver, B.C. V6H 3S4
Tel. (604) 689-5926

Ocean Pacific Marine Supply Ltd
871 A Island Highway, Campbell River, B.C. V9W 2C2
Tel. (250) 286-1011 or 1-800-663-2294

Eco-Treks Kayak Adventures
203 Cow Bay Road, Prince Rupert, B.C.
Tel. (250) 624-8311

Kaien Sports
344 2nd Ave. W., Prince Rupert, B.C. V8J 1G6
Tel. (250) 624-3633

Tongass Trading Company
201 Dock Street, Ketchikan, AK 99901
Tel. (907) 225-5101

SeeQuest Adventures
P.O. Box 155, Waglisla, B.C. V0T 1Z0
Tel. (250) 957-2619
Web site: www.seequest.com

Action Charters
Mike Patterson, P.O. Box 881, Wrangell, AK 99929
Tel. (907) 874-3813/2554
Tours up the Stikine River and the Anan Bear Observatory.

Alaska Waters, Inc.
P.O. Box 1978, Wrangell, AK 99929
Tel. 1-800-347-4462
Tours up the Stikine River and the Anan Bear Observatory.

Aqua Sports
P.O. Box 681, Wrangell, AK 99929
Tel. (907) 874-3811/3061

Breakaway Adventures
P.O. Box 2107, Wrangell, AK 99929
Tel. (907) 874-2488 or 1-888-385-2488
Web site: www.breakawayadventures.com

Stickeen Wilderness Adventures
Todd E. Harding, P.O. Box 934, Wrangell, AK 99929
Tel. 1-800-874-2085

Tongass Kayak Adventures
P.O. Box 2169, Petersburg, AK 99833
Tel. (907) 772-4600
Web site: www.alaska.net/~tonkayak

Alaska Boat & Kayak
101 Dock Street, P.O. Box 20173, Juneau, AK 99802
Tel. (907) 586-8220

Alaska Paddle Sports & Outdoor Center
800 Sixth Street, Juneau, AK 99802
Tel. (907) 463-5678

Auke Bay Landing Craft
P.O. Box 210562, Auke Bay, AK 99821
Tel. (907) 790-4591
Kayak transport.

Lodging & Vehicle Storage

Bay Vista B&B
Fran Borhek
4617 Darien Drive N., Tacoma, WA
Tel. (253) 759-8084

Sunny Sanctuary Campground
8080 Goodspeed Rd., Port Hardy, B.C.
Tel. (250) 949-6753

Park Avenue Campground
1750 Park Ave., Prince Rupert, B.C.
Tel. (250) 624-5861

Anchor Inn
1600 Park Ave., Prince Rupert, B.C.
Tel. (250) 627-8522

Pineridge B&B
1714 Sloan Ave., Prince Rupert, B.C.
Tel. (250) 627-4419

Mountainside B&B
Sloan Ave., Prince Rupert, B.C.
Tel. (250) 627-1000

Northcoast Pacific Mini Storage
Seal Cove, Prince Rupert, B.C.
Tel. (250) 624-5879

Park Avenue Corner Store, FAS Gas
1665 Park Ave., Prince Rupert, B.C.
Tel. (250) 624-3201

Rupert Towing and Lowbed Dispatch
101 Shawatlans Road, Prince Rupert, B.C.
Tel. (250) 624-2722

Totem Lodge Motel
1335 Park Ave., Prince Rupert, B.C.
Tel. (250) 624-2273

Parkside Resort Motel
#101, 11th Ave. East, Prince Rupert, B.C.
Tel. (250) 624-9131

New York Hotel & Café
207 Stedman St., P.O. Box 9112, Ketchikan, AK 99901
Tel. (907) 225-0246

Fennimore's Bed, Breakfast & Bikes
Across from AK Ferry Terminal, P.O. Box 957, Wrangell, AK 99929
Tel. (907) 874-3012

Stikine Inn
107 Front St., P.O. Box 990, Wrangell, AK 99929
Tel. (907) 874-3388

Thunderbird Hotel
223 Front St., P.O. Box 110, Wrangell, AK 99929
Tel. (907) 874-3322

Wrangell Hostel
1st Presbyterian Church
220 Church Street, P.O. Box 439
Wrangell, AK 99929
Tel. (907) 874-3534

Petersburg Bunk & Breakfast Hostel
P.O. Box 892, 805 Gjoa Street
Petersburg, AK 99833
Tel. (907) 772-3632
Web site: www.bunkandbreakfast.com

Le Conte RV Park
P.O. Box 2133, (4th & Haugen Drive) Petersburg, AK 99833
Tel. (907) 772-4680

Scandia House
110 N. Nordic Drive, P.O. Box 689, Petersburg, AK 99833
(907) 772-4281

Savikko Park RV Camping
Douglas, AK 99802
Tel. (907) 586-5255

The Breakwater Inn
1711 Glacier Avenue, Juneau, AK 99801
Tel. (907) 586-6303 or 1-800-544-2250 (Lower 48) or
    1-800-478-2250 (AK)

Juneau International Hostel
614 Harris Street
Juneau, AK 99801
Tel. (907) 586-9559
Web site: www.juneauhostel.org

Glacier Bay Lodge
P.O. Box 199, Gustavus, AK 99826
Tel. 1-800-451-5952

Parks & Native Reserves

Meadowdale Beach County Park
Tel. (425) 745-5111

B.C. Parks
Ministry of Environment, Lands and Parks,
B.C. Provincial Parks Division
5th floor, 2975 Jutland Road, Victoria, B.C.
P.O. Box 9339, STN PROV GOV, Victoria, B.C. V8W 9M1
Tel. (250) 387-4550 or (March 15–Sept. 15) 1-800-689-9025
Web site: www.bcparks.gov.bc.ca

Penelakut Band
P.O. Box 3601, Chemainus, B.C. V0SS 1M0
Tel. (250) 246-2321

Mamaleleqala Que'Qua'Sot'Enox Band
1400 Weiwaikum Rd., Campbell River, B.C. V9W 5W8
Tel. (250) 287-2955

Anan Creek Wildlife Observatory
U.S. Forest Service, Wrangell District,
P.O. Box 51, 525 Bennett Street
Wrangell, AK 99929
Tel. (907) 874-2323 or 1-877-444-6777
Web site: www.reserveusa.com

Pack Creek Bear Observatory
U.S. Forest Service Information Center, Centennial Hall, 101 Egan
    Drive, Juneau, AK 99801
Tel. (907) 588-8790

Misty Fjords National Monument
3031 Tongass Avenue, Ketchikan, AK 99901
Tel. (907) 225-2148

Admiralty National Monument/Kootznawoo Wilderness
8461 Old Dairy Road, Juneau, AK 99801
Tel. (907) 586-8041

Glacier Bay National Park and Preserve
P.O. Box 140, Gustavus, AK 99826
Tel. (907) 697-2230, or (after hours, emergency) (907) 697-2322

Klemtu Tourism,
Kitasoo Indian Band
General Delivery,
Klemtu, B.C. V0T 1L0
Tel. (250) 839-2346 or 1-877-644-2346
Web site: www.klemtutourism.com

Appendix C: Basic Marine Radio Protocol for Kayakers

"Anybody out there?"

THE US FEDERAL Communications Commission and the US and Canadian Coast Guards require that all commercial vessels carry marine radios, monitor the airwaves, and respond to emergencies in their area. Private vessels are exempt, but if they do carry a radio, they too must monitor the designated calling and distress channel. Consequently, a ubiquitous, intricate, and invisible network of communications is constantly aware of everything that transpires on the briny main. You too can participate, but only if you're connected. To prevent congestion and maximize efficiency in emergencies, the FCC and Coast Guards have designated certain channels for certain purposes.

Channel 16: This is the channel that all vessels use to monitor the airwaves. Use it to make contact. Once communication in a nonemergency is established, you must move to another channel that is mutually agreeable to you and otherwise unoccupied. Sometimes the Coast Guard uses Channel 16 for special announcements and weather advisories.

Channel 22: Channel 22 is reserved for the Coast Guard.

Weather Channel: Varies. Continuous and constantly updated weather reports are usually broadcast on single-digit channels.

There's a whole lot more to VHF marine radios. Some channels are designated for highly specialized and esoteric uses; others are purposefully left open for informal use. Plus there's a whole specialized lingo associated with radio communication. Radios can even be used to connect to a phone operator and make long-distance telephone calls. There's an entire body of law that applies to VHF radio use. For a more detailed exposition on marine radios and kayaks, consult David Burch's *Fundamentals of Kayak Navigation* and "VHF and FRS Radios: A New Generation" by Kent Barber in *Sea Kayaker* magazine's August 1999 issue. Out on the water, your best bet for information is to contact the nearest monitoring vessel and ask away.

Appendix D: Salmon & Mustelid Varieties Identification Charts

The Salmon Chart

"Salmon" is an imprecise vernacular term that refers to an ancient, broad, and deep fish lineage. Even the word is old, having come into English from the Old French *saumon* after the Norman invasion of England in 1066. Most salmon are anadromous, that is, they breed in fresh water, migrate downstream to spend part of their lives in the sea, then return to spawn in the freshwater streams where they were born.

The Atlantic salmon, *Salmo salar,* is the largest. Although they average about 15 pounds, specimens of more than 100 pounds have been caught. Unlike Pacific salmon, Atlantic salmon do not always die after spawning and may live to reproduce many times. It is the only species of salmon successfully domesticated so far, and there are several aquaculture operations growing Atlantic salmon along the British Columbia sections of the Inside Passage.

Pacific salmon spawn only once and die after depositing and fertilizing their eggs. The Chinook or king salmon, *Oncorhynchus tshawytscha,* is the largest of the Pacific species. Chinooks average about 20 pounds, but specimens of nearly 100 pounds have been caught.

Salmon Identification Chart

nonbreeding fish and breeding male with kype

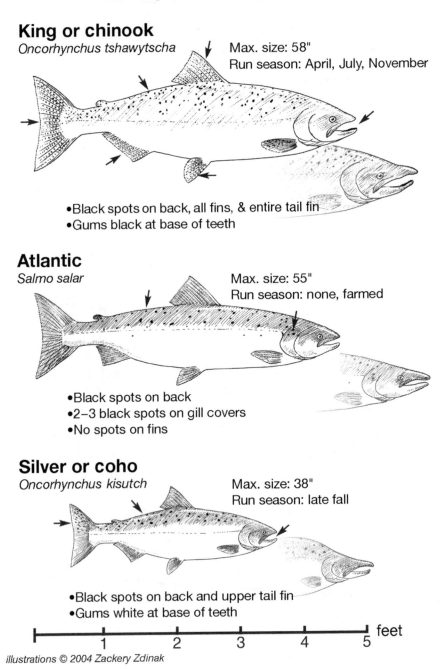

King or chinook
Oncorhynchus tshawytscha

Max. size: 58"
Run season: April, July, November

•Black spots on back, all fins, & entire tail fin
•Gums black at base of teeth

Atlantic
Salmo salar

Max. size: 55"
Run season: none, farmed

•Black spots on back
•2–3 black spots on gill covers
•No spots on fins

Silver or coho
Oncorhynchus kisutch

Max. size: 38"
Run season: late fall

•Black spots on back and upper tail fin
•Gums white at base of teeth

1	2	3	4	5	feet

illustrations © 2004 Zackery Zdinak

Chum or dog
Oncorhynchus keta

Max. size: 36"
Run season: early to late fall

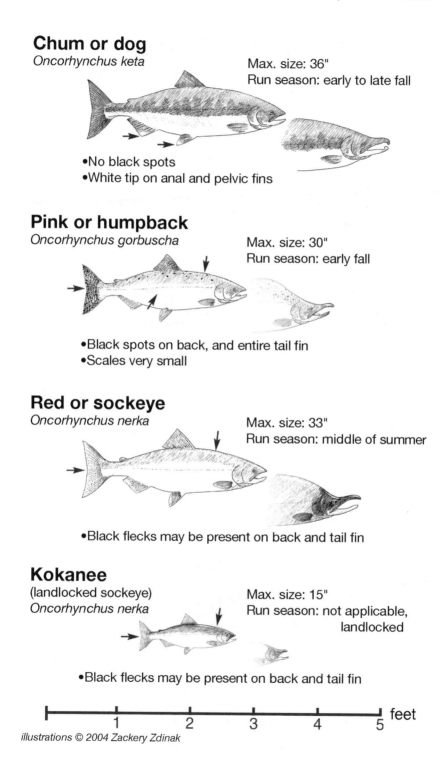

- No black spots
- White tip on anal and pelvic fins

Pink or humpback
Oncorhynchus gorbuscha

Max. size: 30"
Run season: early fall

- Black spots on back, and entire tail fin
- Scales very small

Red or sockeye
Oncorhynchus nerka

Max. size: 33"
Run season: middle of summer

- Black flecks may be present on back and tail fin

Kokanee
(landlocked sockeye)
Oncorhynchus nerka

Max. size: 15"
Run season: not applicable,
landlocked

- Black flecks may be present on back and tail fin

1   2   3   4   5   feet

illustrations © 2004 Zackery Zdinak

Mustelid Identification Chart

Short-tailed weasel
Mustela erminea

Length: 7–13"

- Black tip on tail all year
- Brown above, light below in summer
- White in winter

Marten
Martes americana

Length: 19–27"

- Rusty brown
- Arboreal, usually active above ground in trees

Mink
Mustela vison

Length: 19–28"

- Dark brown above and below
- Semiaquatic, good swimmer

Fisher
Martes pennanti

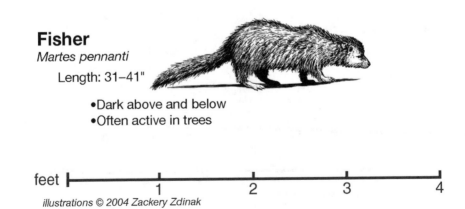

Length: 31–41"

- Dark above and below
- Often active in trees

feet |————————|————————|————————|————————|
         1   2   3   4

illustrations © 2004 Zackery Zdinak

Wolverine
Gulo gulo

Length: 31–44"

- Stocky build
- Shaggy; short tail
- Blond stripe on each side

River otter
Lutra canadensis

Length: 35–52"

- Long, thin body and tail
- Short legs
- Aquatic, usually found in or near water

Sea otter
Enhydra lutris

Length: 30–71"

- Thick bodied
- Short tail and legs
- Usually found in kelp beds
- Rarely comes ashore

feet
1   2   3   4

illustrations © 2004 Zackery Zdinak

Bibliography

*Education is the road from
obstinate ignorance to
thoughtful uncertainty.*
—Unknown

Guidebooks & Maps

The following resources include sailing guides, coast pilots, specialty maps, general travel guides, and kayaking guides that I have found helpful.

Backlund, Gary & Paul Grey. *Kayaking Vancouver Island.* Madeira Park, B.C., Canada: Harbour Publishing, 2003.

————. *A Sea Kayaker's Guide to South Puget Sound.* Tacoma, WA: Little Bay Press, 1999.

————. *A Sea Kayaker's Guide to North Puget Sound.* Tacoma, WA: Little Bay Press, 2002.

Campbell, Ken. *Shades of Grey: Sea Kayaking in Western Washington.* Tacoma, WA: Little Bay Press, 1999.

Chappell, John. *Cruising Beyond Desolation Sound.* Surrey, B.C., Canada: Naikoon Marine, 1992.

Coastal Cruise Tour Guides. *Alaska & Canada's Inside Passage Cruise Tour Guide.* Seattle, WA: Coastal Cruise Tour Guides, 2000.

Douglass, Don & Reanne Hemingway-Douglass. *Exploring the South Coast of British Columbia.* Anacortes, WA: Fine Edge Productions, 1999.

————. *Exploring Southeast Alaska.* Anacortes, WA: Fine Edge Productions, 2000.

————. *Exploring the North Coast of British Columbia.* Anacortes, WA: Fine Edge Productions, 2001.

DuFresne, Jim. *Glacier Bay National Park: A Backcountry Guide to the Glaciers and Beyond.* Seattle, WA: The Mountaineers, 1987.

Eppenbach, Sarah. *Alaska's Southeast: Touring the Inside Passage.* Guilford, CT: The Globe Pequot Press, 1994.

Fisheries and Oceans Canada. *Sailing Directions, British Columbia Coast (South Portion).* Ottawa, Ont., Canada: Minister of Fisheries and Oceans Canada, 1999.

————. *Sailing Directions, British Columbia Coast (North Portion).* Ottawa, Ont., Canada: Minister of Fisheries and Oceans Canada, 1991.

Fortier, Dennis. "The Kayaker's Course Plotter." *Sea Kayaker,* December 2003.

Hilson, Stephen. *Exploring Puget Sound & British Columbia.* Seattle, WA: Evergreen Pacific, 1996.

————. *Exploring Alaska & British Columbia.* Seattle, WA: Evergreen Pacific, 1997.

Howard, Jim. *Guide to Sea Kayaking in Southeast Alaska.* Guilford, CT: The Globe Pequot Press, 1999.

Ince, John & Hedi Kottner. *Sea Kayaking Canada's West Coast.* Vancouver, B.C., Canada: Raxas Books, 1982.

Malin, R.O. *The Northwest Coast.* Olympia, WA: Sobay Co., 1984.

McGee, Peter, editor. *Kayak Routes of the Pacific Northwest Coast.* Vancouver, B.C., Canada: Greystone Books, 2004.

McRae, Bill, Judy Jewell & Jennifer Snarski. *Pacific Northwest.* Oakland, CA: Lonely Planet, 1999.

Morris, Frank & W. R. Heath. *Marine Atlas, Volume 2.* Renton, WA: Bayless Enterprises, Inc., 1999

Mueller, Ted & Marge. *British Columbia's Gulf Islands, Afoot & Afloat.* Seattle, WA: The Mountaineers, 2000.

Scherer, Migael. *A Cruising Guide to Puget Sound.* Camden, ME: International Marine, 1995.

Skillman, Don. *Adventure Kayaking, Trips in Glacier Bay.* Berkeley, CA: Wilderness Press, 1998.

Snowden, Mary Ann. *Island Paddling.* Custer, WA: Orca Book Publishers, 1997.

Stevens, K. *Coastal Waters Recreation Maps.* Victoria, B.C., Canada: Coastal Waters Recreation, 2000.

Upton, Joe. *The Coastal Companion: A Guide for the Alaska-Bound Traveler.* Seattle, WA: Coastal Publishing, 1995.

US Department of Commerce. *United States Coast Pilot 7.* Washington, DC: National Ocean Service, 2000.

————. *United States Coast Pilot 8.* Washington, DC: National Ocean Service, 1994.

Van der Ree, Frieda. *Exploring the Coast by Boat, Vol. 1.* Seattle, WA: The Writing Works, 1979.

Washbourne, Randel. *Kayaking Puget Sound, the San Juans, and Gulf Islands.* Seattle, WA: The Mountaineers, 1990.

————. *The Coastal Kayaker.* Seattle, WA: Pacific Search Press, 1983.

Washington Water Trails Association. *The Cascadia Marine Trail Guidebook.* Seattle, WA: Washington Water Trails Association, 2003.

Wood, Charles E. *Charlie's Charts North to Alaska.* Surrey, B.C., Canada: Charlie's Charts, 2001.

Kayaking — How-To

These resources include general and highly specific references detailing kayaking techniques.

Alderson, Doug. "The Vertical Storm Roll: Trick or Skill?" *Sea Kayaker*, December 2001.

Barber, Kent "VHF and FRS Radios: A New Generation." *Sea Kayaker*, August 1999.

Burch, David. *Fundamentals of Kayak Navigation.* Guilford, CT: The Globe Pequot Press, 1993.

Cunningham, Chris. "Yakers Breathing System." *Sea Kayaker*, October 2002.

Dowd, John. *Sea Kayaking, A Manual for Long-Distance Touring*, 5th ed. Vancouver, B.C., Canada: Greystone Books, 2004.

―――. "Seamanship for Kayakers." *Canoe & Kayak*, May 2004.

Hume, Bob. "Gauging High Tides: The Rule of 12s." *Sea Kayaker*, June 1999.

Hutchinson, Derek C. *The Complete Book of Sea Kayaking.* Guilford, CT: The Globe Pequot Press, 1994.

Lai, Gary. "Keeping in Touch from Anywhere: Two Affordable Hand-held Satellite Phones for Sea Kayakers." *Sea Kayaker*, December 2003. Seattle, WA.

Moyer, Lee. *Sea Kayak Navigation Simplified.* Seattle, WA: Alpen Books Press, 2001.

Stamer, Greg. "The Petrussen Maneuver." *Sea Kayaker*, August 2000.

Voyage Accounts

These trip accounts include canoe, sailing, and kayak voyages, not all necessarily along the Inside Passage but all helpful to me, in some way or another, in the compilation of this book. Comments on some books follow.

Bossiere, Pierre. "Kayak Smuggling in the San Juans." *Paddler,* November/December 2001. Not an account of one particular trip but rather of a modern trend.

Broze, Matt. "Thrown a Curve by the Surf." *Sea Kayaker,* December 1997. Accident account near Cape Caution.

Doig, Ivan. *The Sea Runners.* New York, NY: Penguin Books, 1983. Extraordinary fictionalized account of three indentured servants' escape from Sitka, Alaska, to Astoria, Oregon, in a stolen Tlingit canoe during the Russian administration of Alaska.

Duff, Chris. *On Celtic Tides.* New York, NY: St. Martin's Griffin, 1999.

Fisher, Robin. *Vancouver's Voyage.* Seattle, WA: University of Washington Press, 1992.

Fons, Valerie. *Keep It Moving: Baja by Canoe.* Seattle, WA: The Mountaineers, 1986.

Giddings, J. Calvin. *Demon River Apurimac.* Salt Lake City, UT: University of Utah Press, 1996.

Gillet, Ed. "Chilean Channels." *Sea Kayaker,* summer 1985.

Hahn, Jennifer. *Spirited Waters.* Seattle, WA: The Mountaineers, 2001. Account of partial—and solo—Inside Passage kayaking trip with emphasis on natural history.

Kologe, Brian. "John MacGregor: A Victorian-era Paddler." *Sea Kayaker,* August 1999.

Lamb, Dana, with June Cleveland. *Enchanted Vagabonds.* New York: Harper & Brothers, 1938. Depression-era account of newlyweds on a kayak sailing trip from San Diego, CA, to Cocos Island, Panama, with little more than a .22 and a gold pan. Absolutely engrossing.

Lydon, Tim. *Passage to Alaska.* Blaine, WA: Hancock House Publishers, 2003.

Poole, Michael. *Ragged Islands: Paddling the Inside Passage.* Vancouver, B.C., Canada: Douglas & McIntyre, 1991.

Queen, Randall. "When Does It End?" *Sea Kayaker,* February 1997. Instructive account of how not to approach the Inside Passage.

Raban, Jonathan. *Passage to Juneau.* New York: Pantheon Books, 1999. Some really good writing.

Rasmussen, Greg. *Kayaking in Paradise.* Vancouver/Toronto, Canada: Whitecap Books, 1997.

Ricks, Byron. *Homelands: Kayaking the Inside Passage.* New York: Avon Books, 1999.

Robertson, Dougal. *Survive the Savage Sea.* New York: Praeger Publishers, 1973.

Rodgers, Joel W. *Watertrail.* Seattle, WA: Sasquatch Books, 1998. Portrait of kayaking the Cascadia Marine Trail in Puget Sound and the San Juans.

Schmidt, Peter. "North to Alaska." *Appeal Tribune,* Silverton, OR: August 21, 2002. Account of traveling the Inside Passage in a cruise ship.

Stiller, Eric. *Keep Australia on Your Left: A True Story of an Attempt to Circumnavigate Australia by Kayak.* New York: Forge Books, 2000.

Steinbeck, John. *The Log from the Sea of Cortez.* New York: Bantam Books, 1971.

Upton, Joe. *Journeys Through the Inside Passage.* Vancouver, B.C., Canada: Whitecap Books, 1992. Vignettes from a commercial fisherman that capture particularly well the Inside Passage.

Vancouver, George. *A Voyage of Discovery to the North Pacific Ocean and Round the World: In which the Coast of North-West America has been Carefully Examined and Surveyed.* London, UK: J. Stockdale, 1801.

Wade, John McLaughlin. *The Hopeful Journey.* Unpublished manuscript, 1997.

Wise, Ken C. *Cruise of the Blue Flujin.* Fowlerville, MI: Wilderness Adventure Books, 1987. Depression-era account of three boy scouts who canoe the Inside Passage. Fascinating.

History & Anthropology

Not all these pertain directly to the Inside Passage, though they were all very helpful. Of those that do, some are annotated.

Anderson, Hugo. *The Inside Passage to Alaska: A Short History.* USA: Anderson Publishing Co., 1998. Excellent—and short. There is no better overview.

Bauer, K. Jack. *The Mexican War, 1846–1848.* Lincoln, NE: University of Nebraska Press, 1992.

Benton, William, Publisher. *Encyclopaedia Britannica.* Chicago, IL: University of Chicago Press, 1979.

Bobrick, Benson. *East of the Sun: The Epic Conquest and Tragic History of Siberia.* New York: Poseidon Press, 1992. The definitive—and engrossing—account.

Brodie, Fawn M. *No Man Knows My History.* New York: Alfred A. Knopf, 1973. Biography of Mormon leader Joseph Smith.

Brown, Craig, editor. *The Illustrated History of Canada.* Toronto, Ont., Canada: Key Porter Books, Ltd., 2000.

Chevigny, Hector. *Russian America, The Great Alaskan Venture 1741–1867.* Portland, OR: Binford & Mort Publishing, 1992 (Originally 1965). A page-turner and excellent overview, but suffers factually from pre-glasnost lack of accurate detail.

Christensen, Carol & Thomas. *The U.S.–Mexican War, 1846–1848.* San Francisco, CA: Bay Books, 1998.

Conquest, Robert. *Kolyma: The Arctic Death Camps.* New York: Oxford University Press, 1979.

De Voto, Bernard, Ed. *The Journals of Lewis and Clark.* Boston: Houghton Mifflin Co., 1953.

Diamond, Jared. *Guns, Germs, and Steel.* New York: W. W. Norton & Co., 1999. Excellent. A true integration of history, anthropology and biology.

Drucker, Philip. *Indians of the Northwest Coast.* Garden City, NY: The Natural History Press, 1955. Good, accurate and basic reference.

Eisenhower, John S. D. *So Far from God: The U.S. War with Mexico, 1846–1848.* Norman, OK: University of Oklahoma Press, 1989.

Fenn, Elizabeth A. *Pox Americana: The Great Smallpox Epidemic of 1775–82.* New York: Hill and Wang, 2001.

Ferguson, Will. *Canadian History for Dummies.* Toronto, Ont., Canada: CDG Books Canada, 2000. If you thought Canadian history was dull, tackle this extremely entertaining tome.

Frankevich, Joan. *NPCA Comments on Glacier Bay EIS on Vessel Quotas and Operating Requirements.* National Parks Conservation Association. Anchorage, AK: 2002.

Ginzburg, Eugenia Semyonovna. *Journey into the Whirlwind.* New York: Harcourt Brace Jovanovich, 1967. This, and its sequel (below), is a memoir of one prisoner's life in Kolyma. Both are excellent.

———. *Within the Whirlwind.* New York, NY: Harcourt Brace Jovanovich, 1979.

Gough, Barry. *First Across the Continent.* Norman, OK: University of Oklahoma Press, 1997. Short account of Alexander MacKenzie's trek across Canada.

Hamilton, William. *The Crown of Shakes.* Kearney, NE: Morris Publishing, 1998. Written accounts of Wrangell, Alaska area, Tlingit oral traditions, and stories. Suffers from a lack of good editing.

Hays, H. R. *Children of the Raven.* New York: McGraw-Hill Book Company, 1975. Ethnographic portrait of Northwest Coast Indians focusing on religion, myth, and drama.

Hester, James J. & Sarah M. Nelson. *Studies in Bella Bella Prehistory.* Burnaby, B.C., Canada: Simon Fraser University Archaeology Press, 1978.

Holm, Bill. *Northwest Coast Indian Art: An Analysis by Form.* Seattle, WA: University of Washington Press, 1998. Classic in the field.

Hough, Richard. *Captain James Cook: A Biography.* New York: W. W. Norton & Co., 1997.

Jewitt, John R. *White Slaves of the Nootka.* Surrey, B.C., Canada: Heritage House Publishing Company, Ltd., 1987. Account of the captivity of an American sailor by the Nootka of Vancouver Island. Short and good.

Kramer, Pat. *Native Sites in Western Canada.* Canmore, Alberta, Canada: Altitude Publishing, 1998

Lillard, Charles. *Seven Shillings a Year: The History of Vancouver Island.* Ganges, B.C., Canada: Horsdal & Schubart, 1993.

MacIsaac, Ron; Don Clark & Charles Lillard. *The Devil of DeCourcy Island: The Brother XII.* Victoria, B.C., Canada: Porcepic Books, 1989.

Malcolm, Andrew H. *The Canadians.* New York: St. Martin's Press, 1992.

McGinnis, Joe. *Going to Extremes.* New York: New American Library, 1980. Great portrait of Alaskan characters.

McPhee, John. *Coming into the Country.* New York: Bantam Books, 1985. An even better portrait of the type of person that goes to Alaska with the added bonus of a slice of Alaskan politics.

Montefiore, Simon Sebag. *Stalin: The Court of the Red Tsar.* London, UK: Weidenfeld & Nicholson, 2003.

Morton, Desmond. *A Short History of Canada.* Toronto, Canada: McClelland & Stewart Ltd., 2001.

Naske, Claus-M. & Herman E. Slotnick. *Alaska, A History of the 49th State.* Norman, OK: University of Oklahoma Press, 1994. Not the most engrossing read, but about the only easily accessible work on Alaskan history after the Russians and native life after the Alaska Native Claims Settlement Act.

Oswalt, Wendell H. *This Land Was Theirs.* New York: John Wiley & Sons, Inc., 1966.

Rennick, Penny. *Alaska Geographic: Russian America.* Anchorage, AK: Alaska Geographic, 1999. Good history of Russian America. Short and with wonderful illustrations.

Roppel, Patricia. *An Historical Guide to Revillagigedo and Gravina Islands, Alaska.* Wrangell, AK: Farwest Research, 1995.

Rosen, Yereth. "Alaska to Cruise Ships: We're not your Sewer." *Christian Science Monitor*, July 12, 2001.

Stewart, Hilary. *Looking at Indian Art of the Northwest Coast.* Seattle, WA: University of Washington Press, 1979.

Sword, Wiley. *President Washington's Indian War.* Norman, OK: University of Oklahoma Press, 1985.

Van Wagoner, Richard S. *Mormon Polygamy: A History.* Salt Lake City, UT: Signature Books, 1989.

Weber, David J. *The Mexican Frontier 1821–1846, The American Southwest Under Mexico.* Albuquerque: University of New Mexico Press, 1982.

Zimmerly, David W. *Qayaq, Kayaks of Alaska and Siberia.* Fairbanks, AK: University of Alaska Press, 1989. There is no book like this. Well illustrated.

Zuehlke, Mark. *The B.C. Fact Book.* Vancouver/Toronto, B.C., Canada: Whitecap Books, 1995.

Natural History

Barash, David P. & Judith Eve Lipton. *The Myth of Monogamy: Fidelity and Infidelity in Animals and People.* New York: W. H. Freeman and Company, 2001.

Bernd, Heinrich. *Ravens in Winter.* New York: Vintage Books, 1989. Account of an ethologist attempting to understand ravens and raven natural history.

———. *Mind of the Raven.* New York: HarperCollins, 1999. More of the same.

Buchsbaum, Ralph. *Animals without Backbones.* Chicago and London: The University of Chicago Press, 1948. What can you say about the natural history of invertebrates? Buchsbaum says it all.

Buchsbaum, Ralph & Lorus J. Milne. *The Lower Animals: Living Invertebrates of the World.* Garden City, NY: Doubleday & Co. Inc., 1972. More of the same, but less academic and with great photographs.

Hamlyn, Paul. *Larousse Encyclopedia of Animal Life.* London, UK: The Hamlyn Publishing Group, Ltd., 1967.

Herrero, Stephen. *Bear Attacks: Their Causes and Avoidance.* Guilford, CT: The Lyons Press, 2002. *The* definitive book on bears.

Keen, Richard. *Skywatch: The Western Weather Guide.* Golden, CO: Fulcrum, Inc., 1987. Through illustrating western North American weather, Keen explains the phenomenon of weather.

Koerner, Michael. "When Seals 'Attack.' " *Sea Kayaker,* April 2002.

McPhee, John. *Animals of the Former World.* New York: Farrar, Straus and Giroux, 1998.

Muir, John. *Travels in Alaska.* Boston: Houghton Mifflin Company, 1979.

Redfern, Ron. *The Making of a Continent.* New York: Times Books, 1983.

———. *Origins: The Evolution of Continents, Oceans, and Life.* Norman, OK: University of Oklahoma Press, 2000.

Scheffer, Victor B. *The Year of the Seal.* New York: Charles Scribner's Sons, 1970.

Sibley, David Allen. *The Sibley Guide to Birds.* New York: Alfred A. Knopf, 2000.

Storer, Tracy & Robert Usinger. *General Zoology.* New York: McGraw-Hill, 1965.

Trefil, James S. *A Scientist at the Seashore.* New York: Collier Books, 1987. Want to know how tides work? Why there's sand on beaches? Why the sea is salty, and much more? Trefil is clear, concise, and fun.

Wynne, Kate. *Guide to Marine Mammals of Alaska.* Fairbanks, AK: Sea Grant, 1997.

Index

O

O'Higgins, Bernardo, 324
Oolichan, 215, 269
Oona River, 271
Orca (*Orcinus orca*), 30, 80,
  199–200, 225, 236. *See also*
  Whales
Orcas Island, 122–123
Oregon Territory annexation,
  95–96
Orthodox Church, Russian, 35,
  367, 381
Outer Island Kayak, 66
Outfitters, 419–421
Outside Passage, 19, 27
Owikeeno First Nations, 241
Oysters, 178, 294

P

Pace, 20
Pacheco de Pedilla, Juan Vicente de
  Guemes, 315
Pacific Marine Heritage Legacy,
  151
Pacific Weather Centre, 305
Pack Creek Bear Observatory, 360,
  425
Paddles, 83–84
Paddling tops, 86
Park Avenue Corner Store, 311
Parking, long–term, 53, 136, 230,
  275, 311, 422–424
Parks and native reserves, 425–426
Parkside Resort Motel, 275, 311
Passage to Alaska (Lydon), 240
Passage to Juneau (Raban), 92–93,
  222
Passports, 135
Pasteur, Louis, 66, 210, 293
Pavlutsky, Dmitry, 378
Pawlatta roll, 66
Pearson, Lester, 145
Penelakut Band, 152, 164, 425
Pepper spray, 72, 74, 100, 133, 178
Perez, Juan, 34, 146
Petersburg, 343–344, 346; to
  Juneau, 349–368; from Ketchikan,
  321–348; map, 345
Petersburg Bunk & Breakfast
  Hostel, 344

Petersburg Fisheries, 344
Peter the Great, Czar, 34, 374, 377,
  385
Petrussen maneuver, 66
"Petrussen Maneuver, The: A New
  Twist on an Old Technique"
  (Stamer), 66
Pettigrew, Pierre, 287
Phones, cell vs. satellite, 64–65
Pineridge B&B, 275
Pinnipeds, 75, 78–80, 239,
  386–387. *See also* Wildlife
PI Outdoors, 87
Piscatelli, Frank, 239
Planning, 21–23, 39–40. *See also*
  Routes
Pleasant Island, 395
POD, dual–bladder hydration
  system, 87
Poggies, 85
Point Higgins, 323–325
Point Highfield from Watkins
  Point, 336–340
Polk, James K., 96–97, 142
Portages, 41
Port Hardy, 207–208; map, 209;
  to Rivers Inlet, 228–237; from
  Robson Bight, 197–208
Portland Canal, 312–313
Portland Island, 160
Port Simpson, 312
Port Townsend, 125–130
Potlatch, 203, 204, 219–220,
  335
Powell, John Wesley, 22
Powell River: to Big Bay, Stuart
  Island, 176–186; from New-
  castle Island Provincial Park,
  172–176
Precipitation, 29; average annual,
  43; Central British Columbia,
  224–225; Puget Sound, 99; Van-
  couver Island, 149
President Point to Deception Pass,
  125–130
Prevost Island, 161–162
Prince of Wales Island, 325–326
Prince Rupert, 273, 275; from
  Butedale, 262–275; to Ketchikan,
  309–320; map, 274
Princess Line, 300
Princess Royal Channel: Bella Bella

Fear the Light

Also available in Large Print
by E. X. Ferrars:

The Root of All Evil
Something Wicked
Witness Before the Fact
Furnished for Murder